Christianity and Jerusalem:
Studies in Modern Theology and Politics
in the Holy Land

Christianity and Jerusalem:
Studies in Modern Theology and Politics in the Holy Land

edited by Anthony O'Mahony

GRACEWING

First published in 2010

Gracewing
2 Southern Avenue, Leominster
Herefordshire HR6 0QF

All rights reserved. No part of this publication may be reproduced, stored in a retrieval system, or transmitted in any form, or by any means, electronic, mechanical, photocopying, recording or otherwise, without the written permission of the publisher.

Compilation and editorial material © Anthony O'Mahony, 2010
Copyright for individual chapters resides with the authors

The right of the editor and the contributors to be identified as the authors of this work has been asserted in accordance with the Copyright, Designs and Patents Act 1988.

ISBN 978 0 85244 646 1

Typesetting by
Action Publishing Technology Ltd, Gloucester, GL1 5SR

Contents

Preface	by Anthony O'Mahony	vii
Chapter 1	Contemporary Jewish Israeli Views on Christianity and Christians *David M. Neuhaus, SJ*	1
Chapter 2	Hebrew Catholicism in Modern Israel *Leon Menzies Racionzer*	31
Chapter 3	The *Intifada* and Palestinian Christian Identity *Drew Christiansen, SJ*	44
Chapter 4	Palestinian Christians and Liberation Theology *Leonard Marsh*	69
Chapter 5	The Greek Orthodox Patriarchate of Jerusalem: Church-State Politics in the Holy Land *Sotiris Roussos*	92
Chapter 6	Indigenization and contextualization – the example of Anglican and Protestant churches in the Holy Land *Michael Marten*	115
Chapter 7	Jewish Fundamentalism, the *Halacha* and the Palestinian Christians: the use of Maimonides's Theology in Modern Israel (1967–2003) *Nur Masalha*	138
Chapter 8	The Jewish-Muslim Encounter in the Holy Land: the Theological and Political Implications for Christianity *Robert M. Johnson*	183
Chapter 9	Jerusalem, the Holy City in selected documents of the Holy See and in writings of Michel Sabbah, Latin Patriarch of Jerusalem *Charles H. Miller, SM*	216

Chapter 10	The Plural Significance of Jerusalem as seen *ex infra*: Kenneth Cragg on the Interrelated Jerusalem 1987–2008	
	Bård Mæland	245
Chapter 11	A Possible Way to Share Jerusalem in Peace	
	David Kitching	265
Chapter 12	Christianity and Jerusalem: Present and Future Perspectives	
	Michel Sabbah, The Latin Patriarch of Jerusalem	302
Notes on Contributors		310
Index		315

Preface

Anthony O'Mahony

Christianity in the Holy Land has found its presence significantly challenged from a number of directions – war, interreligious and ethnic conflict, emigration, and a fragmented ecclesiology – for almost all of the twentieth century and into the first decade of the twenty-first century. As a sacred city Jerusalem has a global significance: for Muslims: the Haram-al-Sharif is a symbol of victory; for Jews the Wailing Wall a symbol of loss; and for Christians, the Holy Sepulchre a symbol of victory through loss. Theology and politics have interacted in this sacred story. Political theologies remain at least implicit in the histories of all major faith communities: Jewish, Christian and Muslim.

For the Christian community and in particular for the Christians of Jerusalem, the principal holy spaces are the Church of the Nativity in Bethlehem, the churches and Holy Places in Nazareth, and especially, the Church of the Holy Sepulchre in Jerusalem, which remains an important symbol of Christian presence and custodian-ship in Jerusalem. For Christianity the Holy Land is not only of local significance, but is of importance to the identity of the two and a half billion strong world community of churches which make up Christendom. Christians have not always enjoyed the right of freedom to make pilgrimage to and worship in the Holy Sepulchre, however, access to the sanctuary has always remained a symbolic anchor for Christians in Jerusalem. Perhaps no single place speaks more eloquently of the diversity of Christianity in Jerusalem than the Holy Sepulchre, with multiple side chapels belonging to Greeks, Armenians, Latins, Syrians, Copts, and Ethiopians, competing liturgical rites and celebrations and the aroma of many shades of incense upon the air.

It is not difficult for the modern pilgrim or traveller to Jerusalem to imagine the naturally cosmopolitan character of what was Christian Palestine during its early centuries, where cultural and religious exchange had been woven into the very fabric of the landscape. Christian Jerusalem would have been dominated by pilgrims and monastic houses bringing together people from east and west, south and north: from Africa and Asia, including Ethiopia, Nubia, Egypt and as far away as the western Atlantic coast of Africa; from Arabia, Armenia, Byzantium, Georgia, Central Asia, Persia and India; from all over Europe: Ireland, Gaul, Spain, Britain; Scandinavia, Iceland and Russia. The Judean desert was populated with monks from all over the Christian world who, whilst acting as carriers of their own religious culture, would have known no other identity other than their heavenly civitas or polis. During the Byzantine period the monks of Palestine inhabited some sixty monastic settlements across the hills and plains of the Judean desert. The development of monasticism was made possible by economic prosperity and political stability, which characterized Palestine during the Byzantine period and by the flow of pilgrims, which not only provided financial support, but also provided new members for monastic foundations. It is during this time of expansion that the Judean desert, a region delimited by Jerusalem, the Jordan River and the Dead Sea, is fully assimilated into the religious and monastic geography of the Holy Land.

A modern expression of this long historical continuity in the complex makeup of Christianity in the Holy Land is that in Jerusalem today there are three Patriarchs: Greek Orthodox, Armenian and Latin; five Catholic patriarchal vicars: Maronite, Greek Catholic, Armenian Catholic, Syrian Catholic and Chaldean Catholic; four archbishops: The Church of the East, Syrian Orthodox, Coptic Orthodox and Ethiopian Orthodox; and two Protestant bishops: Anglican and Lutheran. These Christian communities have come under the rule of numerous political entities: Islamic, the Ottoman Empire, the British Mandatory Administration, and the modern states of Jordan and Israel.

It is against this background that the contributors to this volume have undertaken a wide-ranging historical, political and theological enquiry into the Christian presence in modern Jerusalem and the Holy Land. The chapters have an ecumenical, even interreligious, instinct and focus. The political landscape is ever changing which, whilst severely threatening the Christian presence in the Holy Land, continuously challenges and demands a Christian response. The primary responsibility for articulating a Christian response to these political and religious challenges has been that of the Christians of the Holy Land, however it is not solely their burden. This book bears witness to an ongoing theological reflection whilst its immediate concern in the contemporary significance of Jerusalem has a much wider significance. The studies gathered here represent a stream of current research on Christianity in the Holy Land, which was initiated by the conference jointly organized by Heythrop College, University of London and The Catholic Bishops' Conference on Christianity in the Holy Land in 2001. The chapters represent 'snap-shots' of the situation of Christianity and Jerusalem at various points in recent times which, taken as a whole, give a unique insight into a wide range of vital reflections in theological and political thought.

I would like to specially thank Revd Dr Frank Turner, SJ, at the time head of the Department of International Affairs of The Catholic Bishops' Conference of England and Wales with whom the enterprise was intially undertaken. I would also like to thank my colleague Dr John Flannery at Heythrop College who greatly assisted in preparing this text for publication. Grateful thanks must also go to Tom Longford and Jo Whale of Gracewing for their patience and support which has been vital for to the success of the project. The lecture given at the beginning of our collective endeavours by the then Latin Patriarch of Jerusalem, Michel Sabbah (emeritus since 2008) is included in this collection by way of honouring his contribution to helping us all understand the importance of Jerusalem for Christianity. It is hoped that the contributions gathered here will stimulate further research on Christianity in the Holy Land and a continuing dialogue between the worldwide Church and Jerusalem.

Chapter 1

Contemporary Jewish Israeli Views on Christianity and Christians

David M. Neuhaus, SJ

Introduction

The focus of this chapter is on contemporary Jewish Israeli views on Christians and Christianity in Israel today as observed by one reasonably attentive Christian Israeli: myself. My aim here is neither historical nor socio-political. Rather I will seek to sketch impressionistically the contemporary scene. At the outset it is worthwhile noting the unique context of Christians in Israel: they are the only Christian community to live as a minority in a context where the majority is Jewish.[1]

Jews in Israel are very heterogeneous. There are believing, practising Jews and non-believing, non-practising Jews and many varieties in between. Well-known is the division among ultra-Orthodox, modern Orthodox, traditional, Conservative, Reform and Reconstructionist Jews. As important for understanding Jewish life in Israel are the diverse cultural backgrounds of the Jewish communities that originate in Western and Eastern Europe, North America, Latin America, the Middle East etc. A helpful distinction with regard to our subject is the distinction between Jews that come from the countries of Christendom and those that come from the Islamic world. Each community has its own history, a history that moulds attitudes towards Christians and Christianity. Jewish Israeli society is still in formation and this does not always facilitate relations with those defined as outsiders. The historical context of European anti-Semitism and its culmination in the Holocaust is formative for the attitudes of many Jewish Israelis towards 'non-Jews'[2] in general and Christians in particular. Zionism, the motivating ideology behind the establishment of the State of Israel, is, in many ways, a reaction against what is perceived as the inability of Christendom to accept Jews, Judaism and Jewish life in its midst.

Christians in Israel are a small statistical minority, officially less then 2% of the general population.[3] They are also far from homogeneous including Orthodox (Greek, Russian, Rumanian, etc.), Catholic (Uniate and Latin Catholics), Eastern non-Chalcedonians (Syrian and Coptic Orthodox) and Protestants (Anglican, Lutheran, Evangelicals, etc.). Here, though, I will distinguish among four groups of Christians in Israel defined by social, political and cultural factors rather than by the denominational breakdown of Christians in Israel.

1. A first group consists of the Christian Arabs, who, according to the official statistics, make up more than 90% of the Christians in Israel. The Christian Arabs who reside within the 1948/9 borders are citizens of Israel whereas those living in the Palestinian Territories (in East Jerusalem too) are either Palestinian or Jordanian citizens.

2. A second group of Christians resident in Israel consists of expatriates (many being priests and religious), mostly of European and North American provenance, attached to the numerous Christian religious institutions. Most are not citizens of Israel although some are long-term residents.

3. A third group, less clearly identifiable and of yet unknown proportions, consists of Christians who have immigrated to Israel in recent years, particularly from Russia, the countries of the former Communist bloc and also from Ethiopia within the waves of predominantly Jewish immigration. Many have family ties to Jews and receive citizenship or permanent resident status.

4. A fourth group consists of tens of thousands of Christian foreign workers (many from the Philippines, Latin America, Eastern Europe and Africa) who have found employment in Israel. Although the vast majority may be considered a temporary population, among the foreign workers there are those who have families in Israel, speak Hebrew and seem to be establishing a more permanent presence in the country.

Jewish Israelis often seem to give priority in their perception of Christians and Christianity to the Roman Catholic Church. In fact, it often seems that the Pope is perceived as the leading representative of all Christians and that the diversity of Christian churches and groups goes unnoticed. This was particularly evident in the March 2000 pilgrimage of Pope John Paul II to the Holy Land. The Holy Father fascinated secular Israelis in particular and many attitudes and issues about Christians and Christianity surfaced during this visit. It must be stressed though that there is a wide diversity on all issues in Jewish Israeli society and a presentation of attitudes towards any subject certainly risks being stereotypical. What will be outlined here is necessarily an over-simplified picture of Jewish Israeli attitudes towards Christians and Christianity.

General attitudes to Christianity

A prominent Israeli journalist described the visit of Pope John Paul II to Israel in these terms:

> He has left behind a series of pictures that will not be quickly forgotten: Catholic Christianity standing at attention to the strains of Hativka (the national anthem), Catholic Christianity standing up before the Palestinian refugees and announcing that it is on their side, Catholic Christianity descending from the Popemobile into Heikhal Shlomo, the seat of the Chief Rabbinate and shaking the hands of the rabbis, Catholic Christianity entering the gates of Jewish sovereignty, the President's House, Catholic Christianity at Yad Vashem and at the Western Wall.[4]

The Pope's moving addresses and, even more importantly, his symbolic acts: his visits to the Western Wall, to the Chief Rabbis, to the President and to *Yad VaShem*, were followed with close attention. These acts drove home for many Jewish Israelis, as never before, that the Catholic Church and many other branches of the Christian Church have evolved in their attitude to Jews and Judaism, having worked hard to eradicate certain Christian traditional teachings of contempt for Jews and Judaism.[5] One Jewish Israeli activist in Jewish-Christian dialogue commented: 'Following the Pope's recent pilgrimage it will be easier for Jewish Israelis to understand that Christianity is not only a negative phenomenon in history but that it is a positive redemptive force'.[6]

However, Israeli Jewish attitudes towards Christianity have been formed over long centuries of a difficult relationship between Jews and Christians. Rabbi Hayyim David HaLevy, late Chief Rabbi of

Tel Aviv, in a fascinating article on relations between Jews and 'non-Jews', wrote about Christianity in these terms:

> The people of Israel has an old and bitter grievance with Christianity as a religion. This is not only because in its name much Jewish blood has been shed – the Holocaust too, in which six million Jews were slaughtered is a result of Christianity's historical attitude towards the Jews – but also, and mainly, because Christianity distorted beyond recognition the fundamental principles of Judaism (...). The pure belief in God, who is one and whose Name is one, was corrupted into belief in belief in the Trinity. And with an easy sweep of the hand, Christianity uprooted all those commandments and Jewish practices observed under the covenant that God made with His people in the wake of the exodus from Egypt.[7]

I present here some of the negative attitudes, which are still widespread, but I will also present some perspectives for change that were heralded during and after the Pope's visit.

First and foremost, there is a problem of general ignorance. Jewish Israelis tend to have little knowledge about Christianity in general and even less knowledge about the Christian minority that lives in their midst. The Hebrew press pointed to this ignorance before the Pope's visit.[8] In a survey of attitudes carried out just before the papal visit, it was shown that many Israelis were unaware of any common ground between Christianity and Judaism.[9] In a study of the education system, it was shown that Jesus is hardly mentioned at all during the twelve years of elementary schooling.[10] Many Jewish Israelis have never consciously met a Christian Israeli or a Christian Palestinian. Some would not even know that there is such a thing as a Christian Israeli or a Christian Arab.

Secondly, there is the problem of a monochromatic reading of the historic relations between Jewish and Christians. The little Jewish Israelis do know about Christianity and Christians relates directly to the negative side of the history of Jewish-Christian relations in Europe. Two national museums, *Yad VaShem* (the Holocaust Museum) and *Beth HaTefutsot* (the Diaspora Museum) tend to focus predominantly on the darker side of Christian intolerance of Jews and point directly to the link between Christianity and Nazism. Visits to these museums are integrated into the Israeli educational curriculum. Little distinction is made between Christian religious identity and European national identities or between manifestations of modern anti-Semitism and Christianity at large. Debates within the Catholic Church like those about the canonization of Pius XII and Edith Stein or the establishment of the

Carmel at Auschwitz perpetuate the perceived link between Christianity, especially Catholicism, and the Holocaust. In addition, Christians are suspected of being missionary, seeking to convert Jews whenever possible. Even today many Jewish Israelis have a more positive attitude towards Islam than towards Christianity, Islam still being widely perceived as a religion that offered a relative tolerance to Jews in history as compared with Christianity.

Thirdly, there is a problem of traditional Jewish hostility towards Christianity. The general ignorance about Christianity builds upon a relatively widespread religious popular anti-Christian polemic. When Jesus is mentioned he is most often called *Yeshu* (a rabbinic acronym for 'May his name and memory be erased') instead of *Yeshu'a* or *Yehoshua* (Jesus-Joshua). Mythic fabrications about his birth and career as contained in polemical tracts like *Toldot Yeshu* (an early rabbinical anti-Christian tract) are known. Even well meaning, educated Jewish Israelis repeat the polemical inventions of these tracts, inherited from tradition, without questioning them (or being questioned about them). Traditionally, Islam is considered closer to Judaism than Christianity, seen as monotheist, respectful of Law and having a history of tolerance for Jews whereas Christianity is perceived as polytheist, idolatrous, antinomian and profoundly anti-Jewish.

Fourthly, this all goes hand in hand with a fascination about Christianity in its more traditional and exotic forms among secular Jewish Israelis. On Saturdays (the Israeli day off), monasteries are swamped by visitors who seek out the atmosphere of 'overseas' right at home. This is part of a general secular Jewish Israeli fascination with non-Jewish and esoteric spirituality whether Buddhism, Hare Krishna, New Age sects or Christianity. This fascination is usually for a Christianity as 'other-worldly' as possible, celibate monks and nuns often swathed in monastic garb, chanting angelically in unknown languages, in incense filled and dimly lit churches.

Fifthly, the State of Israel has a clearly defined denominational ('ethnic') character.[11] Israelis are registered in the Interior Ministry according to 'ethno-denominational' (defined as 'nation' – Jewish, Arab, Druze, Armenian, Samaritan etc.) rather than 'national-civic' identity (Israeli). The Jewish majority in Israel tends to perceive society and State as being intrinsically Jewish. The Jewish character of the state is rooted in official Zionist ideology and through the use of national symbols (the flag, the anthem, etc.) which are drawn exclusively from the Jewish tradition. This is true for Israelis who regard Jewish identity as primarily religious as well as for many of those who are secular Jews. Christians and

Muslims are most often defined as 'non-Jews' or 'minorities' and in this context the identity tag 'Jewish' is preferred to that of 'Israeli'. Discrimination based upon ethno-denominational identity (Jewish or 'non-Jewish') is widespread and moulds attitudes as well as motivates official policy in many cases. Discrimination affects funding of all services (schools, medical clinics, local councils, etc.), holding public office, buying land, rights of residence, education, development, etc.

Finally, the creation of a Jewish majority state in Israel has also begun to influence Jewish attitudes towards 'non-Jews' in more positive ways. The self-confidence of a majority liberates some Jews to interact with 'non-Jews' in general and Christians in particular in less self-defensive and more interactive and dialogic ways. Even an Orthodox religious authority like Rabbi HaLevy, cited above with regard to a traditional Jewish approach to Christians, points out that within the context of the State of Israel:

> Regarding all aspects of the relations between Jews and 'non–Jews' (*nokhrim*), whether in the Land of Israel or abroad, whether in the relations of political society to its gentile citizens or in the relations of an individual to his gentile neighbour or fellow, all these relations need not be maintained merely 'on account of the ways of peace', because by the halakhic (Jewish legal) definition these people are not considered idolaters. Consequently, sustaining them, visiting their sick, burying their dead, comforting their mourners, and the like, may all be performed out of a human, moral duty...[12]

Some Jewish Israelis are becoming more aware that ignorance and prejudice are not helpful in understanding the Jewish relationship with Christians and the Christian world. It is becoming more acceptable to challenge both the monochromatic reading of history and traditional anti-Christian attitudes in a search for a new approach towards Christianity in general and the Christians in Israel in particular. I will develop some of these aspects at the end of this chapter.

One might conclude in general terms though by saying that Christianity and Christians are generally perceived as foreign and extraneous to the Israeli reality.

Attitudes to specific issues concerning Christianity in Israel

Ethno-denominational identity (Jewish, Christian, Muslim, etc) plays a central role in civic life in the State of Israel. The state itself is defined as Jewish and despite extensive guarantees of democracy and equality for all citizens within a series of basic laws,[13] in practice those who are not Jews are considered at best marginal in the society and at worst as outsiders. Very few Christians, whether Arab, of Jewish origin or expatriate, have managed to achieve positions of prominence in Jewish Israeli society.[14] In general, however, the Christian presence is restricted to closed-off communities, which have formed according to culture, language and rite. Here I will deal with Jewish Israeli attitudes concerning a number of issues which are of direct concern to Christians in Israel: religious freedom, the 'new' Christian Israelis, Christian positions on the Israeli-Arab conflict and Jewish-Christian dialogue.

a) Freedom of religion

Israel does guarantee extensive religious freedom and there is no religious persecution in the State of Israel.[15] At the same time, there are a number of issues that are cause for concern in the general Jewish Israeli attitude to religious freedom.

Jewish Israelis are generally proud that the State of Israel is a Western-style, liberal democracy and that it guarantees religious freedom to all its citizens. The claim is often made that Israel is the only Western-style democracy in the Middle East. At the same time, religious identity and practice play a central role within the formal apparatus of state. An agreement, known as the Status Quo, reached by the Zionists and the Jewish orthodox community in 1948, defines the central role religious authorities play in the personal status of every citizen, especially with regard to registration of birth, performance of marriage and burial. Many Jewish Israelis are painfully aware of the limitations of the Status Quo. The system was created within the context of a struggle between Jewish 'secularists' and Orthodox Jews regarding the exact character of the 'Jewish' state. The civil and political system in Israel today remains under constant pressure as a result of this continuing conflict. In the resulting denominational system, denominational communities (Jewish, Muslim, Christian, Druze, etc.) are granted extensive autonomy, but every individual, like it or not, belongs to a community defined along religious lines, and the clerics of that community control his or her personal status. The system, partly inherited from the Ottomans and partly based upon the idea that Israel is a 'Jewish' state, limits the freedom of individuals especially on issues of personal status, birth registration, marriage, divorce, burial etc. In fact, the Israeli political system in its present form does not allow for the separation of religion and state, so fundamental to most Western style liberal democracies.

Christians, however, enjoy more freedom in the selection of their leadership than any other religious community. Jewish, Muslim and Druze religious leaders and functionaries are selected by Israeli government ministries whereas Christian religious functionaries are selected by and from within their own church organs. Whereas Jewish, Muslim and Druze religious functionaries are bureaucrats of the state and receive state stipends, Christian clergy remain outside the structures of state bureaucracy. Within the realm of education and healthcare, Christians have retained their network of private schools and hospitals, receiving certain subsidies from the state whereas no such parallel private education or healthcare facilities have been developed for Muslims or Druze.

Jewish Israeli attitudes toward the entirety of the 'non-Jewish' population in Israel are affected by the definition of the state as 'Jewish'. There is discrimination, both legal and social, against non-Jews, particularly against the Arab citizens of the state and the Christian Arab citizens among them.[16] I am not referring here to the population in the Palestinian territories who are struggling for political independence but rather to the population that is, by definition, Israeli, living within the borders of Israel since 1948 and having full citizenship. The question of whether Israel should be a state that is 'Jewish' and/or 'democratic' is debated continuously among Jewish Israelis but the reality of second-class citizenship is lived by the population defined as 'non-Jews', predominantly Arab in its composition. Many Jewish Israelis are unaware that the lack of separation between religion and state is also a major impediment to the full guarantee of civil and political rights for Israel's non-Jewish citizens, Christians included.[17]

Although attitudes and even official policies towards Christians sometimes seem to be based upon specifically anti-Christian prejudices, many Jewish Israelis are sensitive to the issue of Israel's reputation as a Western style democracy. This is often seen as linked to maintaining good relations with the West and most particularly with the US and the Israeli administration is cautious about harming Christian interests. In general, Western countries are often perceived as Christian and good relations with them are seen as linked to Israeli treatment of local Christians. Specifically anti-Christian policies and laws have been rare yet certain steps to restrict religious freedom can be noted. In 1977, an anti-missionary law was passed, limiting traditional Christian missionary activity. A more recent proposal to enact restrictions on the distribution and even possession of the New Testament was scuttled due to extensive outside pressure, particularly from pro-Israeli evangelical groups in the US. Israel has known sporadic violent attacks against Christians and Christian places of worship by extremist Jewish groups. Groups that are suspected of being missionary have been particularly targeted. This anti-Christian (and anti-'non Jew') sentiment seems to be increasing in some circles because of the general context of fear and suspicion generated by the present violence and political crisis. Violent acts that target Christians are generally presented as acts of marginal individuals.

The claim of guaranteed religious freedom goes hand in hand with the claim that Israel guarantees freedom of access to the Holy Places. This is often taken as a basis for Israeli demands to administer the Holy Places of not only Judaism but also of Christianity and even Islam within the territories occupied by Israel after the 1967 war and especially those in Jerusalem.[18] The pervasive idea is that only Israel has guaranteed freedom of access to the Holy Places. This is often based upon the additional claim that access to the Holy Places was restricted under Jordanian rule in Jerusalem. Although Jewish Israelis insist that freedom of access to the Holy Places is guaranteed and this is generally scrupulously upheld for foreign Christians, freedom of access has been severely restricted for both Christian and Muslim Palestinians on what has been defined as security grounds. It is not uncommon to meet young Christians from Bethlehem who have never visited the Church of the Holy Sepulchre in Jerusalem, twenty minutes away, because freedom of movement for Palestinian Arabs from the Palestinian territories has been drastically limited for long periods of time. Limiting access of Muslims to the al-Aqsa Mosque has been at the centre of much of the violence in these past years.

The sensitivity to Israel's reputation as a guarantor of religious freedom only marginally influences attitudes to Christian Arabs. Towns at the centre of Christian consciousness like Nazareth and Bethlehem were indeed treated with special care by the Israelis when they were occupied in 1948 and 1967 respectively.[19] However, the rural Christian Palestinian Arab population, far from the important Christian sites, met with the same fate as their Muslim compatriots. Christian Arabs were an integral part of the exodus of refugees particularly from Galilee and from major Palestinian towns like Jaffa, Haifa, Acre, West Jerusalem, Ramleh, Lydda, Bisan etc. Yet it would be true to say that Israeli Jews are often more 'embarrassed' by acts of hostility committed against Arabs when they happen to be Christian. In the recent events in the Palestinian territories this was clear in the way that the Israeli press presented the repeated bombardment of Beit Jala, a town with a large Christian population. Many Israeli commentators insisted that the town was suffering because of the Muslims who came from out of town and used the town to force the Israelis to bombard Christian homes and churches.[20]

Israeli policy and attitudes towards the Christian Arabs in Israel are marked by attempts separate them from their Muslim neighbours and to fragment them according to denominations (Orthodox, Catholic, Protestant, etc.). Denominational (Christian) identity is underlined rather than civic (Arab or Palestinian) identity is underlined. Furthermore, the Israeli administration has tended to separate Christians according to their extraction, non-Arab expatriates or Arabs. Many Jewish Israelis feel more comfortable talking about Muslim, Christian and Druze minorities rather than about an Arab (or Palestinian) minority in Israel. One of the most effective means of fragmenting the Arab minority by the state has been the imposition of military service on certain denominational groups. For example, since the early 1950s the Druze have been enlisted in the army and later certain Bedouin tribes were also subject to compulsory military service. Israeli officials have repeatedly formulated the idea of enlisting Christian Arabs into the army and although compulsory military service has never been imposed there are increasing numbers of Christian Arab youths who have joined the Israeli army. The two main incentives for these youths are the high unemployment in the Arab sector and a strong sense of denominational identity when there are tensions with Druze or Muslim neighbours. The attempts by Arab civic leaders and intellectuals to combat denominational fragmentation and to forge national unity on the basis of Arab (or Palestinian) identity is repeatedly undermined by active state involvement in the fanning of denominational fragmentation. Most recently this has been seen in the official state positions on the construction of a mosque by a group of Muslim activists alongside the basilica in Nazareth.[21]

Jewish Israeli officials have often courted the expatriate Christian presence in Israel in order to promote Israeli interests. Recently this courtship has been institutionalized in what has been named the Christian Allies Caucus, co-chaired by two rightwing members of Knesset and founded to promote a deeper understanding among government officials of pro-Israeli Christian activity in the country.[22] There are special areas of interest that motivate Israeli courtship of Christians. Firstly, there is the issue of foreign pilgrim groups that visit the Holy Land. The desire to be perceived as trustworthy custodians of Christians and Christian Holy Places means that Israel is particularly interested in influencing these groups as much as possible. There has been a long and unresolved struggle regarding who has the right to lead these pilgrim groups during their sojourn in the Land. Needless to say Israeli-trained Jewish guides and Christian Arab guides tend not to present the history of the Land; the Christian presence in the Land and the present conflict in the same light. Secondly, the Israelis have continually co-opted expatriate Christians living in Israel for official 'information' campaigns overseas. The use of expatriate clergy as semi-official Israeli spokespeople has drawn mostly on the Protestant and evangelical churches but a number of Catholics have been mobilized too. Thirdly, the various traditional Churches (particularly the Greek Orthodox, the Armenians and the Franciscan Custody of the Holy Land) own extensive property all over Israel. Israel, which gained control over the extensive Muslim religious endowment land in 1948, has continuously tried to gain control strategic parts of this church land too. The factor of land has been particularly evident in the Israeli attitude towards the Greek Orthodox Church, a major landowner in Israel, which is still lead by almost totally Greek expatriate bishops despite the fact that the faithful are overwhelmingly Arab.[23] In the ongoing negotiations between the Vatican and Israel property rights and property tax are at the centre of ongoing friction.[24]

A further problem is the periodic refusal of the Israeli administration to grant entry visas to some foreigners who come to study in the Holy Land or serve the institutions there. This is particularly the case for those from the surrounding Arab countries.[25] The Christian Allies Caucus has addressed this problem however it links Christian attitudes towards Israeli policies with the granting of visas. The implication seems clear: with regard to granting visas the Israeli administration might begin distinguishing between Christians friendly to Israel and those critical or hostile to Israeli policies. This practice could severely limit if not totally undermine the functioning of church institutions especially in the Arab sector both in Israel and in the Palestinian Territories.[26]

The context of the continued hostilities between Israel and her neighbours certainly explains to some degree the attitudes to and limitations on religious freedom described above. At the same time, the fact that Israel is by definition a denominational state, defined as 'Jewish' in both popular opinion and by law, means that

Israel is not yet the state of all its citizens and this constitutes an obstacle to the full realization of religious freedom.

b) The 'New' Christian Israelis

So far, we have spoken mostly of Christians who are either Arabs or expatriates, however there is a new and little-known Christian reality in Israel today; the myriad of new Christian immigrants, mostly from the former Soviet Union (and also from Ethiopia).[27] As most of these immigrants have identified themselves in some way as Jews on entering the country, it is difficult to estimate how many Christians there are among them and what is the nature of their religious identity. A figure published for 1999 illustrates the complexity of this phenomenon: out of about 86,000 new immigrants that year, 53% were not Jewish according to Jewish Law (i.e. did not have a Jewish mother) and 38% did not even have a Jewish father.[28] The official general population statistic of 2001 included this population by stating that a total of 225,000 new Israelis were not registered as Jews because they were not Jewish according to Jewish religious law. Of these, however, only 25,000 were registered officially as Christian.[29] These statistics illustrate well the problematic: the primary definition of these immigrants to Israel is that they are 'non-Jews' i.e. they do not meet the criteria for being Jewish according to the rabbis: they do not have a Jewish mother and they have not converted to Judaism. For many, 'non-Jew' has become synonymous with Christian although most of these 'non-Jewish' immigrants have no religious link with either Judaism or Christianity.[30]

Population statistics that traditionally broke down the population into Jews, Muslims, Christians, Druze, etc., now have an additional breakdown of the ostensibly Jewish population into Jews and non-Jews. This has created a new category in Jewish Israeli parlance: 'the non-Jewish Jewish Israeli'. These 'new' Israelis sometimes wear crucifixes under their shirts, hide icons in their bedrooms and put up Christmas trees at Christmas time. One of their representatives, the former government minister Yuri Edelstein, a newly observant Orthodox Jew, is the son of a Russian Orthodox priest of Jewish origin. Suspicion regarding the Jewish identity of these immigrants has led many Orthodox Jews to propose amending the Law of Return in order to guarantee the Jewishness of those who are receiving Israeli citizenship. Others are proposing new processes by which this large population of non-Jews might be formally incorporated into the Jewish people by individual or mass conversion or some other process of civil incorporation.³¹ The reality of a non-Jewish or even explicitly Christian immigrant community in Israel living among the Jewish Israeli population is not new. Since 1948, Christians, particularly from Eastern Europe, have found their way to Israel within the waves of predominantly Jewish immigration. In the past, the vast majority of these Christians have had close family links to Jews and either assimilated into the (secular) Jewish population or left Israel for other countries. It remains to be seen though whether the professing Christians among this population will remain in Israel and whether their children will retain a Christian identity.³²

Arguably the best known 'new' Israeli Christian is the late Carmelite Father Daniel Rufheisen, a Polish Jewish convert to Catholicism, who tried to emigrate to Israel in the late 1950s, because of his role in challenging the Israeli legal decision to deny automatic Israeli citizenship to Jewish converts to Christianity. All Israeli school children know about '*HaAkh* (Brother) Daniel' and the 1962 court decision about 'Who is a Jew?'³³ In 1970, in the wake of this case, the Israeli Law of Return, which grants automatic citizenship to Jews from the Diaspora who immigrate to Israel, was amended in order to prevent converted Jews from receiving automatic citizenship.³⁴ The debate about who is eligible for Israeli automatic citizenship under this law has not ended and since the 1970 amendment, further debates have been conducted about Jews who define themselves as Messianic believers in Jesus but not as Christians.³⁵

Christian communities for immigrants to Israel, some clandestine, have been formed (evangelical Protestant, Orthodox and Messianic) and many Israeli Jews realize that it is becoming increasingly important to deal with the issue. Most of these Christians live in neighbourhoods that are defined as Jewish. Many hide their Christian identity and even tend to adopt external Jewish identity markers in order to fit in. The children of these immigrants often hide their Christian identity at school and some children, who have explicitly Christian names, have been renamed by their parents or by school authorities. It is not uncommon for these Christians to go through the Jewish rites of passage in order to pass as Jews: children are circumcised, marriage is performed according to Jewish rites and burial is in Jewish cemeteries.³⁶

The state has promoted mass immigration to Israel in order to increase the Jewish (by definition non-Arab) population of the state as part of the 'demographic struggle' against the Arab population growth. Emissaries who are sent to promote immigration do not have strict scruples about the 'Jewishness' of candidates for immigration but on arriving in Israel those who are overtly Christian have met obstacles to the preservation of their religious identity.[37] In one illustrative case, for example, two Ethiopians who frequented Christian prayer services were threatened with expulsion from the country on the basis of having claimed to be Jewish and yet prayed as Christians.

Clearly, Jewish Israelis hope that the majority of these Christians (particularly those who have family ties with Jews and who are not overtly believing or practising Christians) will assimilate themselves into the Jewish secular majority. Even Ben Gurion, the first Prime Minister of the State, considered the possibility of mass conversions of different populations to Judaism. Yitzhaq Ben Zvi, the second state president, an ethnographer, sought out different ethnic groups who might be descended from the Ten Lost Tribes of Israel and even proposed that the Druze in Israel were one of these peoples.[38] The enthusiasm to find the lost 'ten tribes of Israel' or 'crypto-Jewish' remnants of the Inquisition has led Israeli Jews to seek out potential brethren in the jungles of South America and Africa as well as among the teeming millions of Asia.[39] There has been a limited academic debate on the exact religious identity of the Ethiopian Falashas. Most Israelis have accepted without question that this group should be considered fully Jewish, even if the Orthodox rabbis were very reluctant to do so and have tried to forbid inter-marriage between Jews and Falashas without the Falashas undergoing a ceremony that affirms Rabbinic Judaism.[40]

In 1999, the state established a Joint Institute for Jewish Studies which promotes formal conversion for new Israelis who are not Jewish. The Institute is an official government body and is staffed by representatives from different streams of Judaism.[41] 250,000 immigrants to Israel who are not considered Jewish according to Jewish law are envisioned as the target population of this Institute. In 2000, about 4,600 immigrants were converted to Judaism.[42] Conversion to Judaism courses do not only attract immigrants to Israel who are not Jewish according to Jewish religious law but also attract potential immigrants especially from poorer Third World countries especially in Latin America and Asia.[43]

Resisting assimilation into the Jewish population, small groups of Christian immigrants have tried to establish permanent institutional frameworks in order to guarantee Christian survival and one of the best known of these groups is the '*Œuvre de Saint Jacques*' (Work of St James), founded in the 1950s. The *Œuvre* has

Hebrew-speaking Catholic communities in the main cities of
Israel. In August 2003, the presiding prelate of the *Œuvre*, Dom
Jean-Baptiste Gourion, the Benedictine Abbot of the Monastery
in Abu Ghosh, near Jerusalem, was named an auxiliary bishop to
the Latin Patriarch of Jerusalem. This step gave unprecedented
exposure to the community of Hebrew-speaking Catholics.
Interviewed in an Israeli daily, the new bishop explained that part
of his new task was 'to build relationships with those of the
Christian immigrants who seek such a relationship with the
Church'. The new bishop also called on the Israeli establishment
to stop trying to convert the non-Jewish immigrants.[44] The overt
aim of this group is to assimilate culturally and nationally into
Israeli society while preserving a Christian faith identity.
Alongside the Catholic expression, the Orthodox Church has also
named a pastor for the mainly Russian Orthodox Christian immigrants.[45]

Evangelically linked groups of 'Messianic Jews' have sprung up
too, recently reinforced by their outreach to the tens of thousands
of Russian and other Eastern European Christians who have found
their way to Israel as immigrants or as foreign workers.[46] These
believers in Jesus Christ reject the appellation 'Christian' and insist
on their Israeli and Jewish identities. They tend to adopt the Jewish
calendar and highlight the Old Testament and contemporary
national significance of their religious practices. The Messianic
Jews and their Evangelical Protestant allies meet with utmost ambiguity on the part of many Israelis. While their unswerving Zionist
sympathies and right-wing Israeli politics assure them friends
among the Israeli right wing, their missionary activities are greeted
with hostility and sometimes even violence.[47]

Within this complexity, the questions for the state are numerous.
Among them, one might ask:

1. Is he/she a Jew? There is a general confusion regarding the
   identity of this new group of Christian Israelis. Some do have
   Jewish ancestry. Are they 'Jewish Christians'? Many Jews find
   this term offensive.
2. Is he/she an Israeli? Is Israel a Jewish state? What does this
   mean in terms of integrating these Christians? Can the children of these Christians be educated as Christians? What
   would this type of education entail within the context of a
   Jewish majority? Can Hebrew be used as a medium of
   Christian instruction?

It should be mentioned in this context that Jewish Israelis who convert to Christianity (or any other religion) are free to do so according to a Basic Law that deals with religious freedom. There is a small number of such cases and whereas conversion to Christianity is odious to all traditional Jewish sources, these Christians of Jewish origin remain registered as Jews unless they explicitly seek to change their 'ethno-denominational' identity. Most conceal their religious identity to some extent although some have entered religious orders and communities.

In addition to the 'new' Christians who are Israeli citizens, there is an important presence of Christian foreign workers from Eastern Europe (Poland, Rumania, Ukraine, etc.), South America, Africa and Asia (particularly Philippines and Sri Lanka). Although most of these workers are in Israel on limited work contracts, there are some who clearly hope to stay on in a country considered substantially more affluent than their countries of origin.[48] These foreign workers are served by the traditional churches (Orthodox, Catholic, Protestant) to some degree but have also established a new and as yet fragile presence in Israeli cities where previously there was no visible Christian presence. In Israel it is extremely difficult to attain citizenship as a non-Jewish expatriate[49] however some of these foreign workers stay on illegally, marry in Israel and have children here. Some of the children born in Israel are now claiming citizenship.[50] The presence of a large foreign worker population is one factor that Israel has in common with many other countries in the Middle East and throughout the world.

c) The Israeli-Palestinian conflict

Some Jewish Israelis believe that Christians are by definition foreigners. There is a general ignorance among Jews in Israel about local Arab Christians and many Jewish Israelis think that Arabs are by definition Muslims. According to this perception, Christians are perceived as foreign also to Arab culture and as having been consistently persecuted by Muslims. The popular version of the events in Lebanon or in Sudan as wars between Christians and Muslims is often used to direly predict what the fate of Christians in the Muslim Arab world will be. This leads to a position, sometimes formulated by Israeli government officials, that Christians need Israeli protection from supposed Arab or Muslim aggression.[51] Israeli policy was aimed supposedly to protect Christians in Lebanon and similar arguments are used in order to justify Israeli claims to sovereignty over parts of the Palestinian

Territories and especially the Old City of Jerusalem – the claim is that the Christians will not be safe in a Palestinian state.

Some Jewish Israelis perceive that the whole world is against the State of Israel and that includes the local Christians. Despite this rather monolithic attitude, a distinction is often made among pro-Palestinian, neutral and pro-Israeli Christian positions. The traditional churches, Orthodox, Catholic and Protestant, are considered pro-Palestinian. The reasons given by some Israeli officials for this supposed pro-Palestinian position are:

1. Muslim pressure on local Christians particularly on Arab Christians.
2. The Christian Arab desire to prove that they are as loyal as Muslim Arabs to the national cause.
3. The indigenization of the Christian leadership that has led to the mixing of religion and politics as Christian Arab nationalists have gained key leadership positions in the traditional churches.

Recently, at a public reception, the Israeli President vocally accused the Latin Patriarch of justifying Palestinian terrorism.[52] This accusation has been repeatedly used by the Israeli administration against Christian Arab leaders of the Churches in the Holy Land.

Among the various Evangelical Protestant churches[53] and in some still limited expatriate Catholic circles[54] there is a counter-trend known as Christian Zionism. Evangelical fundamentalist groups, which are attracted to Israel because of its Biblical significance, are increasingly present in Israel. Their strong support for even extremist Zionist positions goes hand in hand with a barely concealed missionary drive towards the Jews. Whereas some Jewish Israelis welcome the political support, these groups are kept at arm's length by many because of their missionary agenda. They are primarily encouraged to influence the foreign policy of their own countries (particularly the USA) through their lobbying. The subject of Christian Zionism has been of some concern to the local Christian churches as the Christian Zionists have often spoken out in support of Israeli political claims in the name of all Christians. In addition, many of these Christian Zionist groups seem to encourage local indigenous Christians not only to throw in their lot with Israel, but to deny their own Arab identity, express hostility towards Islam and to emigrate.

The Israeli government has consistently opposed the indigenization of the local church leadership. The Israeli state has an understandable preference for expatriate Christians as representatives of Christian interests. The extent to which the Christian community is headed by expatriate Europeans or Americans is also often considered the extent to which it might be friendly towards Israeli political interests or at least be indifferent to the Arab-Israeli conflict. Until recently, foreign Christians controlled all church institutions and even now constitute an important part of church personnel within many of these institutions. The Greek Orthodox Church is still exclusively controlled by expatriate Greek bishops[55] and the Franciscan Custody remains under Italian leadership,[56] these two institutions constituting the most important Christian land owners in the Holy Land. This creates sporadic tension between the foreign hierarchy and the indigenous Palestinian Arab faithful. Most of the traditional church hierarchies (Roman Catholic, Anglican, Lutheran, etc), however, have undergone extensive indigenization. Local Christian church leaders who have adopted a more political discourse and taken stands on peace and justice are consistently condemned by state officials. A few Christian leaders have been accused of terrorist activity and have been imprisoned, exiled or placed under various restrictions.[57] The Israeli press recently followed with great interest the hosting of nuclear engineer turned anti-nuclear protester, Mordechai Vanunu, by Anglican Bishop Riah Abu El-Assal. Vanunu, a convert from Judaism to Christianity, reviled as a traitor for his revealing of Israel's nuclear capacities and sentenced to a long prison term, was released in April 2004 and found refuge at the Anglican Cathedral in Jerusalem. This only seemed to strengthen Israeli suspicions that Christians, especially Arab Christians, were hostile to Israel.

Within the context of the conflict between Israelis and Palestinians and the broader Israeli-Arab conflict, there is a consistent Israeli attempt to seek foreign Christian support based upon the historic and often troubled relations between Jews and Christians. In addressing Christians about the present conflict, Jewish Israelis often insist on the following:

1. True repentance for the history of Christian anti-Semitism necessitates support for Jewish aspirations today, including Jewish political aspirations.
2. The biblical heritage, shared by Jews and Christians, unequivocally supports the Jewish God-given right to the Land, land which is at the centre of the Jewish religion, like Rome for Catholics and Mecca for Muslims.

3. The Jews are a bastion of Western democratic and liberal political and cultural presence in the Middle East, the only guarantee of religious freedom and access to the Holy Places.

d) Jewish-Christian dialogue in Israel

Jewish-Christian dialogue has been increasingly important in Europe and the US in the past decades. In Israel, the dialogue is hardly at the centre of Jewish Israeli consciousness due to the fact that most Jewish Israelis rarely meet identifiable Christians in their day-to-day lives. Yet, some Israelis do recognize the importance of dialogue with Christians.[58] Israel's insistence that it is at the centre of the Jewish world today has meant that there has been an increasing attempt by Israeli Jews to take leadership roles in the official and institutional Jewish-Christian dialogue internationally. Some themes of this dialogue include:

1. How is the Bible read? How can Christians become more aware of their 'Jewish' roots?
2. What is anti-Semitism? What is its link with anti-Judaism? How did the Holocaust come about? Is the attitude to the Jews in certain New Testament passages anti-Jewish?
3. What is the significance of the State of Israel for the dialogue? What are Christian attitudes to Zionism?
4. How can Christians reformulate their theological discussion about Judaism and Jews in order to promote respect for Jews and appreciate God's 'ongoing covenant with Israel'?

Within the dialogue, Jews are often expected to teach Christians and help them change. For the moment, this is rarely mutual. Within these frameworks the Jewish side is perceived as the embattled minority whereas the Christian side is perceived as the dominant majority. Needless to say, this is the most significant difference when it comes to such dialogue in Israel where Jews are the dominant majority and Christians are the embattled minority.

In Israel there are numerous organizations that promote interreligious dialogue and recently they have been searching out more and more indigenous (i.e. Muslim and Christian Arab) partners in dialogue.[59] In almost all these organizations, Western (often foreign born) Jews or expatriate Christians are the dominant figures. This often means that the agenda for dialogue is the same as that used in Western countries where Jews are the minority. However, the fact that Jews are a dominant majority has not yet been fully assumed within the Jewish-Christian dialogue in Israel. In Israel, the dialogue must now include an evaluation of the experience of the Israeli reality from a Christian point of view. Jews often insist on this, pointing out that Christians must deal theologically with the return of Jews to their Land and their empowerment there. According to this view, such a Christian reflection on Israel will overturn deeply rooted Christian ideas about the perpetual wretchedness of the Jews because of their rejection of the Christ.[60] This is not a one-way reflection though as a Christian reflection on the reality of Israel as a state brings to the forefront the voices of those Christians who live in Israel.

Dialogue between the indigenous Jews and indigenous Christians in Israel is still in its initial stages. The obstacles are great, most significantly the fact that most Christians are Palestinian Arabs and without peace and justice, Jewish-Christian dialogue seems an unaffordable luxury. However, within the Pastoral Plan of the Catholic Churches in the Holy Land, the result of a five-year synod which ended in 2000, a ground-breaking document calls for the nurturing of exactly this kind of dialogue.[61] Latin Patriarch, Michel Sabbah, has done pioneering work in establish a forum for the development of Israeli-Jewish and Palestinian Christian dialogue in the establishment of a special diocesan commission for relations with Judaism. This forum brings leading local Roman Catholics into contact with Jewish Israeli personalities and institutions. An agenda that could be imagined for just such a Palestinian Arab-Jewish Israeli dialogue is substantially different from that which is proposed for Europe or the US:

1. What has been the experience of the 'non-Jewish' minority within the Jewish state? How has the Israeli state dealt with issues of pluralism? democracy? religious freedom? What are the patterns of coexistence, co-operation, domination, discrimination, prejudice?
2. How does one read the history of the Holocaust, Zionism and the establishment of the State of Israel within the context of this dialogue? What is the future of the Palestinian people?
3. How can Judaism and Christianity (and Islam too) contribute to the values of democracy, pluralism, justice and peace in Israel?
4. What role does the Bible play within the political context of the State of Israel?[62]

5. This particular type of Jewish-Christian dialogue also gives rise to its own theological issues. What is the Christian understanding of the election of Israel? the connection between Israel and the Land of Israel? What does the Christian commitment to peace and justice imply within the Israeli-Palestinian context?

One initiative in the area of Jewish-Christian dialogue that captured the hearts and minds of Israelis in 2003 was the organization of a voyage by Jews and Arabs to Auschwitz. The initiator of the voyage, Christian Israeli Arab Greek Catholic priest Emile Shoufani has insisted that Arabs in general and Christian Arabs too must come to grips with the Holocaust if they are to engage Jewish Israelis in dialogue.[63]

There are other elements of the Jewish-Christian dialogue which are particular to the Israeli context and can not be overlooked. First and foremost, Jewish-Christian dialogue in Israel is faced with the reality of Islam and the Muslim world. The State of Israel exists at the centre of the Islamic Arab world. Whereas Christians involved in dialogue often argue for the privileged place of the Jews in dialogue, Jewish Israelis often see Muslims as equal, if not preferred, partners in the dialogue. Not only is Islam seen as religiously and theologically closer to Judaism, but the long centuries of Jewish co-existence with Muslims were often less traumatic than the centuries spent with Christians. In addition, almost half the Jewish Israeli population (those with their cultural roots in Morocco, Iraq, Yemen, Egypt, Tunisia, Algeria, Syria, Lebanon, Iran, Turkey etc.) share a cultural world with Muslim and Christian Arabs. This shared heritage is still evident among these Jews in Israel (particularly in liturgical, folk, musical and culinary culture). Arabic was a very significant language of Jewish life for hundreds of years during which dialogue with Muslims and Christians was conducted with greater or lesser ease depending on the period.

A second element particular to the Israeli context, is that religion, in and of itself, is often perceived as contributing more to the tensions between communities than to understanding and coexistence by many Jewish Israelis. Among both Jewish Israelis and Christian Arabs, many participants in the inter-religious or inter-cultural dialogue are either marginal in their own communities or non-practising. Many practising (Orthodox) Jews are not interested in dialogue and the various streams of Liberal Judaism are still small and marginal on the Jewish Israeli scene.

Within Jewish-Christian dialogue, Jews have been particularly helpful to Christians in an evaluation of the price paid for the Christian embrace of political empowerment at the time of Constantine and thereafter. At present, the dialogue in general and Israeli-Christian Palestinian dialogue in particular, can and should help Jews in evaluating the current embrace of power by contemporary mainstream Judaism in the context of Zionism and the State of Israel.

Conclusion: perspectives and new trends

In conclusion, it must be repeated that Jewish Israeli attitudes are far from static or monolithic and many factors might transform these attitudes in the period ahead. I would like to briefly mention, in conclusion, a few of the perspectives and new trends in Jewish Israeli life that might modify and even transform the attitudes towards Christians and Christianity which have been presented above.

a) *The need for education*

Ron Kronish, a leading Israeli activist in Jewish-Christian dialogue commented on the Pope's visit, saying that the visit was a watershed. 'What particularly impressed me was what we call "the great educational opportunity". During the month before the Pope's visit and during the visit itself there was more about the Pope and Christianity on television and in the newspapers than during the last thirty years.'[64] Some Jewish Israelis are becoming aware that ignorance about Christianity is an impediment, on the one hand, to general culture and, on the other hand, to respect for the local Christian community. Slowly small steps are being taken to rectify this. The Hebrew University of Jerusalem inaugurated a Centre for the Study of Christianity in 2000 although no departments for the study of Christianity or the New Testament exist in any of the Israeli universities. There is still much work to be done, particularly collaborating with local Christians, especially Christian Arabs, in the task of educating the general Jewish Israeli public about Christians and Christianity.

b) *Israeli secularism*

The increasingly strident formulation of an Israeli secularism that has begun to challenge the Jewish identity of the state will undoubtedly affect attitudes towards 'non-Jews'. The question, already clearly formulated, is whether the state will recognize 'Israeli' identity as the dominant and defining civil identity, thus privatizing denominational identities, particularly 'Jewish' identity. The de-denominationalization of the state is not only presented by some Israelis as a condition for its democratic character but also as a condition for putting an end to discrimination against Christians and all 'non-Jews'.[65] However, it should be pointed out that important work on developing a religious Jewish *modus vivendi* with democracy, pluralism and modernity is also being carried out in Israel.[66]

c) Rereading Islamic-Arab culture

It is difficult to imagine how peace with the Arab world might influence the Israeli scene. Undoubtedly, peace will necessitate a re-reading of Islamic-Arab civilization from the Israeli point of view. The reclaiming of Jewish rootedness in the Islamic-Arab world is already current in certain circles and is expressed in the rebirth of interest in Arabic-speaking Judaism, a dominant form of Judaism of the medieval period. Jews and Christians have both played an important role in the formation of Islamic Arab civilization and their continued existence within the larger context of the Middle East depends on a re-evaluation of their respective relationships with the diversity of Islamic Arab culture. Within the context of Middle Eastern Arab Islamic civilization, Jews and Christians have found a common language on many issues in the past and this might also be a fruitful context for a dialogue today.

d) Hebrew-speaking Christians

Since the inception of Zionism, some have asked whether a Hebrew-speaking Christianity will emerge in Israel.[67] The seeds have been sown. Orthodox, Roman Catholic, Protestant and Messianic congregations already exist where Hebrew is the language of prayer and communication. The coming years will certainly be decisive in the emergence of a Hebrew-speaking, Israeli Christian community that is not only inculturated in Israel but also integrated within the Jewish milieu in the country. This community might then act as a bridge with Christianity in general and with the Christians and Muslims of the Arab world in particular.

e) Rereading the history of Jews and Christians

Jews as a dominant majority in Israel are faced with the challenge of re-writing and teaching their own history.[68] Embattled minority Jewish communities have focused almost exclusively on the negative and dark sides of the relationship between Christians and Jews, particularly Christian failings in this relationship. Part of the challenge is to now uncover more positive modes of relationship that did and do exist. Some very interesting trends can be seen in contemporary Israeli literature in Hebrew.[69] Hamutal Bar Yosef, a Jewish Israeli professor of literature, points out:

> The State of Israel, though full of various tensions, enables a Jew to become interested in Christianity without ever experiencing anti-Semitism and without living in the midst of Christians. This is a completely new experience for the Jew and for writers of Hebrew literature. In a country where the visible manifestations of Christianity have a limited presence, there is no urgent need for Jewish-Christian dialogue, nor for the rehabilitation of Judaism in the eyes of Christians. The growing interest in Christianity in Israeli literature must therefore be explained by intellectual curiosity and emotional attraction, almost free from the burden of victim psychology, leaving blame and guilt to be cured through time.[70]

In addition, the prickly subject of anti-Christian trends in Judaism must be dealt with in order to facilitate a change in Jewish attitudes towards non-Jews in general and Christians in particular.[71] Some Israeli Jews and some Christians in Israel are indeed willing to embark on this journey of dialogue and discovery of the other.[72]

It is important for Christians in Israel to engage themselves fully in the full range of social, educational, political and cultural domains in order to transform the attitudes of the majority society. In a recent document published by the Latin Patriarch of Jerusalem and his theological commission, this engagement is outlined:

> We are deeply conscious of the vocation of the Church of Jerusalem to be a Christian presence in the midst of society, be it Muslim Arab or Jewish Israeli. We believe that we are called to be a leaven, contributing to the positive resolution of the crises that we are passing through. We are a voice from within our societies whose history, language and culture we share. We seek to be a presence that promotes reconciliation, helping all peoples towards a dialogue that promotes understanding and that will ultimately lead to peace in this Land.[73]

It is my experience that many Jewish Israelis are ready to enter into dialogue with Christians about their attitudes and perceptions. A Christian witness to the values of peace and justice on the one hand and unity, democracy and human rights on the other hand has a significant role to play in Israeli society today. Meanwhile, some leading Jewish intellectuals and educators ask important questions that challenge traditional Jewish attitudes and contemporary Israeli negative patterns:

> The State of Israel provides a model opposite to that of the Diaspora communities. Here the Jews are a majority, and there are non-Jewish minorities who are members of the Jewish polity. Does Judaism or Jewish culture have sufficient resources to allow for a political project that is not wholly subsumed by religious or national affiliation? Must the product of Zionism be the creation of a Jewish version of the state that has no room for the Jews? Can Jews free themselves of their complementary demonization of the 'goy' [derogatory term for 'non-Jews' – author's note].[74]

I might conclude here with the words of Pope John Paul II pronounced during his 2000 visit to the seat of the Israeli Chief Rabbis:

> We must work together to build a future in which there will be no more anti-Judaism among Christians or anti-Christian sentiment among Jews. There is much that we have in common. There is so much that we can do together for peace, for justice, for a more human and fraternal world. May the Lord of heaven and earth lead us to a new and fruitful era of mutual respect and cooperation for the benefit of all.[75]

Notes

1. According to the 2003 official Israeli statistics, 81% (5.4 million) of Israelis are Jews, 19% (1.3 million) are 'non-Jews' of whom 82% are Muslim, 9% are Christians and 9% are Druze. These statistics apply to the territory of the State of Israel and East Jerusalem but do not include the Palestinian Territories. See also D. M. Neuhaus, 'New Wine into Old Wineskins: Russians, Jews and non-Jews in the State of Israel', *The Journal of Eastern Christian Studies*, vols in 57. no. 3–4, 2005, pp. 207–6.
2. The most common term used in Israeli parlance is not Christian or Muslim but rather 'non-Jew'. The Hebrew word *goy* tends to be derogatory. The word *nochri* (alien) or *toshav ger* are often used in more religious discourse.
3. According to the 2003 statistics, 2.1% of the population of Israel is Christian. It should be noted however that this figure includes Christians from East Jerusalem, annexed in 1967, most of whom are Jordanian rather than Israeli citizens.

4   Ari Shavit, 'The road to reconciliation', *HaArtez*, 27 March 2000.
5   The Anti-Defamation League published a full page statement in all the important Israeli newspapers acclaiming the 'historic visit to the Jewish state' and informing the public of the 'Pope's views on Israel, Judaism and the Shoah', underlining the profound changes in Catholic Church teaching.
6   Y. Landau quoted in 'Envisioning the Future of Jewish Christian Relations in Israel,' *SIDIC* XXXIII, 3 (2000), p. 10.
7   From a 1988 article cited in M. Walzer, M. Loberbaum, and N. Zohar, (eds), *The Jewish Political Tradition: volume 2, Membership*, New Haven, 2003, pp. 534–5.
8   See in particular the article of O. Coussins, 'It is time for Israelis to learn that Jesus was Jewish', *HaAretz*, 23 December 1999.
9   Survey conducted by Hanoch and Rafi Smith for the Elijah School, 15 March 2000.
10 See Coussins in *HaAretz*, 23 December 1999.
11 In a recent High Court decision the option of registering simply as Israeli on the official identity card was refused. All Israelis are registered officially according to denominational, ethnic or cultural categories (of which there are 135 possibilities) but being registered simply as Israeli is not an option. See *HaAretz*, 19 May 2004. In 2002, the Jewish Orthodox Minister of Interior, after a conflict with the judiciary, refused to recognize the legitimacy of certain (non-Orthodox) conversions to Judaism and consequently annulled the registration of 'nation' on the identity card.
12 Cited in M. Walzer, et al. (eds), *The Jewish Political Tradition: volume 2*, 536–7.
13 The State of Israel has no constitution. Basic freedoms are rooted in the Declaration of Independence. Orthodox Jews have resisted the formulation of a constitution, arguing that Jewish Law is that constitution.
14 There have been prominent Christian Arab members of the Knesset (Israeli parliament), among them the currently serving Azmi Bishara, but generally they are identified as Arabs and not as Christians. One of the rare examples of a Christian Arab active in Israeli cultural life is the author Anton Shammas who writes in Hebrew and is considered one of the most innovative writers of Hebrew today. Shammas now lives in the US. There have been some noted Christian expatriates who are Hebrew-speakers and have held positions within academic and scientific institutions: the best known case is that of Marcel Dubois, OP who served for many years as head of the Philosophy Department at Hebrew University. Another Dominican, himself of Jewish origin, Bruno Hussar, OP was the founder of the Israeli Jewish-Arab peace village of Neve Shalom.
15 For an Israeli perspective on religious freedom see R. Lapidoth, 'Freedom of Religion and Conscience in Israel' in R. Lapidoth and O. Ahimeir (eds), *Freedom of Religion in Jerusalem*, Jerusalem, 1999, pp. 3–46.
16 For a detailed analysis see I. Lustick, *Arabs in the Jewish State: Israel's Control of a National Minority*, Austin, 1980. See also (in Hebrew) *Erets Aheret*, no. 16 (May–June 2003) on the Arab citizens of Israel.
17 Important recent studies include R. Gavison, *Israel as a Jewish and Democratic State: Tensions and Opportunities*, Tel Aviv, 2000 (Hebrew) and A. Yakobson and A. Rubinstein, *Israel and the Family of Nations: Jewish Nation-State and Human Rights*, Tel Aviv, 2004 (Hebrew).
18 For coverage of a document circulated by an official of the Israeli Ministry of Foreign Affairs to the Israeli participants in the Camp David negotiations

concerning the Holy Places see *Kol HaIr* (Hebrew), 14 July 2000.
19 See B. Morris, *The Birth of the Palestinian Refugee Problem, 1947–1949*, London, 1987, p. 201.
20 See, for example, Hila Altschuler in *HaAretz* magazine, 22 December 2000 or *Kol HaIr* (Hebrew), 4 May 2001.
21 For the details of this controversy see D. Christiansen, 'Nazareth journal' in *America*, 4/182 (12 February 2000), pp. 8–13. Finally, after extensive US pressure, the construction of the mosque was forbidden and its foundations were destroyed in 2003.
22 The Christian Allies Caucus was founded in January 1994 and is co-chaired by Yuri Stern (National Union Party) and Yair Peretz (Shas), both on the right side of the political spectrum. The Christians involved include mainly representatives of Evangelical Protestant organizations with strong Christian Zionist agendas. Attempts have also been made to draw in representatives of the traditional churches.
23 According to many sources conflict over land is what is at the basis of the Israeli government's refusal to recognize the Greek Orthodox Patriarch Ireneos who was elected in 2001. The Patriarch has been recognized by the other authorities involved, both Jordanian and Palestinian. See D. Rubenstein, 'The patriarch and his property', *HaAretz*, 29 February 2004.
24 See A. Barkat, 'Spiritual needs and practical purposes', *HaAretz*, 8 December 2003.
25 This endangers the continuity of Christian institutional life particularly for the Orthodox and Catholic Churches as Jerusalem is the church centre. The Roman Catholic diocesan and Franciscan seminaries have numerous vocations from Jordan, Lebanon, Syria, Iraq and Egypt and these seminaries are periodically refused visas.
26 See *HaAretz* coverage, 30 March 2004, 8 April 2004, 28 May 2004.
27 For an excellent survey of this immigration from Russia and the former USSR, see *Eretz Aheret* (Hebrew), 19/2003, titled 'One million Russian immigrants: How we have changed and how we will change even more' that is consecrated to the subject.
28 See *HaAretz*, 31 January 2000.
29 See *HaAretz*, 17 September 2001. Those not registered as Jewish or Christian are registered as Russian, Ukranian, etc. Some, it was revealed, have no registration at all on their identity cards (see *HaAretz*, 17 January 2000). The 2002 statistics counted 27,000 official Christians among the new immigrants. According to Dr Z. Khanin of Bar Ilan University the number of self identified Christians is slighter higher than the official statistic (see *HaAretz* (Hebrew), 11 June 2002 and *The Jerusalem Report*, 26 August 2002, p. 22).
30 The strikingly secular and often anti-religious identity of many of the Russians is featured in *Eretz Aheret* (Hebrew), 19/2003.
31 See the fascinating discussion (in Hebrew) in the issue of conversion to Judaism in *Eretz Aheret*, 17/2003.
32 There is already a noticeable trend of emigration to other Western countries by some of the Russians in Israel who are indeed Christian. One group even asked for political asylum in Canada, claiming that they were not free to practise their Christian faith in Israel.
33 For an account of this case see another late Carmelite of Jewish origin, then resident in Israel, E. Friedman, *Jewish Identity*, New York, 1987, pp. 11–25.
34 The ammendment added the new distinction of not belonging to another

religion to the definition of a Jew that had previously only held that a Jew is someone 'born of a Jewish mother'.

35 In December 1989, the Supreme Court decided that Messianic Jews, who profess belief in Jesus as Messiah, are also not eligible for citizenship under the Law of Return. See *Jerusalem Post*, 5 May 1990.

36 As publicly known non-Jews cannot be married to Jews, some are forced to marry outside Israel. Non-Jews cannot be buried in Jewish cemeteries and so there are now 'civil' cemeteries in which burials with no religious rites can take place.

37 For a description of the work of these emissaries see the article of Yossi BarMuha, 'The Sixteenth Tribe of Israel has been discovered', *HaAretz*, (Hebrew) 8 August 1997.

38 See *HaAretz*, 3 January 1999.

39 About 'crypto Jews' in Majorca, see *The Jerusalem Report*, 8 November 1999; in Peru, see HaAretz 10 Febuary 2000; in Spain, see *Jerusalem Post*, 22 November 2002; in Mexico, see *HaAretz*, 6 January 2001 and 29 March 2002; in the Caribbean *HaAretz*, 4 October 2002; and descendants of the ten tribes in India and Burma, *The Jerusalem Report*, 17 November 2003.

40 Public debate in Israel still rages over the fate of the Falasha Mura, Ethiopian Falasha who adopted official Christianity. Some of the Falasha Mura have relatives in Israel and many seek to immigrate to Israel. For details on the Falasha and Falasha Mura see the articles of Yair Sheleg in *HaAretz*, 4 March and 6 March 2003.

41 For background to this Institute see 'The Birth of Israel's New Jews,' *The Jerusalem Report*, 29 January 2001.

42 See *HaAretz*, 24 December 2000.

43 For two feature stories on such conversions see the story of Creole Catholics from Reunion in *HaAretz*, 7 February 2003; Filipinos in *The Jerusalem Report*, 15 July 2002 and indigenous tribesmen from Peru in *HaAretz* (Hebrew), 19 July 2002 (and the commentary of H. Goodman, 'Zap – you're Jewish' in *The Jewish Report*, 12 August 2002.

44 *HaAretz* (Hebrew), 14 October 2003.

45 For the Russian Orthodox community and the work of Father Alexander Winogradsky see L. Gelfond, 'The New Israelis' in *The Jerusalem Post* magazine, 1 November 2002.

46 See *The Jerusalem Report*, 11 August 2003, pp. 17–19. For an excellent survey of the Messianic Jewish communities see: K. Kjaer-Hansen and B. Skjott, *Facts and Myths: About the Messianic Congregations in Israel*, Jerusalem, 1999.

47 See R. Zimmer, 'For the love of Jesus', *The Jerusalem Report*, 11 August 2003.

48 A foreign worker made her appearance for the first time in an important Israeli novel published by the well known Israeli author, A. B. Yehoshua. The novel, *The Mission of the Human Resource Man: A Passion in Three Parts* (2004), also presents the sense of religious belonging of Christian foreign workers in Jerusalem. The central character, a Russian woman working in Jerusalem, is killed in a terrorist attack and after her body is returned to Russia for burial, her mother demands that her daughter be buried in Jerusalem.

49 Whereas Jews are granted citizenship automatically under the provisions of the Law of Return and can retain their previous citizenship, non-Jews who make application have to wait many years and eventually have to give up their original citizenship. See L. Susser, 'Who gets to be Israeli', *The Jerusalem Report*, 20 June 2003.

50 A recently established government committee is to decide on the rights of children of foreign workers born in Israel and their eligibility for permanent residence in the country, see *HaAretz*, 7 July 2004.
51 See important article of Danny Rubinstein, 'Who will defend the Christians' in *HaAretz*, 13 September 2000 and the strident response of Father Raed Abusahlieh in *Al-Quds*, 24 September 2000. Also, Danny Rubinstein, *HaAretz*, 6 November 2001 and Nitzan Horowitz, *HaAretz*, 30 December 2001. A video cassette, titled 'Holy Land: Christians in Danger', has recently been circulated in France. It argues that Christians are being persecuted by Muslims in the Palestinian Territories and that the Israeli Army defends Christians.
52 See *HaAretz*, 15 January 2004.
53 For Evangelical Protestant Christian Zionism see the illiminating series of five articles by D. Wagner in the Lebanese *Daily Star*, 7, 8, 9, 10, and 14 October 2003.
54 For Catholic philo-Zionism see the interesting analysis of P. Lenhardt, 'La fin du sionisme?' *Sens*, 3/22004, pp. 99–138.
55 See the extensive coverage of the election of the new Greek Orthodox Patriarch, Ireneos I, in 2001 in the Israeli press (eg. *Jerusalem Post* 16 September 2001, *HaAretz*, 1 September 2002).
56 The appointment of Italian Rev. Rierbattista Pizzaballa OFM as Custos in May 2004 led to much speculation regarding a significant pro-Israeli turn in the constitution of the local Roman Catholic hierarchy. Pizzaballa is the first Custos who speaks no Arabic but rather Hebrew and has had no experience of the local Arabic-speaking Church. See *Franciscan News* (www.ofm.org) for interview with Pizzaballa.
57 Anglican Revd Elia Khoury was accused of terrorist activity and expelled in 1969, Greek Catholic Patriarchal Vicar of Jerusalem, Hilarion Cappucci, was convicted of gun running for the PLO and condemned to prison in 1974 (and released after extensive Vatican intervention in 1977), Greek Catholic Revd Fawzi Khoury was accused of belonging to a terrorist organization and briefly imprisoned in 1983 and both he and Anglican Rev. (now Bishop of Jerusalem) Riah Abu al-Assal were subject to severe limitations on their freedom of movement in the 1980s. More recently Greek Orthodox Father Atallah Hanna (an Israeli citizen from the Galilee was questioned by the police and had his travel documents confiscated (see *HaAretz*, 23 Augaust 2002).
58 In the former Israeli government, a minister in the government, Rabbi Melchior, was made responsible for contacts with the Christian world as well as being responsible for Jewish Diaspora affairs.
59 The *Guide to Interreligious and Intercultural Activities in Israel* (published by the Interreligious Coordinating Council in Israel, 2000) lists about sixty-seven organizations working in dialogue.
60 See David Hartman in *HaAretz*, 25 April 2000.
61 See Assembly of Catholic Ordinaries in the Holy Land, *The General Pastoral Plan*, n. 13, 'Relations with believers of other religions', see 'Our relationship with Jews', pp. 153–7.
62 See the Pastoral Letter of H. B. Mgr Michel Sabbah, Latin Patriarch of Jerusalem, *Reading the Bible Today in the Land of the Bible*, November 1993.
63 For interview with Shoufani see E. Shoufani, *Comme un veilleur attend la paix*, Paris, 2003. In May 2003, the Pope appointed another Christian Israeli Arab Greek Catholic priest, Father Elias Chacour, to the liaison committee that

promotes dialogue between the Vatican and the Chief Rabbinate in Israel, a committee that already included Mgr Boulos-Giacinta Marcuzzo, Latin auxiliary bishop of Nazareth.

64. R. Kronish quoted in 'Envisioning the Future of Jewish Christian Relations in Israel', *SIDIC* XXXIII, 3 (2000), p. 10.
65. See L. Susser, 'Who gets to be an Israeli', *The Jerusalem Report*, 30 June 2003.
66. One of the most important Jewish think tanks in Israel is the Shalom Hartman Institute, founded by Orthodox rabbi and philosopher, David Hartman. This institute confronts the problems of the encounter between Judaism and modernity in all its forms including the encounter with other faith traditions.
67. For the earliest history of this question see G. Nerel, 'Hebrew Christian Associations in Ottoman Jerusalem: Jewish Yeshua believers facing Church and Synagogue', in *Revue des Études juives*, 161 (3–4), 2002, pp. 431–57.
68. A pioneering series of books on this subject has already been published by the Open University. The head of the editorial board is Dr Ora Limor. The first volume was published in 1993.
69. Already mentioned above is the very moving portrayal of a Russian Christian foreign worker in A. B. Yehoshua's 2004 novel, *The Mission of the Human Resource Man: A Passion in Three Parts*. More recent novels dealing with Christianity and Christians include Yonatan Ben Nahum, *Confession* (1991), Benjamin Shvili, *Kastoria* (1998), Eyal Meged, *Eternal Life* (2001) and David Grossman, *Someone to Run With* (2002). Meged's father, renown Israeli author Aharon Meged wrote a novel about a Jewish convert to Christianity who became a Jesuit, *The Bat* (1975).
70. H. Bar Yosef, *Jewish-Christian Relations in Modern Hebrew and Yiddish Literature*, Cambridge, 2000, p. 31.
71. A recent contribution to this kind of study is the book by Hebrew University historian Israel J. Yuval, *Two Nations in Your Womb: Perceptions of Jews and Christians*, 2000, (Hebrew).
72. See for example the article by A. Kleinberg, 'O brother, where are thou?' and the debate it provoked in *HaAretz* (Passover supplement, 5 April 2004 and reactions 16 April 2004 and 23 April 2004). See also R. Fontana, 'Gentils en Israël: entre démocratie et Torah', *Sens*, 3/2004, pp. 139–50.
73. M. Sabbah, Latin Patriarch of Jerusalem and Latin Patriarchate theological commission, 'Reflections on the presence of the Church in the Holy Land', 3 December 2003.
74. M. Lorberbaum in M. Walzer, M. Loberbaum, and N. Zohar, (eds), *The Jewish Political Tradition: Volume 2, Membership*, New Haven, 2003, pp. 542–3.
75. Speech of Pope John Paul II at the Chief Rabbinate of Israel, Jerusalem, 23 March, 2000.

Chapter 2

Hebrew Catholicism in Modern Israel

Leon Menzies Racionzer

There are many Jews in modern Israel who believe in Jesus as the Messiah but only a tiny fraction of these are rooted in the Catholic Church.

The largest number of Jewish believers in Jesus is in the Messianic Movement; various sources claim there are between 3,000 and 5,000 of them in Israel alone and many thousands in other countries, United States and France particularly. They are not associated with any recognizable church and are perhaps most appropriately described as a religious movement, composed of faith groups that are mainly attended by ethnic/cultural Jews but there are among their numbers non-Jewish believers and non-Jewish spouses.

There is a striking contrast between those Jewish believers in the Messianic Movement[1] and the Catholic Jewish believers in Jesus, Hebrew Catholics, who according to official diocesan statistics number 250–400. However, other sources suggest there are as many as a thousand in the *Oeuvre de Saint Jacques l'Apôtre* or *kehilla*.[2] Apart from the vast difference in numbers, unlike the Messianic Jews, the Hebrew Catholics are a non-proselytizing community. It is largely due to the efforts of some of their founding members that the Church no longer believes in the conversion of the Jews.[3] This is not to say however, that they will not accept into their numbers any Jew who freely chooses baptism and enters into a covenantal relationship with the Catholic Church. It is the non-missionary nature of the *kehilla* that sets this group apart from all other Jewish believers and may explain why they and indeed the Catholic Church conflict less acrimoniously with Israeli society than the Messianic Jewish Movement.

This chapter will present an account of the origins and the uniqueness of the cultural, theological and ecclesiological situation of Hebrew Catholicism in modern Israel.

Origins of Hebrew Catholicism

The *kehilla* exists within the jurisdiction of the Latin Patriarchate. The former Patriarch Albert Gori approved its creation in 1955, after several years of discussion and preparation and it received warm encouragement from Cardinal Tisserant, then prefect of the Sacred Congregation for the Oriental Churches.[4] The decision to found the *Oeuvre* was prompted principally by the patriarchs' pastoral solicitude for the Catholics, apparently some several thousand of them at that time who arrived in Israel as refugees or immigrants in the years following the Second World War and the creation of the State of Israel (1948)[5] and who continued to arrive throughout the 1950s. They came also invariably from the countries of Eastern Europe and were either converted Jews or descendants of such converts or Catholic spouses in mixed marriages. In a few cases they had no connection at all with Jews and Judaism and were simply anxious to emigrate from their countries, now Communist or in the process of becoming so. The Patriarchate, especially in the person of the then patriarchal vicar for Israel, Mgr Vergani, was conscious of its duty to those immigrants and fearing that because of differences of mentality and language, as well as of the complexity of the socio-political situation, they might not easily find their place within the normal parochial organization, favoured the creation of a distinct framework within its jurisdiction specially designed to meet their needs. It was accepted that the pastoral centres envisaged would adopt Hebrew, as being the lingua franca for immigrants originating from a number of different countries.[6] The statutes of the *Oeuvre* approved on 11 February 1956, exhort its members to:

> Acquire an understanding of the mystery of Israel. 'We insist upon a Biblical formation; we try to promote a Jewish Christian culture and spirituality in conformity with that culture ... (We aim) to combat all forms of anti-Semitism, attempting to develop mutual understanding and friendly relations between the Catholic world and Israel.

The majority of those who supported the creation of the *Oeuvre* seemed to have felt that, even though an open missionary drive among Israeli Jews would in the circumstances be unthinkable, their task was to make the Christian faith accessible to those Hebrew-speaking Israelis whom God might prompt to seek membership of the Church. A smaller number of the 'founding fathers' were (and still are) motivated by a much larger vision, which could be summed up as a desire to implant the Church within the Jewish people 'in such a way that Jews who become Christians should be able to preserve their national character, in much the same way that members of any other people or nation are invited to do'.[7] Extensive autonomy was granted to the *Oeuvre,* which until his demise on 23rd June 2005 was under the pastoral supervision of the Patriarch's Auxiliary Bishop the Benedictine Abbot, a Jew, Jean-Baptiste Gourion at Abou-Gosh, Église de la Résurrection. Gourion had been responsible for the pastoral care of Hebrew-speaking Catholics for some ten years prior to his election as Auxiliary bishop on 14 August 2003 and his subsequent consecration by the Patriarch, H. B. Archbishop Michel Sabbah, on 9 November 2003. There are four *foyers* (or communities) in Tel Aviv, Haifa, Jerusalem and Beersheva.

Unique issues of culture, politics and theology

Members of the *kehilla* may be characterized as Catholic Christians of both Jewish and Gentile origin, who are Israelis or residents in Israel and live in the Jewish milieu, praying and giving expression to their faith in Hebrew, with a profound appreciation of the Jewish roots of their faith and practice. They seek to understand the relationship between contemporary Judaism (in all its diversity) and the Christian faith today.

They live in a unique cultural, political and social environment. Nowhere else in the world and never before in history have Christians encountered the Jewish people in a state that is defined as Jewish and where Jews are the dominant and empowered majority, a reality that dates from 1948.[8] The Hebrew Christians living and working in the State of Israel may be differently affected than their gentile co-religionists by the ongoing conflict between the State of Israel and the Arab world, and in particular between Israelis and Palestinians. Maintaining their national identity as Jewish Israelis, which they seek to do without ignoring the plight of their Palestinian co-religionists, could cause them to be separated both physically and spiritually from the majority of Catholics, the Arabic-speaking Catholics, in the Holy Land, whilst at the same time being mistrusted by the Israeli authorities as being supportive of the Palestinian cause.

The statutes of the *kehilla* recognize the particular vocation of a Catholic coming from Judaism[9] in that they are a prophetic witness to the Church but they must also witness to Israeli society in a manner that does not suggest they have abandoned their roots. A patriotic Hebrew Catholic then, is charged to show pride, devotion and collaboration with the terrestrial homeland,[10] which is increasingly difficult in the current environment emanating from the six-year-old second *intifada*. The dilemma is how to put into practice on a day-to-day basis, in the work place, the schools and colleges and on social occasions,[11] the firmly held belief that one's Christian identity transcends cultural, political and geographical boundaries.[12]

The Israeli perception of Christians is marked by the anguished and difficult history of relationships between Jews and Christians culminating in the Holocaust. How much more then a Jewish Christian?

Israelis are generally ignorant about Christianity[13] and harbour negative images accompanied sometimes by certain hostility when the Christian is seen as a potential enemy or a missionary.[14] Missionary activity fuels in the minds of the Israeli population the two greatest fears of world Jewry: assimilation and annihilation.[15] Hebrew Catholics therefore suffer this additional negative perception that they have deserted their people, they are considered *meshumadim*: apostates and renegades, who for some have joined the enemy and are no longer Jewish.

In spite of the negative Jewish perception there are those in the *kehilla* who regard the emergence of a Hebrew Christian Church as a positive and prophetic sign for both Jews and Christians. For them it is the inevitable return to the 'Church of the circumcision' of the first century and the return of that which has been lost in 'the Church of the Nations'. 'The Church will only be 'Catholic', that is complete, when the two sisters of the mosaic of Saint Sabine in Rome will be side by side again in the world.'[16]

Perhaps it will be the Jewish Catholic Church in Israel that will fulfil the prophetic role of gathering in the exiles from all the nations. [Jer 29:14], [Ezek 28:25, 39:27] If that is to be so then it is appropriate that it must be, as its members intend, a church that has a Jewish culture consisting of Jews and Gentiles, an Oriental Church that is completely absorbed in the Israeli milieu as part of the local indigenous Catholic Church and yet 'part of the Universal Catholic Church united in faith with Catholics throughout the World'.[17]

Many factors militate against the growth of the *kehilla* and its full blossoming as a recognizable Hebrew Christian Church. The community is a small minority within the local Palestinian Arab Church, which in its turn is a tiny minority among the Arabs of Israel, Palestine and Jordan; it lives in a radically different universe to that of its Arab brothers and is confronted by a different pastoral and spiritual situation.[18] Questions arise as to the nature of the needs of a heterogeneous community and the ecclesiastical and liturgical structure that would best serve those of different cultural and national origins such as Western and Eastern Europeans, many from the former Soviet Union, but also from the Middle East, North Africa, Egypt, Ethiopia etc. Israeli society as a whole is extremely heterogeneous and it too is still in the process of finding a homogenous political and social structure.

The *kehilla*, following the suggested vision of Cardinal Tisserant, has adopted Hebrew as the lingua franca for immigrants originating from a number of different countries but many of these immigrants do not speak Hebrew and even some regular mass attendees at the various centres do not speak the modern Hebrew language into which the liturgy of the mass has been carefully translated by two of the *kehilla's* founding fathers.[19]

Other proposals made by some of the members, in the interests of acculturation, such as a celebration of the Jewish New Year [*Rosh Hashanah*] and Tabernacles [*Sukot*], finding a way perhaps to incorporate these feasts into the liturgy, recognizing *Yom Kippur* with fasting and a day of adoration and prayer, even recognizing *Shabbat* as well as Sunday, have not been adopted. [20]

The Israeli political system does not allow for the separation of religion and state; the defining characteristic of belonging to the country is Jewish rather than Israeli, thus there are Jewish Catholics who would avoid being seen as members of the *kehilla* in order to maintain Israeli citizenship and the privileges attaching thereto. It is extremely difficult to attain citizenship in Israel as a non-Jew and a Jew who practises a faith other than Judaism, in whatever form, is classified as a non-Jew.[21] Many Jewish Catholics therefore, in order to forego the lengthy process of making application and in order to avoid the discrimination associated with being non-Jewish, may have applied for and been granted citizenship automatically under the provisions of the 'Law of Return'. Whilst the law guarantees liberty of conscience and worship the terms of entry in these cases restricts their overt practice of Christianity. This applies particularly to the unknown number of those in mixed marriages from the former Communist bloc, in particular the former Soviet Union, Russia and Ethiopia.

The *kehilla* has within its membership a high percentage of religious, priests and nuns, however it would seem that there are very few young people and families. It is perhaps not surprising that there are few young Christians remaining in a land 'crushed by the weight of two diverse extremisms',[22] which create such difficult conditions of life as to compel them to emigrate[23] to Europe or the United States of America in ever-increasing numbers.[24]

The politics of ecclesiology

The re-emergence of Hebrew Catholicism in the Holy Land excites those who see in it a prophetic sign that heals the wounds of the great rupture between the Church of the Circumcision and the Church of the Gentiles. For them the resultant imbalance that saw the *Ecclesia ex Circumcisione* swallowed by the *Ecclesia ex Gentibus* in less than a century could again in modern times overwhelm this fragile shoot thus losing the benefits for all time of the Hebrew traditions and culture upon which the Early Church was founded.

For over forty years those that feared the overcoming of this tender shoot, or at least restrictions to its full blossoming, have proposed ecclesial, and liturgical innovations for its wellbeing within the Israeli milieu.[25] Cardinal Ratzinger, writing to a member of the *kehilla* in 1992 says it is necessary that the Church be extended to cater for its original double structure that must shape the Church again from the inside.[26] The main proposals were intended to show the Israeli people that a Hebrew Christian Church of Israel participates in the life of the country, understands the culture and values of Judaism and also to help 'deepen [the Church's] understanding of itself'.[27]

The criticisms that this movement for change[28] made of Hebrew Catholicism's character in modern Israel, is that it did not show itself to be part of Israeli society. It appeared and still does appear foreign in its nationality, culture and language. In the opinion of some this was due to the continued use of the Roman liturgical style, symbols, and the ecclesial structure. The symbol of the cross particularly serves only as a reminder to Israeli society of the horrors inflicted upon them under this sign[29] and the statues of saints are perceived as idols that Christians worship.[30]

Cardinal Daoud, Prefect of the Sacred Congregation for the Oriental Churches is reported[31] to have observed at the meeting on the future of Christians in the Holy Land, Vatican City, 13

December 2001, that the character of the *kehillot* is that the Church is not actually very visible and has no voice within the ethnic-cultural majority but he asked 'What in practice would be the "ecclesial structure" best adapted to resolving the problem?'

This movement for change seemed to consider that many of the issues of inculturation etc. would be resolved if separate jurisdiction for Hebrew-speaking Catholics in Israel was established – directly dependent on Rome and independent of the predominantly Arab Latin Patriarchate. In the past the Patriarch has not ignored the requests for more autonomy and authority for the *kehilla*. Since 1999 the patriarchal vicar[32] to the *kehilla* has been an invited member of the assembly of Catholic Ordinaries[33] of the Holy Land. But this issue became an extremely complex mix of ecclesiastical and secular politics.[34]

Ironically the 'Roman' intervention that claimed to be motivated by pastoral concern for the growing numbers of non-Arab Catholics among Israel's immigrant population, of whom many are temporary residents who do not speak Hebrew, could well have been the final blow that would restrict the re-emergence of the *ecclesia circumcisione*. The largest immigrant group is Russian, of which an estimated 250,000 to 400,000 are listed as 'non-Jewish.' Of these, only 27,000 to 30,000 acknowledge being Christian, and for the most part these are Orthodox.[35] If the intention had been to set up a church of Israel; a Hebrew-speaking church that would supplant the fledgling Hebrew Catholic Church and be primarily concerned with non-Arabs and non-Jews, the gentile imbalance already existing in the *kehilla* would once again have overpowered the *ecclesia circumcisione*.

There were and still are vigorous attacks on the Patriarch, Michel Sabbah, in the French Catholic press by some French churchmen who supported the idea. These attacks would not appear to have been out of solicitude for the pastoral care of the immigrant population. Immigrant Christians are already well served by chaplains speaking the language of their country of origin. Nor is it conceivable that the strong support by some in the Israeli government for the establishment of a church within the Jewish State did not have a wider political agenda.

Michel Sabbah is the first Palestinian cleric to rise in the Catholic hierarchy and to be named patriarch,[36] and he has spoken out for Palestinian rights and national aspirations and against the Israeli occupation and human rights violations. He has also taken seriously the concerns of Catholics within the State of Israel. As the leading Catholic churchman in Israel, his views are taken seriously throughout the Catholic world. Some in the Israeli government may regard his current position that straddles the geopolitical and ethnic divide as too powerful from a public relations point of view. Therefore, the motives of the Israeli government in their support for what effectively would have divided the Church in the Holy Land would seem to have been to undermine the Patriarch who has been portrayed by some as the 'Islamic patriarch'[37] who, if the Patriarchate were divided, would no longer have been regarded as the head of a united Church in the Holy Land.[38]

The supporters of the move in the French Church for a separate jurisdiction were perhaps unwittingly playing into the hands of a government that is not averse to interfering in ecclesiastical appointments.[39]

Any person who expresses criticism of Israeli policies tends to be accused of anti-Semitism[40] even if they go out of their way to create an environment that encourages mutual understanding and respect for Jews as they are, and dialogue with them as a fundamental Christian priority.[41] The Patriarch's efforts in this respect seem to have gone unnoticed; his condemnation of both violence and of the provocative situations that lead to violence[42] are seen as supportive of the violence of the Palestinians in spite of his continual condemnation of all violence. He states, 'Terrorism is illogical, irrational and unacceptable as a means of resolving conflict.'[43] Ironically his anti-violence stance,[44] and dialogue with the Israelis,[45] alienates him from the very Arabs that the Israelis accuse him of supporting.

The issue of inculturation of the *kehilla* into Israeli society whilst keeping it within the Universal Church so that it might shape it again from the inside, could not have been more appropriately resolved than by the appointment, as previously reported above, of the first Jewish bishop[46] in the Holy Land since James the Apostle. Jean Baptiste Gourion was appointed auxiliary bishop to the Patriarch with special responsibility for Hebrew-Speaking Israeli Catholics on 14 August 2003 and consecrated by the Patriarch on 9 November 2003. Perhaps we can regard this appointment as a rejection by the Vatican of the criticisms of Patriarch Michel Sabbah and of the Latin Patriarchate of Jerusalem as the dominant Catholic ecclesiastical voice in Jerusalem and in the Holy Land. Perhaps too it is a prophetic move in nurturing the rebirth of the *ecclesia circumcisione*.

Notes

1 These are mainly Jews who have come to believe in Jesus as the Messiah through Protestantism; they are not recognized by the Israeli authorities as Christian or as Jews and have alienated themselves from Israeli society by their missionary vocation. They are, nevertheless, a visible Christian presence integrated into Israeli society. They are not dependent on any Western Church and, therefore, are disassociated from the regrettable history of Christian anti-Semitism. They courageously and overtly practise their faith, as did the Apostles, in spite of the trouble that their proselytising brings upon them.
2 The term '*kehilla*' is singular meaning 'The Community' but there are in fact four communities in the *Oeuvre*. The research done by the author disagrees with the suggestion that there may be more than 400 at the most in the *kehilla*.
3 See Nostra Aetate (n. 4.) also, 1985 'Notes on the Correct Way to Present the Jews and Judaism in Preaching and Catechesis of the Roman Catholic Church'. See also Anna Rist, 'An interview with Père Marcel Dubois, OP', *New Blackfriars*, March 1997, p. 189.
4 Cardinal Silvestrini, 'Eugéne Tisserant et la Congrégation pour l'Église Orientale', *Le Cardinal Eugéne Tisserant (1884–1972), Une grande figure de lÉglsie, Une grande Figure Française*, Toulouse: Institut Catholique, 2003, pp. 101–15.
5 A few Catholic thinkers immigrated to Israel because they saw the founding of the State of Israel as perhaps the prophetic fulfilment of [Psalm 147:2] the ingathering of the Jews in *Eretz-Israel*. This naive Zionism, as described by Père Marcel Dubois, OP, had more of a religious element than that of some of the original Jewish Zionists. The influence of these thinkers during the years prior to and after the 1955 approval was a major factor in the establishment of the *kehilla* and has a lasting effect on it in modern times. See Bruno Hussar, 'The beginnings of the Hebrew Church' in *When the Cloud Lifted*, Veritas, 1989.
6 In fact the *Oeuvre* was granted permission by the Patriarchate and the Vatican to have the liturgy in Hebrew as early as 1957. For the pioneering work of the French Jewish convert Priest, Jean-Roger Henné in creating a Hebrew Catholic culture, see Dominique Trimbur 'Les Assomptionistes de Jerusalem, les Juifs et le sionisme', *Tsafon: Revue d'études juives du Nord*, no. 48 (1999–2000), pp. 71–111.
7 David-Maria Hunter (D-MA. Jaeger): 'Holy land Christians: Hebrew-speaking communities', *The Tablet*, 7 January 1978 pp. 5–7.
8 H. B. Latin Patriarch of Jerusalem, Michel Sabbah and members of the diocesan Theological Commission, Jerusalem, 3 December 2003 in his Christmas message '*Reflections on the Presence of the Church in the Holy Land*'. http://www.paxchristi.org.uk/Documents/Sabbah_Advent%20Message%202003.pdf
9 Statutes no. 3.
10 (*Summi Pontifaicatis* 1939).
11 For example how might a Hebrew Catholic behave on Independence Day? Does he celebrate the end of Jewish exile or mourn the harbinger of much of the contemporary Palestinian misfortune that affects the majority of his co-religionists?
12 Jean-Baptiste Gourion: Presentation for the meeting of presidents of

Episcopal Conferences Jerusalem, January 2002, http://www.lpj.org/Nonviolence/Conf/Gourioneg.htm.

13 There are signs that this may be changing. 'The pilgrimage of Pope John Paul II to the Holy Land in March 2000 roused a great enthusiasm among many Israelis and marked a positive turning point between the Church and Israel, moving from an a priori negative to a positive approach to the Church. The evolution of the relationship with the Jewish world is perceived as authentic. The Pope gave a witness of humility, truth and openness of heart, thus showing Israeli society a face of the Church of which it was completely ignorant. It is for us to take up the baton and continue the Holy Father's witness. Jean-Baptiste Gourion: Presentation for the meeting of presidents of Episcopal Conferences Jerusalem, January 2002, http://www.lpj.org/Nonviolence/Conf/Gourioneg.htm. See also David Neuhaus, 'Jewish Israeli Attitudes Towards Christianity and Christians in Contemporary Israel', in Anthony O'Mahony and Michael Kirwan (eds), *World Christianity: Politics, Theology, Dialogues*, London, Melisende, 2004, pp. 347–71.

14 Jean-Baptiste Gourion: Presentation for the meeting of presidents of Episcopal Conferences Jerusalem, January 2002, http://www.lpj.org/Nonviolence/Conf/Gourioneg.htm

15 Père Marcel Dubois, OP speaking to Anna Rist, *New Blackfriars*, March 1997, p. 195 says, 'I said to Cardinal Lustiger that his conversion is seen as more destructive of the Jewish people than the Nazi persecution ... Because to them to become Christian is to lose Jewish identity.

16 Fr Jochanan Elichai, unpublished paper, *réponse à une demande du Patriarche au course du Synode*, Jerusalem, 15 October 1995.

17 David Neuhaus: '*Kehilla*, Church and Jewish people', *Mishkan* No. 29, 1998, 36/2002, p. 79.

18 Jean-Baptiste Gourion: Presentation for the meeting of presidents of Episcopal Conferences Jerusalem, January 2002, http://www.lpj.org/Nonviolence/Conf/Gourioneg.htm

19 The *Oeuvre* was granted permission by the Patriarchate and the Vatican to have the liturgy in Hebrew as early as 1957. The liturgy was translated into Modern Hebrew by Fr Johanan Elichai a French, gentile, De Foucauld brother, and the Polish, Jewish, Carmelite priest, Oswald Rufeisen, more popularly known as Brother Daniel (born 1922, died August 1998). Elihai is also the author of, among other works, the great Hebrew-Arabic dictionary, and is an expert in the field of the Arabian language used by the Palestinians. In the first part of his small book *Juifs et chretines d'hier r demain, Juifs et chretines d'hier r demain*, Cerf, Paris, 1990, Frère Yohanan, gives a fascinating account of a supper in the summer of 1984 that went late into the night with Pope John Paul II at which the Pope became visibly moved at the graphic accounts Frère Yohanan gave of the many crimes of the Church committed against the Jews.

20 Some members may regard such introductions as Judaizing and not inculturation. It is perhaps worth noting that the Messianic Jews celebrate all of these feasts yet are more alienated in Jewish society than the *kehilla* and the Catholic Church.

21 Father Daniel, Oswald Rufeisen, a Polish, Jewish Carmelite priest had his application for automatic citizenship in December 1959 turned down as a consequence of 'the excluding clause' that excludes from automatic citizen-

ship any Jews who have changed their *dat*, religion. Daniel's appeal to the Supreme Court against this decision attracted worldwide attention because it challenged modern Zionism to resolve the different understandings of the various factions of moderate secular Zionists, extreme secular Zionists of which Daniel was one, and the religious Zionists. Daniel's understanding of modern Zionism was that it intended to divorce Jewish nationality from the Jewish religion. On 12 June 1962 the Supreme Court upheld the 1959 decision thus establishing a fusion of religion and state so that even a non-believer claiming to be Jewish by origin is entitled to automatic citizenship but not a Jew who professes another religion. For details of the Supreme Court ruling see *Verdicts of the Supreme Court of Israel* (Heb.) (Abbreb. Verdicts), Government Printers, Jerusalem No. 16 (1962) 2428–2455 also Fr Elias Friedman, '*Jewish Identity*', pp. 11–25, New York, Miriam Press [1987] and Nechama Tec '*In the Lion's Den*' pp. 222–31, Oxford University Press, 1990.

22 Pope John Paul II speaking at the meeting on the future of Christians in the Holy Land, Vatican City, 13 Dec 2001. See Vatican information Service AC/CHRISTIANS:HOLY LAND/...VIS 20011213 (840) at http://www.katolsk.dk/nyheder/december01.html

23 The Cardinal Secretary of State Angelo Sodano said at the 13 Dec meeting 'Statistics tell us, that (the number of Christians) is not many, due to the continual emigrations to which they are compelled by the difficult conditions of life. See Vatican information Service AC/CHRISTIANS:HOLY LAND/...VIS 20011213 (840) at http://www.katolsk.dk/nyheder/december01.html

24 There has been a massive exodus of Christians from the Holy Land throughout the whole of the twentieth century. In 1914 according to the Ottoman Empire census the percentage of Christians in the population of the whole of the Middle East is said to have been 24%. The British mandate census in 1915 after the defeat of the Ottomans puts it at only 13% but whichever is correct the present day undisputed figure of 2% illustrates the extent of emigration. Whilst there were many who left during the closing years of the First World War, due to increasingly harsh treatment of non-Muslim minorities, there is no question of an escalation since 1948 when many fled Jerusalem for example and have never been allowed to return. The Christian population of Jerusalem in 1944 was said to be 30,000; in 1967 it was 12,000 and by the year 2000 it was no more than 8,000. Whilst the original reasons for emigration were mostly economic there has been a shift in more recent years especially following the second *intifada* toward considerable discrimination from both Arab and Israeli majorities. Cf. Charles M. Sennott, *The Body and The Blood*, Perseus Books, 2001 pp. 22–5, 245–48.

25 Cf. Fr Johanan Elihai, unpublished paper, *réponse à une demande du Patriarche au course du Synode*, Jerusalem, 15 October 1995.

26 Ibid.

27 The words of Cardinal Martini in 1984. Ibid.

28 What I refer to, as a movement for change is only a small number of the *kehilla* members in Israel supported by only a few sympathetic voices in Rome and the French Church. The members are not united with regard to ecclesial change, liturgical form etc.

29 Edward Flannery in the foreword to his book *The Anguish of the Jews*, McMillan, Quest Book series, 1965, tells how he was walking down Park

Avenue in New York in the company of a young Jewish couple. Behind them was a large, brightly lit cross, which is raised over the Grand Central Building every Christmas. Turning round suddenly the young woman, never being hostile towards the Christians whatsoever, said: 'This cross makes me shudder, makes me sense some evil presence.' He writes that the symbol that is to Christians one of common love – was for this Jewish woman a symbol of fear and a curse. Her reaction of terror followed what she knew about the great pain that her people suffered through twenty centuries because of the Christians.

30 Elihai, ibid.
31 See the well-informed American Jesuit, counsellor for international affairs to the United States Conference of Catholic Bishops, Drew Christiansen, `A Campaign to Divide the Church in the Holy Land', *America*, 19 May 2003.
32 The Abbot of Abu Gosh, Dom Jean-Baptiste Gourion was patriarchal vicar since 1990 until his appointment as Auxilliary Bishop with special responsibility for Hebrew-speaking Israeli Catholics in 2003.
33 This gave greater authority and autonomy to the Patriarchal Vicar in matters concerning Hebrew-speaking Catholics in the Holy Land.
34 Drew Christiansen, 'A Campaign to Divide the Church in the Holy Land'.
35 Ibid.
36 The Latin Patriarchate was re-established in 1847 when Giuseppe Valerga was appointed to the See. Since then there have been seven European Patriarchs until 1987 when His Beatitude Michel Sabbah, a Palestinian Arab originating from Nazareth was appointed. His appointment was controversial not only in some Hebrew Christian quarters but also to Jews because the perception is that an Arab Patriarch is biased in favour of the Palestinians. European patriarchs have not raised the same objections on account of their being seen as ethnically neutral in the Holy Land.
37 Ambassador Gadi Golan, head of the Israeli Foreign Ministry's Department of Inter religious Affairs, declared that the establishment of 'a Catholic church in Israel' would make it clear that Michel Sabbah is 'the Islamic patriarchs'. Quoted by Drew Christiansen, 'A Campaign to Divide the Church in the Holy Land', *America*, 19 May 2003.
38 Drew Christiansen, ibid. Michel Sabbah has been seen as not only speaking for Catholics but has successfully united all Christians in the Holy Land so that his influence around the world is very considerable. He is fully aware, as is the Israeli government, that he speaks to all Christians around the world. In his Christmas message 2003 he comments, 'These questions might also be of interest to our brothers and sisters in the different Churches around the world.'
39 In the mid-nineties the government tried to prevent the appointment of what they considered a pro-Palestinian as the Melkite Archbishop of Akko. Cf. Drew Christiansen, 'A Campaign to Divide the Church in the Holy Land', *America*, 19 May 2003.
40 The worldwide Catholic Church teaches that dialogue with the Jewish people is distinct from the political options adopted by the State of Israel. Cf. The Patriarch's Christmas message, 23 December 2003. Independent Catholic News. http://www.indcatholicnews.com/latgrt.html
41 The diocesan synod of 2000 led by Sabbah introduced all this and more in its General Pastoral Plan.
42 The Patriarch's Christmas message, 23 December 2003. Independent

Catholic News. http://www.indcatholicnews.com/latgrt.html.
44 Michel Sabbah, *Seek Peace and Pursue It: Questions and answers on Justice and peace in the Holy Land*, September 1998, n. 15.
45 Michel Sabbah led a delegation of Christian clerics to the spiritual leader of the militant Hamas movement, Sheikh Ahmed Yassin, on 10 August 2002 in a bid to stop suicide bombings against Israeli targets. Cf. Independent Catholic News, Jerusalem, 12 August 2002.
46 On 23 March 1998 in preparation for the Pope's 2000 visit, Patriarch Sabbah met with Israel's chief Ashkenazi rabbi, Meir Lau, and the chief Sephardi rabbi, Eliyahu Bakshi-Doron to discuss issues ranging from the Holocaust to the status of Jerusalem's holy sites. While the two sides disagreed in several areas, all participants agreed that the meeting itself was a positive development. Cf. *Daily Catholic World News*, 25 March 1998.
47 Gourion is the first Catholic Jewish bishop; the first Jewish bishop in Jerusalem was the Anglican Bishop Michael Solomon Alexander appointed on 7 November 1841. See Gershon Nerel, 'Hebrew Christian Associations in Ottoman Jerusalem: Jewish Yeshua-Believers Facing Church and Synagogue', *Revue des Études juives*, 161 (2002), pp. 431–57.

Chapter 3

The *Intifada* and Palestinian Christian Identity[1]

Drew Christiansen, SJ

Taking history's long view, the 1990s marked a significant transformation of the Christian presence in the Holy Land, as significant perhaps as the imposition by the Ottomans of the millet system of autonomous community governance more than five centuries ago.[2] By that I mean the manner of being church in the public square has been definitively altered. As a result of the first *intifada* (1987–93) the Greek, Latin and Oriental Churches set aside their traditional divisions and rivalries in a series of joint initiatives on behalf of justice, peace and human rights. These ecumenical actions represented an unprecedented movement of the churches from the margins of society into public life, a role they had been denied in the Ottoman centuries and under more than a millennium of Muslim rule.[3] Their common public witness also ended the de facto silence of the local Christian churches during the first forty years of Israel's existence.

The prolonged political crisis begun in the first *intifada*, starting in 1987, and continuing through the long and now failed 'interim' period (1993–2000) after the Oslo Accords, was the occasion for the churches of the Holy Land to move away from the model of minority religious existence toward a new, self-conscious form of Christianity. That transformation was captured for me in an exchange at a reception a few years ago at Notre Dame of Jerusalem Center between Mme Diana Safie and His Beatitude, the Latin Patriarch Michel Sabbah. Mme Safie was imploring the Patriarch to organize the Palestinian Christians around some issue. Exactly what I have now forgotten. The Patriarch dismissed her plea with a mischievous smile. 'Diana,' he said, 'that's the old way. We are no longer ethnarchs,' that is leaders of distinct ethno-religious communities. 'We must speak for the Church. Lay people must organize politically.'

As ethnarchs the patriarchs had dealt with political authorities on behalf of their separate communities, often making special arrangements in the interests of their own congregations. In the new situation, they speak in concert for all the Christians, often pleading for the rights of Palestinians generally, and sometimes for Palestinians and Israelis alike. But, they do so as churchmen, appealing to universal standards of human rights and justice and gospel norms like forgiveness and love of enemies, leaving explicitly political action to lay people. Of course, their statements and actions are often interpreted as being political, particularly by the Israeli government officials, but the patriarchs and heads of churches in Jerusalem adhere to a tight line defined by recognized standards of human rights and universal claims of justice, a range of concerns that impinges on politics but stands outside it as well. (On the defence of human rights by Catholic bishops after Vatican II, see 'Justice, peace and politics', p. 59, below.)

What do I mean by a self-conscious Palestinian Christian identity? First, there is identification with a particular people and its history. Like Polish Catholics or Irish Catholics, Palestinian Christians identify with the Palestinian people's history of displacement and oppression and with their struggle against occupation and on behalf of independence. Unlike some religious nationalists of an earlier generations – and I use the term 'nationalist' in a broad sense – Palestinian Christians also share a broad ecumenical commitment to human rights and justice for the oppressed rooted in the Gospel. The outlook that connects the Gospel with the promotion of justice is a new one for the Middle East. Ecumenical agreement and cooperation themselves are also new in a region long divided by denominational differences. Just as important, however, is a universalistic pluralism that is concerned for justice for Israel as well as for the Palestinians and for the rights of Jews as well as those of Christians and Muslims. Palestinian Christians' passion is for justice for the Palestinians, but not to the exclusion of justice for others. The universalism inherent in the justice commitment of Christian Palestinians, therefore, has the potential to temper some of the problematic aspects of nationalist ideologies, fostering respect for the rights of all people and discouraging the use of force in resolving disputes.

For the Catholics among them, who have often played a leadership role in forging this new, social ecumenism, their witness participates in the post-Vatican II Catholic Church's way of being church. That is, they are a community of believers who see 'action on behalf of justice and participation in transformation of the world' as 'a constitutive dimension of preaching the Gospel' in today's world.[4] It is also a church that holds 'a preferential option for the poor' which creates a special form of solidarity with oppressed peoples.[5] This combination of Palestinian experience and Christian commitment to justice and non-violent social change has created a new role for the Church to exercise in the public square without entering directly into politics.

In addition, there are aspects of Palestinian Christian identity which are distinctive to the Middle East as a region and to the Holy Land in particular.[6] Along with other Christians in the Middle East, Palestinian Christians glory in their Arab culture and believe they have a special role to play in the dialogue between Christianity and Islam.[7] In the case of the Holy Land, moreover, Catholics, at least, affirm they have a special responsibility because of their situation for dialogue with Jews.[8] While accepting the teaching on Judaism found in *Nostra Aetate*, Vatican Council II's Decree on Non-Christian Religions (1965), they insist that because of Palestinians' painful involvement in the history of modern Israel, the terms and content of the Christian-Jewish dialogue in the Holy Land will be different than the dialogue in Europe and America.[9] Palestinian Christians regard themselves, for example, as co-victims with the Holy Land's Jews of western European aggression in the Crusades and under nineteenth and early twentieth-century imperialism. For most of their history, like Jews, the Christians of the Holy Land were, moreover, a religious minority fated to live under Islamic rule, and have, therefore, had a different historical experience than Christians in Western Europe. Accordingly, they view the Holocaust as a European phenomenon for which they ought not be asked to accept responsibility, especially as guilt-driven western support for the State of Israel has already exacted a high price in suffering from the Palestinian people.[10]

Thus, while the *intifada* of 1987 was a key process in bringing about a distinctive Palestinian Christian identity, several other factors were also involved in shaping that identity: the shared suffering of the Palestinian people, for all Catholics and especially Latin (Roman) Catholics the reforms of Vatican II, the movement of the churches to work on behalf of justice and human rights, the effort of the churches to place themselves in their Arab and Muslim environment, and in the Holy Land a complex relationship to Judaism and to Christian-Jewish dialogue.

It is hard to tell whether the al-Aqsa or second *intifada* begun on 29 September 2000, will allow the processes which formed Palestinian Christian identity over the years from 1988 to 2000 to continue to advance, or whether the renewed pressures of low-intensity conflict and the consequent migration of Christians will sap the strength from these new developments. If that were to happen, we would see the retreat of the churches to the sanctuary, a disappearance of Christians from public life, and perhaps renewed fragmentation among the different Christian communities. After the first three months of fighting more than four hundred people from the village of Beit Sahour alone had already left their homes for Canada and the United States.[11] Semi-official figures at the beginning of 2004 put the total in the excess of 2,000 émigrés.[12] Unofficial estimates put the figures even higher, with as much as one third of the 50,000 pre-*intifada* Christian population of the West Bank having emigrated. Even before the fighting, in relatively prosperous Galilee, one quarter of the Christian population indicated to pollsters that, given an opportunity, they would emigrate. In the words of the First Congress of Patriarchs and Bishops of the Middle East, emigration is 'an open wound, weakening our countries and churches, and consequently the Christian presence in the East'.[13] The al-Aqsa *intifada* has opened that wound still further.[14]

For years, commentators have worried about the disappearance of Christians from the Land of Jesus. Pope John Paul II himself has warned that without the living Christian communities around them, the Holy Places would become vacant museums. Political and social pressures are such that a crippling diminishment of the churches is a real possibility. Despite adverse pressures, the evolution of the churches over the 1990s had given them new strengths and tools with which to face this struggle, even, if God wills, in diminished numbers. Who is to say that the maturation of the Church in the decade of the 1990s cannot, by God's grace, continue in the decade ahead, flowering into a 'second spring' for the Christians of the Holy Land.

I want to focus here on a single point, namely, how the political crisis has created an ecumenical Palestinian Christian identity and stimulated united public witness on part of the churches of the Holy Land. My remarks will fall into four parts:

1. a brief exposition of the ecumenical witness of the churches since the first *intifada*;
2. a survey of the impact of the al-Aqsa *intifada* on the Holy Land's Christians,

3. a short discussion of the churches' witness on justice and peace as distinct from and in relation to politics, and
4. some thoughts, by way of conclusion, about how to secure the future of the Christian presence in the Holy Land.

1. The *Intifada* and Palestinian Christian identity

Intifada. The first *intifada* (1987–93) marked a major transition in the evolution of Palestinian Christianity. Popular pressure drew the churches into the struggle of the Palestinian people. Christians did not want to be left out of the striving of their people for liberation.[15] The Palestinians' 'shaking off' (*intifada*) Israeli occupation, moreover, coincided with the appointment in December 1987 of a Palestinian, Michel Sabbah, a native of Nazareth, as the Latin or Roman Catholic Patriarch. Sabbah's appointment meant that for the first time a Palestinian was leader of one of the principal churches in Jerusalem. Under local Palestinian leadership, the Catholic, the Anglican and Lutheran Churches became advocates for their people. At critical moments, they joined other church leaders in Jerusalem in speaking out on behalf of their people's rights, the pursuit of peace, and Christian rights and interests in the Holy Land.

Another unintended consequences of the *intifada* was to foster grassroots ecumenism among the churches of the Holy Land. Identifying themselves as Palestinians, the Christian laity and clergy tended to put aside the traditional denominational badges that had divided them and to refer to themselves simply as 'Christians'. Political solidarity gave rise to signs of church unity. For example, outside the major centres, in the villages, Latins (Roman Catholics) adopted the Orthodox calendar for major feasts. (In Nazareth, Bethlehem, Jerusalem, however, locales where pilgrims and international audiences expected the observance of the western calendar, the churches continued to meet those expectations.)

Despite its positive influence on ecumenical cooperation, the *intifada* exacted a high price from the Palestinian people. An uprising of young people, the movement disrupted the traditional authority of fathers over their families, spawning a variety of social ills, including incidents of family violence. Curfews and school closings interrupted and sometimes ended educational careers. Unemployment, confinement and other factors contributed to drug problems that had previously been unknown. Closures, restrictive housing policies, demolitions and confiscations led to late marriages and emigration by young people. These and other social ills created a demand for pastoral care and for social interventions on the part of the churches to stabilize the Christian presence in the Holy Land. But, even as church-based aid gave relief to the Palestinian poor and assisted economic development in hard times, some observers believed that the need for Christians to rely on the church institutions for support re-enforced older relationships of dependency and sometimes resulted in resentment on the part of the laity toward the institutional church.

Tension between the Arab faithful and the hierarchy was particularly strong in the Greek Orthodox community. The Greek Orthodox Patriarchate's often secret sales of church-owned property to the Israelis infuriated Palestinians. Furthermore, while the western churches (Latin, Anglican and Lutheran) had local Palestinian leadership, which represented a de-colonization of nineteenth-century church (re-)foundations, the Greek Orthodox Patriarchate remained firmly in the hands of a confraternity of Greek monks. Since only celibates may be ordained bishops in the Orthodox tradition, the married Arab parish clergy, with very few exceptions, were excluded from advancement.

With the death of Patriarch Diodorus I in 2001 and the election of Metropolitan Ireneios in his place, a new era seemed to dawn. Ireneios promised to do business openly and to make public the secret transactions of the past. According to still applicable Ottoman law, his election had to be ratified by the political authorities in his jurisdiction: the Jordanian, the Palestinians and the Israelis. Jordan and the Palestinian Authority gave the necessary approval, but Israel, which had previously blocked his nomination to the office, withheld approval. He was accused of pro-Palestinian leanings, but many believed his desire to open past business dealings to public scrutiny aroused opposition from Israeli businessmen with influence on the government. Finally, in January 2004, the Israeli cabinet approved his election.

After Ireneios took office, he joined the other patriarchs and heads of churches in joint statements and for the first time the Greek clergy could be seen in demonstrations against the Israeli occupation of the Palestinian territories. After a short time, however, the Patriarch fell silent and there were no more joint statements from the patriarchs and heads of churches in Jerusalem. The initiative fell to church leaders of Palestinian origin: the Latin Patriarch, Michel Sabbah; Lutheran Bishop, Munib Younan and Anglican Bishop, Riah Abu Assal. It remains to be seen what margin of freedom the Greek Patriarch will have in the wake of Israeli recognition or what degree of discretion he feels he needs to exercise in return for Israeli good will.

Ecumenical initiatives

As we have seen, the *intifada* forced the Christian churches to overcome their traditional rivalries in support of the Christian Palestinian people. Together the hierarchs of the Jerusalem churches published pastoral statements and took initiatives on common problems. They continue to meet regularly to discuss common business, and they convene on an emergency basis to address crises like the opening of the Hasmonean Tunnel and the final status talks at Camp David. Allow me now to review four such initiatives.

1. Memorandum on Jerusalem

In the period after Oslo, cooperative efforts among the patriarchs and heads of churches grew visibly. In November 1994, the patriarchs and heads of churches published a joint memorandum entitled 'The Significance of Jerusalem for Christians'. They wrote, 'The experience of history teaches us that in order for Jerusalem to be a city of peace ... it cannot belong exclusively to one people or to only one religion. Jerusalem should be open to all, shared by all.'[16] The document went on to affirm the rights of the Christians of Jerusalem as well as the rights of Jews and Muslims in the city. It also proposed 'a special statute for Jerusalem' 'in order to satisfy the national aspirations of all its inhabitants, and in order that Jews, Christians and Muslims can be 'at home' with one another ...'[17]

Like the Holy See, the Jerusalem church leaders called for international guarantees to help implement the statute. 'Jerusalem,' they wrote, 'is too precious to be dependent solely on municipal or national political authorities, whoever they may be.'[18]

2. Hasmonean Tunnel

In 1996 in a highly provocative move, the government of Israeli Prime Minister Binyamin Netanyahu opened the Hasmonean Tunnel under the Haram al-Sharif or Temple Mount, a site theretofore accessible only to archaeologists, and to the public. The heads of churches joined Muslim leaders in protesting the government's action as a stimulus to incitement. They also censured the move as a unilateral change in Jerusalem contrary to the spirit of the Oslo Accords. Latin Patriarch Michel Sabbah led a silent, candlelit procession of Christians of all denominations through the Old City in prayer for peace. Responding to the procession, Mr Uri Mor, director of Christian Communities Affairs in the Israeli Ministry of Religion, charged Patriarch Sabbah with meddling in politics. The United States Catholic Conference defended the Patriarch, as it had done before, affirming the duty of bishops to defend human rights, and to promote justice and peace.

3. Denial of Jerusalem residency

Israel's withdrawal of Jerusalem residency from Palestinians who claimed Jerusalem as their home was another issue which pitted the patriarchs and heads of churches against the Israeli government. The Likud government of Binyamin Netanyahu had been confiscating residency permits from Palestinians who according to Israeli no longer made Jerusalem 'the centre of their lives'. Couples who had to move to have space to raise a family due to the prohibitive housing conditions created for Arab Jerusalemites by the government, those who had married spouses from the West Bank, those who had to move abroad to find remunerative work, even graduate students out of the country for more than a couple of years, all were denied the right to make Jerusalem their home.[19]

For church leaders in Jerusalem, the denial of residency was a pastoral and ecclesial issue as well as a political one. As pastors, they were committed both to promoting a strong family life for their people and to maintaining 'the living Christian presence in the Holy Land'. The lack of housing deliberately created by Israeli policies resulted in overcrowded homes and family tensions. Most of all, it forced young people to delay marriage, frequently to their mid- and late thirties, and, when couples planned to marry, it built pressures for emigration. Subsequent Israeli government policies denied recognition to marriages celebrated in Palestinian territories in Israel, forcing spouses to leave the city to take up family residence on the West Bank. In an effort to relieve these pressures, the churches had built hundreds of units of housing for young families, but these church-sponsored projects could only meet a small part of the need.

In a recent survey, more than a third of respondents on the West Bank and in Jerusalem, and a quarter of the respondents in Israel agreed with the statement, 'If I could, I would emigrate myself.'[20] Among Christians in Israel more than 40% thought 'Israeli restrictions' were the primary motive for emigration, with lack of employment and Islamization as the next most important factors. For West Bank and Jerusalem residents, however, lack of employment was the number one factor, followed by Israeli restrictions and lack of housing.[21]

The withdrawal of residency permits and adverse Israeli housing policies for Palestinians were a principal cause of the emigration of Christians from the Holy Land. From the point of view of the churches, the crisis of emigration was particularly acute in Jerusalem, the site of Jesus' ministry, passion, death, resurrection and ascension, and, therefore, Christianity's foremost holy place. By the year 2000, there were only about 5,000 Palestinian Christians (perhaps as few as 4,500) living in Jerusalem, down from 10,000 in 1967, and from more than 30,000 in 1948. Without a 'living Christian presence', as church officials did not tire of repeating, the Christian Holy Places in Jerusalem were threatened with becoming mere museums and tourist stops. After a dramatic increase in the rate of confiscations, the patriarchs and heads of churches wrote in 1999 to Israeli Interior Minister Eli Suissa, protesting the policy. Subsequently the heads of corresponding churches in the US, including Bishop Joseph Fiorenza, president of the National Conference of Catholic Bishops and United States Catholic Conference, wrote a joint letter in support of the Jerusalem church leaders. The Catholic Bishops' Conference of England and Wales, likewise, registered its concern with the Israeli government.

In the spring of 2000, Israeli Justice Minister Yossi Beilin and Infrastructure Minister Natan Sharansky announced the confiscation policy would be rescinded and thousands of cancelled permits would be re-issued. Church officials report, however, that at the bureaucratic level little has happened to reverse the policy. Confiscations continue, but at a slower pace, and there has been no progress on restoration of the invalidated papers.

4. Final status talks

The last joint actions by the leaders of the Jerusalem churches, prior to the al-Aqsa *intifada,* came during the July 2000 final status talks between Palestinian President Yasser Arafat and Israeli Prime Minister Ehud Barak at Camp David Maryland. After first writing to the negotiators to offer their prayers for the success of the talks, the three patriarchs sent an urgent message to Israeli Prime Minister Ehud Barak, Palestinian President Yasser Arafat and US President Bill Clinton on 20 July, opposing a well-reported proposal for annexation of the Armenian Quarter to Israel. They also requested a consultative status in the talks. According to several sources, the Palestinian side had already agreed in negotiation to the annexation in discussions over the future of Jerusalem.

Days after, as the talks themselves were about to collapse, Palestinian and Israeli officials met separately with the three churchmen. Palestinian officials assured them that Christian concerns would be taken into account in future negotiations, that they or their representatives would be consulted in discussions over Jerusalem and particularly the disposition of the Old City. Israeli Justice and Religious Affairs Minister Yossi Beilin promised that international guarantees as part of arrangements for Jerusalem were admissible. Progress had been made, it appears, in placing Christian concerns for Jerusalem on the agenda. Following the collapse of Camp David talks, moreover, US, Palestinian and Israeli representatives visited Rome to consult with Vatican officials, and promised further consultations with the churches.

Ecumenism and the Great Jubilee

For the Christian churches, and especially for the Roman Catholic Church, the year 2000 marked the Great Jubilee of the Birth of Jesus Christ. In a 1994 apostolic exhortation, *Tertio Millennio Adveniente*, Pope John Paul II made the preparation for the jubilee a major effort in church renewal.[22] He exhorted the whole Church to self-examination and reconciliation, especially in relation to offences against other churches and other world religions. He himself led the way with a special service of pardon at Saint Peter's on the first Sunday of Lent, 2000, which included a 'confession of sins committed against the people of Israel' and for 'sins committed in the service of truth', i.e., religious intolerance.[23] This followed a controverted 1998 reflection from the Vatican's Commission for Relations with the Jews on the Shoah or Holocaust, entitled *We Remember*.[24] At a meeting of the International Catholic-Jewish Liaison Committee, the Jewish co-chair, Dr Gerhard Riegner had expressed serious disappointment that the document '[avoided] taking a clear position on the direct relation between the teaching of contempt and the political and cultural climate that made the Shoah possible'.[25]

The Holy Father made public his desire to be a pilgrim to the

Holy Land as part of his observance of the jubilee. Explicit commitment for the visit, however, was a matter of on-again-off-again talks between the Holy See and the government of Israel, with a firm decision being taken only late in 1999. The visit became one of the great successes of Pope John Paul's pontificate. His meetings with Israeli leaders, his visit to *Yad Vashem*, the Israeli holocaust memorial, and his prayer at the Western Wall, won over the Israeli public and politicians, and Jews abroad. Suspicions raised by *We Remember*, the service of pardon, the proposed canonization of Pius XII and other issues were mooted. Jewish-Catholic relations entered a new era of good feeling with a higher level of mutual confidence. 'Here, right now,' Israeli Prime Minister Ehud Barak told the Holy Father at Yad Vashem, 'time itself has come to a standstill.' The Prime Minister also noted that 'the righteous gentiles' who risked their lives to save Jews from the Holocaust were 'mostly children of your faith'.[26]

The first full day of the pilgrimage took place in Palestinian Self-Rule Area of Bethlehem. It included a papal Mass in Manger Square, a visit with Palestinian president Yasser Arafat, and an appearance at the Deheisheh refugee camp in the vicinity of Bethlehem. Local Christians took pride in the celebration of parts of several multi-lingual liturgies in Arabic. They were delighted too that the largest public event ever held in Israel was a Mass for Youth at Tabghe near the Mount of Beatitudes where 150,000 pilgrims from around the world joined with them in prayer. In addition, at Nazareth, the Holy Father received the acta of the recently concluded synod of the Latin Church, thereby approving plans for renewal of the local church.

In accepting the welcome of PNA president Yasser Arafat, the Pope acknowledged the suffering of the Palestinian people. 'No one can ignore how much the Palestinian people have had to suffer in recent decades. Your torment is before the eyes of the world. And it has gone on too long.'[27] The Holy Father went on to affirm the right of the Palestinians to a national homeland and the right of Palestinian refugees to homes of their own.

Elusive ecumenical concord

With regard to religious relations between the Christian churches, especially the Greek Orthodox and Roman Catholic Churches, however, the Jubilee was only a modest success. The restoration of the dome of the Holy Sepulchre, completed in 1997, with the help of the Pontifical Mission (and Catholic Near East Welfare

Association), seemed to open an auspicious period of cooperation among the churches which had to agree to the work-plan for the restoration. But, similar cooperation was not forthcoming for the restoration, or even the cleaning, of either the Church of the Holy Sepulchre, known in the East as the Church of the Resurrection, or the Church of the Nativity in Bethlehem.

With a vision of throngs of pilgrims crowding the Holy Sepulchre for the jubilee, Uri Mor of Israel's Department for Christian Community Affairs pressed the churches to agree to the opening of an emergency exit to the church. For centuries, there has been only one door to the Church, and during the Orthodox Holy Fire ceremony on Holy Saturday the door is barred shut. During the 1998 ceremony, Israeli police had to intervene to break-up a mêlée between Greeks and Syrians over questions of precedence at the holy site, creating very reasonable apprehension of a conflagration. But, after two years of negotiation, no agreement could be reached over opening the exit. Old ecclesiastical rivalries continued to rule. As agreement seemed to be at hand, the Greek Orthodox demanded control of the key to the fire door, a demand which would have rendered any emergency exit unworkable. The church leaders, on the verge of accepting the Israeli proposal, reversed themselves, and no emergency exit was opened.

Jerusalem church leaders did come together to mark the opening of the Jubilee in Manger Square on 4 December, 1999. They could not agree, however, to recite the Lord's Prayer together. Furthermore, in welcoming Pope John Paul II, Greek Orthodox Patriarch Diodoros I warned Catholics against proselytizing through their work in education and social service. For his part, the Pope urged that 'In the Holy Land where Christians live side by side with the followers of Judaism and Islam, where there are almost daily tensions and conflicts, it is essential to overcome the scandalous impression given by our disagreements and arguments.'[28] Ecumenism, it turned out, was easier to achieve in matters of public concern than in activities proper to the churches.

2. The impact of the al-Aqsa *intifada* on Palestinian Christians

In the early weeks of the al-Aqsa *intifada*, after Palestinian demonstrators sacked Joseph's Tomb in Nablus, the conflict threatened to spill into inter-ethnic and religious fighting reminiscent of the Balkans or the Indian subcontinent. In retaliation for the destruction of the shrine and for public support for it among Israeli Arabs, Israelis attacked mosques in Tiberias, Jaffa and Haifa. At the last report, some mosques in those cities still remain closed to worshippers. Within three nights, rioting settlers from Pisgot Zev and Neve Yakov twice attempted to attack the Church of Saint James in Beit Hanina, an Arab suburb north of Jerusalem. Gangs from Nazaret Illit, or Upper Nazareth, attacked poor areas of Nazareth, Israel's largest Arab city and a major Christian centre. Police offered no protection to the residents. Rather, they stood aside until the victims appeared to be getting the better of their attackers. To their credit, Israeli journalists, like Joseph Algazy of *Ha'aretz,* and other public figures decried these attacks as 'pogroms' which the Israeli public should deplore, and for which the Israeli government ought to demand accountability.[29]

The Israeli Defence Force may have even greater responsibility to bear for its attacks against Palestinian Christian population centres. Early in the second *intifada* thirteen Arab Israeli demonstrators were killed in clashes with the Israeli military, an event that shocked Israeli society generally and left Israeli Arabs deeply disaffected from their country. Subsequently, the northern command surrounded Nazareth, Israel's largest Arab city, with tanks, apparently in an attempt to prevent the uprising from spreading into Israel proper. The sorest impact on Palestinian Christians came, however, in the region of Bethlehem where the largest Christian population in Palestine resides. There in response to sniper attacks on Israeli military personnel near Beit Sahour and on the Jewish settlement at Gilo opposite Beit Jala, the Israelis repeatedly shelled residential areas. Both the Beit Sahour and Beit Jala are majority Christian towns.

After some highly visible night-time firefights in the early days of the uprising, the Israeli tactics varied from week to week and day to day. In the early weeks, the IDF would sometimes give warnings to allow families to retreat from neighborhoods marked for retaliatory attacks. Sometimes only a symbolic shell or two would be lobbed. At others, only concussion grenades would be used. At still others, sustained shelling attacks would be resumed. By the late Fall, shelling of civilian areas in the Bethlehem triangle became routine. On 11 December 2000, the Latin Seminary and nearby parish in Beit Jala were subjected to attack for three hours. In the same week, the Greek Orthodox churches of Saint Nicholas and Saint Michael in Bethlehem came under attack from Israeli gunners. After the Church of the Nativity, they are the two most ancient churches in Bethlehem.

The fear among observers has been that prolonged attacks would add to the pressure for Christians living in the Bethlehem region to emigrate. Fear for one's family can be very real. Maher Attrash, the deputy director of schools for the Latin Patriarchate, and his family barely escaped a direct hit on their Beit Sahour home in the first weeks of the present *intifada*. He and his three daughters had spent the early evening at Shepherds' Fields in prayer. The family returned to their home, where for safety they had been sleeping together in the living room. For unexplained reasons, Mr Attrash that evening decided they would take refuge instead in a bedroom. Within minutes a shell crashed into their living room destroying everything. They escaped, grateful to God for their lives.

Part of the conflict may actually be to incite Christians to emigrate. In October, the *Jerusalem Post* ran a story about a sudden rise in Christian emigration from the Bethlehem area.[30] The report referred to sources in the Israeli Foreign Ministry. Church sources, in calls to foreign embassies and consulates, were unable to confirm stories about the rise of requests for visas.[31] Independent sources also failed to verify the account. The story itself may have been a bit of psychological warfare, crafted, if not to speed emigration, then perhaps to put the *intifada* in a poor light for its adverse impact on Christians.

By January 2001, however, four hundred Christians were reported to have left Beit Sahour alone over the first three months of the *intifada*.[32] Church officials made inquiries with the United States officials over reports that the US consulate had been expediting visas for Palestinians seeking to flee. So, one consequence of the al-Aqsa *intifada* was certainly a rise in Christian emigration from the Holy Land. Today 'the living Christian presence' in the Holy Land finds itself under intense pressure.

Meanwhile, the response of the churches to the al-Aqsa *intifida* has been largely supportive. In his 2000 Christmas message, His Beatitude the Latin Patriarch of Jerusalem, Michel Sabbah declared:

> In this feast, we have one main wish: that Palestinian freedom be born ... Palestinians have been under Israeli military occupation for thirty-three years, and they say: 'Give us our freedom back.'

A few weeks earlier the three Jerusalem patriarchs affirmed, 'The Church believes it is the right as well as the duty of an occupied people to struggle against injustice in order to gain their freedom.'

Lest they be mistaken as warranting an armed uprising, the patriarchs added, 'It also believes that non-violent means of struggle remain stronger and more efficient.'

Their commitment to non-violence distinguishes the church leaders and many Christians from a large part of the Palestinian population.[33] In a survey released in December 2000, for example, 18½% of the interviewees supported the continuation of 'a military-resistance *intifada*' and 54½% backed a combined 'popular and military' resistance. Two-thirds of those polled, moreover, regarded so-called 'suicide operations' as 'a suitable response within current political conditions'.[34] By contrast, a peace catechism issued in 1998 by the Latin Patriarchate rejects terrorism as 'illogical, irrational and unacceptable as a means to resolve conflict'.[35] Citing *The Catechism of the Catholic Church*, it describes terrorist acts as criminal.[36] While the peace catechism admits of the use of force in a legitimate armed uprising, it places terrorism, defined as violent acts against innocent third parties, among the acts never permitted either to established authority or to insurgent groups.[37] I should also note that forbidden acts also include measures which apply mainly to Israel, namely, bombardment of civilians, collective punishment, and indiscriminate attacks, among others.[38]

Faced with mob attacks on Arab Israelis in Christian neighborhoods, the Church has continued to uphold a stance of non-violence. Speaking at a prayer vigil at the Dominican's Saint Stephen's Church, following the attacks on Beit Hanina and Saint James Melkite Church, Patriarch Sabbah chose as his text lines from Romans 12: 'Bless those who persecute you; never curse them, bless them ... Never repay evil with evil ... Do not be mastered by evil, but master evil with good.' The Patriarch continued, 'To this kind of speech one could say, how can we live up to it, today and in these circumstances?' He told the congregation that it gathered not just in solidarity with the suffering of the Palestinian people, but primarily 'before God, not men'. He concluded, 'If we are true believers in God, let us ponder how our freedom, our political freedom, relate[s] to the word of God, who says that love must be the guide of man in the worst and darkest circumstances, such as we are living today.'[39] In December 2004, the Theological Commission of the Latin Patriarchate issued a statement confirming once again the Christian commitment to nonviolence.[40]

In short, the Church hierarchy with Christians generally have supported the *intifada* as a legitimate rising against an occupied power. After seven years of a flawed and one-sided peace process, the *intifada* might be said to be 'a remedy of last resort' to put an end to 'an evident and prolonged tyranny which affects the common good'. [41] Christians support the objectives of the second *intifada*, and they insist on unity with the Palestinian people. But they distinguish themselves from the larger Palestinian population by their preference for non-violence and their opposition to terrorism. For all their commitment to the Palestinian cause, however, Palestinian Christians have begun to show the strain of conflict and the disproportionate burden their communities have born from heavy Israeli reprisals in the first months of fighting. The more than 2,000 people who have fled the West Bank and especially the Bethlehem area are an indication of the cost that the occupation and resistance will continue to exact from the Holy Land's Christians until peace comes to their land.

3. Justice, peace and politics

The role of the churches, church leaders generally, and particularly the Latin Patriarch, in the Israeli-Palestinian conflict deserves some special comment. Their outspokenness has been an occasion for denunciation by Israeli authorities, displeasure on the part of many Jewish leaders, and vocal doubts on the part of some outside observers. Unlike the Ashkenazi and Sephardic Chief Rabbis and Islamic officials in Jerusalem and Israel, the heads of the Christian churches are neither chosen nor supported by the Israeli government. For that reason alone, they have a measure of political independence. From time to time, as in the delayed recognition of Patriarch Ireneios, Israeli officials have tried to appeal to Ottoman legal precedent to curb that independence and have even attempted to meddle in the appointments of bishops.[42] In the rough and tumble of Israeli public life, where every shade of opinion is openly voiced, and rabbis are highly visible in public life, government officials often seem to expect that the heads of the Christian communities should be silent. They appear not to understand the duties of church leaders to speak out on behalf of justice, peace and human rights. At the same time, one must acknowledge that, whatever the Israeli preferences, their pressures on Christian leaders and their spin about them, in the end the Israeli polity permits Christian leaders to speak their views openly.

In the case of Catholicism, at least, bishops' responsibilities to advocate on behalf of justice, peace and human rights emerged from the Second Vatican Council.[43] Prior to the Council, the Church's strategy had been primarily to secure the institutional rights of the Church to exercise its religious ministry in preaching and administration of the sacraments. Beginning with *Pacem in terris*, the landmark encyclical of Pope John XXIII on human rights, published in the midst of the Council, and even more after the conclusion of the Council, the Church's commitment has been first to secure the human and civil rights of all people, including freedom of religion, and only then to seek guarantees for the Church's institutional life.[44]

Gaudium et Spes, the Council's Pastoral Constitution on the Church in the Modern World, identified the defence of human rights as one of the principal ways in which the Church serves the world.[45] The arrangement of articles in both the Holy See-Israel Fundamental Agreement (1993) and the Holy See-PLO Basic Agreement (2000) exemplify this new priority: first defence of the human, civil and religious rights of (all) believers, only then protection of specific church interests. In addition, the Vatican's formulation of the requirements of an internationally guaranteed special statute for Jerusalem during the 1990s would appear to follow the same pattern. First mention goes to the human and civil rights of believers, then to those of the religious communities, and only last to rights relating to the Holy Places, for so long the Church's primary concern.

Bishops have a special role as part of their office to proclaim the Church's gospel, especially in situations of injustice. The Council declared:

> [I]t is always and everywhere legitimate for [the Church] to preach the faith with true freedom, to teach her social doctrine, and to discharge her duty without hindrance. She also has the right to pass moral judgments, even on matters touching the political order, whenever basic personal rights or the salvation of souls make such judgments necessary. (GS 76)

In its decree on the role of bishops, the Council also made clear that their teaching responsibilities include addressing grave public problems including 'the ownership, increase and distribution of material goods, peace and war, and brotherly relations among all peoples'.[46] The Council specifically proposed that bishops are to 'set forth the ways by which (these) very grave questions are to be solved'. Thus, in addressing the deprivation of basic rights and conditions of oppression, church leaders are executing their proper responsibilities. In addition, defending human rights, while inevitably regarded as meddling in politics by offending parties, is a matter of fundamental moral importance. According to contemporary Catholic social teaching, as we have seen, it is a religious duty as well. So, the pronouncements of the patriarchs and heads of churches on essential matters of justice, human rights and peace, while touching on the political order, are an integral part of their religious mission. It is not surprising that, because the Church has articulated the defence of human rights as one of its primary issues, the Latin Patriarch, as a bishop of the Catholic Church and in his role as president of the Assembly of Catholic Bishops of the Holy Land, would be conspicuous in his public leadership on such issues.

In the case of the Holy Land's church leaders, and again especially the Latin Patriarch, one must also address the accusation of partisan nationalism. At times critics laid the charge because the moral criticism of the churches was allegedly aimed one-sidedly at the government of Israel and not at the Palestinian Authority. As evidence rose of rights abuses, misrule and malfeasance on the part of the Palestinian Authority, however, the Palestinian Authority has also come under criticism, most notably by Patriarch Sabbah in his 1999 Christmas homily. Advocacy of a Palestinian homeland, a goal also envisioned in international law and various peace efforts, is hardly grounds for reasonable objection. Likewise, to plead for an end to a prolonged occupation, in gross violation of the Geneva conventions by reason of annexations, settlement of populations and denial of services to the occupied population, can scarcely be regarded as an objectionable act, however, discomfiting as such pleas may be.

Moreover, while Christianity is a universal faith and can play a critical, purifying role with respect to national culture, recent church teaching also recognizes that the culture of a nation or people plays a role in humanity's search for the truth about itself and in the work of evangelization.[47] In that sense, Palestinians' claiming of their own national identity, including the suffering and struggle of the last half century, is appropriately part of the Church's insertion in the life of the Holy Land. Affirmation of the rights of Palestinians and of their national aspirations is accordingly a legitimate role for the Church of the Holy Land. At the same time, Christianity rejects ethnocentrism and encourages a universalism which demands 'a shared responsibility for all humanity'.[48] For that reason, even as it supports Palestinian aspirations, the Church in the Holy Land encourages respect for Israeli rights and non-violent forms of conflict resolution. 'The Church,' as Pope John Paul II wrote, 'promotes those aspects of human behaviour which favour a true culture of peace ... and the search for ways to resolve international conflicts other than by war.'[49] The Church in the Holy Land and its leaders must walk a narrow path advocating on issues of justice and peace and human rights without intervening inappropriately in politics on behalf of a nationalist ideology. Yet, within the parameters of Pope John Paul II's teaching on nationalism and culture, a discerning embrace of the Palestinian cause and Palestinian nationalism is justifiable as essential to a people's spiritual development and to the inculturation of the Gospel.

4. The future of the Christian presence in the Holy Land

The future of Palestinian Christianity remains in question. The next decade will be crucial in determining whether Palestinian Christianity has a future in the land of its birth. The Christian presence may not be reduced to the ecclesiastic's nightmare of a cluster of museums bereft of local worshippers and attended by internationals with no ties to the land or its Christian heritage. Yet, if something approximating that nightmare is to be avoided, action will have to be taken, both in Israel and in the Palestinian areas, to prevent the further diminution of the Christian population and to secure a viable future for the Church in the Holy Land.

Until the outbreak of the second *intifada* (September 2000), Christian discontent seemed to be the greatest in Israel, where between 1948 and 1990 the Christian population had grown fourfold. Resentful of second-class treatment, fearful of an Islamic resurgence that is abetted by Israeli officials, Israel's Christians are showing a lack of faith in the future and a corresponding readiness to emigrate. At the same time, the Barak's government's plans to dissolve the Religious Affairs Ministry as part of a plan to secularize governance in Israel in the short term will hamper church activities until alternate structures to handle their needs are developed.[50] In the long run, it may help contribute to greater equity for Christians in Israel.

At the same time, for Catholics, at least, the legal basis for securing the Christian presence has been secured with the Fundamental Agreement between Israel and the Holy See.[51] Institutionally, the Catholic Church has also been strengthened by the united leadership provided by the Assembly of Catholic Bishops of the Holy

Land, the appointment of a Palestinian to head the local church, and the renewal of the Latin Church through its synod. These are formidable resources, but whether these developments are enough to preserve a sizeable lay presence in the face of economic disadvantage, Islamist agitation, and the political tensions inherent in the situation, is very hard to predict. The probability of success at preserving a Christian presence in the Holy Land would be greater were the Greek Orthodox Church more united internally. The disaffection between the Arab laity and the Greek hierarchy will continue to be a serious liability for the entire Christian community. The survival of Christianity in the Holy Land demands that both the major churches to which Palestinians belong be strong and internally united.

Inevitably the fate of the Palestinian Christians in Israel will depend very much on Israeli and Jewish public opinion. Normalization of life, in the wake of an Israeli-Palestinian final status agreement, which one can safely say will probably not be achieved now for some years, may permit more enthusiastic implementation of the Vatican-Israel agreement and reduce the incentives for Israelis to place pressures on Christian Arabs. But, given the independence of Israeli bureaucrats and the readiness of people on the fringe to make trouble, trusting in normalization may be naive. The future of Palestinian Christianity may depend, rather, on altering general Israeli popular opinion and, therefore, energizing the local Jewish-Christian dialogue at several levels. The al-Aqsa *intifada*, I must admit, dims even these very modest hopes. The uprising has stirred up Israeli anxieties about future co-existence to an unimaginable degree, as witnessed by mob violence in Israel and vigilante executions by both sides on the West Bank and in Gaza. Reservoirs of trust have been depleted on both sides.

In the Palestinian Self-Rule Areas, Muslim-Christian dialogue may be hard to build, though it certainly must go forward. Such dialogue has a relatively short history and has yet to prove seriously productive. The one notable exception was the successful diplomatic campaign in 1999 by the Vatican to rouse international Muslim opinion against the construction of the Shehab al-Din mosque adjacent to the Basilica of the Annunciation in Nazareth, and the parallel success by the local church in winning influential Muslim opinion in the immediate region. The forty-day occupation and siege of Bethlehem's Church of the Nativity in 2002, however, shook the confidence of many lay Christians in their Muslim neighbours. While a few people had sought refuge in the basilica, Muslim gunmen forced their way in, thereby violating one of Christianity's holiest shrines. Palestinian chairman Yasser Arafat, often a protector of Christians in the past, moreover, proved himself extraordinarily mercurial and unhelpful in remedying the crisis. While Bethlehem's Christians prefer not to talk about their troubles, *Newsweek* reporter Joshua Hammer has provided a chilling account of the violence of Bethlehem's Muslim militias and their intimidation of Christians in his recent book *A Season in Bethlehem: Unholy War in a Sacred Place*.[52]

In Palestine, however, the means to secure the Christian future are more likely to be political and social than inter-religious. A strategy for Christian survival in Palestine may call, above all, for the maintenance of secular government and for institutional as well as religious pluralism. The Basic Agreement between the Holy See and the PLO (2000) provides a legal structure for guaranteeing freedom of religion and assuring the rights of Christians governed by the Palestinian Authority. The implementation of the agreement will be more reliable, however, in a pluralistic institutional context rather than in one where implementation must be effected as an exception to the general, autocratic style of governance. A pluralistic society is one in which Christian communities are more likely to have room to live and thrive. Further hope for Christians may lie, ironically, in their very small numbers, their institutional service to Palestinian society, their role in secular politics, and the churches' ties to the West.

Before the al-Aqsa *intifada*, Palestinian Christianity was, in many ways, stronger, more united, more confidant than it was two decades ago. But the collapse of Christian confidence in the Galilee over the past five years, symbolized by the Nazareth mosque controversy, shows how vulnerable Christians remain to adverse social pressure, religious prejudice and manipulation even in less troubled times. The al-Aqsa *intifada*, especially the occupation and siege of the Church of the Nativity, has added significantly to that vulnerability as the Christian emigration from the Bethlehem area suggests. Some months ago, before the *intifada*, it appeared to me that Christianity's future, in the short term at least, might be brighter in Palestine than in Israel. After the punishing shelling of Bethlehem, Beit Jala and Beit Sahour, Muslim harrassment of Christians, the controversy over the Nazareth mosque, and the occupation and siege of the Church of the Nativity, that no longer seems possible. The challenges and burdens will be different, but, whether in Palestine or in Israel, a time of extreme trial is at hand for the Christians of the Holy Land.

While the predictions of the disappearance of Palestinian

Christians may be premature – and God forbid it should ever come to pass – given the conflicting currents in which it finds itself, one can truly say that the future of 'the living Christian presence' in the Holy Land lies in the hands of God. At times like this, as Saint Ignatius of Loyola taught, we must pray as if everything depended on God and work as if everything depended on ourselves.

Notes

1 Portions of this chapter have been adapted from a longer study, 'Palestinian Christians: Status 2000' in Marshall Breger (ed.), *The Vatican Israeli Accords: Legal, Political and Theological Contexts* Notre Dame, In., University of Notre Dame Press, 2004, pp. 307–42. The current version of this chapter has been updated from the original lecture offered in London 24 January, 2001.
   I also must acknowledge my indebtedness for the premise about the role of the *intifada* in shaping a common Christian identity to my Jesuit confrère Peter De Bruhl, SJ in his 'The Crisis of Palestinian Christians' in David Burrell and Yehezkel Landau (eds), *Voices from Jerusalem: Jews and Christians Reflect on the Holy Land*, New York, Paulist, 1992, 118–58.
2 On the millet system, see Anthony O'Mahony, 'Palestinian Christians: Religion, Politics and Society, *c.*1800–1948' in Anthony O'Mahony (ed.), *Palestinian Christians: Religion, Politics and Society in the Holy Land*, London, Melisende, 1999, pp. 17–22.
3 Under Islamic law, Christians were *dhimmi*, i.e., members of a protected minority, excluded from full participation in Muslim societies.
4 On justice as a 'constitutive dimension of preaching the gospel', see the 1970 Synod of Bishops, 'Justice in the World' in David J. O'Brien and Thomas A. Shannon, *Renewing the Earth: Catholic Documents on Peace, Justice and Liberation*, Garden City: Doubleday/Image, 1977, p. 391.
5 On the preferential option for the poor, a term first developed in liberation theology and later adopted by the magisterium, see Pope John Paul II, *On Social Concern: Sollicitudo rei socialis*, Washington, DC, United States Catholic Conference [1987]), no. 42.
6 For more extensive treatment of Arab Christianity, see Kenneth Cragg, *The Arab Christian: A History of the Middle East*, London, Mowbray, 1992 and *Palestine: The Prize and Price of Zion*, Washington, Cassell, 1997.
7 See, for example, Conseil des Patriarches Catholiques d'Orient, *Ensemble devant Dieu pour Le Bien de la Personne et de la Societe: La coexistence entre musulmans et chretiens dans le monde arabe*, 3eme Lettre Pastorale des Patriarches Catholiques d'Orient, Bkerke, Liban, Secretariat General du Conseil, 1994.
8 The churches in communion with Rome, and particularly the Latin Patriarchate, have undertaken steps to dialogue with Israel's Jews. Of particular note were two meetings of the Latin Patriarch with Israel's Chief Rabbis. In 2000, moreover, Patriarch Sabbah accepted the invitation to serve as co-president of an Israeli interreligious association. The Greek Orthodox and Oriental Churches, drawing their authority from anti-Jewish the writings of some Church Fathers, refuse to engage in such dialogue.
9 Thus, the Catholic Patriarchs of the East in their sixth pastoral letter (Christmas 1999) accepted the proposition of the First Congress of Catholic Patriarchs and Bishops of the East (May 1999) that the Catholic Churches of

the Orient should '[a]t the same time [as they deepen relations with Muslims] develop the dialogue with Judaism in the present circumstances taking into account the exigencies of justice, peace, reconciliation and the religious heritage [of our two religions]'. *Nostra Aetate* had called for dialogue with Jews. In addition, it had recognized the common Abrahamic spiritual patrimony of Christians and Jews, affirmed the permanence of God's covenant with the Jewish people, and declared that Jesus' 'passion cannot be blamed upon all Jews then living, without distinction, nor upon the Jews of today'. See Declaration on the Relationship of the Church with Non-Christian Religions: *Nostra Aetate* in Walter M. Abbott, SJ, general editor, *The Documents of Vatican II*, New York, Association/America Press, 1966, n. 4.

10 The inclusion of the Oriental Churches in Christian responsibility for the Holocaust is a problematic issue. First, most are distinctive churches, even those in communion with Rome, and hold to ancient differences between their churches and the Latin West. Secondly, the historical experience of Oriental Christians is decidedly different from that of those in the West. Thirdly, the Christian leaders of the Middle East object to the presumption of Western European and American Catholics engaged in the dialogue that they speak for the whole Church, East and West, a presumption which is further augmented by the common Jewish projection that the Western Catholic Church speaks for all Christianity without condition or exception. Holy Land Catholics who accept *Nostra Aetate's* rejection of the collective responsibility of the Jews for the death of Jesus, nonetheless, feel unjustly pressured to accept collective ecclesial responsibility for the European anti-Judaism that was a contributing factor to the Holocaust.

11 For reporting that captures the pain of the emigration crisis ensuing from the al-Aqsa *intifada*, see Judith Sudilovsky, 'Family v. duty to the Holy Land: Christians leave, feeling guilty', Catholic New Service, 8 February 2001.

12 Mayor Hanna Nasser of Bethlehem in remarks to visiting bishops at Bethlehem University, 13 January 2004.

13 *Actes du 1er Congres des Patriarches et Eveques Catholiques du Moyen-Orient, Mai, 1999*, Bkerke, Lebanon, Secretariat General, 2000, ch. III, no. 15.

14 The al-Aqsa *intifada* has been particularly difficult for Palestinian Christians because from the beginning the uprising has taken on a militant Islamic color, inspired by groups like Hamas and Islamic Jihad, and because its preferred methods have been violent. Christians for the most part have preferred non-violent means of resistance, and in the first *intifada* the mostly Christian population of Beit Sahour carried out a nonviolent tax revolt against the Israeli occupation. See Charles M. Sennott, *The Body and the Blood: The Holy Land's Christians at the Turn of a New Millennium*, New York, Public Affairs, 2001, pp. 135–65.

15 See De Bruhl, 'The Crisis of Palestinian Christians', note 1 above.

16 'On the Significance of Jerusalem for Christians: Memorandum of Their Beatitudes the Patriarchs and the Heads of Christian Communities in Jerusalem' [Private printing], 14 November 1994, 2 (no. 5). In addition, see the joint Christian-Muslim declaration 'The Jerusalem Appeal: Muslims and Christians Together for Jerusalem Sake,' Beirut, 16 June 1996 signed by senior religious leaders from around the region.

17 'On the Significance of Jerusalem for Christians', 5, no. 14.

18 Ibid.

19 On housing and other forms of Israeli discrimination against Arab residents

of East Jerusalem, see Amir S. Chesin, Bill Hutman, and Avi Melamed, *Separate and Unequal: The Inside Story of Israeli Rule in East Jerusalem*, Cambridge, MA, Harvard, 1999; on the housing issue, pp. 29–37, 50–55.
20 Untitled survey by Bernard Sabella [typescript], p. 4. Mr Sabella, a Christian, is a leading Palestinian sociologist.
21 Ibid., p. 13.
22 See 'As the Third Millennium Draws Near,' Origins 24:24, 24 November, 1994, pp. 401, 403–16.
23 'Service of Pardon' in *Origins* 29:40, 23 March 2000, p. 647.
24 Commission for Religious Relations with the Jews, 'We Remember: A Reflection on the "Shoah"', *Origins* 27:40, 26 March 1997, pp. 669–75.
25 Joint Communique, International Catholic-Jewish Liaison Committee, Sixteenth Meeting, Vatican City, 23–26 March 1998, p. 3.
26 Ehud Barak, 'A Nation That Remembers', *Origins* 29:42, 6 April 2000, p. 680.
27 Pope John Paul II, 'Toward a Just and Lasting Peace in the Holy Land', *Origins* 29:41, 30 March 2000, p. 667.
28 Pope John Paul II, 'The Difficult but Essential Road to Christian Unity', *Origins* 29:42, 6 April 2000, p. 690.
29 See Joseph Algazy, 'Mon Etat tue mon peuple', *Le Monde Diplomatique*, November 2000, pp. 14–15.
30 'Hundreds of Christian Arab Families Fleeing PA Areas', by Margot Dudkevitch, *Jerusalem Post*, 25 October 2000.
31 'Hundreds of Christian Arab Families Are Still Here and Will Remain Forever Here', Press Release, Latin Patriarchate of Jerusalem [n.d., probably 25 or 26 October 2000].
32 Obtaining statistics on Christian emigration is exceedingly difficult. Estimates range from 'more than 2000' (Bethlehem mayor Hanna Nasser, January 2004) to 15,000 or more. Figures on the higher side are quite probable.
33 For the role of non-violence in the *intifada* of 1987–1993 from western eyes, see James W. Douglass, *The Non-Violent Coming of God*, Maryknoll, NY, Orbis, 1991, especially pp. 181–204.
34 'Public Opinion Polls on Palestinian Attitudes toward Politics Including the Current Uprising', No. 39, Jerusalem Media and Communications Centre, December 2000, questions no. 2 and 5.
35 *Recherche la paix et poursuis-la: Questions et Responses sur la Justice et la Paix en Notre Sainte Terre*, Jerusalem, Latin Patriarchate, 1998, p. 14.
36 Ibid, p. 15, *The Catechism of the Catholic Church*, n. 2297.
37 *Recherche la paix*, pp. 15–16.
38 Ibid., p. 14.
39 Michel Sabbah, Homily, 'Ecumenical Peace Prayers', Saint-Etienne, Dominican Fathers, 12 October 2000.
40 Theological Commission of the Latin Patriarchate, 'Reflections on the Presence of the Church in the Holy Land', [Latin Patriarchate, Internet Communication] 3 December, 2003, nos. 7 and 17.
41 Ibid., pp. 14–15.
42 In 1998, the government of Prime Minister Binyamin Netanyahu unsuccessfully opposed the appointment of Boutros Mouallem as the Melkite Archbishop for Galilee and failed in its attempt to have its own candidate installed in his place.
43 The leading role of the Catholic Church and the Latin Patriarch in speaking

on behalf of justice and human rights is increasingly recognized even by secular observers. See William A. Orme, Jr., 'Jerusalem Christians Now Back Palestinian Sovereignty', *New York Times* (World Wide Web edition), 24 December 2000.

44 See 'Peace on Earth: *Pacem in terris'* in David J. O'Brien and Thomas A. Shannon, *Renewing the Earth: Catholic Documents on Peace, Justice and Liberation*, Garden City, Doubleday/Image, 1977, pp. 117–70. On the shift in Vatican approaches to church-state relations, see Marshall Breger (ed.), *The Vatican-Israel Accords: Legal, Political and Theological Contexts* Notre Dame, In., University of Notre Dame Press, 2004, especially David-Maria A. Jaeger, OFM. David-Maria A. Jaeger, OFM, 'Fundamental Agreement between the Holy See and the State of Israel: A New Legal Regime of Church-State Relations', pp. 51–66.

45 See 'The Pastoral Constitution on the Church in the Modern World: *Gaudium et spes'* in *Renewing the Earth*, pp. 171–284, especially no. 41.

46 'Decree on Bishops' Pastoral Office in the Church' in *The Documents of Vatican II*, no. 12.

47 See *On the One Hundredth Anniversary of Rerum Novarum: Centesimus annus*, Washington, DC, United States Catholic Conference, 1991, no. 50.

48 Ibid., no. 51.

49 Ibid.

50 In January 2004, the government of Prime Minister Ariel Sharon abolished the Religious Affairs Ministry and integrated the Office of Christian Communities' Affairs into the Ministry of the Interior.

51 But, on the difficulties facing the implementation of the Fundamental Agreement and the continuing negotiations between the Vatican and Israel, see 'Blocks in the Road: [Subtitle]', *America*, 9 February 2004, [vol., no., pp.], an interview with the Holy See negotiation, Father David-Maria Jaeger, OFM, on the tenth anniversary of the accord.

52 Hammer, *A Season in Bethlehem: Unholy War in a Holy Place*, New York, Free Press, 2003.

Chapter 4

Palestinian Christians and Liberation Theology

Leonard Marsh

Introduction

14 May 1998 marked the jubilee of the founding of the State of Israel. For Zionists, both Jewish and Christian, it was an occasion to celebrate. However, as Michael Prior observes,[1] a price has been exacted for the realization of Zionist hopes:

> The fundamental problem of the Palestinians is the price they have had to pay and continue to pay for the encroachment on their land by Zionists from the Diaspora. The creation of the state of Israel was not brought about without the destruction of some 400 Arab villages, and the exodus, and the expulsion, of more than 700,000 Arab inhabitants. At least a further 300,000 left Palestine as a result of the 1967 six-day war.

The displacement of large numbers of people as a result of warfare justified by an assertive nationalism is not a unique or unusual phenomenon. Yet, this situation has generated a remarkable response of interest in Christian theological reflection from within the Palestinian Christian communities, a discourse that can be characterized as belonging to the wider tradition of Christian liberation theology.

To a great extent, Christian liberation theology has been concerned with issues resulting from economic deprivation and the dehumanization of the poor, particularly in the Third World. While it is true that liberation theology also has addressed such issues as cultural and ethnic marginalization (e.g., in the writings of James Cone, a black American theologian), and inter-religious and cultural questions arising from Asia (such as in the writings of the Sri Lankan priest Tissa Balasuriya), '... most of the excitement of liberation theology comes from South America and reflects a fundamental concern with issues of economic poverty'.[2]

Palestinian Liberation Theology has emerged out of the Palestinian Christian experience, above all from a history of expulsion and occupation. Their predicament has been refined perhaps uniquely because other (non-Palestinian) Christians have felt they must support the State of Israel.

This chapter attempts to explore the unique dimensions and dilemmas of the Christian Palestinian experience and the Christian theological reflection that has emerged from it, to ask

a) What is Palestinian Liberation Theology?
b) What has brought it about?
c) What has been its inner tensions and external factors bearing upon it?
d) How does Palestinian Liberation Theology relate to the larger context of liberation theology world-wide?

The main example of Palestinian Christian theology used here will be the writings of Canon Naim Ateek, an Anglican Palestinian priest.

This chapter will put forward the argument that only through an awareness and appreciation of the multidimensional nature of the Palestinian Christian crisis can the significance and validity of Palestinian Christian Liberation Theology be adequately assessed.

1. Palestinian Christianity and Palestinian nationalism

Arab nationalism emerged out of the political disintegration of the Ottoman Empire, reaching its culmination at the end of the First World War. It became obvious that the Young Turk revolution would not bring about self-determination for non-Turkish areas of the Ottoman Empire. Arab nationalist societies such as *al-Fatat* and *al-Ahd* grew in strength among the military and intellectuals in areas such as Syria, the Lebanon, and Palestine.

During the First World War, the Turkish Empire had allied itself with Germany and the Austrian-Hungarian Empire. British foreign policy officials, chiefly represented by Lord Balfour and the famous Balfour Declaration of 1917, made conflicting agreements with Zionists promising a Jewish homeland. Meanwhile, along with the Russians and the French, the British undertook to divide the Middle East territorially.

The Balfour Declaration, and the period of the British mandate over Palestine (1920–1948) saw an intensification of a sense of Palestinian national identity.[3] This sense of national identity was partly focused as a result of religious factors. As Rashid Khalidi points out:

> Although Muslims and Christians had somewhat different conceptions from one another about what made Palestine a Holy Land, and of its boundaries and extent, they shared a similar general idea of the country as a unit, and as being special and holy.[4]

The jurisdictions of the Latin and Greek Orthodox Patriarchates, and the Protestant Episcopate of Jerusalem which covered Palestine entirely, reinforced this sense of identity even when Ottoman administrative units changed.

The British mandate over Palestine ended on 14 May 1948. The State of Israel was immediately proclaimed and Arab forces entered Palestine. The extent of the defeat of the Arabs allowed the new Israeli state to expand its boundaries almost at once. Just a year later, the Palestinians seem to have disappeared as a national movement.[5]

The impact of what Palestinians refer to as *Al-Nakba* (the Catastrophe) is exemplified by the experience of a leading Palestinian Christian writer, Father Elias Chacour (born 1939). Father Chacour is a Greek Catholic (Melkite) priest who chronicled his personal experience of being forced as a child from Biram, a village in Galilee destroyed by Israeli troops in 1948, in two important works, *Blood Brothers*[6] and *We Belong to the Land*[7]. Chacour was trained for the Greek Catholic priesthood in Nazareth and St Sulpice in Paris, ordained in 1965, and has a degree in Biblical Studies, including the Talmud, from the Hebrew University in Jerusalem. The title, *Blood Brothers*, is significant in that it stresses the Semitic unity of Arabs and Jews. Chacour does have sympathy for a Jewish Israel but contrasts the hopes and aspirations of pre-Holocaust Zionism with the brutality and oppression he himself has experienced as a Palestinian.

Blood Brothers, a reflective autobiography, relates his growing radicalization as a Palestinian Christian activist. His conviction that Palestinians have a right to live in Israel on the basis of equality – even if Zionists believe *they* have the right to the land to the exclusion of others by the authority of scripture – was enhanced by his pastorate of the Melkite Church in Ibillin in the Galilee. He witnessed and documented the oppression of Palestinians in this community.

Another contemporary Christian thinker from the Holy Land, Naim Ateek, a Palestinian Anglican theologian, sees the 1967 Six Day War as a crucial moment in the history of the Israeli state. The occupation of Gaza, along with parts of Syria and Egypt was, according to him, attributed by most Jews and many western Christians to 'God's purposeful and powerful intervention on the side of Israel and against the Arabs.'[8]

Ateek believes that, after 1967, Palestinians faced a Zionism that was based less on a secular ideology than a religious one. This development has been important in the growth of a specifically Palestinian Christian response to the nationalist question.

The eruption of the first *intifada* (the Uprising) in the refugee camps beginning in the Gaza Strip in December 1987, was not supported initially by Palestinian Christians in the main. This situation changed, however, when on 9 February 1988, Khalid Tarazi, a Christian boy from Gaza, died after interrogation following his arrest by the Israelis.

Daphne Tsimhoni, a Senior Researcher at Ben Gurion University in Israel, sees this event and similar occurrences as symbolizing 'their [Palestinian Christians] common fate with their Muslim counterparts'.[9] Tsimhoni notes the contribution of Palestinian Christians in bringing the Palestinian cause to Western public opinion – such figures as Hanna Siniora, editor-in-chief of *al-Fajr*; Dr Hanan Ashwari, a prominent delegate to the peace talks; Elias Freij, Bethlehem mayor; Jonathan Kuttab, a Palestinian civil rights lawyer, and the expelled Mubarak Awd, who organized non-violent protests against Israeli occupation. Tsimhoni notes that 'these contributions are not meant to represent the Christian but rather the national cause'.[10]

The Latin Patriarch Michel Sabbah, Greek Catholic Archbishop Lufti Laham, and the now retired Anglican Bishop Samir Kafity, organized a collective effort of the Jerusalem Christian churches supporting the Palestinian national cause. In April 1989, they issued a joint statement against injustice and oppression of the Palestinian people:

> In Jerusalem, on the West Bank and in Gaza our people experience in their daily lives constant deprivation of their fundamental rights because of arbitrary actions deliberately taken by the authorities.
> Our people are often subjected to unprovoked harassment and hardship.

> We are particularly concerned by the tragic and unnecessary loss of Palestinian lives, especially among minors. Unarmed and innocent people are being killed by the unwarranted use of firearms and hundreds are wounded by the excessive use of force.
> We protest against the frequent shooting incidents in the vicinity of holy places.
> We also condemn the practice of mass administrative arrests, and of continuing detention of adults and minors without trial.
> We further condemn the use of all forms of collective punishment, including the demolition of homes and depriving whole communities of basic services such as water and electricity.[11]

Such joint statements continue to be made at Christian festivals and special occasions. This identification with the Palestinian national cause, and the society in which Palestinian Christians live in Israel/Palestine, is a paramount factor in development of Palestinian Christian liberation theology.

2. Christian Palestinians: a declining minority?

An important consequence of the conflicts since the establishment of the State of Israel has been the emigration of considerable numbers of Palestinians. Christians have shared in this emigration in disproportionate numbers in relation to their Muslim counterparts.

Michael Prior observes the acute difficulty emigration poses for the Christian community: 'A recent survey in Israel has shown that the intention to emigrate is three times higher for Christians than for Muslims.'[12]

This evidence regarding the intention to emigrate compounds the fact that 7% of the 714,000 who had been made refugees in 1948 were Christians. Since the occupation of the West Bank and Gaza in 1967, nearly 40% of Palestinian Christians have left the country.[13]

An additional factor undermining Christian Palestinians is that alone among the states of the Middle East, Christians are a minority not just in relation to Muslims but also to the Jewish majority which identifies itself with the Israeli state.[14] Andrea Pacini notes that although the Arab Christian legal position is guaranteed by the state, Arab Christians are not, in practice, integrated into Israeli society, nor do they enjoy equal opportunities in social and political life. High unemployment and an inordinately low percentage of university students among Arabs in Israel further add to the general disillusionment with the Israeli state among Arab Christians.[15]

A further factor depleting the strength of Palestinian Christians in proportion to the Muslim population has been a lower birth rate among Christians: Muslims are recorded as having 4.7 children per family, compared to 2.4 for Christians.[16] It is still in dispute as to how much the position of Christians as a minority – within the Muslim majority situation in the Palestinian national movement – has been undermined.

In a statistical analysis of the reasons given by Palestinian Christians for emigration, the Palestinian Christian sociologist at the Pontifical Bethlehem University, Bernard Sabella, concludes that Palestinians leave because of a lack of economic and educational opportunities. Palestinian Christians are particularly vulnerable because they tend to occupy more middle-class occupations and have a higher educational achievement.[17]

Sabella contends that the notion that Islamic radicalism per se has brought about Christian emigration is unfounded according to statistical evidence among different surveys.[18] He does suggest that Christian emigration has lead to an ageing of the Christian population left behind (with a high median age of thirty years), and tends to weaken the social position of churches in society.[19] However, Tsimhoni asserts that 'The dilemma of the Christians as a minority within the Palestinian Arab national movement has existed since the movement's inception.'[20]

This dilemma has been obscured because of the Israeli occupation of Jerusalem and the West Bank, but the *intifada* brought this out into the open.

Tsimhoni's view of the situation would tend to be supported by Said K. Aburih in his book, *The Forgotten Faithful*. Based on a series of interviews following the *intifada*, many interviewees reported a growing antagonism toward Christians based on an attempt to redefine Palestinian identity in Islamic terms.[21] This book's methodology is anecdotal, but supported by Tsimhoni's insistence that, despite intentions of those in leadership positions to promote harmony among Christians and Muslims, mutual suspicion remains. The role radical Islamists play where secular nationalism is perceived as having failed in achieving its goals increases Christian apprehension. The election of Hamas in January 2006 may be indicative of such disillusionment.

Yet such misgivings and conflict have encouraged Christians to more firmly assert their identity as Palestinians. Indeed, this is the major basis of an indigenous Palestinian Christian Liberation Theology.

3. Zionism and Christianity

An important concern in the work of Naim Ateek, particularly in his text, *Justice and Only Justice*, has been to question the endorsement certain elements among Western Christianity have given to Zionism, even to the point of affirming a scriptural mandate for the State of Israel, i.e., that the land of Israel has been given by God to the Jews.

Specifically addressing Christian Zionism, Ateek takes to task three figures treated as representatives of alleged Christian traditions sympathetic to the State of Israel and the so-called theology supporting such attitudes.[22]

The first and perhaps least compelling case is that of Howard A. Johnson, former canon of the Cathedral of St John the Divine in New York, who after a visit to Israel in 1960 published *Global Odyssey*.[23] Ateek regards Johnson's criticisms of indigenous Palestinian Christians as 'harsh and most erroneous',[24] and Ateek perhaps may be more sensitive because they are both Anglicans. Furthermore, Ateek views Johnson's writings as an irresponsible mixing of spurious theology and politics. For example, Johnson had criticized an Arabic edition of the revised Anglican *Book of Common Prayer* for the editing-out of a number of Psalms (some 50 to 100), and Johnson inferred they were deleted because of their mention of Israel. Ateek corrects this claim, showing that at least fifteen other Psalms referring to Israel were retained in the revised prayer book, and that of the fifty-odd psalms omitted, at least thirty do not refer to Israel at all. Ateek remarks such misrepresentation 'only makes the work of the church more difficult'.[25]

Ateek's attack may seem a condemnation of mere inaccuracy or ignorance on the part of a casual visitor taking the pulse of Palestinian Anglicanism. He mounts a more serious theological challenge to a volume by the American theologian Paul van Buren, entitled *Discerning the Way*,[26] a prolegomenon to a projected four-volume work, *Theology of the Jewish-Christian Reality*. Van Buren (1924–1998) had already made his reputation in the 1960s as a 'Death of God' theologian, having begun his theological career as a former research student of Swiss Reformed theologian Karl Barth.

The principal objection Ateek has to van Buren's methodology is his imprecise use of the term *Israel*, and his failure to distinguish between the Israel of the Bible and the modern state. According to Ateek, van Buren seems to give divine legitimacy to the modern State of Israel. Here is van Buren himself:

> If the Holocaust is a negative revelation of God's requirement of human responsibility, the founding of the state of Israel says the same thing in positive form. Israel was founded not by divine intervention from heaven or the sending of the messiah, but by Jewish guns and Jewish efforts against seemingly insuperable numerical and material odds. Had the early pioneers, the fugitives from the Holocaust or the supporters of the project from the Diaspora, waited upon a so-called act of God, instead of daring to *be* the act of God, they would in all likelihood be waiting still, those who were still alive. This event which has begun to reorient the church, this event of the founding of Israel and Jewish return to the land, was one of humanly assumed responsibility for history, yes, for God's history with His people and their history with Him.[27]

Ateek challenges these words, and this way of thinking both as naive, suggesting that God ignores all other nations, and immoral. In effect, van Buren regresses to the image of a *tribal* deity.[28]

Rosemary Radford Reuther, a Roman Catholic feminist theologian, examines van Buren's Christian Zionist theology in some depth. She believes that van Buren transfers the 'Christological monism' he inherited from Barth to God's biblical covenant with the Jewish people. Instead of God being known only in Christ – as with Barth – God is only perceived as the God who chose the people of Israel as his own people.[29] Van Buren has maintained Barth's rejection of natural theology and affirmed God's election of the Jewish people at Sinai as 'foundational and normative' in creation and redemption,[30] and made this a cornerstone of his work.

Incidentally, this seems a long way from the attitudes which characterized van Buren's text from the 1960s, *The Secular Meaning of the Gospel*. Commenting on this work, Alistair Kee observed that

> In *The Secular Meaning of the Gospel*, we are confronted with two kinds of reduction. In the first, certain dimensions of theology are arbitrarily (by positivist assumptions) cut off. Whatever they meant, they are not allowed to mean anything today. Having cut off these dimensions, which might easily be the most significant, he then employs to the remainder the now familiar God-to-man reduction.[31]

This God-to-man reduction again may be linked to van Buren's Barthian rejection of natural theology, and what Reuther had referred to as 'Christological monism'. Now, however, van Buren suggests another form of reductionism in that the Christian Church has no covenant of its own, its identity being an extension of God's covenant with Israel.[32] Furthermore, because Christianity developed under Gentile influence, a supercessionary relationship to Judaism and an hostility to Jews followed, demanding of [Jews] that they abandon obedience to the Torah and find salvation through Jesus Christ.[33] The end result of this alleged Christian attitude toward Jews has been the Holocaust.[34] Van Buren alleges that his view of the relationship of the Christian message as rooted primarily in the Jewish covenant with God is compatible with the New Testament.[35]

At last, van Buren regards Palestinian claims as unfounded.[36] It would seem that his 'theology' can be conceived of as a serious attempt to address the issue of Christian anti-Semitism, but it ends in disallowing Palestinians – even Palestinian Christians – to have an identity of their own. An inference from van Buren's argument might be that Palestinians should be required to pay the penalty for the history of European anti-Semitism despite the fact that they played no part in it.

Ateek also criticizes a more recent form of Christian Zionism evinced in the writings and pronouncements of the Reverend Jerry Falwell, self-proclaimed founder of the Moral Majority in the US. Falwell appropriated this term – Moral Majority – from the presidential election campaign of Richard Nixon – but it continues to resonate with a decided *minority* today. Falwell claims that Christian Zionism is an aspect of following Jesus.[37] Ateek notes that this curious fundamentalist ideology has found expression since the 1980s in the establishment of 'the International Christian Embassy' in Jerusalem. This organization is expressly dedicated to supporting and sustaining the State of Israel.

Falwell needs to be seen in the wider context of North American Christian fundamentalism, where Israel and its role in prophecy are believed to have a crucial function. Many Christian fundamentalists in the US see prophetic trends in history; their idiosyncratic readings of Ezekiel, Daniel, and the Book of Revelation provide them with reassurance that divine providence is at work in contemporary affairs. Circa 1912–1915, a twelve-volume work titled *The Fundamentals*[38] was published in Chicago, Illinois. It is strongly premillenarial in outlook. Premillenarianists believe that Jesus Christ will return bodily to earth, wage a battle against Satan and the anti-Christ, and establish a 1,000-year reign. This 'dispensationalist' theology has its origins in the writings of the founder of the Plymouth brethren, John Nelson Darby, in the early nineteenth century, and celebrated in Cyrus I. Scofield's *Reference Bible* (1909). Scofield talks of a theology of seven 'dispensations', or periods of time in which God deals with the world.

Fundamentalists and dispensationalists have come together to develop a re-working of the biblical text in which a specific chronology emerges: Jews having rejected Jesus, the kingdom He came to establish had to be delayed. Thus we are in a period of abeyance, as it were, until the Rapture (1 Thessalonians 4:7). The founding of the State of Israel, according to Scofield's followers, is a sign that we are moving towards the final dispensation. In their interpretation, the founding of the State of Israel is referred to in the Bible (Ezekiel 30–40). God is bound to bring about his final purposes *through* Israel. Because the modern Israeli state is central to Christ's return, it follows that Israel must be protected at all costs.

In *Prophecy and Politics: Militant Evangelists on the Road to Nuclear War*,[39] American writer Grace Halsell perceives a relationship between recent US evangelists such as Falwell, and his supporters and an emphatically uncritical support of the State of Israel.

Naim Ateek is typical among the mainstream of Middle Eastern Christians in rejecting such arcane notions as described above. In a booklet on Christian Zionism, the Middle Eastern Council of Churches rejected dispensationalist ideology as bound up with premillenarianism – and both as biblically unfounded and as having allowed Christian faith to become subservient in the modern Israeli context.[40]

4. Biblical exegesis and Palestinian Christianity

Palestinian Liberation Theology has to address the central issue of biblical interpretation. All liberation theologians need to engage with the interpretation of the Bible, but Palestinian Christians need to address the central issue of the Bible and the land. This is because, as Michael Prior points out,

> The Bible at face value provides not only a moral framework which transposes Jewish claims into a divinely sanctioned legitimacy, but postulates the taking possession of the promised land and the forcible expulsion of the indigenous population as the fulfilment of a biblical mandate.[41]

The problem this poses is one which Prior himself, Naim Ateek, and the former Anglican Assistant Bishop of Jerusalem, Kenneth Cragg, have addressed.

In the Hebrew Bible, Yahweh addresses Abram with a promise of the gift of the land to him and his descendants (Genesis 12:6–7). This promise is repeated when Abram comes to stay at Hebron and a 'covenant' is established (Genesis 15:18–21). Later, the promise also is made to Isaac, Abram's son. Isaac prays this his son Jacob may see this promised land realized (Genesis: 28:4). The dying Joseph tells his brothers that God will bring them into the land that he had promised to Abraham (formerly Abram), Isaac and Jacob. (Genesis 30:24).

The Exodus tradition has been congenial to liberation theologians seeking to harness the theme of liberation from bondage and exploitation.[42]

> I have come down to deliver them from the Egyptians, and to bring them up out of the land to a good land, a land flowing with milk and honey, to the country of the Canaanites, the Hittites, the Amorites....
> (Exodus 3:8; also Exodus 6:6–8)

The gift of the land to the Hebrew people is restated in Leviticus 14:34 and is emphasized in Deuteronomy 1:6–8. Yahweh is presented as requiring the destruction of the inhabitants of Canaan Deuteronomy 20:16–18, a perspective that runs through the Books of Joshua and Judges.

The relationship of the Promised Land to the people of Israel in the perspective of the Hebrew Bible continues to be reflected in the Book of Psalms: 'And he brought them to this holy land, to the mountain which his right hand had won' Psalms 78:54–55. Or again: 'Thou didst bring a vine out of Egypt, thou did drive out the nations and plant it' (Psalms 80:8).

Such observations are not meant to represent an exhaustive treatment of the question of land and settlement in the Hebrew Bible, but do provide a sense of the significance of the divine promise of the land as referred to in the Bible.

Naim Ateek recognizes that the biblical text represents a major challenge to any Palestinian Theology of Liberation. For Palestinians, the Bible itself is not a source of strength offering an encouragement to faith and the gift of salvation. Rather, Jews and some Christians have used the Bible in a way that can be said to support injustice and inequality. Understood in a literalistic way, the Bible appears to Palestinians to enslave them and undermine their hopes for a national homeland.

When Christians recite the Benedictus including the words 'Blessed be the God of Israel ...', Ateek asks what does this mean?[43] Which *Israel* is being referred to? What redemption is being promised, and to whom? One problem facing Palestinian Liberation Theology is how the Bible itself is to be appreciated by Palestinian Christians. Conflicting issues in the biblical text put the question, Is God partial to the Jews and is the God of the Bible a God of justice and peace?

Ateek believes it is necessary to undertake a process of 'contextualization' in relation to the Bible. An awareness of what Palestinians face in approaching the biblical text seems to be what Ateek refers to when he writes of the need to 'contextualize'.[44] According to Ateek, such a perspective is a necessary preliminary task in any process of interpretation. At the same time, he is also keen to be faithful to the 'biblical message'.[45]

Ateek is aware that one previous approach to the problem of interpreting the Old Testament in Christian terms has been that of allegory or what he calls 'spiritualization'.[46]

The allegorical interpretation of the Bible has been prevalent from the days of the Early Church, but from the eighteenth century onward it has more or less disappeared as a hermeneutical tool in interpreting scripture.

An earlier, classical example of allegorical methodology is Augustine's reading of the New Testament parable of the Good Samaritan:

> A certain man went down from Jerusalem to Jericho. Adam himself is meant, Jerusalem is the heavenly city of peace, from whose blessedness Adam fell; Jericho means the moon, and signifies our mortality, because it is born, waxes, wanes, and dies. The thieves are the devil and his angels 'who stripped him', namely, of his immortality, and beat him by persuading him to sin.[47]

Ateek does not define what he means by allegorization but the example above, from Augustine, is representative of this tradition. Nor does Ateek define 'spiritualization'; it may be he is referring to an approach which makes use of typology – taking events from the Old Testament which can be read as prefiguring or foreshadowing the New Testament. In typological terms, Old Testament scenes may be seen as 'types' contrasting with New Testament 'anti-types'. An example often cited is the contrast of Eve tempted by the

Serpent in Genesis (the type) with Mary at the Annunciation (the anti-type). The comparison here is between the disobedience of Eve and Mary's obedience to God's invitation to be the mother of Christ in Luke's Gospel.

Ateek believes that such an approach fails to address the problem of the political misuse of the Bible, while acknowledging the value of 'critical methodology' in clarifying ambiguities in such areas as authorship, context, and sources. These need to be guided by a 'larger theological understanding'.[48] It may be observed here that critical methodology can be of greater theological significance than Ateek allows.

Ateek believes that the 'authentic' word of the Bible and the 'true' meaning of biblical texts can only be found in Jesus Christ himself. Christ is the key to understanding the Bible and God's action in history. It is only in Jesus Christ that 'objective' knowledge of the God is found.[49]

If theological suppositions and assertions exist in the Old Testament which conflict with the understanding of God as Christians believe has been revealed in Christ, then these suppositions and assertions must not be regarded as revelatory, at least in Christian terms. In other words, Ateek identifies different traditions in the Hebrew Bible that he evaluates only according to the revelation given in Jesus Christ.

One tradition is essentially tribalistic in nature, based on the election of the Jews to be God's people and allowing for the forcible ejection of others from the land. This and other traditions have a pedagogical value in a *negative* way: they clarify what God is not.[50] For Christians the normative or positive picture of God is given in Jesus Christ.

Ateek favours the prophetic tradition that finally opposes the tribalistic understanding of deity (Kings 1:21). Using the story of Naboth's vineyard, he interprets this narrative as embodying the experience of Palestine and the suppression of human rights. The prophet Elijah pronounces God's judgement against King Ahab who had appropriated Naboth's land unjustly. Ateek claims three lessons from this passage:

The story reveals God's passionate concern for justice; He places the State of Israel in the same position as King Ahab, and, Ateek asserts, Palestinians identify with the injustice done by Ahab against Naboth.

In the story, Ahab is killed in battle, and his wife dies in a particularly horrific way. Ateek wishes, in the light of his Christocentric, hermeneutical method, to plead for justice with mercy.[51] Lastly,

Ateek sees the development of a legal tradition in the Hebrew Bible as both embodying the specialness of the Jews, and relating them to a more inclusive, ethical Judaism. These ideas have developed more concretely with the emergence of reform Judaism, which is more inclusive than orthodoxy – also reflecting the possible influence of the European Enlightenment.[52]

The preference for the prophetic strand in Hebrew scripture is put in the context of belief in a God who has a commitment to the underprivileged, the disadvantaged and the vulnerable. Thus, this can be seen as a theology of hope and compassion.[53] Although Ateek rejects typology and allegory as hermeneutical tools, he is prepared to use 'parallelism' in linking Old and New Testament stories to the contemporary situation where God is revealed as a God of justice and truth.

Ateek observes that Eastern Christians have experienced a heavy price historically because they shared the name 'Christian' with Crusaders of a previous epoch, living as a minority among different countries in the Middle East.[54] The task of Palestinian Christians is to undertake a two-dimensional ministry entailing elements of prophecy and non-violence.[55]

Ateek sees the Church in Israel-Palestine in terms of a rich heritage of Orthodoxy, Catholicism and Protestantism. Most Arab Christians are united by a common faith, even if some church hierarchies may be preoccupied with past differences.[56] Ateek sees the theological implications of his exegesis as a matter of faith in an inclusive God of truth, justice and peace; choosing to regard the Incarnation as the basis for involvement in the world and the Church being the conscience of the nation.[57]

In evaluating Ateek's approach, it ought to be acknowledged that its strength lies in the placing of emphasis on *forgiveness* in a Christ-centred hermeneutic. Kenneth Cragg sees this as the distinctive contribution that Palestinian Christianity can bring to the intractable history of the Israeli-Palestinian conflict.[58]

It may be observed, however, that this approach has its weaknesses. Ateek's vision is rooted in an approach to Scriptures that has its origin in the Protestant Reformation. This Reformation saw a renewed emphasis in the interpretation of the Bible. A major proportion of the works of both Luther and Calvin were commentaries and expositions of biblical text. The emphasis on *literal* interpretation, rather than allegory, in understanding the entire biblical text, and the conviction that the Bible is Christocentric, is not easy to reconcile. The problem of the Old and the New Testaments and their relationship remains. For Luther, the unity to be found was in the God who revealed himself in Christ. The contrast between the Testaments was asserted as one between law and gospel.

In his 'Preface to the Old Testament' from 1523, Luther wrote:

> And what is the New Testament but a prophetic preaching and proclamation of Christ, set forth through the sayings of the Old Testament and fulfilled through Christ.[59]

This approach is committed to seeing Christ *within* the Old Testament and tends to ignore what does not fit in with such a scheme. Ateek may not acknowledge this, but his methodology bears a striking resemblance to this way of thinking.

It has two major deficiencies. For one thing, it can be said to deprive the Old Testament of any significance in its own right apart from Christianity. Another crucial difficulty is that it fails to adequately face the historical and critical questions that biblical scholarship has addressed over the last two hundred years. In his treatment of the Bible, Ateek readily recognizes the contribution of biblical scholarship, but he sees its concerns as limited to issues of authorship, origins and dating. Ateek ignores any option in evaluating the Hebrew Scriptures that may take seriously the literary text, the circumstances of the composition, and any possibly relevant evidence from extra-biblical sources.

One relevant consideration might be to show some awareness of a widespread view among scholars that the narratives of Genesis, including the history of the patriarchs, do not in fact accord with historical reality, but are retrospective reflections guided by the authors' intentions in attempting to construct a religious and national identity following the Babylonian exile.[60] It also needs to be acknowledged that, apart from the Bible stories, we cannot historically reconstruct any alleged Hebrew conquest of Canaan.

This also is true of the Exodus narrative, which represents a stylized attempt to inculcate faith in the God of Israel rather than record actual history. There may be a vital distinction to be made between real history and literary expressions which may evince a culture's self-understanding under particular circumstances.

Ateek's approach may commend itself to those who stand in a particular Christian interpretative tradition; but it can be shown that this approach lacks the tools to undertake a more universally acceptable and independent evaluation of biblical texts.

5. Palestinian Liberation Theology in action: *Sabeel*

Christopher Rowland has drawn attention to the emphasis in liberation theology on the experience of the everyday world and its injustices as an essential part of the knowledge of God.[61] It needs to be appreciated that Palestinian Liberation Theology is a wider movement than that represented in purely academic terms.

An important aspect of this is an organization called *Sabeel*. *Sabeel* is the Palestinian Liberation Theology centre which originated at Jerusalem in 1989 to realize liberation theology in practice in the Palestinian context. The first *Sabeel* newsletter, dated 1994, traces the impetus of the centre initially with pastoral concerns experienced by clergy 'working with the people at the grassroots and listening to their cries'.[62] Although in the first instance the concern was to respond to physical sufferings, there was a growing awareness that these sufferings were 'being aggravated by a religious argument in the political conflict'.[63]

Questions that were being raised by the Israeli-Palestinian conflict informed the writing and activity of *Sabeel*: where is God in all of this? Why does God allow the confiscation of our [Palestinian] land? Why does God allow the occupation and the oppression of our people?[64] Another important need was to reflect upon biblical text – to question where Scripture, particularly the Old Testament, could be perceived as instrumental in justifying or rationalizing the suffering of Palestinians.

A committee of clergy and lay theologians came together to explore how liberation theology could be practically applied to the experience of Palestinian Christians. The early work of this committee resulted in an international conference in 1990 held at the Tantur Ecumenical Theological Centre situated between Jerusalem and Bethlehem. The conference looked at such issues as Palestinian Christian identity, power, justice, and the Bible; women, faith, and the *intifada*.

Workshops were held on topics including Holy Land Christians and Survival; Reclaiming Our Identity and Redefining Ourselves; Biblical Justice; among others. It included presentations by liberation theologians from the United States, the Philippines, and Ireland.

The work of the first conference was published through an editorial team of Naim Ateek; Marc Ellis, a Jewish American writer, and Rosemary Radford Ruether. The resulting work, titled *Faith and the Intifada*, led to a permanent centre being established for the work of the new organization, *Sabeel*.

Another international conference was held on the campus of Bethlehem University, 10–15 February 1998. The work of this conference was published as *Holy Land Hollow Jubilee*, edited by Naim Ateek and Michael Prior.[65] The theme of the conference was 'The Challenge of Jubilee: What Does God Require?' Its aim was to look at the fifty years since the founding of the modern State of Israel and evaluate this history and learn from it. Sessions concerned a wide variety of issues: religious fundamentalism, Christian-Muslim relations, jubilee and the biblical tradition, the Bible and Zionism, human rights, and pilgrimage alternatives. Although primarily a theological conference, the participants were transported to different sites on the West Bank where they were able to witness first-hand the reality of checkpoints, destroyed villages, and confiscated land.

The conference was addressed by the late Edward Said, Professor of English and Comparative Literature at Columbia University, New York, and an internationally-known Palestinian academic who had been raised as a Protestant Christian. Professor Said drew an analogy between the Palestinian movement with opposition to apartheid in South Africa and called for a sustained campaign in universities and churches in order to demonstrate that that was and is a public and moral cause. Without such a sustained campaign, Said was pessimistic about the Palestinian situation, 'which is more bleak than it has ever been'.[66] He claimed 'We are getting weaker, we are slowly being overtaken and forgotten … Our resolve is in danger of succumbing to the solemn silence of other defeated native peoples.'[67]

Sabeel holds a continual series of Ecumenical Bible study sessions. The first of these was held in January 1994, focusing on the text, *The Upside Down Kingdom*, by the American Mennonite author Donald Kraybill. The book relates Jesus' teaching about God's kingdom, where the poor are elevated and the wealthy brought down, to contemporary society. Forty representatives from Anglican, Latin Catholic, Lutheran, Greek Catholic, Coptic, Armenian and Greek Orthodox Churches participated.

Workshops form a vital part of *Sabeel*'s activities. In 1991, following the Gulf War which had a seriously negative impact on Palestinians, a workshop on 'The Bible and the War' looked at theological concerns related to that conflict. It was followed by a workshop on 'The Bible and War – The Just War Theory' in Nazareth in March 1992. The wider context of Jewish-Christian relations was addressed by Dr Marc Ellis, a Jewish liberation theologian in a lecture titled 'Ending Auschwitz and the Renewal of Palestine in the Jewish Imagination.'

Sabeel also organizes extensive youth programmes. It arranges summer camps on such subjects such as what it means to be a Christian here and now, and attempts to develop leadership and planning skills for Palestinian youth. Themes addressed here have included violence/non-violence, democracy and freedom, the environment, the role of women, and the example of Jesus.

Sabeel also acts as a bridge for mutual information exchange among liberation theology movements in other areas of the world. It held a recent meeting with Mike Mailula, the Exposure Coordinator of the South African-based Theology Exchange programme. This organization provides educational opportunities for people involved in development and justice issues within South Africa, and learning from comparable situations in other parts of the world regarding theology and human rights.

Through its newsletters, *Sabeel* provides commentaries and reflection on the perspective of liberation theology in Palestine and contemporary political developments. In its first newsletter it states that Palestinians 'had to face the formidable task of formulating and disseminating their understanding of Christianity and the Gospel of Christ within the lives of Palestinian Christians today'.[68]

Following the Hebron Massacre, 25 February 1994, *Sabeel* issued a theological reflection on its significance. At least twenty-nine Muslims were killed at the Mosque of Abraham in Hebron while at prayer during the third week of Ramadan. Baruch Goldstein, a Jewish settler from Kiryat Arba, was responsible.

Sabeel claims that three misconceptions of a theological nature can be discerned with respect to this atrocity: A first misconception is *a faulty theology of God*. A God that is exclusively Jewish encourages the belief that in killing Palestinians, God's will is being done. A single or narrow-minded interpretation of the Old Testament obviously generates such ideas. According to *Sabeel*, Baruch Goldstein, the attacker had absorbed these ideas; they provide the evidence of an interview Goldstein had given to an American documentary filmmaker published in the Jerusalem Post on Sunday, February 27 1994. A second misconception is *a faulty theology of humanity*. Baruch Goldstein's understanding of humanity did not include Palestinians. A third misconception is *an erroneous view of freedom and democracy*. Simply put, it is a view that does not accept others, especially Palestinians, as having human rights and freedoms.

Sabeel's commentary on the Hebron massacre goes on to observe that a cycle of violence has developed, pointing to the Hamas suicide attack of 6 April 1994 (just a couple of months after Hebron), where seven Israelis were killed in the city of Afula. According to *Sabeel*, all extremists share a highly exclusive character contributing to bigotry and alienation.

In May 2000, four months before the second *intifada* began (September 2000), *Sabeel* issued the Jerusalem Sabeel Document: Principles for a Just Peace in Palestine-Israel. This document sets out the theological, moral and legal bases for a peace with justice in the Israeli-Palestinian conflict. It calls for a Palestinian state to be established on the West Bank (including East Jerusalem) and the Gaza Strip. It affirms the grave injustice that has been done to the Palestinian people and calls for this to be acknowledged by Israel, allowing the right of return of refugees and reparation to be made as the only basis for a settlement based on the establishment of two sovereign and fully democratic states.

In February 2001, *Sabeel* organized a conference entitled *Speaking Truth, Seeking Justice*, inviting 250 delegates from twenty-one countries. The political context of this conference was the continuation of the second *intifada*, which had begun in September 2000, and the election of Ariel Sharon as Israeli Prime Minister.

Recently, in correspondence with the Friends of Sabeel in North America,[69] *Sabeel* expressed sorrow and outrage at the 11 September tragedy in the US, noting that 'Now is the time to work with more determination to deal with the root causes that create violence, a violence that is consuming our world.'

Conclusion

Palestinian Liberation Theology has emerged out of a multi-dimensional crisis for Palestinian Christians. Its problems partly result from Palestinian Christians being a declining minority within a context of oppression and expulsion following the establishment of the modern state of Israel. They exist in a situation where their genuine Arab identity is questioned by other Palestinians. Palestinian Liberation Theology is an unambiguous statement of identification with the Palestinian national cause, and an expression of the need for unity over past divisions and solidarity with non-Christian Palestinians. This need has been all the greater because past internal divisions and a troubled relationship with the Western Church have complicated and even compromised the identity of the Palestinian Christian.

The specific difficulties in theological terms are summed up by Kenneth Cragg:

> We need to grasp the mystique by which it is opposed, the divine mandate which – in the eyes of many in the west and in Christian quarters – its adversary commands and wields. The sense of what the Palestinians are up against in the massive yet elusive sanction Israel enjoys is no small part of their travail. How it may be demystified, how spiritually counterbalanced by more prosaic meanings of justice and peace, is a profound problem for the Palestinian soul – a problem that leads back into vexed areas of biblical interpretation and theology.[70]

Palestinian Liberation Theology is a significant response to these problems of Palestinian Christian life. All Liberation Theology is contextual and emerges out of specific social and cultural situations. The classic 'ideal type' is that of Latin America which springs from a history of colonialism and economic deprivation. This is easily transferable to similar situations in South Africa and the concerns of black theologians in the United States of America.

What is unique about Palestinian Liberation Theology is not that it has emerged out of a particular context of oppression or deprivation. It is distinctive principally because it is a defence against a pervasive theological tradition that identifies with Jewish history and the Old Testament as part of the Christian revelation. Extreme manifestations of this identification, in cases such as Christian Zionism, have had the effect of isolating Palestinian Christians in their own society, linking them potentially if not actually – in the minds of their fellow Palestinians – with Western hostility to the Palestinian cause and with support for Zionism and the State of Israel. Western Christians and others need to be made more self-aware and critical through engagement with Palestinian Christian thinking, and the extent to which Palestinians have had to suffer under the impact of Western Christian anxieties with its anti-Semitic history, particularly since the Holocaust/Shoah has so intensified western guilt in this area.

The strength of Palestinian Christian Liberation Theology lies in calling attention to the existence of an authentic *Arab* Christianity with a long and distinguished history. Another aspect of its strength is an approach to biblical exegesis, as shown in the work of Naim Ateek, that emphasizes the justice and universality of the God of the Bible over an exclusive tribalism. In engaging with those elements of the biblical text it finds problematic, and capable of being used in an oppressive way, such as the land tradition, Ateek is, however, insufficiently aware of contemporary biblical scholarship. This is this work's major weakness.

Modern critical scholarship can distinguish between historicity, or what actually happened, and the development of the texts as an expression of religious identity at a later period. An awareness of such issues might suggest new possibilities for the evaluation of these texts which may pose acute difficulties for Palestinian Christians.

Like all Liberation Theology, Palestinian Christian Theology should not be appreciated as a purely academic concern. It has generated an impressive activist response that addresses unfolding events of complexity and pathos in a fast-moving situation in a volatile part of the world. It seeks to 'conscientize' – to use the word of Paulo Freire in his *Pedagogy of the Oppressed*[71] – Palestinian Christians about their faith and situation, and engage apathetic or naive Western Christians in order to make them more alert about their theology, more responsible to Palestinian Christians and in relation to the Israeli-Palestinian conflict.

Perhaps Palestinian Christian theology's greatest contribution could be to bring to bear on the Israeli-Palestinian conflict in the future not just its own claims for justice, but that it has something to offer concerning Christian thinking on reconciliation and forgiveness. For, in an intractable situation where the legacy of the past hangs so heavily, this disinherited and dwindling Christian community survives as a prophetic sign that reconciliation and renewal only will occur when enemies can forgive and be forgiven.

Notes

1 Michael Prior, 'Palestinian Christians and the Liberation of Theology', *The Month*, December 1993, p. 483.
2 Ibid.
3 Rosemary Radford Reuther and Herman J. Reuther, *The Wrath of Jonah, The Crisis of Religious Nationalism in the Israeli-Palestinian Conflict*. San Francisco, Harper, 1989, p. 103.
4 Rashid Khalidi, *Palestinian Identity*, Columbia University Press, p. 150.
5 Rosemary Radford Reuther, and Herman J. Reuther, *The Wrath of Jonah, The Crisis of Religious Nationalism in the Israeli-Palestinian Conflict*, p. 112.
6 Elias Chacour, *Blood Brothers*, Grand Rapids, Michigan, Chosen Books, Baker Bookhouse Company, 1984.
7 Elias Chacour, *We Belong to the Land*, San Francisco, Harper, 1990.
8 Naim Ateek, 'The Emergence of a Palestinian Christian Identity', in Marc Ellis and Radford Rosemary Reuther (eds), *Faith and the Intifada*, Maryknoll, New York, Orbis Books, 1985, p. 1.
9 Daphne Tsimhoni, *Christian Communities in Jerusalem and the West Bank Since 1948*, Westport, Connecticut, Praeger, 1993, p. 168.

10 Ibid.
11 Ibid., p. 69.
12 Michael Prior, 'The Future of the Christian Community in the Holy Land', *The Month*, 1 April 1996, p. 141.
13 Michael Prior, 'The Future of the Christian Community in the Holy Land', *The Month*, 1 April 1996, p. 277.
14 Andrea Pacini, *Socio-Political and Community Dynamics of Arab Christians in Jordan, Israel and the Autonomous Palestinian Regions*, in *Christian Communities in the Arab Middle East*, Oxford, Clarendon Press, 1998, p. 272.
15 Ibid., p. 272.
16 Ibid., p. 277.
17 Bernard Sabella, 'Socio-Economic Characteristics and Challenges to Palestinian Christians in the Holy Land', in Anthony O'Mahony (ed.), *Palestinian Christians, Religion, Politics and Society in the Holy Land*, London, Melisende, 1999, p. 92.
18 Ibid., p. 94.
19 Ibid., p. 93.
20 Daphne Tsimhoni, *Christian Communities in Jerusalem and the West Bank Since 1948*. Westport, Connecticut, Praeger, 1993, p. 182.
21 Said K. Aburish, *The Forgotten Faithful*, London, Quartet Books, 1993, pp. 77–95.
22 Naim Ateek, *Justice and Only Justice: A Palestinian Theology of Liberation*. Maryknoll, New York, Orbis Books, 1989, p. 62.
23 Howard A. Johnson, *Global Odyssey*, New York, Geoffrey, 1963.
24 Naim Ateek, *Justice and Only Justice: A Palestinian Theology of Liberation*, p. 62.
25 Naim Ateek, Ibid., p. 63.
26 Paul Van Buren, *Discerning the Way*, New York, Seabury, 1980.
27 Naim Ateek, *Justice and Only Justice: A Palestinian Theology of Liberation*, p. 64.
28 Ibid.
29 Rosemary Radford Reuther and Herman J. Reuther, *The Wrath of Jonah, The Crisis of Religious Nationalism in the Israeli-Palestinian Conflict*. p. 211.
30 Ibid.
31 Alistair Kee, *The Way of Transcendence*, London, Penguin Books, Ltd., 1971, p. 178.
32 Rosemary Radford Reuther and Herman J. Reuther, *The Wrath of Jonah, The Crisis of Religious Nationalism in the Israeli-Palestinian Conflict*, p. 212.
33 Ibid., p. 213.
34 Ibid.
35 Ibid.
36 Rosemary Radford Reuther, and Herman J. Reuther, *The Wrath of Jonah, The Crisis of Religious Nationalism in the Israeli-Palestinian Conflict*, p. 214.
37 Ateek, Naim *Justice and Only Justice: A Palestinian Theology of Liberation*, p. 65.
38 *The Fundamentals*, series of pamphlets published 1910–1915, authors including B. B. Warfield, Jay Orr, Bishop H. C. G. Moule and Morgan, G. Campbell.
39 Grace Halsell, *Prophecy and Politics: Militant Evangelists on the Road to Nuclear War*, Westport, Connecticut, Lawrence Hill, 1995.
40 Middle East Council of Churches, *What is Western Fundamentalist Christian Zionism*, Limassol, Cyprus, 1998 (from preface).
41 Michael Prior, *Zionism and the State of Israel*. London, Routledge, 1999, p. xiv.
42 Gutierrez, Gustavo, *A Theology of Liberation*, London, SCM Press Ltd., 1974,

pp. 155–9.
43 Naim Ateek, *Justice and Only Justice: A Palestinian Theology of Liberation*, p. 76.
44 Ibid., p. 78.
45 Ibid.
46 Ibid.
47 Northrop Frye, *The Great Code: The Bible and Literature*, London, Routledge, 1982, p. 81.
48 Naim Ateek, *Justice and Only Justice: A Palestinian Theology of Liberation*, p. 78.
49 Ibid., p. 82.
50 Ibid., p. 83.
51 Ibid., p. 89.
52 Ibid., p. 95.
53 Ibid., p. 134.
54 Ibid., p. 135.
55 Ibid., p. 151.
56 Ibid., p. 152.
57 Ibid., p. 157.
58 Kenneth Cragg, *Palestine: The Prize and Price of Zion*, London, Cassell, 1997, p. 222.
59 Martin Luther, Preface to the Old Testament. English Translation of *Luther's Works (American Edition, Volume 35)*, Philadelphia, 1960, pp. 233–333.
60 R. N. Whybray, *The Making of the Pentateuch*, Sheffield, Sheffield Academic Press, 1987.
61 Christopher Rowland, *The Cambridge Companion to Liberation Theology*, Cambridge, Cambridge University Press, 2000, p. 10.
62 *Sabeel* newsletter, 1994.
63 Ibid.
64 Ibid.
65 Ibid., p. 94
66 Edward Said, Keynote address in *Holy Land, Hollow Jubilee*, Ateek and Prior (eds), 1999, p. 30.
67 Ibid.
68 *Sabeel* newsletter, 1994.
69 Correspondence from Sabeel to Friends of Sabeel in North America, 12 September 2001.
70 Kenneth Cragg, *The Arab Christian*, London, Mowbray, 1992, p. 235.
71 Paulo Freire, *Pedagogy of the Oppressed*, Penguin Books, 1970. Revised, 1993.

Chapter 5

The Greek Orthodox Patriarchate of Jerusalem: Church-State Politics in the Holy Land

Sotiris Roussos

The Greek Orthodox Church of Jerusalem is distinct for two main reasons: first for its monastic character and second for its mission to safeguard and preserve a large number of the Christian Holy Shrines in Jerusalem the Holy Land. These characteristics are shaping its history and its relations with both the state and the local Arab Orthodox Christians. Another salient feature of the Patriarchate is the exclusively ethnic Greek make-up of the senior clergy. The governing body of the Patriarchate is the Confraternity of the Holy Sepulchre; although the Confraternity was already well-known in the fifth century, its Rules, *Katastatikon*, date from the reign of Patriarch Dositheos in 1662. According to the *Katastatikon*, the Patriarch is the head of the Confraternity and is customarily elected from among the members of the Confraternity. Custom restricted the choice of bishops to members of the order who had to be Greeks. The faithful, on the other hand, were overwhelmingly Arab.[1]

Under Islamic rule, the Greek Orthodox Patriarchate followed a co-optation policy in Church-State relations, which shaped the attitude of the members of the Greek Orthodox upper-clergy. The Patriarchate co-operated closely with state policies in political, social and economic spheres in exchange of church autonomy in its internal matters.[2] The *millet* system of the Ottoman Empire institutionalized this behaviour, which became the main guideline of the Patriarchate's policy towards the state.[3]

From the first half of the sixteenth century the Patriarch of Jerusalem resided in Constantinople whereas the Confraternity remained in Jerusalem. Each Patriarch designated his successor during his active lifetime, subject to the approval of the Confraternity. Contrary to the Canonical rules of the Orthodox Church, the Ecumenical Patriarch of Constantinople, who should not take part in the election, effectively influences the result through his connection with the Porte.[4]

This policy enabled the Patriarchate to face growing Catholic, Anglican and Protestant European influence in the Holy Places maintaining its predominance among the Churches in the Holy Land. In the nineteenth century, the Greek Orthodox Patriarchate found itself in the midst of Russo-Turkish antagonism in the Levant. In the struggle for control of the Holy Places, the Patriarchate managed to exploit the Ottoman suspicion for Russian plans in the Near East and the influence of ethnic Greek elite members of the central Ottoman administration, the *Phanariotes*, in order to enlist Ottoman support. The predominant position of the Greek Orthodox Church in the Holy Land was crystallized and secured in what is called the Status Quo on the Holy Places.

The Status Quo referred mainly to the rights and privileges of the Christian communities in the Holy Places, particularly to the possession and use of the Holy Sepulchre, Calvary, the Church of Nativity and the Church of Mary. The Status Quo had been set by a series of Ottoman *firman* and international agreements, From the seventeenth century onwards a series of decrees issued by Sultan Murad IV in 1631 and Mahmud son-of-Ibrahim made clear that only the Sublime Porte could regulate the status of the Greek Orthodox Patriarchate of Jerusalem and that any intervention of local authority regarding either disputes with other Churches or collection of taxes should be stopped immediately.[5] The *firman* of 1757 gave the Greek Orthodox Patriarchate the supremacy in the Holy Places. The *firman* of 1852 maintained the regulations of 1757 and constituted the official declaration of the Status Quo. Finally the Treaty of Paris after the Crimean War, and the Treaty of Vienna in 1878 confirmed the arrangements of 1852.[6]

After the First and Second World Wars the creation of the State of Israel and the Arab-Israeli conflict changed the situation. Nation-states replaced multi-ethnic empires. The Palestinian struggle for self-determination and statehood now included the antagonism between laity and Greek upper-clergy. For those of the Greek Orthodox Palestinians who participated in the national struggle, nationalizing the hierarchy and the church land became part of the national agenda.

This chapter will identify three major crises of the Patriarchate from the nineteenth century till the present day: the deposition of Patriarch Cyrillos in 1872; the attempts to depose Patriarch Damianos in the period 1908–1920 and finally the crisis with Patriarch Ireneos in 2005. All three of them involve intra-Church rivalry, serious concern of the Arab Orthodox faithful and state intervention and reveal the main undercurrents that shape the Patriarchate's attitude. The main argument that persists in these crises is that the flourishing of the Confraternity is a *sine qua non* precondition for the guardianship of the Holy Places on behalf of the Greek nation. This responsibility is a moral concern that is foundational to the Confraternity and supercedes any other individual or collective concern.[7] In such a pattern the individual – be it monk or Patriarch – gains its significance only as part of a collective action.

The members of the Confraternity form a collective entity as it is termed by Keith Graham. Firstly, they act in ways whose significance can be adequately captured only by reference to their corporate body, the *klima*, that is the religious and social establishment of the Confraternity. Secondly, whatever this social and religious establishment does is distinct from anything which the individual monks, bishops or patriarchs can do and thirdly, the establishment's survival is relatively indifferent to the particular members which compose it at any particular moment.[8] The luck of corporate solidarity and discipline can be thus explained with reference to the survival and self-preservation of the establishment.

This moral concern is tightly linked to the sense of forcible separation from Jerusalem holiness felt by the Christians especially after the Muslim conquest and the pilgrims' reparation of this loss by experiencing Jerusalem with the help of certain shrines and rituals performed by the monks and the bishops in the Holy Places.[9] As Adrian Hastings pointed out, during the first century of Christian pilgrimage to the Holy Land, '... the vehicle and living proof of this holiness was to be found in the monks inhabiting these places and in the liturgies celebrated in their churches'.[10]

Pius contributions and financial donations also provided one route for a 'sense' of inhabiting the Holy Land. A large number of monks travelled in various places of the Ottoman Empire calling for financial support, *ziteia*, for the Patriarchate of Jerusalem. The custom of travelling and fundraising for the Holy Sepulchre was firstly inaugurated by Patriarch Germanos in the mid-sixteenth century and was followed all through the Ottoman period. The Ecumenical Patriarch issued several Synodical Letters to all

Orthodox in Greek, Turkish, Wallachian and Slavic, calling them to support the fundraising of the Patriarchate of Jerusalem.[11] The donations were not always in money but included land, houses and estates – even shares of ship-ownership. The *Phanariotes* governors of the semi-autonomous Principalities of Moldavia and Wallachia (Rumania) granted the Patriarchate of Jerusalem twenty-one monasteries with all their lands and revenues.

Caught between Istanbul and Russia

Turning now to the first crisis of the Patriarchate in question, we should emphasize that from the sixteenth century the Patriarchate resided in Istanbul and was closely controlled by the Ecumenical Patriarchate and the ethnic Greek elite of *Phanariotes*. The death of Patriarch Athanasios in 1844 coincided with the ascent of Russian influence on the Orthodox Church in the Middle East. In 1847, a Russian Ecclesiastical mission was established in Palestine in the context of the antagonism between the Great Powers to acquire the protection of the Holy Places and the pilgrims.[12]

Russian influence continued to affect the Patriarchate and reached its peak with the establishment of the Imperial Orthodox Palestine Society in 1882. The founding members of the Society included Russian scholars who supported the Society as a purely educational institution, others who saw it as a means to improve the life of the fellow Orthodox in the Levant, and a small group of Panslavists who saw it as an instrument of Panslavist aims in the Near East. The Greeks in both Greece and Palestine believed that Russian involvement and, in particular, the Society, was to do in the Levant what the Slavonic Benevolent Society had been doing in the Balkans since 1858. That is, to assist native Orthodox Christians to develop their own religious, educational and other national institutions at the expense of the influence of the Ecumenical Patriarchate.[13] In the meantime, Russia pressed upon the Ottoman authorities that the Holy Synod of Jerusalem and not the Ecumenical Patriarch and the *Phanar* should elect the new Patriarch. The Ottoman authorities agreed and eventually Cyrillos, Bishop of Lydda, against the wishes of the *Phanar*, was elected new Patriarch in 1845.[14] Cyrillos took up residence in Palestine and his election marked the end of Jerusalem's subordination to Constantinople.[15]

In 1872, Cyrillos refused to sign the Protocol of the Orthodox Council, which declared the Bulgarian Church schismatic. He was afraid that such a move would cause the loss of the Patriarchate's income in Russia. The Council turned against him and called for his deposition. This was the beginning of a long controversy between on the one hand, the Confraternity and the Ecumenical Patriarchate, and on the other, Cyrillos, Russia and the indigenous Arab Orthodox. However, both Russia and the Arab Orthodox had not been able to prevent the deposition of Cyrillos by the Jerusalem Synod.

Neither Russian diplomatic pressure on the Porte, nor control of the Patriarchate's income in Russia were enough to induce the Greek-dominated Synod and Confraternity to accept Cyrillos. The *Phanariotes* and the Confraternity found a valuable ally in the Ottoman authorities. The Porte was against the spreading of Russian influence in the Middle East. Thus, the Ottomans helped the Greeks to dominate the Orthodox Church in order to thwart Russian plans. The Ottoman government recognized the deposition of Cyrillos and the Synod elected a member of the Confraternity, Procopios, new Patriarch, in December 1872.

The missionary work of the Russian Church challenged the supremacy of the Confraternity on two fields; the landed property by the acquisition in Jerusalem and by its effort to introduce Russian clergymen and prelates performing services for the local Arab Orthodox Christian community.[16] Most importantly the Russian missionary enterprise purchased land close to the holy sites in Jerusalem, Bethlehem and Nazareth. The Confraternity has shaped itself around the holy shrines and the growing authority of its members was fortified by the connection with and control of them and of the land surrounding them.[17] It was, hence, these activities that threatened the wellbeing of the Confraternity and led to Cyrillos' deposition. The antagonism between the Ecumenical Patriarchate and the Russian Church in the Levant can be termed as 'geopolitics of pilgrimage'. Notwithstanding his enlightened and regenerating reign for almost thirty years, Cyrillos was judged and deposed for the position he took concerning pilgrimage geopolitics. His stance against the 1872 Council harmed the Greek interests in this pilgrimage by weakening the Ecumenical Patriarchate.

This deposition sparked the Arab Orthodox national consciousness. Encouraged and assisted by the Russians, the Arab Orthodox advanced demands for greater participation in the affairs of the Patriarchate.[18] In March 1875, a new Constitution of the Patriarchate gave a greater say to the Arab Orthodox on Church affairs through a Mixed (lay-clergy) Council, but they had no participation in the patriarchal election. The main change that occurred after Cyrillos the crisis was the change in the notion of the Holy Land: until then the Holy Land was the land of pilgrims. As Rashid Khalidi maintains, the constant efforts of the European powers – Russia, in the case of the Arab Orthodox – to expand their influence over Palestine throughout the nineteenth century affected the self-view of the inhabitants of the country. Reinforced by Ottoman administrative changes regarding the *sanjak* of Jerusalem, the Arab Orthodox and the Arab Christians began to formulate a sense of community and belonging to the land of Palestine.[19]

National and international dilemmas in the Holy Land: the reign of Patriarch Damianos

The Christian communities had played an important role in the development of a Palestinian Arab concept of Palestine. The Greek Orthodox contribution to this concept as distinct from that of Syrian Arab nationalisms, into which Palestine was often included, was significant. Their leading paper, *Filastin,* founded by the Orthodox brothers Al-Isa in Jaffa, had been an advocate of the distinct concept of Palestine since 1911.[20] Palestine for them was the area under the authority of the Greek Orthodox Patriarchate of Jerusalem. Strong anti-Zionist trends, which were developed among the Christians, strengthened the Arab national consciousness.[21] It was this anti-Zionist trend that brought Orthodox Christians and Muslims together in the building up of the Palestinian Arab national movement. The Jewish community in Palestine acquired equal educational virtues to the Arab Christians and thus posed a threat to their material existence.

In the case of the Greek Orthodox community, the struggle for greater control over the Patriarchate led the community to seek an alliance with the Muslims. In this struggle, the traditional leadership preferred co-operation with the British, stressing the communal Greek Orthodox identity. On the other hand there was a younger generation of Arab Orthodox who stressed the Arab identity and supported Arab unity. Their strategy was to promote a notion of 'secular' nationalism by downgrading the importance of their communal affiliation. In order to secure a position equal to Muslims they raised the banner of common fatherland, language and history rather than religion. This strategy meant that religion was not constitutive of a society and that it had no political significance.²² It also meant abandonment of the communal organization and diminishing the influence of the Church. However before following this strategy, the Greek Orthodox communities had to pass through internal strife between advocates of traditional communal distinctiveness and those promoting Arab nationalism. This division still existed in the 1930s.²³

The Young Turks Constitution in 1908 urged the Arab Orthodox to launch a new campaign for greater participation in the Patriarchate. A committee of forty members was set up in order to press upon the Patriarch demands for certain church reforms including the establishment of a mixed council of lay and clerical members to administer the property of the Patriarchate.²⁴ In September 1908 Patriarch Damianos proposed to the committee the appointment by both the Patriarchate and the Arab Orthodox community of a mixed committee to discuss their demands.²⁵ The discussions of the mixed committee did not, however, bear any fruit. The Arab Orthodox demanded the establishment of a Mixed Council similar to that of the Ecumenical Patriarchate. Damianos refused and, consequently, caused serious friction.

Due to the local unrest in November, the Grand Vizier directed an investigation into the matter. Damianos explained to him the Rules of the Patriarchate of Constantinople and the fact that the provisions of the Turkish Constitution did not apply to the Patriarchate of Jerusalem, due to its particular monastic character. Despite Damianos' refusal, certain members of the Confraternity suspected that the Patriarch had been lenient to the demands of the Arab Orthodox during his personal conferences with them.²⁶

On 18 December 1908 the majority of the Synod led by Meletios Metaxakis, then Archbishop of Athens and future Ecumenical Patriarch and Patriarch of Alexandria, and Chrysostomos Papadopoulos, who was to become Archbishop of Athens, deposed Patriarch Damianos. The Patriarch declined to accept his deposition. The Ottoman government, however, recognised the new Locum Tenens, *Topoteretes*, and consequently the deposition. Damianos then appealed to the Ottoman government to send a committee to investigate the matter on the spot.²⁷

Despite the recognition of the deposition by the Patriarchates of Constantinople and Alexandria as well as by the Greek government, the violent reaction of the crowd against the deposition and the reluctance of the local military forces to suppress the violence of the crowds complicated the situation. The interference of both the local and central Ottoman administration, backed by Russian influence, led the Ecumenical Patriarch to accept reconciliation with Patriarch Damianos in the face of the group of Meletios and Chrysostomos.

In February 1910, Damianos was again recognized Patriarch by the Synod. As for the Arab Orthodox demands, the resolutions of the committee set up by the Ottoman government did not seem satisfactory. These resolutions provided for a mixed council of six lay Arab Orthodox and six Greek clerics. It also allowed entry of the Arab Orthodox in the Confraternity of the Holy Sepulchre but it did not provide for greater Arab participation in the patriarchal election. In fact the Mixed Council did not function effectively and it ceased sessions in 1913 due to the intransigence of both parties.[28]

After their defeat, Meletios Metaxakis and Chrysostomos Papadopoulos together with Chrysanthos, Metropolitan of Trebizond, Archbishop of Athens, Germanos Metropolitan of Thyateira were active in forming a multi-centred network linking Athens, London and Alexandria. These three ecclesiastical figures constituted the network's leadership. At a lower level stood ecclesiastics such as Nikolaos Metropolitan of Axoum and Archimandrite Arsenios Kakoyiannis, who prepared reports or undertook missions regarding issues in the Orthodox Patriarchates, particularly in Jerusalem and Syria. The members of the network were closely associated with Greek politics and the Greek irredentist ideology. Chrysanthos and Meletios in particular were deeply involved in the political developments during and after the First World War and they undertook missions which although seemed ecclesiastical were chiefly political. For instance, Meletios' involvement in the negotiations over the control of Mount Athos in 1913 and Chrysanthos' mission in Albania in the period 1926–1927 had a distinct political character. They were anticipating the formation of an improbable 'pact' between Greek Orthodoxy and Anglicanism against France, the Holy See and other Catholic powers. The participation of Greek Orthodox delegates in the sixth Lambeth Palace Conference in 1920 and the London Conference between the Orthodox and the Anglican Churches in 1930 were clear signs of the close ties between them.

The ecclesiastic network had developed a certain theory about the affairs of the Patriarchates and the Greek Orthodox communities. As revealed in the reports and memoranda they exchanged, they believed that any development in any single Orthodox Patriarchate would influence the position of the rest of the Patriarchates in the Middle East. This 'theory of dominoes' was prevailing in the attitude of Meletios in the Patriarchate of Alexandria, in the reports of Nikolaos of Nubia and Kakoyiannis on the affairs of the Patriarchate of Jerusalem and in the views of Chrysanthos and Germanos on the situation of the Greek Orthodox in Syria.[29]

They also confounded the ecclesiastical conscience with the modern national conscience: that is they tried '... to represent the modern Greek national conscience as identical with, and a continuation of the Greek [Orthodox] 'national' conscience under Turkish domination'.[30] As George Mavrogordatos points out, '... the identification of the Nation with Orthodoxy proved irresistible. During the [Greek] War of Independence itself, religion was the only fixed line of demarcation between the warring sides, in full conformity with the pre-existing Ottoman system of religiously defined "millets"'[31] The ecclesiastical network was part of the structural-functional interpenetration of religious and political institutions and facilitated the irredentist Greek state's project of the Great Idea (*I Megali Idea*).[32]

The period from 1919 to 1921 was marked by the attempt of the Greek majority of the Holy Synod to depose the Greek Patriarch, Damianos. The involvement of the Greek state, the huge debt of the Patriarchate and the demands of the Arab Orthodox developed a personal feud into major crisis. The majority of the Holy Synod accused Patriarch Damianos of arrogance and misconduct of the Patriarchate's finances. In June 1919 a memorandum of the Confraternity blamed the Patriarch for the crisis in the Patriarchate, described him as a 'bad demon' of the Church and accused him of surrendering Greek rights over the Holy Places and wasting the funds of the Patriarchate.[33] Apparently the Patriarchate was deprived from vital revenues from vast property in Rumania and Bessarabia during and after the First World War. For the first time in the modern history of the Patriarchate, the Holy Synod openly asked for the intervention of the Greek state.

The Greek Liberal Government of Eleutherios Venizelos took two initiatives. Since Damianos was considered Royalist and thus an opponent of Venizelos, the Greek Foreign Ministry supported Damianos' deposition. On the other hand they proposed a loan by the National Bank of Greece. Greek diplomats were concerned about a possible co-operation between Palestinian Arab Muslims, represented by the Mufti of Jerusalem, and the Arab Palestinian Orthodox against Zionism and the Greek Patriarchate. When answering questions about Greek policy towards Zionism, the Greek Consul in Alexandria, Antonios Sactouris, who was in charge of the matter, stated that Greece respected the right of the Jewish people to have a state and that, having no political interest in Palestine, Greece did not oppose Zionism. He also admitted that the Greek government had made no official statement on the issue but that it had provided its diplomats with instructions to be 'friendly' towards Zionism.

The memorandum of the Second Directorate of Greek Foreign Ministry provides a clear view of the main Greek objectives regarding the Holy Places.[34] The Greek Foreign Ministry admitted that Greece had no interest in Palestine based on purely political motives. The main concern of the Greek government was the preservation of the Greek character of the Patriarchate or, as the memorandum put it, the protection of the historical rights of the Greek nation over the Holy Places.

According to the same memorandum, neither an Arab nor a Jewish state could guarantee the preservation of the Status Quo in the Holy Places. It suggested that the Holy Places should be excluded from a future Arab state and that, furthermore, the Christian world would oppose the ruling of the Holy Places by the Jews. The most preferable solution for the Greek interests was the creation of a neutral zone administered by the communities who had rights over the Holy Places, the Greek Orthodox, the Catholics and the Armenians. If this plan was not acceptable to the Allies, then the best alternative was a British Mandate or Protectorate over Palestine. The memorandum seems to rely on the support of the Anglican Church in favour of the Greek Orthodox Patriarchate. The memorandum went further and suggested the creation of Arab parishes and consecration of Arab bishops in case the British favoured the Arab Orthodox element, but that was the bottom line of Greek concessions.

The Arab Orthodox feared that further Greek intervention would strengthen the Greek element at the expense of their participation. Hence they put forward demands for greater Arab Orthodox control over the Patriarchate. The British intervened by appointing the Bertram-Luke commission in 1921. Its resolutions consolidated the position of Damianos and set a financial committee to manage the finances of the Patriarchate, refusing the loan by the National Bank of Greece. They thus prevented the Greek intervention which might have been a dangerous precedent for interference by other foreign powers.[35]

The selling of the Patriarchate's lands to the Zionists infuriated the Arab Orthodox who were now involved in the national movement. Moreover in 1922 the appointment of Bishop Cleopas as

Metropolitan of Nazareth faced the strong reaction of many of the local Orthodox community. Cleopas, though a gifted prelate, did not speak Arabic and supported the participation in elections for the Legislative Council, which were boycotted by the Arabs. Damianos allegedly took the same position.[36] In July 1923 the first Arab Orthodox congress was convened in Haifa. Its resolutions aimed to give the Patriarchate local character and virtually meant 'arabization' of the Church of Jerusalem.[37]

The result was a new commission by A. Bertram and J. W. A. Young, who, in 1925, proposed the participation of the Arab Orthodox in the Confraternity as well as greater Arab Orthodox control on the finances of the Patriarchate.[38] At the same time they turned down new Greek proposals to solve the grave financial problems of the Patriarchate through a loan by either the National Bank of Greece or a consortium of Greek banks. The initial reaction of the Greek Consul was not negative. He thought that the proposals of the commission, especially the provisions for property, education and welfare, were a fair base for negotiation. However the Greek Foreign Ministry and particularly the responsible Second Directorate, had no policy guidelines on the issue of the Patriarchate of Jerusalem. Exploiting the absence of policy the Patriarch managed to dictate his uncompromising line to the Greek diplomats.

The reaction of the Patriarch, supported subsequently by the Greek Consul, and the lack of British resolution prevented the realization of these proposals. The British Mandate was reluctant to accept any major changes in the Greek Orthodox Church. The mandatory government determined all claims related to Holy Places or religious communities on the basis of rights and practices existing during the Ottoman rule.[39]

The Arab Orthodox on the other hand, represented by the Arab Orthodox Executive Committee of the Second Arab Orthodox Congress, asked for proportional representation and participation of the Arab Orthodox in the assembly for the election of the new Patriarch. *Filastin* attacked the Patriarchate and the Greek Consul and declared that the issue of the Arab Orthodox was common for all the Arabs, Christians and Muslims.[40]

In 1929 this newspaper opened a wide discussion on the form of a Palestinian flag, tackling questions concerning the tensions between Palestinian particularism and pan-Arabism, as well as the status of Muslim-Christians relations in a period of increasing islamization of Palestinian identity.[41] During the general strike, in April–October 1936, *Filastin* played an important role in introducing and spreading national messages and influenced considerably the organization and the co-ordination of the strike, earning the wide support of the general public. According to Mustapha Kabha, at this point the Arab Orthodox press reached the peak of its influence on values and processes in Palestinian society at the time.[42] The lack of participation of the Greek Orthodox Christians in the riots of 1929 and the revolt of 1936 indicated the ambiguity of their position towards both the British and the Palestinian Arab national movement.[43]

The 1948 war and the Jordanian rule did not alter substantially the situation in the Patriarchate. The death of Patriarch Timotheos and the new patriarchal election gave the pretext for a new round of Arab Orthodox demands for a greater say in church affairs. Despite the combined pressure by Palestinian Arab faithful and the Jordanian nationalist government of Suleiman al-Nabulsi, the Confraternity and the recently elected Patriarch Benedictos managed to preserve its exclusively Greek character. The new *Katastatikon*, (the Jordanian Law of the Greek Orthodox of Jerusalem No. 27, in 1958) provided for a mixed council of eight lay and six ecclesiastics, who were to observe but not participate in its preparation. It provided also that one third of the Patriarchate's income would supply the charitable and educational needs of the faithful. There should be two Arab ecclesiastics in the Synod chosen by the Patriarch without the approval of the lay community.[44]

Land, identity and Church-State relations after 1967

The 1967 Arab-Israeli war and the Israeli occupation of East Jerusalem, West Bank and Gaza Strip created a new situation. Under Israeli occupation and turbulent relations with Arab regimes, the Palestinians and more importantly Christian Palestinians re-defined their position, raising the banner of secular nationalism over communal identification and sectarianism. Christian Palestinians became leading advocates of nationalism, secularization and radicalization of the Palestinian national struggle. George Habash, founder of the Popular Front for the Liberation of Palestine has been quoted claiming: 'I combine my Arab nationality, my Christianity, my Muslim culture and Marxism.'[45] In general the political terminology, slogans and methods of the post-1967 Palestinian groups indicate a break with domination by the traditional elites. Several leaders of militant leftist groups were middle-class Christian Palestinians. They also acquired command positions in the inner councils of the Palestinian national movement.[46]

Moreover, the election of the Likud coalition in 1977 passed the power over to policy makers whose main priority was to facilitate the programmes of Jewish settlements in and around Jerusalem and to ensure Israeli Jewish predominance in Jerusalem.[47] According to Meron Benvenisti, the Israelis understood that dominion over the physical space of the city must be accompanied by demographic superiority. He added that 'Church domes and buildings to house pilgrims will not determine the identity of the Holy City; homes for people will.'[48] The Arab Orthodox Palestinian will continue to oppose land sales by the Patriarchate. Church land was part of the land of Palestine and any tampering of this land was to be considered national treason. The Arab Orthodox Initiative Committee established in 1992 to revive the demands and claims over the Patriarchate[49] and beliefs about the usurpation of Arab Orthodox rights by the Greek senior clergy became again the prevailing religious and political issue in the community.[50]

There is also a significant demographic eclipse of Christians in the Holy Land. According to analysts, with a conservative estimate of natural population growth of 2% there should have been a population of 425,000 Palestinian Christians in Israel and the Palestinian Territories in the 1990s, up from a pre-independence population of 145,000. Instead according to 1995 census, there were only 110,000 Christians. In 1996, there were 26,473 Greek Orthodox Palestinians out of approximately 50,000 Christians in East Jerusalem, West Bank and Gaza.[51] In 1992 the total faithful of the Patriarchate of Jerusalem were estimated at 145,000 in the Occupied Territories, Israel and Jordan.[52] During the same period there was a constant emigration trend among the Palestinian Christians. Church institutions could employ only 26.5% of them and Christian unemployment reached almost 35% of heads of households.[53] From September 2000, the al-Aqsa *intifada* put a virtual end to tourism and the pilgrimage trade in which 80% of Christians worked. Moreover Israeli security measures and blockades and terrorist operations of Palestinian Islamic militants using Christian towns as their base to oppose the Israelis, increased the pressure to Christian population. As a result 3,000 Palestinians, mostly Christians, have emigrated from Bethlehem area during the four years of *intifada*.[54]

The Oslo Process complicated the matter for the Jerusalem Patriarchate and its strategy towards the state. The formation of the Palestinian Authority as a would-be-state created new facts on the ground. Major issues such as land sales or leasing have surpassed the symbolic patterns of Palestinian nationalism and become part of the negotiations agenda.[55] The land in Abu Ghneim/Har Homa is a case in point. The large Israeli settlement in this area very near to East Jerusalem became one of the major issues of criticism by the Palestinian Authority against Israeli settlement policies, which create facts on the ground and as such violate the Oslo Accords. According to the Arab Palestinian press part of the land in Abu Ghneim belonged to the Greek Orthodox Patriarchate, which sold or leased it to the Israeli state and to business. Notwithstanding the accuracy of these press accusations, it is safe to argue that the Patriarchate and its land were brought again into the centre of not only the national struggle but of the negotiations process.

Despite sometimes fierce criticism by the Palestinian press, the Palestinian Authority and Palestinian leader Chairman Arafat personally dealt with the matter in a rather discreet manner. The Palestinian side did not wish to be misunderstood by a friendly government of Greece, on this issue. Secondly, an open conflict between the Palestinian Authority and the ancient Jerusalemite Christian Church institution might have spoiled its unifying image as representative of all Palestinians, Christians and Muslims. Most importantly, an open controversy with the Patriarchate could have presented Arafat and the Palestinian negotiators with considerable problems during the final status talks on Jerusalem and the political control over the Holy Shrines. However Arafat found indirect ways to send his message of disapproval to the Patriarchate.[56]

The major break, however, with the tradition of 'close co-operation for internal autonomy' came with the patriarchal election after the death of the late Patriarch Diodoros in February 2001. The elections were more or less in accordance with the usual practice in such a process. Personal feuds and shifting alliances around certain prelates and excessive lobbying in Athens, Constantinople, Tel Aviv, Ramallah and Amman is a familiar pattern of patriarchal elections.[57]

Equally familiar were recurring political controversies. The alleged leasing of church property to foreign investment firms including Israeli companies, a conflict between certain segments of the Arab Orthodox and the Greek upper clergy over equitable representation in church property and welfare administration and allegations of corruption and bribery perpetrated by members of Greek clergy, customarily surface prior to elections.[58]

The regional situation had profoundly changed since the 1980s with the Peace Process and the formation of the Palestinian Authority. The *Locum Tenens* now had to submit the list of the candidates to three ruling powers, Jordan, the Palestinian Authority and Israel and seek for their formal approval. After the collapse of the Taba talks and the eruption of violence all interested parties, namely Israel, the Palestinian leadership and the Arab Orthodox were particularly concerned about the outcome of the patriarchal elections. In the international arena, also, the end of the Cold War allowed religious institutions and religious legitimacy to play an active role in international politics.[59]

The Arab Orthodox community was not unified behind common goals. Three main groupings can be discerned: first, well established professionals and notables mainly in Jordan who pressed for the arabization of the Patriarchate, second, Palestinian middle-class professionals, priests, intellectuals, activists or not, aspiring to the Palestinian national goals[60] and close to the Palestinian Authority, who asked for a compromise – better education, communal welfare and higher Arab representation in the Church – and third, the poorer strata, disillusioned with the political situation and ready to forget their communal Greek Orthodox identity.[61] With such a split in the Arab Orthodox community both the Palestinian Authorities and the Jordanian kingdom kept a very discreet and very low profile policy, sending however the message that they wished to see a high profile stance for the Arab Orthodox community with regard to these issues.

The Israeli government of Ariel Sharon could not afford to see a 'pro-Palestinian' Patriarch in the region at such a critical moment. Israel wanted to avoid the arabization of the Greek Orthodox Patriarchate, which would follow the example of the Latin Patriarchate and most importantly they feared possible Palestinian control over the Patriarchate's property. Last but not least they wanted to prevent any kind of non-Greek i.e. Russian interference, in the Patriarchate.[62]

The Israeli government decided to interfere in the internal affairs of the Patriarchate by erasing from five prelates the candidates' list, including Metropolitan Ireneos, who was eventually elected patriarch. It was the first time since the nineteenth century that the sovereign or occupying power intervened directly in the patriarchal election and it constituted a major break with the tradition of church-state relations in the Holy Land.

The dangers emanating from such a decision were almost immediately visible. It could have created a very dangerous precedent of state intervention into the heart of church functions and lead to a schism inside the Church. The majority of the Synod refused to accept it and sought help from Jordan. At the same time leading Arab Orthodox figures from both Jordan and the Palestinian Authority expressed their desire to conduct the election of the Patriarch according to the Jordanian Law of 1958, ignoring the decision of the Israeli government.[63]

Meanwhile there was immense lobbying in Jerusalem and Athens. This lobbying was fruitful in bringing the support of the Greek government which had been rather inactive up to this point, and, most importantly, of the Church of Greece. The latter, and particularly the Archbishop of the Church of Greece, Christodoulos, was very active. It was perhaps the first time that the Church of Greece played a decisive role in the patriarchal election. During the 1980s and the beginning of 1990s there was a growing siege mentality in the Greek society, cultivated by the Orthodox Church. Archbishop Chistodoulos, as G. Mavrogordatos mentions, 'could successfully promote the Orthodox Church as the only "ark" of Greek national identity threatened by European integration and globalisation'.[64]

In the case of Jerusalem, Archbishop Christodoulos claimed, in an article in July 1994, that according to unnamed Middle-Eastern sources an agreement between Israel and the Palestinians on the Holy Places was imminent. This agreement would have provided for Saudi control over the Muslim Holy Places and the Vatican's control over the Christian Holy Places.[65] There was a widespread view in the Greek press that Israel had come to some kind of arrangement with the Holy See which would be detrimental to the preponderant role of the Greek Orthodox Patriarchate in the Holy Land.[66]

Eventually the Israeli Ministry of Justice approved the list of candidates without erasing any of them. However the Israeli government did not formally acknowledge the election of Patriarch Ireneos for two years. Various Israeli officials and experts said that the real issue was the real estate holdings of the Patriarchate, including land on which the Knesset and many other important properties in Israel, Jerusalem and the West Bank stand. The Greek Orthodox Patriarchate is the second largest landowner in Israel after the Israeli state itself. Right wing and pro-settler groups accused Patriarch Ireneos of being a supporter of the PLO and Yasser Arafat personally despite his statement, 'I am not pro-Palestinian, nor pro-Israel, nor pro-anything, I am only pro-God.'[67]

The fate of the Knesset building, the leasing of which is to be terminated in 2051, is not of major concern for Israel. What is more important is the struggle for control of patriarchate land around Mar Elias Monastery, between Jerusalem and Bethlehem. In 2004 the Defence Ministry expropriated about five acres of the land to build a separation fence, but the Patriarchate still holds a good deal of real estate. Israel would very much like to gain control of that land to connect the neighbourhoods of Gilo and Har Homa (both of which are situated across the 1967 line) and create territorial continuity in south Jerusalem.[68] Moreover the Israeli authorities are seeking further 'judaization' and Israelization of the East Jerusalem and the Old City in particular.

Caught between Israeli plans and Palestinian reaction, the Patriarch initially pledged that, contrary to his predecessors, he would not only cease any land sales to Israelis but he would also reclaim land that has been expropriated and restore the Patriarchate's land that had been unlawfully sold.[69] Despite these assurances, it was revealed in the Israeli press that Patriarch Ireneos had granted a proxy to his former financial manager, who sold real estate inside the Old City to Israeli business. The Patriarch denied the report and claimed that this was a conspiracy against him. The incident sparked harsh reaction from both the Arab Orthodox and members of the Synod. It also coincided with a series of scandals in the Church of Greece, which not only weakened one of Patriarch Ireneos' main supporters but also implicated the Patriarchate in those scandals.[70]

The first reaction came from a conference held in Nazareth by the Arab faithful. A considerable part of the Arab Orthodox community in Nazareth had been engaged in a long controversy with the Patriarchate over land leasing of Patriarchate's land in Nazareth from 1992 onwards. The concern of the Arab faithful in Israel also revealed the transfer the centre of gravity of the community from the Palestinian territories to Israel. The Christian Arab population in Israel has quadrupled since 1948 and now constitutes almost all of the Christians in historic Palestine. Moreover the community experienced a period of Muslim-Christians tension and it faced dilemmas as to their relations with the larger Muslim Arab community in Israel.[71] It also sensed a possible change in the character of the Orthodox by the influx of Orthodox Russian-speaking immigrants in Israel.[72] Land dispute with the Patriarchate gave the Arab Orthodox opportunity to have a common national agenda with the Palestinian Christians in Jerusalem and the Palestinian Territories.

The Palestinian Authority's first reaction was to form a Ministerial Investigation Committee to look into the case and it called upon the international community and the Quartet to assume their responsibilities and thwart the Israeli attempt to violate the land and culture of the Holy Land. We can discern two trends in the Arab Orthodox community. One represented by the National Christian Coalition, a group of young Palestinian Christians. The group aims to spread national awareness among the Palestinian Christian masses and to encourage the formation of Palestinian national command to head all churches in the Holy Land. It also aspires to activate the national role of the churches, to build bridges with the Israeli Arab Christians and to consolidate the spirit of Muslim-Christian brotherhood, because they form one body. There is also another trend manifested by the Executive Committee of the Arab Orthodox Conference in Palestine and the Palestine prelate, Archimandrite Attalah Hanna. This trend focuses on land sales, calls for a total halt of Patriarchate land purchases by Israelis and for the re-activation of the provisions of the Jordanian Law provision regarding lay participation in the Patriarchate's management.[73]

The turning point in the dispute between the faithful and the Patriarchate came with the reaction of the majority of the Holy Synod of the Patriarchate against the Patriarch and their decision to depose him. They accused him of being 'incorringly caught up in a syndrome of lying, religious distortion, degradation of the Patriarchate's role and irresponsible mishandling of Patriarchate's property'.[74] They also declared that the issue is closely related to the Greek nation's rights on the Holy Places and, moreover, to the centrality of the Holy Places for the world Christianity. The dispute was also imbued by personal feuds dating back to the period of Ireneos' election. The decline of the influence of the Archbishop of Athens, Christodoulos, brought these feuds to the surface. Though initially inactive after the eruption of the Holy Synod 'revolt', the Greek government feared a schism in the Church and called publicly for the resignation of Ireneos. The exposure of the crisis in the Greek mass media and possible problems in relations with the Arab states prompted the public stance of the Greek government, missing however the opportunity for discrete constructive and possibly more productive diplomacy, which would give it the role of mediator among the three governments and the Church.[75] The Jordanian and the Palestinian authorities were reluctant to take sides at the beginning; they also preferred Ireneos' resignation. Finally after much discussion and distress, the

Orthodox Church demoted Ireneos, its former Patriarch, to the rank of a simple monk. The Ecumenical Patriarch had, hence, to intervene, regaining its supremacy among the Greek Orthodox Churches in the East, after a nearly decade-long challenge by Archbishop Christodoulos.

Conclusion

The Patriarchate is founded upon a configuration of, firstly, land, that is the Holy Places and the authority of the bishops, which is fortified in connection with, and in control of them; secondly, the collective entity of the Confraternity, the survival of which is relatively indifferent to the particular members which compose it at any particular moment and, last but not least, a co-optation policy in church-state relations.

In each of the above-mentioned crises there was a threat to this configuration. In the case of Cyrillos, Russia challenged the authority of the bishops on the land and the central role of Constantinople and Jerusalem in the geopolitics of pilgrimage. Damianos' turbulent reign was due to ruptures in the collective entity of the Confraternity, important members of which failed to reconcile Greek nationalism with the new circumstances in Mandate Palestine. The last crisis seems to be more complicated. The Church finds it difficult to manage its co-optation-with-the-state policy, ignoring the symbolic and strategic importance of land for the Palestinian faithful. It also finds it difficult to break with co-optation policies, insofar as it has yet to build a new configuration of a global and local Greek Orthodox tradition.

Notes

1 F. J. Bliss, *The religions of modern Syria and Palestine*, Edinburgh, 1912, p. 55.
2 P. Ramet, 'Autocephaly and National Identity', in P. Ramet (ed.), *Eastern Christianity and Politics in the Twentieth Century*, Duke University Press, 1988 pp. 14–15.
3 N. J. Pantazopoulos, *Church and Law*, Amsterdam, Adolf M. Hakkert, 1984, pp. 5–7.
4 F. J. Bliss, *The religions of modern Syria and Palestine*, p. 53.
5 S. Vryonis Jr., 'The History of the Greek Patriarchate of Jerusalem as Reflected in Codex Patriarcicus No. 428, 1517–1805', *Byzantine and Modern Greek Studies*, vol. 7, 1981, p. 43.
6 L. G. A. Cust, *The Status Quo in the Holy Places*, Jerusalem, 1929, pp. 9–14. For an account on international politics on Jerusalem in the 19th century see R. Heacock, 'Jerusalem and the Holy Places in the European Diplomacy', in A.

O' Mahony (ed.), *The Christian Heritage in the Holy Land*, London, Scorpion [Melisende] 1995, pp. 201–2 and S. Roussos, 'The Greek Orthodox Community of Jerusalem in International Politics: International Solutions for Jerusalem and the Greek Orthodox Community in the 19th and 20th Centuries' in L. Levine (ed.), *Jerusalem: Its Sanctity and Centrality for Judaism, Christianity and Islam*, New York, Continuum, 1999, pp. 482–93.

7   K. Graham, 'The Moral Significance of Collective Entities', *Inquiry*, vol. 44, 2001, pp. 21–42.
8   Ibid, p. 23.
9   K. Amstrong, 'Jerusalem: The Problems and Responsibilities of sacred space', *Islam and Christian-Muslim relations*, vol. 13, no. 2, 2002, p. 190.
10 A. Hastings, 'Holy Lands and their political consequences', *Nations and Nationalisms*, vol. 9, no. 1, 2003, p. 35.
11 *Booklet of Chrysanthos, Patriarch of Jerusalem*, Bucharest 1768 [in Greek] See also S. Tselikas, 'Katagrafi tou Archeiou tou Patriarcheiou Ierosolymon [Catalogue of the Archives of the Patriarchate of Jerusalem]', *Deltion Istorikou kai Palaiografikou Arxeiou*, vol. 5, Athens, MIET, 1992, pp. 390–5.
12 T. Stavrou, 'Russian interest in the Levant 1843–1848', *Middle East Journal*, vol. 17, 1963, pp. 91–103.
13 T. Stavrou, *Russian interests in Palestine 1882–1914. A study of Religious and Educational Enterprise*, Thessalonica, Institute for Balkan Studies, 1963, p. 206.
14 Ch. Papadopoulos, *Istoria tes Ekklesias Ierosolymon* [*History of the Church of Jerusalem*], Alexandria, 1910, pp. 777–8.
15 D. Hopwood, *The Russian presence in Syria and Palestine 1843–1914*, Oxford, Clarendon Press, 1969, p. 181.
16 R. Kark, 'The Impact of Early Missionary Enterprises on Landscape and Identity Formation in Palestine, 1820–1914', *Islam and Christian-Muslim Relations*, vol. 15, no. 2, April 2004, pp. 209–34; see also K. Anderson, 'Pilgrims, Property and Politics: The Russian Orthodox Church in Jerusalem', in A. O'Mahony (ed.), *Eastern Christianity: Studies in Modern history, Religion and Politics*, Melisende, London, 2004, pp. 388–430.
17 A. Hastings, 'Holy Lands and their political consequences', p. 34.
18 D. Hopwood, *The Russian presence in Syria and Palestine 1843–1914*, p. 183.
19 R. Khalidi, 'The Formation of Palestinian Identity: The Critical Years, 1917–1923' in J. Jankowski and I. Gershoni, (eds), *Rethinking Nationalism in the Arab Middle East*, Columbia University Press, New York, 1997, pp. 173–6. For earlier territorial concepts of 'Palestine' see H. Berger, '"Palestine" and other Territorial Concepts in the 17th Century', *International Journal of Middle East Studies*, vol. 30, 1998, pp. 563–72.
20 R. Khalidi, *Palestinian Identity: The Construction of Modern National Consciousness*, Columbia University Press, New York, 1997, pp. 126–7.
21 Y. Porath, 'The awakening of the Palestinian Arabs', in Moshe Ma'oz (ed.), *Studies on Palestine during the Ottoman period*, The Magnes Press, Jerusalem 1975, pp. 358–60, 380–1.
22 E. Kedourie, *The Chatham House Version and other Middle-Eastern Studies*, University Press of New England, London, 1984, p. 319. The Palestinian Arab intellectual, Khalil Sakakini and his dilemmas between his Christian faith and his belonging to the East is a case in point. See 'Khalil Sakakini's Ottoman Prison Diaries: Damascus (1917–1918)', *Jerusalem Quarterly File*, Winter 2004.

23 17 June 1932, Greek Consul in Palestine, D. Benetatos, to Second Directorate, 'Report on the visit of the Arab Orthodox Executive Committee to High Commissioner', 7103, B/36, A.Y.E. (Greek Foreign Ministry Archives).
24 F. J. Bliss, *The Religions of Syria and Palestine*, p. 70.
25 A. Bertram and H. C. Luke., *Report of the Commission appointed by the Government of Palestine into the affairs of the Orthodox Patriarchate of Jerusalem*, Oxford University Press, London, 1921, p. 251.
26 *Report of the Commission appointed by the Government of Palestine into the affairs of the Orthodox Patriarchate of Jerusalem*, p. 254.
27 Ibid., pp. 257–8.
28 D. Hopwood, *The Russian presence in Syria and Palestine 1843–1914*, pp. 199–200.
29 S. Roussos, 'Diplomacy and Communal Identity: Greece and the Greek Orthodox in Syria and Lebanon 1919–1940', *Chronos*, no. 1, 1998, pp. 33–65.
30 T. H. Papadopoulos, *Studies and documents relating to the History of the Greek Church and People under Turkish domination*, Variorum, London 1990, p. 149.
31 G. Th. Mavrogordatos, 'Orthodoxy and Nationalism in the Greek Case', *West European Politics*, vol. 26, no. 1, January 2003, p. 128.
32 El. Prodromou, 'Democratization and Religious Transformation in Greece: An Underappreciated theoretical and Empirical Primer', in P. M. Kitromilides and Th. Veremis (eds), *The Orthodox Church in a Changing World*, Athens, ELIAMEP, 1998, pp. 107–8.
33 27 June 1919, Cairo to Athens, 14466, B/35/10, A.Y.E.
34 1919, Internal Memorandum of Second Directorate, B/35/9, A.Y.E. The Second Directorate was in charge of Russia, non-European states (apart from Turkey) and religious affairs.
35 See S. Roussos, 'Patriarchs, Notables and Diplomats: The Greek Orthodox Patriarchate of Jerusalem in the Modern Period', in A. O'Mahony (ed.), *Eastern Christianity: Studies in Modern history, Religion and Politics*, Melisende, London, 2004, pp. 372–87.
36 F. H. Kisch, *Palestine Diary*, Victor Gollancz Ltd., London, p. 39.
37 S. Khuri and N. Khuri , *Khulasat ta'rikh kanisat Urshalim al urthudhuksiya*, Jerusalem, 1925. See also A. O'Mahony, 'Palestinian-Arab Orthodox Christians: Religion, Politics and Church-State Relations in Jerusalem, c.1908–1925', *Chronos*, no. 3, 2000, pp. 61–87 and D. Tsimhoni, 'The Greek Orthodox Patriarchate of Jerusalem during the formative years of the British Mandate in Palestine', *Asian and African Studies*, vol. 12, no 1, March 1978, pp. 77–121.
38 See A. Bertram. and J. W. A. Young, *The Orthodox Patriarchate of Jerusalem. Report of the Commission upon certain controversies*, Oxford University Press, London, 1926.
39 M. Eordegian, 'British and Israeli Maintenance of the Status Quo in the Holy Places of Christendom', *International Journal of Middle East Studies*, vol. 35, 2003, pp. 307–28.
40 *Filastin*, 16 October 1931, see also *Echos d' Orient*, vol. XXXI, 1932, p. 91.
41 T. Sorek, 'The orange and the "Cross and Crescent": imagining Palestine in 1929', *Nations and Nationalism*, vol. 10, no. 3, 2004, pp. 269–91.
42 M. Kabha, 'The Palestinian Press and the General Strike, April-October 1936: *Filastin* as a Case Study', *Middle Eastern Studies*, vol. 39, no. 3, July 2003, pp. 169–89.

43 Y. Porath, *The Emergence of the Palestinian Arab national movement*, vol. I 1918–1929, Frank Cass, London, 1974 and vol. II 1929–1939, Frank Cass, London, 1977.
44 D. Tsimhoni, *Christian Communities in Jerusalem and the West Bank Since 1948. An Historical, Social and Political Survey*, Praeger, London, 1993, pp. 36–46.
45 Quoted by Zuheir Andreus in newspaper *Kul al-Arab*, see Y. Stern and J. Khoury, 'Christian-Arab activists face minefield of identity', *Ha'aretz*, 25 March 2005.
46 Don Peretz, 'Palestinian Social Stratification: The Political Implications', *Journal of Palestine Studies*, vol. VII, no. 1, 1977, pp. 70–1.
47 On the Patriarchate's attitude towards Likud policies and Patriarch Diodoros' reaction to *intifada*, in 1987, and towards the takeover of Saint John Hospices by the settler group Ateret Cohanim see S. Roussos, 'The Greek Orthodox Patriarchate and Community of Jerusalem: Church, State and Identity', in A. O'Mahony (ed.), *The Christian Communities of Jerusalem and the Holy Land: Studies in History, Religion and Politics*, Cardiff University of Wales Press, 2003, pp. 38–56.
48 M. Benvenisti, *City of Stone: The Hidden History of Jerusalem*, University of California Press, Berkeley, 1996, p. 149.
49 M. Dumper, 'Church-State Relations in Jerusalem since 1948', in A. O' Mahony, Göran Gunner and Kevork Hintlian (eds), *Christian Heritage in the Holy Land.*, Scropion [Melisende], London, 1995, p. 278 and on land sales by the Patriarchate to Israel National Fund after 1967, see M. Dumper, *The Politics of Jerusalem since 1967*, Columbia University Press, New York, 1997, pp. 187–9.
50 See G. Bowman, 'Nationalising the sacred: Shrines and Shifting Identities in the Israeli Occupied Territories', *Man*, XXVIII, no. 3, 1993, pp. 1–30; S. K. Aburish, *The Forgotten Faithful. the Christians in the Holy Land*, London, 1993; R. Beeston, 'Palestinians want the Greek out of Orthodox', *The Times*, 3 October 1992.
51 Drew Christiansen, SJ, 'Christianity's empty cradle? Relentless pressure drive Christians from the Middle East', Part I: *National Catholic Reporter*, 4 March 2005.
52 Y. Courbage, and P. Fargues, *Chrétiens et Juifs dans l'Islam arabe et turc*, Paris, Fayard, 1992, p. 328.
53 B. Sabella, 'Palestinian Christian Emigration from the Holy Land', *Proche-Orient Chrétien*, XLI, 1991, p. 76.
54 D. Christiansen, SJ, 'Christianity's empty cradle? Relentless pressure drive Christians from the Middle East', Part I *National Catholic Reporter*, 4 March 2005.
55 D. Newman, 'the geopolitics of peacemaking in Israel-Palestine', *Political Geography*, vol. 21, 2002, pp. 629–46.
56 Suleiman al-Akawi, 'The Orthodox Patriarchate and the Peace Prize', *An Nahar*, 18 October 1995.
57 See S. Roussos, 'The Patriarchate of Jerusalem in the Greek, Israeli, Palestinian triangle', *One in Christ: a Catholic Ecumenical Review*, vol. 39, no. 3, July 2004, pp. 15–25.
58 S. Ma'ayeh, 'Jerusalem: Orthodox clergy prepares for election showdown', *The Jordan Times*, 30 May 2001.

59 J. Fox, 'The Influence of Religious Legitimacy on Grievance Formation by Ethno-Religious Minorities', *Journal of Peace Research*, vol. 36, no. 3, May 1999, p. 292.
60 Letter of the Chairman of the Arab Orthodox Benevolent Society in Beit Jala, Dr Simon Araj to the Orthodox Peace Fellowship webmail.earlham.edu/archive/opf-1/April-2002/msg00060.html
61 R. Panzer, 'Die Politische Identifikation griechisch-orthodoxer Christen im Vorderen Orient', *Orient*, 2/98, 39, Jahrgang 2, 1998, p. 240.
62 G. Kalokairinos, 'Behind the scenes in Jerusalem', *Kathimerini*, 22 July 2001 [in Greek].
63 *al-Quds*, July 2001 (Arabic), Wafa (Official Palestine News Agency), 8 January 2002.
64 G. Th. Mavrogordatos, 'Orthodoxy and Nationalism in the Greek Case', p. 133.
65 Metropolitan of Dimitrias, Christodoulos, 'The Vatican and the Holy Places', *To Vema*, 17 July 1994 [in Greek].
66 S. Alexiou, 'Give and Take by the Vatican', *To Vema*, 24 July 1994 [in Greek].
67 *The New York Times*, 26 April 2002.
68 A. Carmel, 'In the name of the fathers', *Ha'aretz*, 3 March 2005.
69 Statement by Patriarch Ireneos in a meeting with Arab Orthodox laymen in Amman, *Ha'aretz*, 3 March 2005.
70 The scandal implicated people of obscure background (ex-police officers and outlaws) that have been closely connected with the Church of Greece and served as Archbishop's Christodoulos envoys to the Patriarchate during the election campaign of Ireneos.
71 Y. Stern and J. Khoury, 'Christian-Arab activists face minefield of identity'. For sectarian politics in Nazareth after 1989 see Ch. F. Emmett, 'Conflicting Loyalties and Local Politics in Nazareth', *Middle East Journal*, vol. 51, no. 4, Autumn 1997, pp. 535–53.
72 D. M. Neuhaus, SJ, 'Jewish Israeli Attitudes towards Christianity and Christians in Contemporary Israel', in A. O'Mahony and M. Kirwan (eds), *World Christianity: Politics, Theology, Dialogues*, London, Melisende, 2004, pp. 347–71.
73 *Al-Ayyam*, 20 March 2005.
74 Petition of the Majority of the Holy Synod, *Ta Nea*, 6 May 2005 [in Greek].
75 With the eruption of the crisis the Turkish Prime Minister offered 150,000 Ottoman documents from 1500 to 1914 regarding property rights in order to help Palestinians claim their property rights In West Bank and Gaza Strip. K. Iordanides, 'The obstinate elder', *Kathimerini*, 8 May 2005 [in Greek].

Chapter 6

Indigenization and contextualization – the example of Anglican and Presbyterian churches in the Holy Land

Michael Marten

Introduction

The Anglican and Presbyterian churches are the only two major Protestant denominations to have had an institutionalized presence in the Holy Land since the nineteenth century. Apart from the two world wars that interrupted their work in the region, this presence has been a continuous one, with relationships developing over time in the ecclesiastical, social and political fields. These have both influenced and caused repeated re-interpretation of theological understandings of the place of the Holy Land. In seeking to understand and relate theological positions on the Holy Land – and perhaps especially of Jerusalem – understanding this long-term presence is essential: it provides a relational and historical context for the pursuit of theological endeavour, and opens the way to a greater understanding of what it means to relate to a territory both imagined and real. I will show how the Anglicans and Presbyterians related differently to their environment, the former moving towards indigenization of the ecclesial community, whilst the latter, although remaining identifiably western, nonetheless seeks to contextualize its theology and work. The primary objects of study will be the English and Scottish 'sending' churches and their theological interpretations, and the institutions in Jerusalem and the Holy Land that they created.

PART I – CONTEXTS AND BEGINNINGS

Theological Origins

The theological origins of the Presbyterian and a significant branch of the Anglican presence in what was then Palestine are notable for their similarity: both traditions sought to pursue the conversion of Jews. Although Jews could easily be identified at home, in both traditions there was a strong sense that if it became possible to convert Jews in Palestine, then Jews elsewhere would more readily convert to Protestantism. This desire to convert Jews arose from specific theological understandings, and despite the differing denominational backgrounds, remarkable similarities exist in this context, the dominant element being the ascendancy of the Evangelical movement. Whilst this can be characterized in a number of ways, two of the dominant features of interest here can be identified as biblical literalism and hostility to liberalism (understood as 'any philosophy of life not built on divine revelation'[1]). Reflecting on the latter element, in a time when formerly-held truths were being questioned in all areas of life in terms of new scientific theories and philosophy, the need for an unwavering belief structure seemed paramount, represented most dramatically perhaps in the context of worship:

> it seems strange that in a society which was so dynamic and a culture so optimistic, most hymn-writers should have remained wedded to a static Aristotelian view of God as the 'unmoved mover' and equated all change with corruption and decay.[2]

Salvation in this context could be achieved only by a return to that which did not alter – the steadfastness of the Divine, the unchanging presence of God in the midst of human change. Furthermore, there was a clear sense that at a time when worldwide missionary activity was capturing the imagination of Western churches, preaching 'this conversion [of the Jews] is most of all to preach the gospel to the weary world'[3] – in many ways, therefore, the most fundamental kind of missionary activity to engage in.

Biblical literalism was represented most dramatically in the various forms of millenarianism that were developed in the Victorian era. It would not serve any useful purpose to elaborate on these in this context,[4] but it is worth noting that Scottish and English Evangelical traditions, despite denominational differences, were again remarkably similar in this regard,[5] and the role of 'the Jews'[6] in Palestine played a central role. Palestine was seen as the natural home of 'the Jews', and the terms were at times almost used interchangeably. Furthermore, Palestine was felt to be known in some intimate way to believers in the Christian Gospel: this imaginary map was felt to be both real and realistic, shaped by biblical and fictional narratives,[7] e.g. the *Arabian Nights*.[8] As Victorian Britain saw itself as the 'Protestant Israel',[9] there was felt to be a deep connection to – and fascination with – the land of Palestine and 'the Jews'.[10] The Bible was read in such a way that the expectation of a 'new Israel', the manifold prophecies of the Old Testament, the belief that God would act in relation to what was perceived to be the 'chosen people' all received prominence – for many who were aware of political events across Europe in connection with Jews, it seemed 'to be prophecy which blended with politics and common humanity to fuel the motor of Protestant evangelism'.[11] By the early twentieth century this had developed into theories about 'restoration', which centred on the conversion of Jews and their being 'restored' to the land – Canaan/Palestine – though in how far this latter element would happen literally was open to dispute.[12] The place of Jews in the divine economy was therefore part of the process of worldwide missionary endeavour: only once the entire world, including Jews, had converted, would Christ return, enabling some form of restoration of 'the Jews' to take place. For many, therefore, engaging in missionary activity but ignoring Jews and their potential conversion made no sense. These thought patterns explain the desire to engage in missionary activity amongst Jews, and also point to the connection to Palestine.

It is important to add that although the conversion of Jews was a focal point for both the Anglican and Presbyterian missions, the Anglicans, in the form of the Church Missionary Society (CMS) at least, had wider ambitions: William Jowett, the first CMS missionary in the Mediterranean area was commissioned to work with 'Jews, Mahometans, and pagans'.[13] Their methods and thinking on this front were severely tested by the circumstances they found themselves in, since proselytizing Muslims was strictly forbidden. However, they were open to the possibility and even desirability of converting Muslims, whereas essentially, the Scots simply saw any potential Muslim converts as an incidental bonus to the main purpose of their missionary work – the conversion of 'the Jews'.

The work of the English and Scottish churches in Palestine

These theological understandings, then, formed the basis of English and Scottish missionary work in Palestine. The complexity of the theology was matched by the complexity of the situation the missionaries found themselves in. Religious communities were grouped into *millets*,[14] and movement between the *millets* themselves as well as to or from Islam declined as religious communities tended to live in the same locales resulting, for example, in relatively few mixed marriages.[15] Proselytizing among Muslims was forbidden, and attempts at converting Jews proved extremely problematic. The CMS response was to approach the situation indirectly, by seeking the 'conversion' of Eastern Christians in Palestine so that they 'would be so imbued with the pure form of Christianity that they would resume the duty, abandoned by their fathers for centuries, of converting the Muslims';[16] the Scots tended to understand the situation in similar terms. The methods that the missionaries used were the standard tools available to the nineteenth-century missionary: apart from direct preaching of the gospel where and when possible, education for children of the communities that were being pursued featured strongly, and in the latter half of the nineteenth century, as medicine became more professionalized, clinics and hospitals were created.[17]

The Anglican approach was in two dimensions: the CMS has already been mentioned, but partly as a result of the lobbying of the London Jews Society (LJS) – more properly the London Society for Promoting Christianity amongst the Jews – there was the creation of the Anglo-Prussian bishopric in Jerusalem. This was a unique creation: there was no Anglican congregation or community of any kind in Jerusalem, and the ordaining of a bishop specifically to further missionary work amongst Jews represented a new departure, particularly since this was primarily at the instigation of an interest group that sought to pursue the conversion of only one, relatively small segment of the population of Jerusalem.[18] However, the level of support among the Establishment for the LJS and the Anglican bishop should not be underestimated: LJS patrons and sponsors had been partly responsible for the first British government consul, William Young, being appointed to Jerusalem, and ensured a secure financial base for the work.[19] The involvement and rivalry of the two Anglican organizations is key to understanding the way in which the Anglican work in Palestine developed: a succession of bishops gradually built up an Anglican community based partly on the ordination to the priesthood of an increasing number of Palestinian Arab converts. Meanwhile, the CMS, partly based on classic imperial racism, tended to resist the local priests, regularly protesting that it was a 'sovereign' or lay society that was not subject to the bishop or his priests, a stance that Bishop Blyth (1887–1914) in particular, worked hard to counter. In contemporary times – particularly after the 1948 creation of Israel and the 1967 Israeli occupation of east Jerusalem and other territories, and then accentuated by the 1976 appointment of the first Palestinian bishop, Faik Ibrahim Haddad, to a new diocese that encompassed Palestine, Jordan, Israel, Lebanon and Syria with Jerusalem as its centre[20] – this situation has to some extent been reversed. There is now a relatively strong diocese rooted in local communities centred on the Cathedral Church of St George the Martyr in Jerusalem, and a Christian-Zionist oriented community based at Christ Church near the Jaffa Gate, which largely rejects the authority of the local church (Christ Church is run by the Israel Trust of the Anglican Church, the sister society of the Church's Ministry among Jewish people (CMJ), itself the successor to the LJS).[21] The diocese now incorporates thirty-one congregations and a considerable number of social institutions in Israel, the Occupied Palestinian Territories, Jordan, Lebanon and Syria.[22]

Scottish work developed in less direct ways: the creation by the Free Church of Scotland of a medical mission in Tiberias/Safad in northern Palestine in the 1880s under the direction of David Torrance followed a long period of inactivity in Palestine, though work had been carried out elsewhere in the eastern Mediterranean at various times. Evangelization, which involved considerable itinerant travel, was a key element from very early on, and the education of children was also quickly adopted. Two further key institutions were acquired: at the turn of the century, a hospital in Hebron originally run by Alexander Paterson for the Mildmay Mission was taken over by the (meantime) United Free Church of Scotland, and shortly before the First World War, Tabeetha School in Jaffa was bequeathed to the Church of Scotland by Jane Walker-Arnott, an independent Scottish woman who had founded it in 1863.[23] These institutions all came under the auspices of Jewish Mission Committees – unlike in the Anglican Church, this was an integral part of the churches' structure, rather than a missionary organization linked to the main church. Whilst conversion of Jews was the aim of these institutions, and this was in some instances translated into preferential treatment of e.g. Jewish children (who paid reduced or no school fees), the work was broadly directed to all communities – and, it is worth noting, was largely unsuccessful in terms of conversions, apart from poaching a small number of Eastern Christians to the Protestant cause.

After the First World War, St Andrew's Memorial Church in Jerusalem was built to remember the Scots who had fallen in the Palestine campaign – the first non-missionary institution of the Scots in Palestine, serving primarily British Mandatory officials based in Jerusalem. The Hebron institution was disposed of in the 1920s, so that by the time of the establishment of the State of Israel and the conclusion of the 1948 war, all the Scots' institutions happened to be in the territory of the new state. As a result of Palestinians being ethnically cleansed from large parts of what had now become Israel, the Church of Scotland found itself with a school in Jaffa which had very few Palestinian children left in it, a hospital in Tiberias devoid of its Palestinian staff,[24] and a church in west Jerusalem that was on the border of no man's land, with a small congregation in part made up of Christians living in west Jerusalem who had no possibility of returning to their own churches, now in Jordanian territory.

Developing theology in encounter

The purpose of this brief historical overview of Anglican and Presbyterian involvement is to highlight the level of involvement of Anglicans and Presbyterians in the Holy Land – views and opinions had very real connections to political and social realities, and these influenced the thinking of the churches.[25] Although missions were initiated with the very specific aim of conversion in mind, and a strong view as to the best means of achieving this aim, the fact is that despite many years of work, relatively few successes in terms of converts were recorded. Instead, a gradual process of localization took place. In the Scottish institutions this was primarily in terms of congregational members and school pupils since there has never been a local Christian appointed to either of the ministerial posts (Jerusalem, Tiberias), although the Jerusalem congregation has for many years now had a Palestinian Christian as the Clerk to its Kirk Session (the congregation's governing body). The Church of Scotland has developed an understanding of its role as much more one of a supportive outsider, not seeking to become an indigenous church in the way that Presbyterian churches originating with American missionary work in Lebanon and Syria, for example, have become, but seeking to contextualize its presence according to the political realities it finds itself in – this is something that will be returned to below. The Anglicans, on the other hand, succeeded in gradually transferring ever more significant parts of the institutional structures to local Christians, with the first ordinations of Palestinian Christians taking place in 1877.[26] In the early part of the twentieth century structures were slowly introduced to enable local involvement in decision-making, so that even though it was 1957 before a Palestinian bishop was appointed over part of the work, a clear process of transfer to local responsibility and indigenization can be seen to have been taking place. This in itself, and the move away from forthright evangelization and the poaching of Christians from other churches (Bishop Blyth refused to accept members who moved from other Christian traditions – a radical transformation of the earlier view that the Eastern churches represented a failed form of Christianity), is an indication of how far the Anglicans have away moved from their original position; in the meantime they have succeeded in creating a wholly new church that is now more or less fully accepted as part of the fabric of local Christian institutions, rather than being an outpost of a western denomination.

PART II – RESPONSES

The question of the State of Israel and the Palestinian Nakba

The political transformation of the country as a result of Zionist-inspired immigration of Jews, the fleeing of many Jews from Axis-controlled territories in Europe to Palestine before and during the Second World War, and the founding of the State of Israel and the Nakba of the Palestinians, profoundly disrupted the work of the churches, including the Protestants.

St George's Cathedral, the headquarters of the Anglican Church, was in Jordanian east Jerusalem, whilst many of the main properties of the church were located in what had become Israel. Most of the congregants connected to these properties had fled, becoming refugees in the surrounding countries. The church engaged in developing emergency facilities for refugees, overseen in part by Bishop Stewart's wife, Alison. This work was a reaction to two distinct elements: firstly, the very obvious needs that were apparent, and secondly, the ill-feeling that existed towards the English-dominated church. There was a strong sense that the church and the country it came from had failed the Palestinian Arab population, and Bishop Stewart sought to act quickly to remedy this, creating numerous institutions and founding refugee villages to try and alleviate the situation.[27]

The gradual moves towards further indigenization of the church hierarchy, outlined above, also entailed a logical move away from the former mission-centred nature of the church. Local educational work increased, with the opening in 1962 of a theological college, and further development of primary and secondary school education. Western pilgrims were catered for in the context of St George's guest house, and the Anglican presence became more of 'an embassy of Anglicanism in the Holy Land, centring on educational and ecumenical ventures'.[28] The ecumenical involvement of the Anglican Church was greatly facilitated by the lack of interdenominational feuding over holy places, but can also be regarded as a necessity for survival: it is a relatively small church in an ever-decreasing Christian community, and in order to at least maintain its position, a level of co-operation with larger denominations is a clear imperative.

The Church of Scotland found itself in a very different situation in 1948, owning institutions (initially occupied by squatters[29]) in a state that declared itself to be Jewish and viewed Christian missionary activity with a degree of hostility. Changes in the Church's outlook took place on practical and theological levels. For example, by the early 1950s it had become clear that there was no longer a need for a mission hospital in Tiberias: the new state created a national health service that made a missionary hospital in what was now an almost exclusively Jewish town redundant.[30] In 1953 Herbert Torrance, the son of the founder of the mission, retired as medical director and the hospital closed, to be turned into a guest house for pilgrims under the same name, the 'Sea of Galilee Centre', a function it occupied until the late 1990s. It was then closed down again, this time for a multi-million pound refurbishment to transform it into a high quality hotel-like establishment. It re-opened in 2004, re-branded as 'The Scots Hotel', a move not without controversy in the Church.[31] Meanwhile, the school in Jaffa continued to function, drawing in pupils from Jewish and Arab communities, as well a number of pupils from international backgrounds: with the state capital being in neighbouring Tel Aviv, the Jaffa school initially represented one of the only English-language schools in the area, and diplomats and others sent their children there. This continues to the present day.

Theologically, the Church of Scotland found itself confronted with a different aspect to the new state/Nakba event than their Anglican colleagues: not only was there a general western re-evaluation of global missionary history and current activity which gradually led to a more participatory and co-operative attitude to indigenous communities, but the horrific accounts of European Jews' fate in the context of the Holocaust led to a wholesale rethink of the place of Jewish missions in Christian theology. No longer was it regarded as acceptable in mainstream Christian circles to openly seek to convert Jews, this being seen as one of the elements of the virulent anti-Judaism that played a role in the devastation of Jewish communities across Europe. One of the consequences of this was structural: rather than most of the work in the new State of Israel coming under the Jewish Mission Committee as had been the case until then, the committee was abolished and by the mid-1960s all responsibility transferred to a committee known by the somewhat incongruous name of 'The Committee on Relations with Israel and Other Faiths' of the Overseas Board[32] – though this full title was not always used (it has now become the more straightforward Middle East and North Africa Committee).

However, this position took time to develop. Although initially a distinct sympathy for Israel predominated in church circles, along with an acceptance of Israeli foundational myths,[33] there was for some time an adherence to what can perhaps best be described as pre-Holocaust positions, evidenced, for example, in the 1954 publication of an essay by a Church of Scotland minister, Clephane Macanna, in which, after lauding the efforts of the early Israelis in creating a state, he proceeds to elaborate on the problems the state will face in seeking to reconcile Orthodox Judaism with the needs of a state. Advocating the implementation of 'freedom of religion' as espoused in the unratified Israeli constitution, he asks what it is that the 'Orthodox [Jewish] bloc' in the Israeli state is afraid of when restricting Christian work to the Christian community, suggesting that 'they cannot yet conceive that the Christian Church only asks what it has given for centuries – religious freedom that is real ... [in] Great Britain, North America, and much of Europe ...'[34] He posits three possible answers to his question: a fear of the appeal of Christianity since Orthodox Judaism is seen to hold little appeal for the majority of Israelis, the continuation of what the author calls the 'protective spirit' (understood as a defensiveness in regard to other traditions), or, 'is it that, for the moment at any rate, Judaism has no message for its own people in their present circumstances and in this day and time?'[35] He then proceeds to suggest that it is precisely in the latter area that the Christian churches in Israel can help, by reflecting 'on the hand of God in history', helping to overcome the problem of 'this spiritual vacuum created by the Rabbinate'.[36] Here, then, an almost totally unqualified support for Israel (and a complete disregard for the situation of the Palestinians) is coupled with a form of Christianity that does not appear to have recognized any fault on the part of the Christian tradition for the Nazi atrocities against Jews and the unwillingness of western Christian states – such as Britain and the United States – to have provided adequate refuge to Jews fleeing Axis countries. Attachment and identification with Israel was clearly not without its problems. These were to become more acute after 1967.

Responding to 1967 – the 'fourth phase' of Zionism

Michael Prior described five distinct phases in Zionism, with the fourth occurring as Israel attempted to absorb the newly-occupied territories of the Sinai, Gaza Strip, West Bank (including east Jerusalem) and the Golan Heights following the 1967 war and the rout of Arab military forces. In 1948 Zionism appeared to have achieved what it set out to do – create a state for Jews, though it was perceived by many Israelis to be a vulnerable creation (Prior's 'third phase') – and so the question might be asked: how could the acquisition of further territory develop Zionism?[37] Firstly, the obvious barbarism of the new occupation needed defending in some way. Clearly state security and the perversion of judicial systems could be brought into play, but for the first time mainstream Zionism became overtly religious, notable especially with the creation of the first Jewish settlements around Hebron, and in ever increasing measure since then. From being a non-religious (at times even anti-religious) ideology which had sometimes made use of religious imagery in furthering its aims, Zionism adopted the religious element of what it meant to be Jewish: mainstream Reform and Orthodox Jewish traditions performed an about-turn and made common cause with a political creed.[38] A key figure in this is Rabbi Zvi Yehuda Kook, who argued that there could be no circumstances under which it would be right to 'sacrifice' any part of 'Eretz Israel' and that settling the newly-acquired land was a sacred duty for Jews. This perhaps becomes more understandable when bearing in mind that 'Eretz Israel' was equated with biblical texts such as Dt 11:24; in other words, the land was interpreted as something that was divinely given, not the result of human history. The elements of this fusion of nationalism and religion are worth noting: it is the extreme right-wing of the Zionist movement that has had most success in relating to the religious element of Israeli society, with movements such as Tehiya, Moledet, Kach, and most famously, *Gush Emunim* (Bloc of the Faithful). Zionism as a nationalist movement became a nationalist-religious movement (notable especially since the 1980s), so that 'what earlier were rejected as extreme nationalistic, ethnocentric, xenophobic and militaristic positions have become respectable, and, often, objects of admiration'.[39]

It is in this context that the Anglican and Presbyterian responses to the 1967 war and its consequences need to be placed. The Anglican Church in Jerusalem experienced the consequences of the 1967 war as a crisis: the membership of the church itself was (and remains) largely urban and made up of middle-class professionals,[40] but many of these left the region in the aftermath of the war, and severe financial difficulties ensued. Coupled with a further wave of refugees, this financial shortfall was covered by appeals overseas.[41] Re-organization of the diocese became a priority, given that access to the East Bank of the Jordan River was now almost impossible, whereas connections to congregations in Israel became somewhat easier. Bishop George Appleton, viewed by some in the Palestinian community with suspicion because of his attempts at forging closer links to Judaism, was the last English bishop in Jerusalem. As already noted, Faik Haddad became the first Arab bishop of the new diocese, one of the four dioceses in the Province of Jerusalem and the Middle East. This ran counter to the interests of the CMJ, which had petitioned for the retention of an English bishop, fearing Arab politics would interfere in the carrying out of the role. In fact, this represented simply a further alienation of the Christ Church community from the mainstream Anglican Church in the Holy Land: Christ Church had warmly welcomed the military occupation of the new territories in 1967 and the illegal annexation of east Jerusalem. When the diocese was reorganized and Haddad appointed, Christ Church was allowed to retain ownership of their properties and pursue their missionary work, becoming ever more distant from the church based at St George's which was rooted in the concerns of its (mostly Palestinian) membership. As the occupation has become more permanent and more devastating to the Palestinians, the relationship between the diocese and Christ Church has continued to deteriorate.

Relations between the mainstream St George's tradition and the Israeli state have often been problematic, primarily because Palestinian Anglicans were often amongst those negatively impacted by the occupation. Two dominant strands are worth picking out here, both related to attempts at resisting the occupation as supported by the nationalist-religious element of Zionism (Prior's fourth phase).

The first is connected to Bishop Samir Kafity and his successor (and present incumbent), Bishop Riah Abu al-Assal, both of whom have sought to deepen links on all levels with other communities. Kafity travelled abroad regularly, and found willing and supportive audiences in many western countries. He also engaged with other local church representatives more frequently and more consistently than the Anglicans had done in the past, leading, for example, to joint condemnations with the Greek, Latin and Armenian heads of churches of the Israeli repression of the first Palestinian *intifada*.[42] The Anglicans, having avoided factional disputes over holy sites, were in a strong position to bring these previously antagonistic communities together in an attempt to prevent Israel dividing them and unilaterally appropriating ecclesiastical and other property. Abu al-Assal has been equally assiduous in pursuing this kind of link, regularly promoting joint Christmas and Easter messages with other church leaders, as well as finding other ways to act together in the face of a common oppressor.

The second significant Anglican element in countering the nationalist-religious tendency of Zionism that furthered the Israeli occupation of Palestinian territory was the creation of Sabeel. Na'im Ateek's groundbreaking book *Justice and only justice: a Palestinian Theology of Liberation*,[43] developed from an academic dissertation written in the early 1980s, envisaged new ways of thinking about theology in the context of the Israeli occupation and oppression. For example, the temptation to conflate 'Israeli' with 'Jewish' (in part as a result of the changes in Zionism that Prior identified) led some in the Palestinian Christian community to consider abandoning the use of the Old Testament; Ateek's book challenged this notion. Of course, this was not a new problem – Kenneth Cragg identified this as a key issue in 1969[44] – but Ateek, an Anglican priest, developed a framework in which this could be thought about and worked on, initiated by a conference in 1990 in Tantur, Bethlehem, that led to the creation of Sabeel, an ecumenical liberation theology centre. Connected to the mainstream churches, and with staff and members from various traditions, Sabeel seeks to encourage adults and youth to 'do' theology in their daily lives as they search for what God is saying to them. Without a theology that is biblically based and relevant to people's daily realities, it is difficult to maintain faith and hope under oppressive circumstances. Indeed, Palestinian Christians have plenty of political analysis but a shortage of theological anchoring. Yet, with organized opportunities for and training in theological reflection, they become empowered by the spirit of God and are filled with new vision. Agonizing over issues of justice and peace has become a theological necessity, not only a political one. Yet, with organized opportunities for and training in theological reflection, they become empowered by the Spirit of God and are filled with a new vision.[45]

Whilst the relationship between Ateek and the bishop is known to have had problematic moments, there can be no doubt that Sabeel's work has enriched the life of Ateek's own denomination, as well as that of other churches. Given the brutal nature of the Israeli occupation, Sabeel sometimes appears to find it easier to relate to international supporters than grassroots activists, but it is to be hoped that the vital connection to what is happening theologically 'on the ground' is not lost, for this would remove the raison d'être of Sabeel – and that would be a great loss to the Anglican and other traditions in the country.

A key element of Kafity's time as bishop was, as already mentioned, his pursuit of relationships with other local churches. One of the results of this was a partnership agreement with the Church of Scotland, initiated in 1992, which allows the development of co-operative work in certain areas, and can be seen as representing a way forward after the 1967 war. Having been cut off from most of the Christian communities in east Jerusalem and the West Bank from 1948–1967, the Church of Scotland in Israel did not find it straightforward to identify its role in the country: it could not leave since there was no indigenous Presbyterian church that could take on the institutions it owned, but equally it was not always sure what its role was in staying. Two key figures emerge in this context: the first is Rev. Robin Ross, who had been the minister in Tiberias and then moved on to become the Secretary of the Middle East and North Africa Committee for the Church. Ross' sensitivity to and understanding of local ecclesiastical contexts, and his ability to coherently relate his theological thinking to the wider political situation, matched similar skills in the second key person on the Scottish side of the partnership arrangement: Rev. Colin Morton, who at the time was the minister of St Andrew's Church in Jerusalem and later, in recognition of his close co-operation with St George's, became one of the only Presbyterians to also be made an Honorary Canon of the Cathedral.

The contemporary context

The move towards partnership helped the Church of Scotland to define more closely why it is in the Holy Land. An articulation of the Committee's aims dated July 2004 begins by stating that the Overseas Board (that the Committee is part of) 'is committed to giving support and encouragement – spiritual, moral and practical – to the Christian presence in Israel and Palestine'. It seeks to do this in a variety of ways, including:

> learning from the experience of the Christian people of the land ..., encouraging work towards justice, reconciliation, forgiveness and peace ..., praying with the peoples of the land ..., serving alongside the local Christian community ..., supporting constructive engagement with other faiths ..., pursuing and supporting non-violent efforts to end the illegal occupation ..., committing ... resources to ... support the Christian community ..., informing people in Scotland of the situation.[46]

On another level of the Church of Scotland, theological reflection on some of the relevant issues has recently come to the fore. The Board of World Mission (to all intents and purposes another name for the Overseas Board, which governs the work of the institutions in the Holy Land), the Panel on Doctrine (dedicated to theological reflection on issues central to faith), and the Committee on Church and Nation (working on the interface between theology and politics) recently produced a joint report entitled *Theology of Land and Covenant*. This covered a wide range of issues, without reaching a definitive doctrinal statement on the issue under discussion. In part, this derives from a diverse mix of representatives from the three participating groups within the church: from those explicitly supporting full and equal rights for both Palestinians and Israelis, to Christian Zionists who valued the position of Israel above all others. Whilst the inability of the group to reach a single conclusion could be construed as a cop out, it could also be understood as a positive sign: it reflects the diversity in the Church of Scotland, and theoretically should encourage further discussion on the issues raised.[47]

The Anglican Church, despite its small size, has clearly established a role for itself in the ecumenical context in Jerusalem. From Bishop Blyth's refusal to accept new members from other Christian churches, one can draw a clear line to the increasing respect given these churches by the Anglicans, and the reciprocity this brings with it. For example, the Anglicans are very clear to describe their bishop as the bishop *in* Jerusalem rather than *of* Jerusalem, acknowledging the primacy of the Greek Orthodox Patriarch as *the* bishop of Jerusalem.[48] Stefan Durst argues that even the position of St George's Cathedral is circumscribed by deference to the Holy Sepulchre: although St George's is described as a cathedral and has the status of a cathedral, it is the seat of the Greek Orthodox Patriarch that is *the* Cathedral of Jerusalem.[49] This acknowledgement of significant local relationships has put the Anglicans in a powerful position in the Holy Land, to the extent that in the recent crisis facing the Greek Orthodox Church over alleged improper land sales, the Anglicans, together with the local Catholic and Lutheran churches, offered to act as mediators.[50] This is indicative of a secure and stable relationship between one church tradition and another, and can be regarded as a significant achievement after less than two centuries in the region.

This integration into the local religious landscape has manifested itself in other ways too: it was the Protestant churches, first and foremost the Anglicans, who were behind the creation of the body that eventually became the Middle East Council of Churches (MECC). Indeed, between 1985 and 1994, Bishop Kafity was one of the three presidents of the MECC, a significant period in which the Council, for example, reflected in various ways on the implications of Israeli occupation of Palestinian territory and some of the theological issues arising from that.[51] However, even beyond this, the place of the Anglicans in one of the 'families of churches' of the MECC has been one of considerable importance.[52]

The ongoing division over the role of Christ Church vis-à-vis the wider work of the Anglican diocese represents an issue that is unlikely to be resolved in the immediate future. A recent example of the ongoing problems can be found in the context of the September 2004 Anglican Peace and Justice Network's *Statement on the Israeli/Palestinian Conflict*, which the bishop and other representatives of the Jerusalem diocese co-signed.[53] Describing Israeli occupation practices, and recognizing the imbalance of power inherent in the conflict, the Statement calls upon Israel to comply with international law regarding the occupation. It concludes by calling not only on the Anglican tradition to engage in 'focused and intentional prayer and advocacy for peace in the Holy Land', but also issues 'a call on the leadership of the Abrahamic Faiths' to 'exercise their authority and influence on the political leadership among the several nations who carry the responsibility for making a just peace.' This recognition of the role played by third parties in the conflict represents an opening for Anglicans worldwide to engage more fully in seeking a just resolution of the conflict. The *ITAC Response to the Anglican Peace & Justice Statement*,[54] authored by Tony Higton, the General Director of CMJ, condemns the Statement as 'biased and unjust'. The Response goes on to argue:

> If it really wants peace, the church should pray about and act upon the needs and failings of both sides in the conflict, without bias. It should be an agent of reconciliation, but that role is undermined by negative or biased criticism, which only fuels the fire. Prayer is vital because there is no obvious human solution to this conflict.

This last statement is perhaps the most telling part of the ITAC Response: it sees the conflict as an intrinsically insoluble situation, rather than recognizing it as a political conflict over land and hegemony, with the dominating power's political imperatives underpinned by religious sentiment (as Prior has shown). In subscribing to the Statement, the Diocese, consisting primarily of Palestinian Christians who are suffering the effects of Israel's occupation, clearly sees ways in which the conflict can be resolved, and thereby opens the way to engage more critically with the events of the day than Christ Church and the CMJ is able to do.

Conclusions

Using broad outlines of the historical links of the Anglican and Presbyterian churches to the Holy Land, I have sought to show how differently the two denominations have related to the environment they have engaged with.

Although the Anglicans face a complex internal situation with regard to the differences between the diocese and Christ Church, it is clear that the mainstream church, represented in the Jerusalem diocese, embodies a living faith tradition embedded in the context of Jerusalem and the Holy Land, a tradition that has adapted itself to the circumstances it has encountered, and that appears broadly comfortable with the role it plays in ecclesiastical life in the region. It is, of course, impossible to say how the

Anglican presence will develop: so much of the church's life in the past has been intimately connected to social and political circumstances beyond its control, and this is likely to continue. Although it would be foolish to diminish the risks to the church, not only from the Israeli oppression of its Palestinian membership, but also from the ever-growing emigration of Christians from the region,[55] it would appear that although the church is not numerically strong, it is well-equipped to deal with what may lie ahead. The indigenization of the church and its connection to the local community seems to have equipped it to deal with the challenges that lie ahead, and to do so at least as well as the more long-standing denominations in the region.

The Church of Scotland, which has not sought indigenization, has for some considerable time recognized the need to contextualize its work in the region. It has sought to do this in a number of ways. With the creation of the new 'Scots Hotel' in Tiberias, a rethinking of the priorities of the Church of Scotland in the Holy Land will undoubtedly become necessary, not least because the immense financial burdens the Tiberias enterprise appears to entail will be a drain on the Church's funds, which could otherwise be used in Scotland or in the wider world. To prevent the protests that have already been raised about this from growing will require theological as well as financial reflection. For example, in relation to the stated desire to pursue 'non-violent efforts to end the illegal occupation': does the Tiberias centre have a theological (and financially acceptable) role to play in this? The challenge for the Church at the present time is to reflect and work on ways in which these issues can be dealt with in a meaningful way, since, for example, there does not appear to be a structured context for reflecting on these matters in a wider context. Very practical questions arise here, such as: at a time when there is growing international awareness of the economic and political pressure that can be brought to bear on Israeli occupation policies by boycotting Israeli settlement goods, the fact that the Scots Hotel sells wines from the occupied Golan Heights is regarded by many in Scotland and elsewhere as severely problematic.[56] Another difficult issue is suggested by the fact that the Scots Hotel website is only available in English and Hebrew – but not in Arabic, suggesting a lack of interest in relating to Palestinian Christians.

The Anglican partners are currently pressing for greater involvement on this wider potential role, but one might detect a certain hesitancy on the part of the Church of Scotland to act decisively in favour of such a commitment, despite the proclaimed intent. The challenge for the Church of Scotland at the present time is perhaps to reflect and work on ways in which these issues can be dealt with in a meaningful way, since, for example, there does not appear to be a structured method for reflecting on these matters in a wider context. The second *intifada* has resulted in a dearth of visitors from abroad and whilst the appointed staff have tried in various creative ways to work through what it means to be a small church operating with a limited local base, it is not at all clear that the mechanisms and structures are in place to guide the church's developing role and to engage with the theological issues that present themselves given their financial and practical obligations and expressions of intent. Despite these problems, the Church of Scotland is clearly still very much part of the process of reflection and action in relation to the Holy Land, and whilst it remains to be seen where this will lead in the future, continued contextualization of its work is clearly a priority for its work in the region.

Both of these churches initiated their work in the region with relatively similar motivations. However, their different approaches to the local population in the past stem from wider understandings of ecclesiology and missionary purpose that go beyond the scope of this essay; there is room for interesting comparative work to be done here. These two approaches have led to a contemporary situation where both indigenization and contextualization represent viable modes of engaging with the complex political, ecclesial, social and economic circumstances that they find themselves in. It is particularly interesting to note the partnership that they have engaged in together, suggesting that both forms of engagement have something important to offer their constituencies. Creative exploration, separately and together, of the opportunities available to them in relation to the other religious and political actors, make for a creative witness to the theological and ethical values they stand for.

Notes

1 David Bebbington, *Evangelicalism in Modern Britain. A history from the 1730s to the 1980s*, London/New York, 1989; p. 99; chapter 3 as a whole provides an excellent overview of Evangelical thinking in the early part of the 19th century.
2 Ian Bradley, *Abide with me. The world of Victorian hymns*, London, 1997, p. 120.
3 Andrew Bruce Davidson, *Old Testament Prophecy*, J. A. Paterson (ed.), Edinburgh, 1903, p. 483.
4 Bebbington describes millenarianism, pre-millenarianism and post-millenar-

ianism, linking these to pessimism and optimism in viewing world affairs: pp. 81–6, 60–3, 102–4 respectively; c.f. pp. 191–4 for the period around the First World War; see also Clyde Binfield, 'Jews in Evangelical Dissent: The British Society, The Herschell Connection and the Pre-Millenarian Thread', in *Prophecy and Eschatology*, series: *Subsidia vol. 10*, Michael Wilks (ed.), Oxford, 1994, pp. 225–70, 233–37.

5 On the influential role played by Scots in London on theology in both Scotland and England, c.f. George C. Cameron, *The Scots Kirk in London*, Oxford, 1979: particularly pp. 107–10 (on Edward Irving) and more generally chapters 8–10.

6 The first chapter of my book offers an exposition of 'the Jews' as a construct in this time; *Attempting to bring the gospel home. Scottish missions to Palestine 1839–1917*, London, 2006. Here, I use inverted commas to signify the particularity of the term.

7 For a later example of similar sentiments c.f. A. J. Sherman, *Mandate Days. British Lives in Palestine 1918–1948*, London, 1997, p. 16. Such thinking permeates all aspects of a culture and is reflected not just in an overtly religious context: Bryan Cheyette examines the literary links to Judaism in the context of 'race' in *Constructions of 'the Jew' in English literature and society: racial representations, 1875–1945*, Cambridge, 1993.

8 Staying overnight in Rosetta, the 1839 Scottish delegation sent to examine the prospects for Jewish missionary work in Palestine noted: 'All was now truly oriental, and the scenery of the Arabian Nights occurred vividly to our mind' – Andrew A Bonar and Robert Murray McCheyne, *Narrative of a Visit to the Holy Land and Mission of Inquiry to the Jews*, Edinburgh, 1843, p. 55. On the confusion of 'the real East with the East of the stories' (Rana Kabbani, *Imperial Fictions. Europe's Myths of Orient*, London, 1986, 1994, p. 29), including an examination of the *'alf layla was layla* and Galland's text, see Kabbani's section on the 'Arabian Nights', pp. 23–36.

9 The term is used by Linda Colley: Britons saw themselves as 'a distinct and chosen people…[For] most Victorians, the massive overseas empire which was the fruit of so much successful warfare represented final and conclusive proof of Great Britain's providential destiny. God had entrusted Britons with empire, they believed, so as to further the worldwide spread of the Gospel and as a testimony to their status as the Protestant Israel.' *Britons: Forging the Nation. 1707–1837*, London, 1992, p. 388.

10 Binfield, 1994, p. 226.

11 Binfield, Ibid., the title of a publication from 1890, printed in Beirut, indicates general Evangelical thought at this time: *The Everlasting Nation: An International Monthly Journal of History, Biography, Prophecy, Literature, Exegesis, and Passing Events Relating to the Jewish People*.

12 Davidson, 1903, gives an overview in his chapter on 'The Restoration of the Jews'.

13 CMS records cited by Abdul Latif Tibawi, *British Interests in Palestine, 1800–1901*, Oxford, 1961, p. 21.

14 Anthony O'Mahony expounds on this in 'The Christian Communities of Jerusalem and the Holy Land: A Historical and Political Survey', in *The Christian Communities of Jerusalem and the Holy Land. Studies in History, Religion and Politics*, Anthony O'Mahony (ed.), Cardiff, 2003, pp. 1–37, 5–10.

15 Children of a Christian/Muslim marriage would automatically be Muslim. More generally, 'The legally tolerated status of *dhimma* … established a

'default' position which amounted to gentle but relentless pressure in smaller internal communities to become Muslim and legitimised a generally hostile attitude to Christians outside the Muslim realms'; Jørgen S Nielsen, 'Is there an escape from the history of Christian-Muslim Relations?' in, *A Faithful Presence: essays for Kenneth Cragg*, David Thomas with Clare Amos (eds), London, 2003, pp. 350–61, 352. This was part of a more general condemnation of Christianity, Nielsen argues on the previous page.

16 Tibawi, 1961 p. 23. Of course, whilst Eastern Christians were seen merely as errant brothers, Muslims were seen as followers of a false prophet, and Islam as a faith tradition was viewed with considerable hostility.

17 For details of the Anglicans' approach, see Tibawi and more recently Rafiq A Farah, *In troubled waters. A History of the Anglican Church in Jerusalem 1841–1998*, Leicester, 2002; for the mandate period, Inger Marie Okkenhaug provides an excellent overview of Anglican work in *The Quality of Heroic Living, of High Endeavour and Adventure. Anglican Mission, Women and Education in Palestine, 1888–1948*, series *Studies in Christian Mission*, Marc R. Spindler (ed.), Leiden, 2002; on the Scots' approach, see Marten, 2005.

18 The uniqueness of the position was further underlined by the need for an Act of Parliament to allow the ordination of a bishop to a non-British territory; Farah, 2002, p. 26. Charlotte van der Leest has described how the second bishop, Samuel Gobat, changed the priorities of his post and focused much of his attention on the local Christian communities; 'The Protestant Bishopric of Jerusalem and the Missionary Activities in Nazareth: The Gobat years (1846–1879)', in *Christian witness between continuity and new beginnings: modern historical missions in the Middle East*, eds. Michael Marten/Martin Tamcke, series: *Studien zur Orientalischen Kirchengeschichte*, ed. Martin Tamcke Hamburg, 2006, pp. 199–211.

19 Tibawi, 1961, p. 15 indicates some of the supporters of the LJS, pp. 32–33 outlines the instructions given to Young.

20 Though there had been other high-ranking appointments of Palestinians prior to this, including Najib Cubain's appointment as bishop for Jordan, Lebanon and Syria in 1957, Haddad was the first Palestinian bishop to oversee the entire territory.

21 When I visited Christ Church in May 2001 and asked Kelvin Crombie, who kindly gave of his time to meet me, about relationships to the diocese, he commented scathingly that 'the Arab bishop' had no 'real' authority over their work because the Cathedral had departed from the original purposes of Anglican work in the region – a contentious interpretation of the historical record, to say the least. His book represents a similar perspective on relations with the diocese: see, for example, his denunciation of Assistant Bishop Elias Khoury as a 'PLO Bishop': *For the Love of Zion. Christian witness and the restoration of Israel*, London, 1991, p. 254 (and the full title of the chapter).

22 Details taken from the diocesan website: *The Episcopal Diocese of Jerusalem – Institutes – Diocesan Offices*, http://www.j-diocese.com/main.html (accessed 17 January 2006).

23 The Tiberias and Hebron hospitals were operated by the (United) Free Church of Scotland, which had split from the main Church of Scotland in 1843. In 1929, the two churches reunited. J. H. S. Burleigh describes the labyrinthine processes of Scottish disunity and reunification in considerable

detail in *A Church History of Scotland*, Oxford, 1960; see especially Part IV.iv – Part V.

24 The hospital was converted to a pilgrims' guest house a few years after the State of Israel was founded.

25 Of course, there are many other connections to Jerusalem and the Holy Land which cannot be elaborated on here in any detail. Examples would include the 'Protestant Holy Sepulchre', the Garden Tomb, as well as the work of the Palestine Exploration Fund, which had numerous connections to Protestant individuals and thought. See on these topics Sarah Kochav, 'The Search for a Protestant Holy Sepulchre: The Garden Tomb in Nineteenth-Century Jerusalem', in *Journal of Ecclesiastical History*, vol. 46, no. 2, April 1995, pp. 278–301, and John James Moscrop, *Measuring Jerusalem. The Palestine Exploration Fund and British Interests in the Holy Land*, London/New York, 2000.

26 It should be noted that this was not as straightforward as it may seem, with CMS missionaries mistrusting local priests: Farah, 2002, p. 53.

27 Farah, 2002, p. 130; Daphne Tsimhoni, *Christian Communities in Jerusalem and the West Bank Since 1948*, Westport/London, 1993, pp. 140–1.

28 Thomas Hummel, 'Between Eastern and Western Christendom: The Anglican Presence in Jerusalem', in *The Christian Communities of Jerusalem and the Holy Land. Studies in History, Religion and Politics*, Anthony O'Mahony (ed.), Cardiff, 2003, pp. 147–70, 166.

29 Robert Deans Kernohan, *Scotland's Life and Work. A Scottish view of God's world through* Life and Work: *1879–1979*, Edinburgh, 1979, p. 177.

30 The Church of Scotland's magazine, *Life & Work*, recorded Robert Mackie, a Church of Scotland minister who was also the WCC's director of the Inter-Church Aid and Refugee Department, visiting Tiberias in 1951 and seeing rows and rows of huts to house Yemeni Jews; Kernohan, 1979, p. 177.

31 As well as considerable debate about this issue within the Church of Scotland, the mainstream media have also reported on it; see for example: Jenifer Johnston, 'Church's hotel in Israel "taking cash away from HIV/Aids work in Africa"', *The Sunday Herald*, 1 May 2005, www.sundayherald.com/49539 (accessed 17 January 2006).

32 Colin Morton, 'Motives for the Scottish Mission in Palestine. 19th and 20th Centuries', in *Patterns of the Past, Prospects for the Future. The Christian Heritage in the Holy Land*, London, 1999, pp. 213–18, 217.

33 Michael Prior describes and analyses the main myths in the seventh chapter of *Zionism and the State of Israel: a Moral Inquiry*, London/New York, 1999.

34 R Clephane Macanna, 'The Emergence of the State of Israel and its Significance for the Christian Church', in *The Church and the Jewish People*, ed. Göte Hedenquist, London, 1954, 77–90 p. 85.

35 Macanna, 1954 p. 86.

36 Macanna, 1954 pp. 87, 89.

37 Prior, 1999: chapters 1 and 3 provide the basis of this assessment.

38 One of the best expositions of this is Prior, 1999: chapter 3. Uri Ram uses the term 'Neo-Zionism' to describe some of these elements: 'From Nation-State to Nation——State: Nation, History and Identity Struggles in Jewish Israel', in *The Challenge of Post-Zionism: Alternatives to Israeli Fundamentalist Politics*, ed. Ephraim Nimni, London/New York, 2003, pp. 20–41, 27.

39 Prior, 1999, p. 83.

40 Tsimhoni, 1993, p. 146.

41 Farah, 2002, p. 147.
42 Hummel, 2003, p. 167.
43 Published in New York, 1989.
44 Kenneth Cragg, 'The Anglican Church', in *Religion in the Middle East. Three Religions in Concord and Conflict*, vol. 1, *Judaism and Christianity*, A. J. Arberry (ed.), Cambridge, 1969, pp. 570–95, 587–9.
45 'Sabeel Center', *Sabeel Palestinian Liberation Theology Center*, 27 October 2003, www.sabeel.org/?page=article&id=11 (accessed 10 May 2005).
46 The Church of Scotland Overseas Board, *Middle East Committee. Israel and Palestine: Aims & Objectives*, July 2004.
47 *Theology of Land and Covenant*, a report presented to the General Assembly of the Church of Scotland by a joint Study Group from the Board of World Mission, the Panel on Doctrine and the Committee on Church and Nation in May 2003. Unfortunately, although it provided a strong basis for discussion, this generally did not take place in the context of the wider Church of Scotland, since it was buried in a volume of committee reports from all branches of the church and never reprinted in separate form. It is, however, available on request from the Church offices, and Rev. Clarence Musgrave, at the time minister in Jerusalem, reported that the report has been debated in churches in the Holy Land, with positive feedback regarding its usefulness and clarity. A level of personal interest in this should be declared here: my wife, Rev. Sigrid Marten, was one of the Committee on Church and Nation representatives on the Study Group.
48 This is clearly stated on the Diocesan website, where reference is made to the 'Bishop in Jerusalem': 'Parishes and Institutions', *The Episcopal Diocese of Jerusalem*, www.jerusalem.anglican.org/p_and_i_ny.htm (accessed 9 May 2005).
49 Stefan Durst, *Jerusalem als ökumenisches Problem im 20. Jahrhundert*, Pfaffenweiler, 1993, p. 170.
50 'Anglicans, Catholics, Lutherans ready to mediate in Jerusalem', *Ecumenical News International*, ENI-05-0337, 9 May 2005, www.eni.ch/highlights/news.shtml?2005/05 (accessed 17 January 2006).
51 For example, the Middle East Council of Churches publication on Christian Zionism: *What is Western Fundamentalist Christian Zionism?*, Limassol, 1988.
52 Uwe Gräbe has described elements of this: 'Mission and Proselytism as a Historical Background to a Contemporary Reformulation of Christian "Presence and Witness" in the Middle East', in Marten/Tamcke, 2006, pp. 247–54.
53 This is available in a number of places online, but the Jerusalem diocesan website version is perhaps most useful as it incorporates a full list of signatories: 'Anglican Peace and Justice Network Statement on the Israeli/Palestinian Conflict', *The Episcopal Diocese of Jerusalem – Diocesan News*, 22 Spetember 2004, www.j-diocese.com/DiocesanNews/view.asp?selected=169#slbl169 (accessed 17 January 2006).
54 'ITAC Response to the Anglican Peace & Justice Statement', *The Church's Ministry among Jewish people – www.cmj.org.uk*, undated, www.cmj.org.uk/rep2APJN.html (accessed 9 May 2005).
55 These two problems are, of course, linked, though the emigration of Christians from the Middle East has other reasons too, which cannot be developed here.
56 The sale of these wines is clearly described on the website as a positive thing.

The problem increases since the website implies that the wines sold are all 'Galilee area' wines, a turn of phrase that appears to be intended to deliberately mislead, since only some of them fall into this category: 'The cellar contains wines from boutique wineries in the Galilee area, including from Chateau Golan, Dalton, Tabor and the Golan Wineries...'; 'The Scots Hotel – Wine Cellar', The Scots Hotel – Tiberias – Galilee, http://www.scotshotels.co.il/wine_cellar.html (accessed 12 March 2009).

Chapter 7

Jewish Fundamentalism, the *Halacha* and the Palestinian Christians: the use of Maimonides's Theology in Modern Israel (1967–2003)

Nur Masalha

Introduction

Over the past two decades the study of religious fundamentalism and politics – and especially of the impact of the first on the second – has witnessed a renaissance.[1] This study is not on Moses Maimonides (1135–1204) or the Jewish religious law (*halacha*) as such. It rather focuses on two currents of Jewish fundamentalist theology in Israel: the Zionist messianic theology and the theology of the ultra-orthodox *haredi* rabbis,[2] both Sephardi and Ashkenazi. It explores the doctrinal differences between these two concerning the 'messianic doctrine', their attitudes towards the Palestinian Christians and their impact on Israeli domestic and foreign policies. The two strands invoke the interpretation of the Jewish *halacha* of Maimonides to justify their respective attitudes towards the Palestinian Christians. This chapter, in particular, explores the contemporary use of Maimonides – one of the most illustrious examples of classical Islam and the age of Arabo-Jewish-Islamic symbioses – by Jewish fundamentalists[3] who metamorphosed him from an enlightened medieval philosopher into a Neo-Zionist and an anti-Arab religious zealot.

There is neither a unified Jewish fundamentalist discourse in Israel nor a monolithic attitude towards Maimonides. Both doctrinally and politically, Israeli religious fundamentalists are not a homogeneous group, and their interpretative use of Maimonides' theology varies from one group to another for political and ideological reasons. Both the National Religious Party (NRP or Mifdal) and *Gush Emunim* represent fundamentalist Jews who are not *haredim*. The following will examine the theological roots of the hostile attitudes to Christianity, its symbols and followers in the Holy Land, adopted by both the Zionist religious camp and the rabbis of the ultra-orthodox *haredim* in the post-1967 period. I will show how the two main currents of Jewish fundamentalism in Israel (militant Zionist and orthodox non-Zionist) justify these attitudes by relying on Maimonides's theological orthodoxy and conservative interpretation of the Jewish *halacha*.

Zionism gave rise to three main offshoots: secular statist (labour), right-wing revisionist, and messianic religious. Beside the common goal of establishing a Jewish state in Palestine, each branch formed a slightly different agenda and strove towards different goals. On the whole, however, political Zionism emerged in Europe in the late nineteenth century with frequently anti-religious dispositions. Although the Hebrew Bible was always in the background as a support, the Jewish state would not be a theocracy. However after the establishment of Israel in 1948 Jewish orthodox religious opposition to political Zionism was on the wane and the rising religious Zionism reflected a radical shift from an orthodox Jewish theology of Diaspora to a settler (Jewish) theology of emigration, conquest and settlement of the 'land of Israel.' While in Diaspora Judaism the concept of the 'land' had largely religious connotations of sanctity and piety, the discourse of both secular and religious Zionism has radically altered the meaning of the land from its traditional religious connotations into its modern Zionist perception, reinventing Judaism and investing it with a new nationalist (settler) tradition of 'land of Israel' and 'the people of Israel'. This settler (Zionist) Judaism was further redefined after the 1967 war – an event which turned out to be a watershed in Israeli history with a profound effect on the country's secular and religious camps. Even for many secular Israelis, who were indifferent to religion until then, the conquest of the West Bank and other Arab territories in 1967 represented a conversion of mystical experience. The war gave huge impetus to religious Zionism, or Neo-Zionism, and the spectacular conquests generated feverish religious messianism and gave rise to a new fundamentalist theology. In the wake of 1967 and the dramatic rise of religious Zionism, the role of the biblical narrative within the Zionist ideology and land settlement increased significantly.[4] Since 1967 the rising religious Zionism, often described as the messianic redemptionist or fundamentalist trend, has transposed the rhetoric of early Zionism from a secular aspiration to create a sovereign 'state for the Jews' to the apocalyptic vision of redeeming the 'whole land of Israel' and the establishment of a theocratic monarchy. Jewish fundamentalism in Israel has developed into a major political and cultural force, with a considerable influence on the attitudes, commitments, and votes of a large number of Israelis.[5]

Several Israeli scholars, who have documented the growth of Jewish fundamentalism in Israel since 1967, have observed a strong element of religious coercion. Already in 1965 a prominent Israeli historian, Professor Ya'acov Talmon, observed the major religious role in the Israeli state and society:

> In Israel today, the Rabbinate is rapidly developing into a firmly institutionalized Church imposing an exacting discipline on its members and facing the general body of laymen as a distinct power. This is not a religious development, but, ironically enough, the outcome of the emergence of the [Jewish] State. The latter has given birth and legitimacy to an established Church.[6]

Talmon pointed out that none of this has roots in Jewish tradition. The theocratic elements in Israeli state and society are often explained in terms of the problems of coalition politics, but the socio-political and cultural reasons are much deeper. Such a theocratic development is hardly surprising in a society in which some basis must be established – in state ideology, cultural attitude, and law – to distinguish the privileged and dominant Jewish population from the non-Jewish citizens of Israel.[7]

In fact until 1967 religious Zionism remained relatively pragmatic in its demand to apply the *halacha* within Israel as well as in foreign affairs. Since 1967, as Israeli scholars (including Yehoshafat Harkabi, Yesha'ayahu Leibowitz, Ehud Sprinzak, Avi'ezer Ravitzky, Uriel Tal) have pointed out, militant religious Zionism has become central to Israel's domestic and foreign policies. The relationship between Jewish religion and Israeli politics has become more intimate: a spreading new theology deployed in the service of settler colonial policies, and Zionist nationalist policies as the implementation of Jewish religious commandments (*mitzvot*) and Jewish theocracy.[8] In 1995, when former President Yitzhak Navon expressed the view that 'there are things to which the *halacha* is not relevant', former Chief Rabbi Avraham Shapira replied: 'Everything is *halacha*.'[9] This fundamentalist theology finds its organized focus in the Zionist religious camp, especially the National Religious Party and the highly influential settlement movement of *Gush Emunim* ('The Bloc of Faithful').

Being the most palpable expression of the new wave of religious messianism that has been sweeping through considerable segments of Israeli society since 1967, *Gush Emunim* leads a 'holy' crusade to 'redeem and settle the whole land of Israel' and activates the entire panorama of Jewish fundamentalists and secular ultra-nationalists, including some of Israel's most powerful leaders.[10] Its theology combines a potent mixture of religious messianism and fascist nationalism and the pronouncements of its rabbis and lay leaders are not limited to the strategic objective of utilizing Jewish settlements to keep control of the occupied territories. The paramount objective of the *Gush Emunim* leaders is to create in their homogeneous settlements models of a new religious society governed by the *halacha* – a society that would spread and eventually absorb the entire Israeli Jewish society, secular, traditional and religious.[11] In their interpretation of the *halacha Gush Emunim* and other Jewish fundamentalist groups make every effort to entrench the notions of inequality and supremacy as the paramount principles defining Jewish relations with non-Jews in the Holy Land.

Gush Emunim has been the most successful extra-parliamentary movement to arise in Israel since 1948 and has had a profound influence upon the Israeli political system.[12] Its practical settlement of the West Bank has been the main vehicle of the political success of Jewish fundamentalism inside Israel. Of *Gush Emunim*, Professor Ehud Sprinzak of the Hebrew University of Jerusalem, writes, 'It is still a very dynamic force, by far the most viable component of the radical right. It may also be the most effective social movement that has emerged in Israel since 1948.'[13] Its rabbis and leaders are predominantly middle class, educated Ashkenazi Zionist Jews. The *Gush Emunim's* single most influential ideologue was Rabbi Tzvi Yehuda Kook (1890–1982), who was the head of Merkaz Harav Yeshiva in Jerusalem – and the son of the first Chief Ashkenazi Rabbi of the Jewish Yishuv in Mandatory Palestine, Rabbi Abraham Yitzhak HaCohen Kook (1865–1935). The latter (often referred to as 'Rabbi Kook the elder') was a prolific author, the founder of the Zionist religious and messianic ideology, and Palestine Chief Rabbi between 1920 and 1935. He was a key figure in accommodating the ideology of secular Zionism to classical Jewish orthodoxy, and is held in great regard not only by *Gush Emunim* but also by many secular Zionists. Most of the *Gush Emunim* rabbis and ideologists are influential figures within the mainstream religious population and beyond and their demand that the *halacha* guide official policies towards the Palestinian population (Muslims and Christians) is widely accepted in religious circles and parties. Moreover the fundamentalist settlers of *Gush Emunim* have always had a disproportionate impact on the official policies of successive Israeli governments. Formally established in February 1974 and wielding tremendous influence over the Likud administrations of Menahem Begin, Yitzhak Shamir, Binyamin Netanyahu and Ariel Sharon, *Gush Emunim* has played a key role in establishing dozens of Jewish settlements throughout the occupied West Bank. The settlements are designed to prevent any territorial concessions in the West Bank or any other areas deemed as being part of the 'divinely ordained land of Israel'.

Among the three main religious communities in the Holy Land, the Christian community is the smallest and weakest. However, Palestinian Christians are an integral part of the Palestinian people. Despite their religious identity as Christians, their national identity is as part of the Palestinian Arab culture and heritage. Palestinian Christians, like Palestinian Muslims, were victims of the 1948 war, the birth of Israel and the expulsion of the Palestinians. 60% of the Palestinian Christians were driven out of what became Israel in 1948. Many of the 418 Arab villages destroyed in 1948 had a mix of Christian and Muslim inhabitants. Many churches and mosques in these villages were also levelled. Also in 1948 23,000 Palestinian Christians were expelled along with 22,000 Palestinian Muslims from the Arab neighbourhoods and villages of west Jerusalem. It is hardly surprising, therefore, that, in the wake of the 1948 war, the number of Palestinian Christians has dwindled drastically and it continues to drop steadily through emigration, as a result of the continuing political conflict and economic instability in the Holy Land.[14]

Despite the small numbers of Palestinian Christians still living in the Holy Land, their presence among the Palestinian people as a whole (in the occupied territories and among the senior officials of the Palestinian Authority (PA), in the Diaspora and among the Palestinian citizens of Israel) is strongly felt qualitatively. In the Palestinian Legislative Council and among the most senior officials of the PA, a good number are Christians. And for the time being, in the territories under the PA control, Christmas, New Year, and Easter have been recognized as official holidays. An outsider visiting the Holy Land would find it hard to distinguish between the Palestinian Christian and Muslim. In spite of this reality, much attention has been devoted in recent years to the 'Islamic threat' to the Christians of the Holy Land. By contrast little research has been carried on the attitudes of the Israeli Jewish fundamentalist groups towards the Palestinian Christians, particularly the use and abuse of Moses Maimonides's theology to justify attacks on Christianity in the Holy Land.

Maimonides: A Jewish Nationalist?

The struggle between Zionist religious nationalists and Arab authors over the celebrated medieval philosopher and theologian Moses Maimonides is one of the most extraordinary episodes of intellectual conflicts in modern times. Now commonly known by the name Maimonides, he is widely recognized as Judaism's greatest theologian. A popular Jewish saying, 'From Moses to Moses there was none like Moses [Maimonides],' expresses the eminent position he has always held in Jewish estimation. In 1985 various conferences were held in Israel and among Jewish communities in the West to commemorate 850 years since the birth of Maimonides. These meetings dealt with his intellectual contribution and considered their relevance for contemporary Jewish thought and practice. Maimonides was never merely a Jewish philosopher in some narrow sense; he was a distinguished medieval rationalist philosopher and the most illustrious example of Arabo-Islamic-Judaic symbiosis of the twelfth century. Modern Arab historians have tended to portray Maimonides not only as a product of Arabo-Islamic-Jewish culture of the twelfth century but have also assessed his work within the context of the chronicles of Arab history itself. In *History of the Arabs*, Philip Hitti, while acknowledging his Jewish background, included Maimonides in the distinguished group of 'Spanish Arab physicians who were physicians by avocation and something else by vocation' and called him Abu 'Imran Ibn Maymun in the Arabic form of his name:

> For first place after ibn-Rushd [Averroes, 1126–1198] among the philosophers of the age the only candidate is his Jewish contemporary and fellow Cordovan ... Maimonides ..., the most famous of the Hebrew physicians and philosophers of the whole Arabic epoch.[15]

More recently several Arab authors described Musa Ibn Maymun as an Arab-Muslim thinker and philosopher.[16]

Ironically, however, in modern day-Israel Maimonides has become the hero of messianic religious Zionism and anti-Arab

Jewish fundamentalism. Maimonides's medieval orthodoxy and contemporary Israeli Jewish fundamentalism have completely different historical contexts and proper settings. Maimonides was neither an Arab nationalist nor a Zionist Jew; he was a man of his medieval time and tradition. To begin with, the religious relationship of medieval Diaspora Jews to the land had little to do with modern Jewish nationalism, neither secular nor religious Zionism. Religious Zionism and *Gush Emunim* have made the sanctity of the 'whole land of Israel' a central tenet of their doctrine and a prime object of their religious passion. Yet for Maimonides the 'land of Israel' was of itself no different from other lands. It was distinctive, however, only because it was sanctified by the Commandments and by events of Israelite history. For him the land was not an object of passion; it wasn't a territory or land that demarcated the cultural identity of Diaspora Judaism. His medieval theology had little to do with modern Zionist nationalism or feverish religious messianism. His theology, which preceded Zionist nationalist idea by 700 years, reflected a confident Jewish religious and social identity away from the 'land of Israel'; returning to, and colonization of, the 'land of Israel' did not constitute the great hope of the Jewish people. Flourishing Jewish identity and culture was safeguarded in an accommodation with the Arab-Muslim civilization. Born in Muslim Spain, Maimonides passed through the land on his way to Muslim Egypt and lived his entire life in the Diaspora;[17] for him Jewish relationship to the 'land of Israel' resembled Muslim relationship to Hijaz and the holy cities of Mecca and Madina.

Maimonides's halachic orthodoxy was particularly illustrated in his typically medievalist approach to Christianity, which he described as "*avoda zara*' ('strange worship' or false worship') and a form of 'idolatry'. However I will show that Maimonides's strict orthodoxy was a product of distinct historical settings and must always be located, studied and understood within its proper medieval context. I will also assess the impact of the growth of anti-Christian theology in Israel, combined with the rise of radical Jewish fundamentalism, on inter-faith relations in Israel and Palestine. The doctrinal differences and dispute between the two fundamentalist varieties over the 'messianic doctrine' and their impact on Israeli foreign and domestic policies will also be considered. I am not a scholar of Maimonides's theology or the Jewish religion and do not offer a new interpretation of classical Jewish religious attitudes towards the Palestinian Christians. My primary concern is to explore the religious fundamentalist manifestations by highly influential segments of the various religious camps in

Israel. It should also be pointed out that where traditional and medieval Jewish sources (especially Maimonides's writings and theology) are quoted, they are quoted because they are widely cited by both orthodox Jews and Israeli-Jewish religious nationalists.

The Medieval Context

Europeans called him Maimonides, the Arabs Musa Ibn Maymun and in rabbinical literature he is named the Rambam, an acronym from Rabbi Moshe ben Maimon. He is generally recognized as Judaism's greatest theologian and halachic authority.[18] He also distinguished himself as an astronomer, physician and above all as a rational philosopher and became the most illustrious example of the Arab-Islamic-Judaic symbiosis of the late Middle Ages. Today he is generally recognized as the most important codifier of Jewish law and as one of the most radical philosophers of the Islamic world. Perceived as the peak and pinnacle of Jewish scholarship and sagacity over the ages, Maimonides was linked in Jewish folksayings to Moses himself. Moses gave the *Torah* and Maimonides gave the *Torah Mishneh*, the second or additional legal code, by which orthodox Jews have conducted their normative religious life for the last 800 years. In the modern era, Maimonides became a hero in Reform Judaism.

Born in 1135 in Cordoba, capital of Muslim Spain, Maimonides's family left the country in the aftermath of the conquest of Cordoba by the Islamic sect *al-Muwahhid*, and lived some time in Fez in Morocco. He emigrated, when in his thirties, to Egypt, where he lived in Fostat, south of Cairo, for most of his life and died in 1204. It is believed that he served as the court physician to Saladin (*sultan* Salah al-Din) and his son al-Malik al-Aziz.[19] Classical orthodox Judaism and the Arabo-Islamic culture were the contexts within which Maimonides worked, although most accounts of his thought are unduly obsessed with his Jewish background and fail to do justice to the outstanding part he played in the development of medieval Arabic thought and culture and Islamic civilization. He was an orthodox rabbi and the leader of his community, but, in philosophical terms, it would be misleading to think of Maimonides as being a specifically Jewish philosopher.[20] Of far more importance when we come to his philosophy is the influence of the tradition of philosophy in the Islamic world. He was a member of a distinguished group of thinkers in the Islamic world who took on board the methodology of Aristotle and applied it to difficult conceptual issues in interesting and perceptive ways.[21] He was highly influenced by the philosophical doctrines of Ibn Sina (Avicenna) and Alfarabi, two of the most famous and greatest medieval Muslim philosophers and his philosophy was a grandiose attempt at a synthesis between the Jewish faith (a monotheistic 'revealed' faith) and rational Greek-Arabic Aristotelian philosophy.

Maimonides, his son Abraham, Sa'adia Gaon and many other famous Jewish personalities were the product of the 'Arabo-Judaic culture' of the Middle Ages and the embodiment of its rational flowering.[22] For the medieval Muslims, Jews and Christians were 'People of the Book' (*ahl al-Kitab*) and as such entitled to religious tolerance and protection within the Islamic community under the covenant (*dhimma*). The Islamic doctrine proudly proclaimed its Judaeo-Christian descent and the Quran, although introducing significant modifications into the biblical narrative, affirmed Islam's adherence to the classical Abrahamic orthodoxy.[23] In the Middle Ages as a whole the position of Jews under Arab Islam was far better than that of the Jews in medieval Christian Europe.[24] The medical professional in Muslim countries was held in high esteem and Jewish doctors are known to have been court physicians to caliphs and other Muslim rulers in practically every Muslim country. Reading Arabic sources on the history of medicine, for example, Ibn Abi Usayba, a colleague of Maimonides's son and successor, Abraham, one is impressed by the spirit of true fellowship which bound together the doctors of various denominations of that time.[25] An observant Jew and a famous doctor, Maimonides was a good example of Jews reaching the highest government posts in Muslim countries. Maimonides's descendants occupied the office of *nagid* (in Arabic *Ras al-Millah*), or head of the Jewish community in Egypt for almost two centuries.

In the Middle Ages the Arab-Islamic civilization linked Hellenic-Roman antiquity with modern times. Its dominant religion was Islam, its language was Arabic. Arabic had ceased to be an ethnic language and became the language of a civilization. Jews and Christians unhesitatingly used Arabic even while expounding sacred topics to their co-religionists. Maimonides's philosophy and theology drew freely and copiously from Muslim civilization and he must have regarded Islam from the flesh and bone of Judaism.[26] Under Islam the Jewish *dhimmi* was permitted to maintain his religious and cultural autonomy and Maimonides's theology is an illustrious example of Arab Judaism and the fact that Judaism inside Islam was an autonomous culture sure of itself despite, and possibly because of, its intimate connection with its Arabo-Islamic environment. Maimonides's generally positive attitudes towards Islam, are often contrasted with his relative hostility towards Christianity which, together with the Greek New Testament, were perceived as at variance with the orthodox Jewish religious culture, while Islam and the Quran, within the context of the Arabo-Jewish symbiosis of the time, were perceived as closely related to Judaism.

Tolerant Muslim pluralism and linguistic integration laid the ground for an extraordinary intellectual symbiosis in which Muslims, Jews and Christians joined together in the discovery, study, imitation, and illustration of Hellenistic philosophy in what Franz Rosenthal called 'the classical heritage of Islam'.[27] This intellectual renaissance created a new theology (*kalam*, in Arabic; *mutakallimun*, theologians) designed to make religious law and philosophy coincide: to rationalize divine Revelation and show that it was in harmony with logic and the natural order. The most basic aspect of the Arab-Jewish symbiosis is the fact that the great majority of Jews adopted the Arabic language, while Hebrew not only retained its position as a second and literary language, but also experienced an unprecedented revival. Writing in literary Arabic, Maimonides justified this: 'Anyone who knows the three languages, Hebrew, Aramaic and Arabic – knows that they are only three branches of one and the same language.'[28] The acquisition of the Arabic language by the Jews meant also their adoption of Arab ways of thinking and forms of literature and well as Muslim religious notions. Arabic was used by Jews for all kinds of literary activities, not only for scientific and other secular purposes, but also for expounding and translating the Bible or the *Mishnah*, for theological and philosophical treatise, for discussing Jewish law and ritual, and even for the study of Hebrew grammar. For writing letters and other non-literary purposes, a more colloquial form of Arabic, interspersed with Hebrew words and phrases, was used.[29]

The Judaic-Arabic symbiosis is reflected in the history of the translation of the Jewish Bible into Arabic. Originally, the reason for this activity was an endeavour to provide by these translations an authoritative interpretation of the texts, in particular in theological matters (e.g., the inculcation of a spiritual-abstract conception of the human-like qualities attributed to God in the Bible). That is why the most famous of the classical translations, which superseded all the others in popular usage, that of Sa'adia Gaon, a linguist, philosopher and theologian, (d. 942), was called by his *Tafsir*, commentary. In order to avoid misunderstanding,

Sa'adia also wrote an Arabic commentary on the Bible. His Arabic translations of the Bible became a sacred text, which was copied, and later printed, beside the Hebrew original. Writing in Arabic and using Arabic methods and terminology, Jewish scholars assiduously explored and described the Hebrew Bible and the *Mishnah*. For the first time, the pronunciation, the grammar and vocabulary of Hebrew were scientifically treated; thus Hebrew and Hebrew Bible studies became a disciplined and well-organized means of expression under the influence of the Arabic language of Arabo-Islamic culture.[30]

Some of the most important medieval Jewish theology was written in Arabic, partly because it had to use Arabic and Muslim concepts for which no words existed in Hebrew. Islam saved Jewish theology of the Talmud from disintegration and gave it a new content, in the image of Islam and the image which Islam had of Judaism. In Muslim theology, Maimonides found a model of a renaissance for Arab Judaism that Islam encouraged and cultivated. With the exception of *Mishneh Torah*, his code of Jewish law, all of Mainonides's major works were written in Arabic, although some were printed in Hebrew characters by simple transliteration from one alphabet to the other in order to get round the Islamic ban on missionary activity by the Peoples of the Book in Ayyubid Egypt. But despite this device his works were read and discussed by theologians of all faiths. In his philosophical work that is considered his *magnum opus*, *The Guide of the Perplexed* (Arabic, *Dalalat al-Hairin*), he debated with Alfarabi and the *mutakallimum* and with the Karaites whom he fought with all the authority of his rabbinical position. Maimonides's translator into Hebrew, his contemporary Yehuda Ibn Tibbon, explained in his preface, written in Provence, to *The Guide of the Perplexed*, that all these great works could only have been written in Arabic, since they used Arabic concepts for which no words existed in Hebrew.[31]

Maimonides's major theological innovation was in the codification of Jewish law; he created a new literary form for the codification of Jewish law, of which his own work, the *Mishneh Torah* was the peak. The creation of a new Arabo-Hebrew legal style is one of the highlights of Maimonides's work. Enlightened though he was, Maimonides reclaimed a traditionalist talmudist theologian for whom science was in the service of religious piety; he was politically opposed to the materialist and dialectical theologies of the Abbasids, but was intellectually formed by them. Although attempting to synthesize philosophy and religion, Maimonides's two monumental works, *The Guide of the Perplexed* and *Mishneh Torah* apparently represent disparate concerns of Maimonides the rabbi and Maimonides the philosopher.

The Crusades may have contributed to strengthening the Arabo-Jewish solidarity of the Middle Ages in the face of the encroachment of Christian Europe. At the time of the First Crusade (1096–1102) Jews living Jerusalem shared the same terrible fate as the Muslims when the city fell to the Crusaders. One medieval Muslim chronicler reported that the Crusaders burned the 'Church of the Jews'. Another put it in more details: 'They collected the Jews in the "Church" and burnt it down with them in it. They destroyed shrines and the tomb of Abraham – on him be peace – and they took the *mihrab* of David peacefully.'[32] Apparently medieval Muslim scholars did not view the Jews living under Islam with same suspicion as that which they harboured on occasions towards Middle Eastern Christians, who might, rightly or wrongly, be expected to side with their co-religionists, the Crusaders.[33]

Theology differs from religion itself; it is thought about religion, its contents and institutions. The centre of Maimonides's theology is the doctrine of the divine. His doctrine of theocentricity (God as the centre) contrasts with what is called in modern times 'religious humanism' or 'ethical monotheism' since any humanistic and moralistic world-view is of necessary anthropocentric (with man at the centre). For Maimonides, who recognized only God as true being and ascribes no value or significance to man except in his knowledge of God, morality has no intrinsic value, but only an instrumental significance. He regarded morality as a means required by man for the purpose of making him free for his great aim, which was the knowledge of God.[34] For Maimonides's theology, the proof of God's existence is incomplete, unless it also establishes His absolute unity. In reflecting on this question, practically all Jewish philosophers and theologians of the Middle Ages came to the conclusion that the unity of God necessarily implies that He must be incorporeal. This conclusion then required them to set forth figurative or metaphorical interpretations of the many biblical passages that ascribe bodily characteristics to God. Maimonides devoted such attention to the arguments for God's unity and incorporeality. He began his *The Guide of the Perplexed* with an elaborate and comprehensive effort to refute all literal interpretations of passages in the Bible that speak God as having corporeal features. Within his medieval context Maimonides – who had no experience of living in a European Christian country was bound to be hostile to the Trinitarian concept of God which he associated with Christianity.

Though Christian theologians interpreted the Trinity as a doctrine of one God in Three Persons, Maimonides perceived it as denial of the divine unity. Most Jewish anti-Trinitarian polemics before and after Maimonides were directed against Christianity.[35]

Maimonides, as befitting a great rational philosopher, was tolerant by nature. But his conservative orthodox theology reflected Jewish thought of the time. Certain of his formulations contain some offensive statements and precepts directed specifically against Christianity. But his theological orthodoxy can only be understood within its historical settings. As a product of a rational philosophy and a tolerant culture, Maimonides significantly lowered the barrier separating Jew and non-Jew; he often referred to the rabbinical dictum of Jews engaging in normal social relations with non-Jews 'in order to pursue the ways of peace'; he also quoted biblical verses like 'His [God's] mercy is on all creatures', in order to incorporate all of humanity within the range of Jewish obligations towards others.[36] Ironically, however, in spite of being one of the most distinguished thinkers of the Arab and Islamic worlds, Maimonides has become the hero of religious Zionism and Jewish fundamentalism in modern-day Israel. In the post-1967 period his theological orthodoxy has been widely used and abused by an array of Jewish fundamentalist groups and parties.

The Reinvention of Maimonides since 1967

For orthodox Jews the *halacha* is binding and Jewish religious ordinances have absolute validity. Moreover many orthodox Jews and Israeli (messianic) religious nationalists claim to find justification for their attitudes towards the Palestinians, often referred to as 'Arabs living in Israel', in Maimonides's theology. For many Israeli Jewish fundamentalists Maimonides's strict orthodoxy and his medievalist interpretation of the *halacha* are the starting point of their politico-religious conceptions of the Arab-Israeli conflict. For Israeli Jewish fundamentalists, the Jewish halachic system reflected in Maimonides's formulations elevated the status, rights and life ('blood') of Jew above the non-Jew. Reinterpreting radically some of Maimonides's rational formulations, many mystical Jewish fundamentalists in Israel have sought the establishment of Jewish theocracy over the entire, biblically described, land of Israel, and the building of the Temple in Jerusalem, as all part of implementing the divinely ordained messianic redemption.

In post-1967 Israel, the general tendency to quote selectively and in a misleading way from Maimonides's theology, is derived from a theology which conceives a radical and sharp distinction between Jew and non-Jew and assumes a basically antagonistic relation between them. For Israeli Jewish fundamentalists, Jewish conflict with 'gentiles', and even war against them, is 'for their own good', because this will hasten messianic redemption.[37] Jewish fundamentalists also envisaged a theocratic regime for Israel based on the *halacha* and spurned universal, humanist and liberal values. The theology that guides *Gush Emunim* is shared by many others in the Zionist religious-nationalist camp who embrace the supremacist notion of Jews as a divinely 'chosen people' ('*am segula*) and the rightful owners of the 'promised land'. The indigenous Palestinians are aliens in this land; they are no more than illegitimate tenants and squatters, and a threat to the process of messianic redemption; their human and civil rights are no match for the divine legitimacy and the religiously ordained duty (or *mitzvah*) of 'conquering, possessing and settling the promised land'. For the *Gush Emunim* settlers in the West Bank, Israel must continue the ancient biblical battles over settlement of the 'land of Israel', to be won by a combination of religious faith and military might. The devotion of an increasingly powerful trend to the total possession of 'the biblical land of Israel' and to messianic redemption has effectively turned the Palestinians into resident aliens on their own soil.

The *Gush Emunim* settlement movement finds justification for the annexation of the occupied territories, or at least the prohibition on withdrawal, in Maimonides's commentary on the *Book of the Commandments*: 'We are commanded to inherit the land that God gave to Abraham, Isaac, and Jacob, and must not leave it in the hand of any other nation or desolate... We must not leave the land in their hands [the seven Canaanite nations] or any other people in any generation.'[38] While Maimonides's theology reflected a traditional Diaspora cultural identity, *Gush Emunim's* Neo-Zionist and revolutionary ideology emphasizes both the 'holiness' and 'territorial wholeness' of '*Eretz-Yisrael*' combined with modern Israeli settler colonialism. In *Gush Emunim's* theology, Israeli Jewish national identity is not just a socio-cultural reality, it is a geo-political and territorial ideal. Israeli-Jewish national identity is born both out of a cultural self-understanding and out of the actual land that the Jews inhabit.[39] The popular slogan of the movement reflects this: 'The Land of Israel, for the People of Israel, According to the *Torah* of Israel.' As Rabbi Tzvi Kook put it, 'The Land was chosen before the people.' The *Gush* philosophy is based on several components: messianic fervour related to the belief in the 'sanctity' of Greater Israel; the establishment of Jewish sovereignty over the 'whole land of Israel' and the building of the Temple in Jerusalem; the ethos of a mystical religious utopia, reflecting the desire to build a nationalist religious state based on the *halacha* as a substitute for Western-style liberal democracy.[40]

Maimonides's rational tradition and his Arabo-Greek philosophy synthesized with Jewish Diaspora orthodoxy stand in sharp contrast with modern messianic Zionism and mystical Jewish fundamentalism. According to the recently deceased Professor Yesha'ayahu Leibowitz, an orthodox Jew and one of the foremost Jewish scholars of his day, Maimonides did not ascribe great significance to the messianic idea, and hardly felt it necessary, although he did not ignore it, since it is an integral part of Jewish tradition, religion and faith.[41] Clearly the writings and teachings of the Kooks (father and son) relied only highly selectively on Maimonides's theology. They integrated the traditional, passive religious longings for the land with the modern, secular, activist and expansionist Zionism, giving birth to a new comprehensive ideology of mystical Jewish nationalist-religious fundamentalism.[42] Their theology is both eschatological and messianic and they tended to sanctify not just the land but almost every secular Zionist enterprise. Their new doctrine was not just derived from orthodox Jewish tradition but also based on theological innovation and revolutionary activism. The doctrine, which was applied to the modern political conflict in the Holy Land, assumes living in a messianic era, the imminent coming of the Messiah and 'the beginning of redemption'. It asserts that the 1967 war represented the Divine Hand at work and that the Jews, aided by God, will thereafter triumph over the non-Jews and rule over them forever. Rabbi Tzvi Kook took over the leadership of the followers of messianic ideology after the death of his father and subsequently all important *Gush Emunim* rabbis were his students. 'Kookist' Neo-Zionism saw the 1967 war as a turning point in the process of messianic redemption and the deliverance of *Eretz-Yisrael* from what it termed the *Sitra Achra*, the 'evil (Palestinian Arab) side'.[43] Tzvi Kook himself rushed with his biblical claims towards the West Bank immediately after the 1967 conquests: 'All this land is ours, absolutely, belonging to all of us, non-transferable to others even in part ... As guaranteed by the word of God ... Therefore ... it is clear and absolute that there are no `Arab territories' or `Arab lands' here, but only the lands of Israel, the eternal heritage of our forefathers to which others have come and upon which they have built without our permission and in our absence.'⁴⁴ Tzvi Kook's politics were described by the Israeli journalist David Shaham as 'consistent, extremist, uncompromising and concentrated on a single issue: the right of the Jewish people to sovereignty over every foot of the land of Israel. Absolute sovereignty, with no imposed limitations. 'From a perspective of national sovereignty', he [Kook] says, 'the country belongs to us ...'.⁴⁵ Immediately after the 1967 war Rabbi Kook demanded the annexation of the occupied territories, in line with explicit *halacha* provisions.⁴⁶ He also said at a conference after 1967:

> I tell you explicitly that there is a prohibition in the *Torah* against giving up even an inch of our liberated land. There are no conquests here and we are not occupying foreign lands; we are returning to our home, to the inheritance of our forefathers. There is no Arab land here, only the inheritance of our God – the more the world gets used to this thought the better it will be for them and for all of us.⁴⁷

The *halacha* concept of *'ger toshav'*

Since 1967 Israeli religious Zionists have been debating the question as to whether Palestinians residing in the 'land of Israel' could qualify for the halachic status of *ger toshav* ('resident alien'). In line with this *halacha* concept of *'ger toshav'* both Palestinian Muslims and Palestinian Christians are viewed by some Jewish religious nationalists, including many *Gush Emunim* rabbis, as temporary 'alien residents' and as a population living, at best, on sufferance. While the relatively moderate members of the NRP categorize the Palestinians as *gerei toshav* ('resident aliens'), the more radical Jewish fundamentalists have pointed out that biblical discussion of *ger toshav* had only meant to refer to non-Jews who adopt Judaism (Numbers 10:14). They also pointed out that Maimonides had made it clear in his law code that the *Torah* concept of *ger toshav* refers to the 'righteous gentile' who becomes a Jew.⁴⁸ That radical position is found a book called *Toward a New Israel: The Jewish State and the Arab Question* (1986 and 1992 Hebrew and English editions respectively), written by Professor Mordechai Nisan, a senior lecturer at the Hebrew University of Jerusalem and a leading fundamentalist intellectual. The halachic legal status of *ger toshav* according to Nisan: *ger toshav* is a non-Jew who accepts the Seven Noahide laws and joins the community of the Jewish people, who lives a rather free life, enjoys a social standing above a man who is a slave to a Jew:

The Gentile in Eretz-Israel who accepts the Seven Noahide Laws becomes a *Ger-Toshav* (a resident alien) and, according to Maimonides, enters the category of 'the righteous nations of the world'. This point is discussed in halachic literature and codified by Maimonides into Jewish Law. The concept of the *Ger-Toshav* refers to a person who has gone through the process of a partial conversion before a Rabbinic court of three. The *Ben-Noah* assumes a more inferior and limited status if his acceptance of Torah is due to a rational decision alone, but not a Divinely fixed obligation. The *Ger-Toshav*, then, is positioned between the *Ben-Noah* and the Jew. He ascends to a level of social and religious performance, he goes through a stage of partial conversion, but limits himself to accepting just the Seven Commandments. The *Tosafot* commentary in the Talmud implies that this individual should go further and consider converting completely to Judaism. However, for the moment, the *Ger-Toshav* assumes a middle position in the Torah order within a Jewish-led society.[49]

'The position of a non-repentant Gentile remains inferior. He refuses to assume a higher life standard as set out by the *Torah* and rejects Jewish primacy in Eretz-Israel. Maimonides explicates that non-Jews (*Bnei Noah*) are to endure a lowly status compounded by elements of servitude and special taxes.'[50]

In August 1984, Nisan, who supports the replacement of Israel's secular law by the *halacha*, repeats the same ideas in an article in *Kivunim* (an official organ of the World Zionist Organization), that, relying selectively on Maimonides, a non-Jew permitted to reside in the land of Israel 'must accept paying a tax and suffering the humiliation of servitude'. In *Toward New Israel*, Nisan bemoans the traditional Jewish *dhimmi* status under Islam: 'The hallmark of the *dhimmi* condition was the precarious and pitiful nature of existence under Islam rule. Subjugated to an inferior status, the Jew paid a special poll tax, the *jizya*.'[51] Yet in *Kivunim*, Nisan demands, supposedly in keeping with a religious text of Maimonides, that a non-Jew in Israel 'be held down and not [be allowed] to raise his head against Jews'. For Nisan, non-Jews must not be appointed to any office or position of power over Jews; if they refuse to live a life of inferiority, then this signals their rebellion and the unavoidable necessity of Jewish warfare against their very presence in the 'land of Israel'.[52]

For a supporter of *Gush Emunim* like Nisan, the struggle against the Palestinians is also part of a wider effort to reinterpret Jewish history and redeem Maimonides;

The struggle over Maimonides between Jews and Arabs is really an instance of the confrontation going back more than a millennium, as the Jewish people try to perpetuate their unique religious and national identity within the extensive Muslim/Arab homeland. An awareness of this historic confrontation conveys the profundity of the rejection of modern Zionism by modern Arab nationalism'[53]

Other *Gush Emunim* supporters and rabbis deny that a Palestinian nation existed and strongly opposed the idea of Palestinian autonomy any sort in the occupied territories. According to the *Gush* spiritual leaders, there is no need to take into consideration the Arab inhabitants since their residence in the country for hundreds of years was prohibited and was based on theft, fraud and distortion; therefore the time has now come for the Arab 'robbers' to depart. As Rabbi Shlomo Aviner, a Parisian-born Jew and the former Rabbi of Bet El settlement on the West Bank and currently the Chief Rabbi of the 'Ateret Cohanim yeshiva in East Jerusalem's Old City, explains:

> To what can this be compared [?] It resembles a man entering his neighbour's house without permission and residing there for many years. When the original owner of the house returns, the invader [the Arab] claims: 'It is my [house]. I have been living here for many years.' So what? All of these years he was a robber! Now he should depart and pay housing rent as well. A person might say: there is a difference between a residence of thirty years and a residence of two thousand years. Let us ask him: Is there a law of limitation which gives a robber the right to his plunder? .... Everyone who settled here knew very well that he was residing in a land that belonged to the people of Israel. Perhaps an Arab who was born here does not know this, nonetheless the fact that a man settled on land does not make it his. Legally 'possession' serves only as evidence of a claim of ownership, but it does not create ownership. The Arabs' 'possession' of the land is therefore a 'possession that asserts no right'. It is the possession of territory when it is absolutely clear that they are not its legal owners, and this possession has no legal and moral validity.[54]

In a similar disposition the afore-mentioned Rabbi Tzvi Kook, who apparently inspired Aviner's apologia, wrote:

> We find ourselves here by virtue of our forefathers' inheritance, the foundation of the Bible and history, and there is no one that can change this fact. What does it resemble? A man left his house and others came and invaded it. This is exactly what happened to us. There are those who claim that these are Arab lands here. It is all a lie and falsehood. There are absolutely no Arab lands here.[55]

In fact this imagery of the homecoming Jew and the Arab invader permeates the writings of the spiritual leaders and ideologists of *Gush Emunim*, particularly the religious extremists, and implies that the Jew has the right to evict the 'alien' Arab 'invader'.

Moreover these rabbis who interpret the classical Zionist assertion of 'historical rights' to the land as meaning that the very fact of Arab residence on, and possession of, the land is morally flawed and legally, at best, temporary, and therefore the Arabs must evacuate the land for the 'legal owners' of the country and depart. Knesset Member Rabbi Meir Kahane (1932–1990, the rabble-rousing founder of the Jewish Defense League in the United States and its Israeli counterpart the *Kach* ('Thus') movement, established in the late 1970s), saw the Palestinians' very residence in the 'land of Israel' as making them criminals; the conclusion that they should be expelled was quick to follow. Although giving widespread publicity to this idea, Kahane did not invent it. It is based on ancient Jewish sources, and first and foremost the biblical verse: 'You shall dispossess all the inhabitants of the land' (Num. 33:52) and the interpretation of it given by classical Jewish commentators. The eleventh-century Rabbi Rashi [Rabbi Shlomo Yitzhaki, a paramount Bible and Talmud commentator], for example, explained: 'You shall drive out the land and you shall dispossess it of its inhabitants, and then you will dwell in it, i.e. you will be able to remain in it [if you dispossess it of its inhabitants], but if not, you will not be able to remain in it.' Thus this biblical verse is interpreted by Israeli Jewish fundamentalists as a standing order binding for the present and future.[56]

If the very idea of Arab residence in Palestine is based on 'theft', is morally flawed and legally temporary, according to the religious messianics, then Arab removal is the logical conclusion. Rabbi Yisrael Ariel bluntly and explicitly demands expelling the Palestinians as necessitated by Jewish religious commandments:

> On the one hand there is a commandment of settling *Eretz-Yisrael*, which is defined by our sages[57] of blessed memory also as the commandment of 'inheritance and residence' – a commandment mentioned many times in the Torah. Every young student understands that 'inheritance and residence' means conquering and settling the land. The Torah repeats the commandment 'You shall dispossess all the inhabitants of the land' tens of times, and Rashi explains that 'You shall dispossess – You shall expel.' The Torah itself uses the term 'expulsion' a number of times such as: 'Since you shall expel the inhabitants of the country with my help'. The substance of this commandment is to expel the inhabitants of the land whoever they

may be .... This is also the opinion of Rashi in defining the commandment. In the same Talmudic passage which mentions the commandment pertaining to the land, Rashi interprets: 'Because [of the commandment] to settle *Eretz-Yisrael* – to expel idolaters and to settle [the people of] Israel there'. Thus according to Rashi the commandment to settle [the land] aims at the expulsion of the non-Jew from *Eretz-Yisrael* and that it be settled with Jews.[58]

Rabbi Meir Kahane, who acquired a reputation for defining the outer limits of both right-wing fascism and Jewish fundamentalism in Israel, was a major contributor to the rise of militant messianic theology in Israel in the post-1967 period. After his assassination in New York in 1990, Kahane's funeral in Jerusalem was attended by two Israeli cabinet ministers, two deputy ministers, and by the Chief Sephardi Rabbi who urged the mourners to 'follow in Kahane's ways'.[59] Kahane's movement *Kach* had connections with *Gush Emunim* settlers and other associated extreme right-wing groups, such as the avowedly terrorist 'Jewish Underground' and the 'Ateret Cohanim yeshiva in the Old City of Jerusalem,[60] which belongs to a fundamentalist group campaigning for rebuilding the Jewish Temple on the ruins of the Muslim mosques on the al-Haram al-Sharif in East Jerusalem. Kahane, unlike some of the rabbis of *Gush Emunim*, made little distinction between Palestinian Christians and Palestinian Muslims. His racist public campaign thrived on media publicity, and concentrated, also, on the Palestinian citizens of Israel and not just on the Palestinians of the occupied territories. As Kahane declared on another occasion: 'No non-Jews can be citizens of Israel', seeking to rescind the citizenship status currently given to Palestinian Christians and Muslims inside the Green Line; if the Arabs refuse to accept the [*halacha*] status of *ger toshav* (paying 'tribute' and living in 'servitude'), 'We'll put them on trucks and send them over the Allenby Bridge ... we'll use force. And if they fire at our soldiers, we'll kill them.'[61]

Kahane justified the expulsion of the Palestinians (Muslims and Christians) as the surest way to bring about the 'redemption of Jews'. In his thinking, the removal of Palestinians would fulfil two main objectives: first, political, to prevent the Palestinian population from becoming a majority in Greater Israel and thereby undermining Israel as a Jewish state from within; second, religious, as a means of hastening messianic redemption. As Kahane put it:

The Arabs of Israel are a stark desecration of God's name. Their non-reconciliation to Jewish sovereignty over the land of Israel is a rejection of the sovereignty of the God of Israel and of his kingdom. Their removal from the country is more than a political affair. It is a religious matter, a religious duty, a commandment to wipe out the desecration of God's name. Instead of worrying about the reactions of the Gentiles if we do act [to remove them], we should tremble at the thought of God's anger if we do not act. Tragedy will befall us if we do not remove the Arabs from the country, since redemption can come immediately and in its full glory, if we do that which God commands ... Let us hasten the redemption.[62]

In the early 1980s, shortly after his election to the Knesset, Rabbi Kahane submitted two draft bills to the Speaker of the Knesset Shlomo Hillel:

1. Proposed Law for Israeli Citizenship and for Jewish and Arab Population Transfer;
2. Proposed Law for the Prevention of Assimilation between Jews and Non-Jews and for the Sanctity of the Jewish People.

This draft law would ban intermarriage and sexual intercourse between Arabs and Jews. According to the first bill, the right of citizenship is reserved exclusively for Jews; the Arab can only obtain the status of 'resident alien in *Eretz-Yisrael*', with no right to vote or hold office.[63] The bill defines a 'resident alien' as a non-Jew who accepts upon himself the seven Halachic Noahide laws, or the seven precepts that the after the Flood Noah's descendants were commanded: the prohibition of idolatry, blasphemy, bloodshed, incest, robbery, and eating of limbs severed from a living animal, as well as the commandment to maintain the laws. The draft bill would also make the *halacha* prohibition on the residence of a 'resident alien' in Jerusalem the law of the State of Israel. A non-Jew who shall not accept the status of 'resident alien', 'shall be removed from the country, either of his own free will, or against his will'.[64] Clearly Kahane was of the opinion that only 'a small percentage [of Arabs] would agree to the conditions imposed on a resident alien, who would not have the status of a citizen. These would be mainly old people. They would remain';[65] the rest would be expelled.

The second draft bill submitted by Kahane to the Knesset Speaker in 1984 would ban intermarriage and sexual relations between a *ger toshav* and a Jew. The bill states that a non-Jew who has any sort of sexual relations with a Jew shall be punished with three years' imprisonment. There is a clear discrimination in favour of Jews in the punishment for breaking such laws: 'A non-Jew who has sexual relations with a Jewish prostitute or with a Jewish male shall be punished with fifty years' imprisonment; a Jewish prostitute or Jewish male who has relations with a non-Jewish male shall be imprisoned with five years' imprisonment.'[66] The two draft bills of M. K. Kahane were disqualified by the Knesset Presidium (the Speaker Shlomo Hillel and his deputies) on 3 December 1984, although the Supreme Court later rule that Kahane had the right to submit them for Knesset debates.[67] Although Kahane attempted to persuade the Israeli Knesset that the above stated differences in the punishment of a Jew and non-Jew for the same crime committed is common in the Talmud and the *halacha*, other Members of the Knesset preferred to compare his draft bills with Nazi proposals made during the Weimar Republic.

Settler colonialism and the biblical narrative

In modern times a whole range of settler colonial enterprises have used the Bible. The biblical narrative has often been deployed by Christian and Jewish fundamentalists as the idea that provides moral authority for, and redeems, modern colonial enterprises.[68] The content of the biblical text is highly problematic; in the narrative of the Book of Exodus, there is an inextricable link between extrication of the Israelites from slavery in Egypt and the divine mandate to plunder ancient Palestine and even commit genocide; the invading Israelites are commanded to annihilate the indigenous inhabitants of Canaan. In the Book of Deuteronomy (often described as the focal point of the religious history and theology of the Old Testament) there is a requirement of the indigenous population of Canaan.

The deployment of the biblical text and the evocation of the exploits of biblical heroes in support of settler colonialism is deeply rooted in Zionism, although secular Zionists have often denied that the Books of Exodus and Deuteronomy have any contemporary relevance to the fate of the Palestinian Arabs. But with the rise of religious Zionism since 1967 the narratives of Exodus have found an explicit relevance in contemporary Israel. Since 1967 many Jewish fundamentalists in Israel, including *Gush Emunim* rabbis and political leaders, have routinely compared Palestinian Muslims and Christians to the ancient Canaanites or 'Amalekites, whose extermination or expulsion by the ancient

Israelites was, according to the Bible, predestined by a divine design'.[69] Although many rabbis refer to Palestinian Muslims as 'Ishmalites' and to the circumstances under which biblical Abraham 'expelled' Ishmael, others prefer to use Joshua's destruction and subjugation of the Canaanites as a model for the determination of Israeli policy towards the contemporary 'Palestinian problem'. For example, in April 1969, in a statement in the journal of the Israeli Army Rabbinate, *Mahanaim*, a certain Shraga Gafni cites biblical authority for driving the 'Canaanite peoples' from the land of Israel and explains the 'relevance' of the judgment of Amalek (1 Samuel 15) to the Palestinian Arabs:

> As to the Arabs – the element that now resides in the land is foreign in its essence to the land and its promise – their sentence must be that of all previous foreign elements. Our wars with them have been inevitable, just as in the days of the conquest of our possessions in antiquity, our wars with the people who ruled our land for their own benefit were inevitable ... In the case of the enemies who, in the nature of their being, have only one single goal, to destroy you, there is no remedy but for them to be destroyed. This is the judgment of Amalek.

Reflecting on the appropriate policy to adopt towards the Palestinians, Rabbi Tzvi Yehuda Kook cited Maimonides to the effect that the Canaanites had three choices: to flee, to accept Jewish sovereignty, or to fight, implying that the decision by most Canaanites to resist Jewish rule justified their destruction.[70] According to the Old Testament, the Amalekites were an ancient nomadic people, who dwelled in the Sinai desert and southern Palestine, who were regarded as the Israelites' inveterate foe, whose 'annihilation' became a sacred duty and against whom war should be waged until their 'memory be blotted out' forever (Exodus 17:16; Deuteronomy 25:17–19). Although the biblical stories mention that the Amalekites were finally wiped out during the reign of Hezekiah in the eighth century BC, rabbinical literature dwells on the Amalekite's role as the Israelites' permanent archenemy, saying that the struggle between the two peoples will continue until the coming of the Messiah, when God will destroy the last remnants of Amalek.

Many of the *Gush Emunim* rabbis and religious messianists talk about the 'new Canaanite era' and insist on giving the biblical commandment to 'blot out the memory of Amalek' an actual contemporary relevance in the conflict between Israelis and Palestinians. In February 1980 Rabbi Yisrael Hess, the former

Campus Rabbi of Bar-Ilan University, published an article in the student bulletin *Bat Kol,* the title of which, 'The Genocide Commandment in the Torah' ('*mitzvat hagenocide batorah*' in Hebrew) leaves no place for ambiguity. The article ends with the following: 'The day is not far when we shall all be called to this holy war this commandment of the annihilation of Amalek.'[71] Hess quotes the biblical commandment according to which he believes Israel, in the tradition of Joshua from biblical times, should act: 'Go and strike down Amalek; put him under the ban with all that he possesses. Do not spare him, but kill man and woman, baby and suckling, ox and sheep, camel and donkey.'[72] Hess adds: 'Against this holy war God declares a counter *jihad* ... in order to emphasize that this is the background for the annihilation and that it is over this that the war is being waged and that it is not a conflict between two peoples ... God is not content that we annihilate Amalek – 'blot out the memory of Amalek' – he also enlists personally in this war ... because, as has been said, he has a personal interest in this matter, this is the principal aim.'[73]

Other Jewish fundamentalist leaders have argued that Palestinian Muslims and Christians face a choice between emigration or conversion to Judaism. As a settler speaker from the *Gush Emunim* settlement of 'Ofra, Aharon Halamish, put it:

> It is not necessary to throw bombs into the casbah or expel the Arabs. There is nothing wrong, however, with making their life difficult in the hope that they will emigrate ... Perhaps in the end only those will remain who genuinely want to be loyal citizens of Israel, and if they really do, let them convert [to Judaism].'[74]

The theology of Israeli religious fundamentalists, including the theory of the 'Amalek of today,' also found an echo in an article published by the Chief Military Rabbi of the IDF Central Command, Rabbi Avraham Zemel (Avidan) who, according to Professor Amnon Rubinstein, gave *halacha* justification for the 'murder of non-Jewish civilians including women and children, during war'.[75] Another soldier, who was also a yeshiva student, asked his rabbi about the subject of '*tohar haneshik*' (the 'purity of arms'). From the answer of the rabbi the soldier concluded: 'During war I am permitted or even obliged to kill every male and female Arab that happens to be in my way ... I must kill them even if this involves complication with the military law.'[76]

Spokesmen of *Gush Emunim* drew satisfaction from the result of the violent attacks on Palestinian mayors Bassam Shaka'a (Muslim) and Karim Khalaf (Christian) in 1980: 'Well organised, very good work'; 'I hope that Jews did it.'[77] In a similar vein Rabbi Haim Druckman, then MK for the NRP and a settlers' leader, declared: 'Let all thine enemies perish thus.'[78] Rabbi Yisrael Ariel, using and abusing Maimonides, justified the campaign of the Jewish Underground terrorist organization, implying that the killing of an Arab was not murder:

> Any one who searches through the code of Maimonides, which is the pillar of the *halacha* in the Jewish world, [and searches for] the concept 'you shall not murder' or the concept 'holy blood' with regard to the killing of a non-Jew – will search in vain, because he will not find [it] ... It follows from the words of Maimonides that a Jew who kills a non-Jew ... is exempt from the prohibition 'you shall not murder'. And so Maimonides writes in the *halachas* of murder: 'An Israelite who kills a resident alien is not sentenced to death in the court of law.'[79]

Israeli religious messianists have forged a convenient alliance with American Christian fundamentalists, both perceiving Israel as the fulfilment of the prophecies of the Jewish Scriptures. American Christian fundamentalists further argue that the establishment of Jewish theocracy in the 'whole land of Israel' is necessary for the second coming of the Messiah.[80] Apparently the genocidal theme of the Bible has sparked off great interest among many American Christian fundamentalists who anticipate the end of the world will be marked by Armageddon, slaughter and devastation.[81] By contrast, however, many liberal Israelis have roundly condemned these genocidal notions. Citing Hess's article, Professor Amnon Rubinstein commented:

> Rabbi Hess explains the commandment which instructs the blotting out of the memory of Amalek and says that there is not the slightest mercy in this commandment which orders the killing and annihilation of also children and infants. Amalek is whoever declares war on the people of God.'[82]

Rubinstein points out that 'No reservation on behalf of the editorial board, the students or the University was made after publishing this article which was also reprinted in other newspapers.'[83] A subsequent issue of *Bat Kol*, no. 2, 16 April 1980, carried two articles written by Professor Uriel Simon and Dr Tzvi Weinberg severely criticizing the article of Rabbi Hess. The same notion propagated by the messianists regarding the synonimity of the

Palestinians with the Amalekites was also criticized in moderate religious circles.[84] The late Professor Uriel Tal, who was a prominent biblical scholar at Tel Aviv University, and who conducted his study in the early 1980s, pointed out that the political messianic stream refers to the Palestinian (Muslims and in three stages or degrees):

a) the reduction of the Palestinians in Israel and the occupied territories to the *halacha* status of *ger toshav*, paying 'tribute' and living in 'servitude';
b) the promotion of Arab 'transfer' i.e., expulsion;
c) the implementation of the commandment of Amalek, as expressed in Rabbi Hess's article: 'The Commandment of Genocide in the Torah', in other words, 'annihilating' the Palestinian Arabs.[85]

Traditional rabbinical attitudes towards Christianity

The reasons for the historical tension between Christianity and Judaism are not to be sought merely in the differences in religious beliefs and dogmas, which also exist in relation to all other religions. Neither are they, moreover, due to the long history of anti-Semitism and persecution of Jews in Christian countries, since anti-Semitism was the result rather than the first cause of the tension between Christianity and Judaism. Jewish scholars often dwell on the negative Christian image of Judaism; they have argued that the tension is due essentially to the ambivalent position in which the Church found itself vis-à-vis Judaism. Christianity had a Jewish beginning and continuing Jewish associations through the Bible. But it has become a distinct form of religious life with its distinct conceptions of salvation, forms of devotion and piety, emotional and intellectual attitudes, and historical consciousness. The ambivalence created by this sense of both relatedness and difference is still far from being resolved both in the Christian world and the State of Israel. By explicitly claiming to be a new religion, and by conceiving itself as the fulfilment of the promises in the Old Testament, the Church placed itself squarely on a Jewish foundation: it was the consummation of the biblical promise. Jesus was the promised Son of David, the Lord's Anointed (*Mashiah ben David*), and hence the Christian community, i.e. the Church, was the 'true Israel' of God.

Rabbinical attitudes towards Christianity have been determined by historical, religious and social factors. Christianity, after it had been seen to be a Jewish 'heretical' sect, became a dominant religion, and assumed its medieval Catholic form (including the cultic use of images), considered by Jewish philosophers and theologians to be 'idolatrous'. The fact that for many centuries medieval Jewish philosophy was influenced mainly by Muslim thought only strengthened this view. Medieval Jewish theologians argued that Islam shared with Judaism a conception of God which could be described as more monotheistic than that of Christianity due to its adherence to the Trinitarian formulation. Rabbinical authorities debated whether the laws and injunctions concerning commerce and contacts with 'idolators' also applied to Christians. To rabbinical authorities of medieval times the Christian world appeared as the incarnation of Rome, symbolized by Edom and Esau, and as the evil power bent on destroying Jacob. Occasionally Jewish thinkers would suggest that Christianity, recognizing the divine character of the Bible and being less polytheistic than classical and primitive paganism, might be a providential instrument used by God to bring the 'gentiles' gradually nearer to true religion.[86] Yet in spite of the traditional attitudes of hostility and mistrust, there was always a certain amount of mutual interest. Jewish thinkers (Maimonides in particular) have influenced Christian theologians and biblical exegetes. The rabbinical theological evaluation of Christianity also had repercussions in the sphere of *halacha* and the exigencies of the latter in turn influenced theoretical attitudes.[87] Rabbinical authorities saw valid distinctions between Judaism and Christianity and criticized concepts such the Trinity, the atoning sacrifice of the Messiah, the Son of God on the Cross; and Christians did not accept rabbinical tradition as the authentic interpretation of a valid divine law.

Maimonides and 'Idolatrous Worship' ('avoda zara)

Rabbinical hostility to Christianity is found in both orthodox Judaism and contemporary religious Zionism. The theological arguments stem from the focus of orthodox Judaism on the 'service of God and obedience to its commandments'. '*Avoda zara*', or 'idolatrous worship', is the grossest rejection of orthodox Judaism. In practice the Jewish laws (*halacha*) dealing with '*avoda zara* covered all relations between Jews and Gentiles.[88] Orthodox Judaism was founded on a total rejection of '*avoda zara*; in the biblical text and Talmudic literature the term '*avoda zara* is found in the following: 'You shall have no other gods but Me' (Exodus 20:3); 'You shall not make for yourself a sculptured image, or any likeness of what is in the heavens above, or on the earth below' (Exodus 20: 4); 'Nothing that has to do with idolatry may be used for healing' (Exodus R); (Aramaic). As for that image – its head was of fine gold, its breasts and arms were silver, its belly and its thighs of brass, its legs of iron, its feet part of iron and part of clay (Daniel 2: 32–33); 'A drunkard who prays is as though he worships idols (Talmud, Berakhot); 'When Jewish elders in Rome were asked: If God has no pleasure in an idol, why does He not make an end of it? They answered: If men worshipped a thing of which men had no need, He would make an end of it, but lo! they worshipped the sun and the moon and the stars and the planets: shall God destroy His world because of fools?' ('Avoda Zara 4, 7); 'Of any sin spoken of in the *Torah*, if a man is told – Commit it and you will not die, let him commit it, save only idolatry, incest and bloodshed!' (Talmud, Sanhedrin); 'If a man be bidden to worship idols on pain of death, let him worship them and not die?' (Talmud, 'Avoda Zara); 'Who denies idolatry is as one that avows the entire *Torah* (Talmud, Qiddushin).

One traditional definition of the term is that everyone who has not accepted the seven Noahide commandments is considered to be a idolator, however in many contexts the term 'Gentile' is synonymous with 'idol worshipper'.[89] The Mishnah (a collection of *halachot*), which consists of five chapters, treats the following subjects:

(a) prohibitions concerning dealings with Gentiles (who are presumed to be idolaters) on their festival periods; objects which may or may not be sold or hired to Gentiles as they may be required for idol worship; prohibitions of sale or lease of real estate in the 'land of Israel' to Gentiles;
(b) (prohibitions arising from Gentiles being suspected of incest and murder; laws concerning articles belonging to Gentiles;
(c) the prohibition of actual idolatrous objects (images, shrines) and the way in which are to be abolished or destroyed;
(d) laws about wine produced or handled by non-Jews, which is presumed to have been used, or intended for use, as a libation before an idol. The tractate in the two Talmuds contains much aggadic material (all the teachings

presented in the Talmud and Midrash that are not directly concerned with *halacha*. These include biblical interpretations, reasons for commandments, anecdotes, etc.) and important historical traditions on the relations between Jews and non-Jews in general and non-Jewish authorities in particular. It also conveys much information on idolatry, including 'oriental religions, on Christianity and Gnosticism'. However in medieval times copies of the tractate were rare, probably because in the course of the centuries it suffered at the hands of Christian censors. This led many Jewish scholars to issue declarations to the effect that statements in the tractate were directed only against the nations of antiquity, not against Christianity, and to adopt a lenient attitude to some of its prohibitions.[90]

These are some of the historical roots of orthodox Judaism's traditionally stern position towards the perceived followers of '*avoda zara*. They must be destroyed less they seduce Jews so as to follow in their footsteps.[91] Maimonides wrote:

> An affirmative precept enjoined for the destruction of any idol, articles and subsidiary to its worship, and everything made for its benefit ... In the land of Israel, it is a duty actively to chase out idolatry until we have exterminated it from the whole of our country. Outside of the holy land, however, we are not so commanded; but only that whenever we acquire any territory by conquest, we should destroy all the idols found there.[92]

Maimonides summed up the Jewish law on the treatment of idolators as follows:

> It is forbidden to show them mercy, as it was said, 'nor show mercy unto them' (Deuteronomy 7:2). Hence, if one see a heathen who worships idols perishing or drowning, one is not to save him ... Hence you learn that it is forbidden to heal idolators even for a fee. But if one is afraid of them or apprehends that refusal might cause ill will, medical treatment may be given for a fee but not gratuitously ... The forgoing rules apply to the time when the people of Israel live reviled among the nations, or when the Gentile's power is predominant. But when Israel is predominant over the nations of the world, we are forbidden to permit a gentile who is idolator to dwell among us. He must not enter our land, even as a temporary resident; or even as a traveller, journeying with merchandise from place to place, until he has undertaken to keep the seven precepts which the Noahides were commanded to observe.[93]

But there is a fundamental difference between the medieval and modern mind. Maimonides was a man of his time and tradition and his theological position on '*avoda zara* was first and foremost a product of a medieval mind. His theological position towards both Islam and Christianity reflected his medievalist approach. He generally regarded Ishmaelites or Muslims as monotheistic Gentiles in spirit and practice and exempted them from the category of idolators,[94] but the Christians were explicitly categorized as such: 'Christians are idol worshippers.'[95] In a letter to 'Ovadia the convert Maimonides set forth the religious status of Muslims from the view point of the Torah:

> These Ishmaelites [i.e. Muslims] are not idol worshippers at all, and it has been removed from their tongues and hearts, and they worship the exalted God as a unity, as is proper, a unity without defect ... Regarding the unity of God they are not in error at all.[96]

Christianity was not, according to Maimonides, a pure monotheistic faith for in it God is *one* in name but *three* in thought and conception – and thus conflicts directly with halachic principles. Maimonides's explicitly anti-Christian prejudices, on the other hand, reflected deeply rooted Jewish attitudes of medieval times. In his interpretation of the Mishnah, Maimonides wrote: 'You should know that the Christian nation ... all of them are idolators.'[97] In another *responsum* Maimonides throws light on his ambivalent view of both Christianity and Islam respectively and the differences between them from the viewpoint of the *halacha*:

> It is permissible to teach *mitzvot* to Christians and to attract them to our religion, but it is forbidden to do this with Ishmaelites based on what their faith teaches them, that this Torah is not of Heavenly origin.[98]

For Maimonides, the Muslims rejected the sanctity of the first Five Books (the Pentateuch) and considered them a forgery and therefore cannot be persuaded of their ideas and ways at all. By contrast he saw positive elements in the fact that Christians believe that the Torah text and its validity had never changed.

Virtually all Israeli Jewish fundamentalists reject the notion of a 'Judeo-Christian tradition', which constitutes, according to many Israeli secular and western commentators, as a basis for a western civilization, although there are differences among Israeli Jewish fundamentalists over what distinctions are worth making among 'gentiles/Christians.'[99] In 1992 at a symposium, organized by the Ministry of Religion on the subject 'Is Autonomy for *ger toshavs* in the Holy Land Feasible? Rabbi Shlomo Min-Harar, had this to say: 'All Christians without exception hate the Jews and look forward to their deaths.'[100] But the marked hostility towards Christianity and its followers in the Holy Land among Israeli Jewish fundamentalists has less to do with the persecution of Jews in Europe or the Holocaust. Although anti-Semitism and persecution of Jews in Christian Europe did contribute to these anti-Christian attitudes, these are not the sole explanation. Sephardi Jewish rabbis, and to a lesser extent their followers who came from Muslim countries and had no experience of persecution by Christians, have expressed more visible hostility towards Christianity and its religious symbols and sites in the Holy Land than fundamentalist Ashkenazi rabbis and their Ashkenazi followers who had actually experienced discrimination in Christian countries.[101]

Many Israeli rabbis make clear distinction between Palestinian Christians and Palestinian Muslims. In discussions on Jewish relations with non-Jews living in the 'land of Israel', several *Gush Emunim* rabbis have distinguished Palestinian Muslims from Palestinian Christians, claiming that the former are 'unquestionably monotheistic', while the belief of the latter in the Trinity suggests they should be regarded as 'idol-worshippers'.[102] The same rabbis (using Maimonides) attack Christianity as a form of paganism and of idol-worshipping which should be discouraged in the 'land of Israel'. Rabbi Moshe Levinger of the Jewish settlement in Hebron, for instance, has always referred to Palestinian Muslims as 'Ishmaelites' (he never says Muslims, Arabs or Palestinians), who basically 'do not worship idols': 'Maimonides determined that Islam is not pagan, like Christianity. If there had been a crucifix here [in the Ibrahimi Mosque of Hebron], it would have been a different matter.'[103]

Doctrinal disputes: *Gush Emunim* and the *haredi* rabbis

The widespread use and abuse of Maimonides's theology in contemporary Israel is also evident from the fact that the deployment of his theological publications cut across religious Zionist and non-Zionist parties and rabbis; Sephardi and Ashkenazi rabbis; modernist nationalist and ultra-orthodox *haredi* communities. Maimonides's enormous influence on *haredi* rabbis is hardly surprising, but their interpretation of his theology is distinctly different from that of the nationalist religious messianics. In some respect the *haredi* communities in Israel are the inheritors of the

Jewish religion in its classical form. The clash between *haredi* orthodoxy and modern, largely secular, Zionism has been central to the evolution of orthodox Judaism in Israel. The ultra-orthodox also remained sworn enemies of the Rabbis Kook (father and son)[104] and have continued to proclaim their opposition to Zionism. The roots of *haredi* opposition to both secular and religious Zionism are found in the Talmudic literature in which Jews were obliged to take 'three oaths', two of them, a) that Diaspora Jews should not rebel against non-Jews; b) that they should not massively emigrate to Palestine 'before the right time', that is before the coming of the Messiah and the end of the exile by God himself. In the past fifteen centuries the vast majority of most important Jewish rabbis interpreted 'the three oaths' as making the continued existence of Jews in exile as a religious obligation.[105] Until the nineteenth century influential European rabbis continued to warn against massive immigration of Jews to Palestine, even with the consent of all the nations of the world, before the coming of the Messiah.

Political Zionism rejected this fundamental tenet of orthodox Judaism. It emerged at the end of the nineteenth century in a fierce struggle with orthodox Judaism which was supported by most influential rabbis of the period. But the reinvention of Maimonides as a 'nationalist religious Zionist' had to wait until the after the establishment of the State of Israel. It was only after the 1967 conquests that Maimonides became the patron saint of the Zionist religious camp.[106] In contrast, in spite of the enormous prestige Maimonides enjoys among orthodox and *haredi* Jews as the first codifier of the *halacha* and as the leading theologian of Judaism, he remains suspect among the *haredim*, mainly because his philosophy attempted to synthesize the Jewish faith and Greek-Arabic Aristotelian rational philosophy. Traditionally the greatest criticism had been levelled at *The Guide of the Perplexed*. Conservative and super-purist sages labelled it a heretical work. In 1230, a group of purists succeeded in persuading the Roman Church to burn *The Guide of the Perplexed*. Some sages banned this work to all but mature Talmudists.[107] Nowadays most *haredi* rabbis in Israel still keep *The Guide of the Perplexed* and other philosophical writings of Maimonides away from most of their people.[108]

The nationalist religious rabbis of the NRP and *Gush Emunim*, in total disregard of the *haredi* and orthodox rabbis' theology, have claimed that the messianic era with the pre-eminence of the Torah in the World has already begun; that the 'three oaths' do not apply in messianic times; and that, although the Messiah has not appeared, a cosmic process called the 'beginning of redemption' has begun. During the beginning of these messianic times some of the previous religious laws should be disregarded and others should be changed. Thus the doctrinal dispute between the NRP and the *haredi* rabbis has centred on the issue of whether Jews are living in normal times or in the period of the 'beginning of messianic redemption.'[109] Other party political and personal rivalries further fuelled the intense mutual hatred between the diverse fundamentalist groups of religious Jews, especially in the personal quarrels between rabbis representing these diverse groups.

While the nationalist religious messianic camp has been expanding in Israel since the early 1970s, the political and electoral successes of the *haredi* sects and parties in Israel came to public attention only from the 1988 general elections onwards. Until then members of the *haredi* communities lived in generally self-sustained and residentially segregated areas of in the cities. *Haredi* Judaism, despite its opposition to Zionism, has changed its stance since the late 1980s; it has demanded a role of leadership, advocating a form of (non-Zionist) Jewish fundamentalism and insisting that both the domestic and foreign policy of Israel be derived from the *halacha*. Moreover becoming self-confident after their electoral gains in 1988 and 1993, the *haredim* strengthened their doctrinal opposition to secular and religious Zionism. In 1989, the two most influential *haredi* rabbis in Israel, Rabbi Menahem Eli'ezer Shach and Rabbi 'Ovadia Yosef (the spiritual leaders of Degel Ha'Torah[110] and Shas parties respectively) held an anti-Zionist convention in Bnei Brak, a town near Tel Aviv. Rabbi Yosef is head of the seven-member *Mo'etzet Hachamei Hatorah* (Council of Torah Sages) and the Lithuanian Rabbi Shach is one of the leaders of *Mo'etzet Gedolei Hatorah* (Council of Great Torah Scholars). For many years Rabbi Shach had been conducting fierce personal, ideological and scholarly rivalry with the late Rabbi Schneerson, the New-York-based messianic Hassidic rabbi.[111] In their speeches, which were published in the *haredi* newspaper *Yated Neeman* (the weekly of Degel Ha'Torah), Rabbi Shach and Rabbi Yosef addressed from an halachic perspective the issue of whether some areas of the 'land of Israel' should be given to non-Jews, that is, to Palestinians. The two rabbis rejected the 'beginning of redemption' doctrine; the messianic time of redemption had not yet arrived; Jews still live in normal times. They also rejected the NRP view that in accordance with the 'beginning of redemption' no land should be given to non-Jews; saving Jewish lives should be more important than holding onto parts of the 'land of Israel'.[112]

The two *haredi* rabbis were lauded by Israeli liberals and peace activists for approving the concept of partial withdrawal from the occupied territories in order to avert war and save Jewish lives, but little attention was paid to other, no less significant, pronouncements made by the rabbis at the convention. For instance, Rabbi Yosef (who is renowned for his halachic erudition and for being a important political figure in Israel) acknowledged that in messianic times Jews would be more powerful than non-Jews and would then be obliged by the *halacha* to conquer the 'land of Israel' and expel all non-Jews and to destroy the 'idolatrous Christian churches'. Yosef stated:

> The Jews are not in fact more powerful than the non-Jews and are unable to expel the non-Jews from the land of Israel because the Jews fear the non-Jews ... God's commandment is then not valid ... Even non-Jews who are idolaters live among us with no possibility of their being expelled or even moved. The Israeli government is obligated by international law to guard the Christian churches in the land of Israel, even though those churches are definitely places of idolatry and cult practice. This is so in spite of the fact that we are commanded by our [religious] law to destroy all idolatry and its servants until we uproot it from all parts of our land and any areas that we are able to conquer ... Surely, this fact continues to weaken the religious meaning of the Israel army's conquests [in 1967].[113]

In a 1994 Knesset debate on 'The Basic Law: Human Dignity and Liberty', a Shas Member of the Knesset, Yosef 'Azran, had this to say: 'The issue of equality [before the law in Israel] is impossible because it is a catastrophe from the standpoint of religion and it says that a Gentile and a Jew are the same.'[114] The spiritual leader of his party, Rabbi Yosef, whose political pragmatism is often admired in Israel, has never concealed his anti-Christian theology: the view that Jews, when sufficiently powerful, have a halachic duty to expel the Christians from the Holy Land and destroy all Christian churches, but only if doing so would not endanger Jewish life.[115] This openly anti-Christian sentiment is also demonstrated by fact that the term 'Red Cross', supposedly associated with Christianity, is prohibited from usage in the *haredi* press.[116] Although *haredi* rabbis continued to express doctrinal opposition to religious Zionism, and especially the doctrine of 'the beginning of redemption', they also continued to advocate a form of Jewish fundamentalism, with its visible hostility towards Christianity and Palestinian Christians.

Burning the New Testament

Jewish fundamentalist theology is increasingly encouraged by thinkers from central religious institutions in Israel. For instance, Ovadia Yosef, ex-Sephardi Chief Rabbi of Israel and spiritual mentor of Shas (an acronym for *Shomrie Torah Sephardim* translated as 'Separdi Torah Gauardians'); this party of the Separdi Jewish *Haredim* seeks a *halacha* state in Israel, and has ruled that the New Testement should be publicly burned because Christianity is a form of idolatry.[117] On 23 March 1980, following Rabbi Yosef's ruling, hundreds of copies of the New Testament were publicly and ceremonially burned in Jerusalem under the auspices of *Yad Leakhim*, a Jewish religious organization subsidized by the Israeli Ministry of Religions.[118] Another impact of the same ruling was revealed in the Hebrew daily *Ma'ariv* in June 1985 when New Testament copies found in the library of the base of the army Chief Education Officer were burned by the military rabbi of the base.[119] Three weeks later *Ma'ariv* reported that the Knesset Foreign Affairs and Defence Committee had referred to the incident and one of its members (Rabbi Haim Druckman, a Member of the Knesset and prominent supporter of *Gush Emunim*) had justified the New Testament burning.[120] Some Jewish fundamentalists (for instance: Moshe Ben-Yosef Hagar), however, advised against burning copies of the Old Testament, but only because, indirectly, Christian beliefs affirm the Jewish people's connection to the 'land of Israel.'[121]

The Question of Jerusalem

The messianic rabbis see the Palestinians' very residence in the Holy Land as making them criminals and imply that Israel's failure to clear out the Palestinian Muslims and Christians from Jerusalem completely is a transgression of the *halacha*.[122] The same rabbis have demanded that the Palestinians should be at least discouraged from living in Jerusalem. They repeatedly cite the following from Maimonides's *Mishneh Torah*: 'Jerusalem is more sacred than other towns surrounded by a wall ... no place allowed in it for *ger toshav*.'[123] Rabbi Shalom Dov Wolpo, who bases his views on both Maimonides and the opinions of the Brooklyn-based rabbi from Lyubavich (the late Rabbi Schneerson, the head of the Habbad Hassidic movement) emphasizes that not even a '*ger toshav*' can live in Jerusalem, and how much less Christians and Muslims who are not included in this category:

> According to *halacha* it is forbidden for a gentile to live in Jerusalem, and in accordance with the ruling by Maimonides it is forbidden to permit even a *ger toshav* in Jerusalem ... True, this applies when Israel has a strong hand, but today, too, although it is not possible to expel them by force, this does not mean that we have to encourage them to live there.[124]

Rabbi Eli'ezer Waldenberg, the Israel Prize winner for 1976, stated:

> It is forbidden for gentiles to live in Jerusalem. I, for example, support upholding the *halacha* prohibition on a gentile's living in Jerusalem, and if we would apply the *halacha* as we should, we would have to expel all the gentiles from Jerusalem and purify it absolutely. Also we must not permit the gentiles to be a majority in any of Israel's cities.[125]

Rabbi Wolpo adds:

> If they [the Israeli leaders] had declared at the time of the occupation of Jerusalem and the territories [in June 1967] that they were going to leave alive the residents and give them financial compensation, but they must cross immediately to Trans-Jordan, they [the Arabs] would have been thankful for this until today ... yet what did the [Israeli] leaders do: they left the Arabs in their location ... but from the beginning they should have removed them from here.[126]

Rabbi Meir Kahane actually submitted to the Knesset a draft bill that would make the *halacha* ban on the residence of a '*ger toshav*' in Jerusalem the law of the State of Israel, but it was disqualified by the Knesset presidium on 3 December 1984.[127]

The *haredi* press described the political change in the Jerusalem City Council in 1993, and the replacement of Labour Mayor Teddy Kollek by Likud Ehud Olmert, as the 'first stage of the deliverance of Israel from the claws of heresy'.[128] The rule of Kollek and his secular colleagues, according to the *haredi* organ *Yated Neeman*, represented a 'Hellenistic heretic culture' and pro-Christian attitudes. Another *haredi* organ, *Hamodia*, was highly critical of Kollek's policies towards Christian institutions in Jerusalem and his support for the idea of a Mormon centre in the city.[129]

'Ateret Cohanim and the St John's Hospice

Since 1967 much of Israeli settlement activity has been undertaken to 'redeem' East Jerusalem's Old City from its Christian and

Muslim inhabitants. The Old City, however, has remained predominantly inhabited by Palestinian Muslims and Christians. In the Old City's Jewish Jerusalem Quarter and its surrounding districts, some 4,000 Palestinians were evicted to make possible the reconstruction of a vastly enlarged and completely Jewish Quarter, excluding its former Arab residents.[130] In order to preserve the ethnic purity of the Old City's Jewish Quarter, in 1981 Israel's High Court ruled that non-Jews could not buy property there.[131] Both the Muslim and Christian quarters of the Old City – in sharp contrast to the Jewish Quarter – have remained religiously mixed and according to Israel's Statistical Yearbook of 1988, 3,900 Christians and 700 Muslims lived in the Christian Quarter.

The messianic rabbis have sought to establish a Jewish theocracy in the 'whole land of Israel' and the rebuilding of the Temple in Jerusalem. In 1983, while serving as Sephardi Chief Rabbi, Eliyahu had sponsored a conference with 'Ateret Cohanim yeshiva on the rebuilding of the Third Temple in Jerusalem. Apparently Rabbi Eliyahu believes that the Third Temple would descend from heaven amidst flames of fire – at that point the Muslim shrines, the Dome of the Rock and the al-Aqsa Mosque, would be burnt and the Third Temple built in their place.[132]

Five years earlier, in December 1978, a group of orthodox Jews and disciples of Rabbi Tzvi Yehuda Kook announced they had set up a yeshiva in the Muslim Quarter of the Old City of Jerusalem, calling it 'Ateret Cohanim: 'the Priestly Crown'. 'Ateret Cohanim was formed to publish and distribute material concerning 'the priesthood and functions of the Temple', and 'to acquire in any manner whatsoever and especially by grant, gift lease or purchase-land, rooms or houses [in Arab East Jerusalem]'. Its members state openly that they want to prepare the way for the Messiah by 'redeeming' the Old City stone by stone, until they have transformed Jerusalem into a holy city in the service of the Third Temple. They also justify the expulsion of Palestinian Muslim and Christians by invoking Maimonides who said that after the Messiah comes, only Jews will be permitted to live in Jerusalem.[133] Since the 1980s Friend of 'Ateret Cohanim in the United States recorded millions of US dollars in donations. Some of the money has come from right-wing Christian evangelicals in the US who view the activities of Jewish Israeli fundamentalists as the prelude to the Second Coming.[134] 'Ateret Cohanim officials stated that most of the money collected in the US goes to its subsidiary, the 'Jerusalem Reclamation Project', founded in the early 1980s, whose primary purpose is to purchase Arab property in East Jerusalem.

The activities included the takeover of the St John's Hospice in the Old City, just a few metres from the Church of the Holy Sepulchre. On 11 April 1990, during the Easter Holy Week and Passover, 150 armed Jewish settlers affiliated with 'Ateret Cohanim moved into the seventy-room St John's Hospice near the Church of the Holy Sepulchre. The hospice is owned by the Greek Orthodox Church, but had been leased since 1932 to an Armenian called Martyos Matossian. The latter, an elusive man, rented hospice rooms to Arab families and European pilgrims, but the Greek Orthodox Church had been trying to evict him since 1980. On 28 June 1989 Matossian sublet the building for $3.5 million to a mysterious Panamanian company called SBC Ltd., which turned over the building to the Jewish settlers. The settlers renamed the site Neot David, put up a Star of David and invited Israeli minister Ariel Sharon to visit the site. The Israeli Housing Ministry, which had been quietly helping 'Ateret Cohanim to purchase Arab property in the Old City since 1986, had covertly channelled $1.8 million to a subsidiary of the Jewish National Fund (JNF). The JNF company then passed the money to subsidize the purchase of the sublease to the Panama-based SBC.[135]

The encroachment by Jewish fundamentalist settlers into the Christian Quarter, culminating in the purchase of the hospice, erupted into a huge controversy in Israel and the West. On 27 April 1990 all the major Christian churches in Israel and the occupied territories closed and rang funeral peals in protest. Also it was the first time that the Church of the Holy Sepulchre had been closed in eight hundred years. In New York Cardinal O'Connor denounced the takeover as an 'obscene' plot to acquire Christian property in the Holy Land. In Jerusalem the Greek Orthodox Church argued that the sublet to SBC was illegal. The Church's claim was subsequently upheld by an Israel court, which then ordered the settlers to vacate the property but permitted twenty security and 'maintenance employees' (who are actually settlers of 'Ateret Cohanim) to remain in the building pending litigation. The settlers and their families are still living in the hospice.[136]

Epilogue

In the 1990s the Oslo process and the Israeli-Palestinian agreements clearly shocked the *Gush Emunim* rabbis and leaders and brought to the surface the deep divisions that had been developing inside Israeli society in response to the peace talks with the

Palestinians. The establishment of the Palestinian Authority in Gaza and the West Bank and the appearance of armed Palestinian police and the sight of Palestinians waving their flags all constituted visible evidence of the weaknesses of the messianic vision of a quick redemption. In recent years the messianic rabbis have turned their hatred to the 'Jewish traitors', whose treason spoiled God's plan and influenced many Israelis to disregard the divine commandments and to follow the traitors, who are prepared to give away parts of the 'sacred' land. A leader of the NRP, Rabbi Yitzhak Levy, who had made clear his opposition to allowing Israeli Arab Knesset members the right to vote on the Oslo Accords of 1993 and who, according to the daily *Haaretz* of 25 February 1998, was reputed to have supported 'exiling Arabs' in the occupied territories to other Arab states.[137]

Rabbi Levy was known to be close to former Sephardi Chief Rabbi Mordechai Eliyahu, another advocate of the 'whole land of Israel', who has called for the rehabilitation of the young messianic Zionist, Yigal Amir, who in 1995 murdered Prime Minister Yitzhak Rabin.[138] In a sense Rabin's assassination in 1995 by a religious Zionist, Yigal Amir, was a religious murder, carried out with rabbinical halachic sanction.[139] In the wake of the murder two influential West Bank rabbis, Dov Leor and Nahum Rabinovich, were accused of issuing a religious edict, declaring the Israeli premier to be a *rodef* – a person whose killing is permissible under *halachic* law.[140] Expressing a fundamentalist theology and echoing Neo-Zionism's hostility towards the symbols of Christianity in the Holy Land, Rabbi Yair Dreyfus, an articulate settlement leader, declared:

> The true Jews, desirous to live as Jews, will have no choice but to separate themselves in ghettos, The new, sinful Canaanite-Palestinian state [Israel after Oslo] will soon be established upon the ruins of the genuine Jewish-Zionist state ... God may even make war against this polluted throne of his. The Jews who lead us into that sin no longer deserve any divine protection ... Our leadership will walk a Via Dolorosa before it understands that we are commanded to resist the [secular] state of Israel, not just its present government.[141]

The deployment of Mainmonides' theology in present-day Israel is evident from the fact that the widespread use of his theological works cut across Neo-Zionist and non-Zionist movements and rabbis; Sephardi and Ashkenazi rabbis; messianic nationalist and ultra-orthodox *haredi* communities. But the reinvention of the greatest symbol of Arabo-Jewish heritage as a religious zealot is an extraordinary phenomenon that is a product of post-1967 imperial Israel. Moreover the fact that the newly concocted Maimonides has become, in a peculiar way, the hero of Neo-Zionism and anti-Arab religious fundamentalism is more indicative of the rise and growing influence of fundamentalist currents in Israeli society.

The reinvention of Maimonides's theology in present-day Israel has been condemned by prominent Jewish intellectuals, including the late Yesha'ayahu Leibovitch, himself an orthodox Jew and an international authority on Maimonides and former editor-in-chief of the *Encyclopedia Hebraica*.[142] There was also a minority of liberal Israelis who saw the activities of Jewish fundamentalist groups, such as Kach and other similar groups as the outcome of a deeply ingrained anti-Arab racism, which permeates and is part of the general brutalization of society. Professor Dan Meron of Tel Aviv University wrote that the fundamentalist phenomenon 'grew out of the well-known' 'home-made' racism. 'This racism is not unique, but exists in all sections of the Israeli public ... it is part of the general brutalisation and behaviour of our society.'[143] Of course a state run by the *halacha* would not be consistent with the basic conceptions of democracy and individual freedom. There is good reason to suggest, however, that the more that Jewish fundamentalism increases (in both its Zionist religious messianic and non-Zionist *hardi* forms), and the greater the role of the *halacha* in the political life of Israel becomes, the more vigorously fundamentalist rabbis will demand that the Palestinians, Christians and Muslims, be dealt with according to halachic regulations, including the imposition of the status of *ger toshav* ('resident alien') on them, and the treatment of Christianity in the Holy Land as a form of 'idolatry' (*'avoda zara'*). However, while the reinvention of Mainmonides is symptomatic of the kind of intolerant new religious politics in present-day Israel, the struggle over Maimonides is also a struggle over reclaiming the classical cultural heritage of Arabo-Judaism and future interfaith relations in the Holy Land. Furthermore the struggle over Maimonides in Israel is only the tip of the iceberg of a more profound conflict between those seeking to strengthen the Jewish religious identity of Israel and those wishing to transform Israel into a secular democratic state.

Notes

1 Keren Armstong, *The Batle for God*, New York, Alfred A. Knopf, 2000; James Barr, *Fundamentalism*, London, SCM Press, 1997; Lionel Caplan, (ed.), *Studies in Religious Fundamentalism in Comparative Perspective: Religion, Ideology and the Crisis of Modernity*, Albany, State University of New York Press, 1987;

Gilles Kepel, *The Revenge of God: The Resurgence of Islam, Christianity and Judaism in the Modern World,* Cambridge, Polity Press, 1994; Martin E. Marty and R. Scott Appleby (eds), *The Fundamentalism Project, Fundamentalisms Comprehended,* vol. 5, Chicago, University of Chicago Press, 1995; Martin E. Marty and R. Scott Appleby (eds), *The Fundamentalism Project, Fundamentalisms Observed,* vol.1, Chicago, University of Chicago Press, 1991; Martin E. Marty and R. Scott Appleby (eds), *The Fundamentalism Project, Fundamentalisms and Society,* vol. 2, Chicago, University of Chicago Press, 1993; Martin E. Marty and R. Scott Appleby (eds), *Fundamentalisms and the State, The Fundamentalisms Project,* vol. 3, Chicago, University of Chicago Press, 1993; Laurence Silberstein, (ed.), *Jewish Fundamentalism in Comparative Perspective: Religion, Ideology, and the Crisis of Morality,* New York, New York University Press, 1993; E. Sivan and M. Friedman, *Religious Radicalism and Politics in the Middle East,* New York, State University of New York Press, 1990; Nazih Ayyubi, *Political Islam: Religion and Politics in the Arab World,* London, New York, Routledge, 1991; Ziad Abu-Amr, *Islamic Fundamentalism in the West Bank and Gaza: Muslim Brotherhood and Islamic Jihad,* Bloomington, IN, Indiana University Press, 1994; Jeffrey K. Hadden and Anson Shupe (eds), *Secularization and Fundamentalism Reconsidered,* New York, Paragon House, 1989; Bruce Lawrence, *Defenders of God: The Fundamentalist Revolt Against the Modern Age,* San Francisco, Harper & Row Publishers, 1989.

2 The name *haredim,* which means 'fearful' or 'God-fearing', refers to those ultra-orthodox Jews who object to modern innovations.

3 The term 'Jewish religious fundamentalist' applies to those individuals, parties and movements with a radical fundamentalist approach to religion and state, wanting Israel to become a *halachic* state, that is, one governed by Jewish religious law.

4 Michael Prior, *Zionism and the Jewish State: A Moral Inquiry,* London, Routledge, 1999, p. 84; Marc H. Ellis, *Israel and Palestine: Out of the Ashes,* London and Sterling, Virginia: Pluto Press, 2002, pp. 57–61.

5 Ian Lustick, *For the Land and the Lord: Jewish Fundamentalism in Israel,* New York: Council on Foreign Relations, 1988.

6 Jacob Talmom, 'Who Is a Jew?' *Encounter,* May 1965, cited in Georges Tamarin, *The Israeli Dilemma,* Rotterdam: Rotterdam University Press, 1973, p. 37.

7 Noam Chomsky, *Peace in the Middle East? Reflections of Justice and Nationhood,* Glasgow: Fontana/Collins, 1975, pp. 37–8.

8 Yehoshafat Harkabi, *Hakhra'ot Goraliyot* [Fateful Decisions], Tel Aviv, 'Am 'Oved, 1986, p. 207.

9 *Davar Rishon,* 27 November 1995.

10 Lustick, *For the Land and the Lord,* pp. ix, 12–6, 153.

11 Israel Shahak and Norton Mezvinsky, *Jewish Fundamentalism in Israel,* London: Pluto Press, 1999, p. 83.

12 Lustick, *For the Land and the Lord,* pp. 8, 12–15; David Schnall, 'An Impact Assessment,' in David Newman (ed.), *The Impact of Gush Emunim,* London, Croom Helm, 1985, p. 15.

13 Ehud Sprinzak, *The Ascendance of Israel's Radical Right,* New York and Oxford, Oxford University Press, 1991, p. 107.

14 Zoughbi Zoughbi, '–Christian-Muslim Relations in Palestine-A Personal View', in *Sabeel Newsletter,* 12 (Summer 1998), p. 12. Also available at: http://www.sabeel.org/news/newslt12/

15 Philip K. Hitti, *History of the Arabs,* London and New York, Macmillan Press

and St Martin's Press, 1956, 6th edition, pp. 576, 584–5.
16 Abdel-Rahim Omran, *Population in the Arab World: Problems and Prospects*, New York and London, Croom Helm, 1980, pp. 18, 23–4; *Time*, 23 December 1985.
17 Prior, *Zionism and the State of Israel*, pp. 56–7.
18 Yeshaiahu Leibowitz, *The Faith of Maimonides*, New York, Adama Books, 1987, p. 68.
19 Hitti, *History of the Arabs*, p. 584; Bernard Lewis, *Islam in History: Ideas, Men and Events in the Middle East*, London, Alcove Press, 1973, pp. 166–76.
20 Oliver Leaman, *Moses Maimonides*, London and New York, Routledge, 1990.
21 Leaman, *Moses Maimonides*, p. x.
22 S. D. Goitein, *Jews and Arabs: Their Contacts Through the Ages*, New York: Schocken Books, 1964, pp. 70–1, 93.
23 *The Quran*, 2.113, 135–6.
24 Goitein, *Jews and Arabs*, p. 84.
25 Ibid., pp. 70–1.
26 Ibid., p. 130.
27 Franz Rosenthal, *The Classical Heritage of Islam*, London, Routledge and Kegan Paul, 1975; Nissim Rajwan, 'Aspects of Jude-Arabic Culture', *New Outlook* 11, no. 1 (1986), pp. 31–42; Isidore Epstein, *Judaism: A Historical Presentation*, London, Penguin, 1990.
28 Quoted in Ilan Halevi, *A History of the Jews*, London, Zed Book, 1987, p. 61.
29 Ibid., pp. 131–2.
30 Ibid, pp. 134–6.
31 Ibid., pp. 73–5.
32 Quoted Carole Hillenbrand, *The Crusades: Islamic Perspectives*, Edinburgh, Edinburgh University Press, 1999, p. 66.
33 Ibid., pp. 66–8.
34 Leibowitz, *The Faith of Maimonides*, p. 59.
35 Marvin Fox, 'Trinity' *Encyclopaedia Judaica* 7, Jerusalem: Keter Publishing House, 1971, pp. 671–2.
36 Mordechai Nisan, *Toward a New Israel: The Jewish State and the Arab Question*, New York, AMS Press, 1992, p. 170.
37 Lustick, *For the Land and the Lord*, p. 120.
38 Cited in Harkabi, *Hakhra'ot Goraliyot*, p. 208.
39 Ian Lustick, 'Israel's Dangerous Fundamentalists', *Foreign Policy* (Fall 1987), pp. 118–39.
40 Yosef Gorny, *The State of Israel in Jewish Public Thought*, London, Macmillan, 1994, pp. 150–1.
41 Leibowitz, *The Faith of Maimonides*, p. 61.
42 Clive Jones, 'Ideo-Theology and the Jewish State: From Conflict to Conciliation?' *British Journal of Middle Eastern Studies* 26, no.1 (May 1999), pp. 11–14; Michael Prior, 'Settling for God', *Middle East International*, no. 565 (19 December 1997), pp. 20–1.
43 Jones, 'Ideo-Theology and the Jewish State', p. 12.
44 Quoted in David J. Schnall, *Beyond the Green Line: Israeli Settlements West of the Jordan*, New York, Praeger & Co., 1984, p. 19.
45 Shaham, in *Yedi'ot Aharonot* supplement, 13 April 1979.
46 See Kook's article in *Hatzofeh*, 23 June 1967.
47 Quoted in Rabbi Pichnik (ed.), *Shanah Beshanah*, 5728 (Hebrew) [Year by Year], Jerusalem, Hekhal Shlomo Publication, 1968, pp. 108–9.

48 Nisan, *Toward a New Israel*, p. 167.
49 Ibid., p. 163.
50 Ibid.
51 Ibid., p. 156.
52 *Kivunim*, no. 24 (August 1984), pp. 151–6; Harkabi, *Hakhra'ot Goraliyot*, pp. 216–7.
53 Nisan, *Toward a New Israel*, pp. 173–4.
54 Shlomo Aviner, 'Yerushat Haaretz Vehabe'ayah Hamusarit' [The Inheritance of the Land and the Moral Problem] *Artzi* 2 [My Country] (Jerusalem, 1983), p. 10.
55 Tzvi Yehuda Kook, 'Bein 'Am Veartzo' [Between People and its Land], *Artzi* 2 (Spring 1982), p. 10.
56 Harkabi, *Hakhra'ot Goraliyot*, p. 211.
57 The term 'sages' is used both to designate all rabbis mentioned in the Talmud and to refer more vaguely to past orthodox rabbis.
58 Yisrael Ariel, 'Devarim Kehavayatam' [Things As They Are], *Tzippiyah, I: Anthology of Contemporary Problems, Israel, the Land and the Temple*, Jerusalem, Hamateh 'Lema'an Ahai ve Rea'ai'' publication, 1980.
59 Amos Elon, *A Blood-Dimmed Tide: Dispatches from the Middle East*, New York: Columbia University Press, 1997, p. 197.
60 Lawrence Joffe, *Keesing's Guide to the Mid-East Peace Process*, London, Cartermill, 1996, p. 151.
61 Cited in Mark Tessler, 'The Political Right in Israel: Its Origins, Growth and Prospects', *Journal of Palestine Studies* 15, no. 2 (winter 1986), p. 31.
62 *Meir Kahane, Lesikim Be'enekhem* [They Shall be Strings in Your Eyes], Jerusalem: Hamakhon Lara'ayon Hayehudi, 1980/81, pp. 244–5.
63 This proposed law is found in Yair Kotler, *Heil Kahane*, New York, Adama Books, 1986, pp. 203–7.
64 Cited in Kotler, *Heil Kahane*, pp. 205–6.
65 Kahane, *Lesikim Be'eneikhim*, p. 234.
66 This draft bill is found in Kotler, *Heil Kahane*, pp. 198–201.
67 Ibid., pp. 198 and 203; Harkabi, *Hakhra'ot Goraliyot*, pp. 220–1.
68 Michael Prior, *The Bible and Colonialism: A Moral Critique*, Sheffield, Sheffield Academic Press, 1997.
69 Shahak and Mezvinsky, *Jewish Fundamentalism in Israel*, p. 73.
70 Kook, 'Bein 'Am Veartzo', p. 19.
71 *Bat Kol*, 26 February 1980.
72 *Bat Kol*, 26 February 1980; (1 Samuel 15:3)
73 Ibid.
74 Cited in *Journal of Palestine Studies* 10, no.1 (autumn 1980), p. 150; Danny Rubinstein, *Mi La-H' Elai: Gush Emunim* [On the Lord's Side: *Gush Emunim*], Tel Aviv, Hakibbutz Hameuhad Publishing House, 1982, p. 91; Yehuda Litani in *Haaretz*, 15 May 1984, p. 15.
75 Amnon Rubinstein, *Mehertzel 'Ad Gush Emunim Uvehazarah* [From Herzl to *Gush Emunim* and Back Again], Tel Aviv, Schocken Press, 1980, p. 124.
76 Ibid.
77 *New York Times*, 4 June 1980.
78 *Newsweek*, 16 June 1980; Rubinstein, *Mi La-H' Elai*, p. 94.
70 Ariel, 'Devarim Kehavayatam'.
80 Avi Raz in *Ma'ariv*, 18 September 1992.
81 Shahak and Mezvinsky, *Jewish Fundamentalism in Israel*, p. 73.

82 Rubinstein, *Mehertzel 'Ad Gush Emunim Uvehazarah*, p. 125.
83 Ibid., p. 179.
84 See for instance *Torah Ve'avodah* [Torah and Work], no.6 (Jerusalem, 1984).
85 Uriel Tal in *Haaretz*, 26 September 1984, p. 27; Hanna Kim, 'To Annihilate Amalek,' *'Al-Hamishmar*, 12 March 1984; Yoram Peri, 'Expulsion is not the Final Stage', *Davar*, 3 August 1984; Yehoshu'a Rash, 'Uriel Tal's Legacy', *Gesher* 32, no. 114 (summer 1986), p. 77.
86 R. J. Zvi Werblowsky, 'Jewish Attitudes Towards Christiniaty', in *Encyclopaedia Judaica* 5, Jerusalem, Keter, 1971, pp. 513–4.
87 Jacob Katz, *Exclusiveness and Tolerance: Studies in Jewish-Gentile Relations in Medieval and Modern Times*, London, Oxford University Press, 1961.
88 Ephraim Urbach, 'Avoda Zara', *Encyclopaedia Hebraica* 26, Jerusalem, Encyclopaedia Publishing Company, 1974, pp. 614–23 (Hebrew).
89 Harkabi, *Hakhra'ot Goraliyot*, p. 221.
90 'Avodah Zarah', in *Encyclopaedia Judaica* Jerusalem, Keter publishing House, 1971, p. 980.
91 Harkabi, *Hakhra'ot Goraliyot*, p. 221.
92 Maimonides, *Halachot Avoda Zara Vehokot Hagoim*, chapter 7, cited in Harkabi, *Hakhra'ot Goraliyot*, p. 221.
93 Maimonides, *Halachot Avoda Zara Vehokot Hagoiym*, chapter 10, cited in Harkabi, *Hakhra'ot Goraliyot*, pp. 221–2.
94 Abraham Haim Friedman, *Teshuvot Harambam* [Maimonides Responsa], Jerusalem, Mekitzi Nirdamim, 1934, p. 335.
95 Maimonides, *Halachot Avoda Zara Vehokot Hagoim*, chapter 9, cited in Harkabi, *Hakhra'ot Goraliyot*, p. 222.
96 *Teshuvot Harambam*, vol. 2, no. 448, p. 726; MT, Laws of Forbidden Foods, XI, 7.
97 Maimonides, *Masechet Avoda Zara*, cited in Harkabi, *Hakhra'ot Golraliyot*, p. 222.
98 *Teshuvot Harambam*, vol. 1, no. 149, pp. 284–5.
99 Lustick, *For the Land and the Lord*, p. 120.
100 Shahak and Mezvinsky, *Jewish Fundamentalism in Israel*, p. 75–6.
101 Ibid., p. 154.
102 Kook, 'Bein 'Am Vertzo', p. 19; Dov Leor, 'The Arabs and Us', *Artzi* 4 (spring 1986), p. 21; *Nekudah*, no. 93, 22 November 1985, p. 26.
103 Quoted in Elon, *A Blood-Dimmed Tide*, p. 70.
104 Gideon Aran, 'The Father, the Son and the Holy Land: The Spiritual Authorities of Jewish-Zionist Fundamentalism in Israel, in R. Scott Appleby (ed.), *Spokesmen for the Despised: Fundamentalist Leaders of the Middle East*, Chicago and London, University Press of Chicago, 1997, pp. 297–8.
105 Aviezer Ravitzky, *Messianism, Zionism and Jewish Religious Radicalism*, Chicago and London, University of Chicago Press, 1996.
106 Shahak and Mezvinsky, *Jewish Fundamentalism in Israel*, p. 19.
107 Gilbert S. Rosenthal (ed.), *Maimonides: His Wisdom for Our Time*, New York, Walker and Company, 1969, pp. xx-xxi.
108 Shahak and Mezvinsky, *Jewish Fundamentalism in Israel*, n. 17, p. 167.
109 Ibid.
110 In Hebrew 'Flag of the Torah', a faction within the *haredi* party of Yahdut Ha-Torah.
111 Rolef, *Political Dictionary of the State of Israel*, p. 372. See 'Habbad' in Susan Hattis Rolef (ed.), *Political Dictionary of the State of Israel*, New York, Macmillan

Publishing Company, 1993, 2nd edition, pp. 371-2.
112 *Yated Neeman*, 18 September 1989, quoted in Shahak and Mezvinsky, *Jewish Fundamentalism in Israel*, pp. 19-20.
113 Shahak and Mezvinsky, *Jewish Fundamentalism in Israel*, p. 20.
114 *Haaretz*, 7 November 1994.
115 Shahak and Mezvinsky, *Jewish Fundamentalism in Israel*, pp. 20-1.
116 Ibid., p. 33.
117 'Amos Ben-Vered in *Haaretz*, 23 October 1979, p. 8.
118 Shahak, *Jewish History, Jewish Religion*, p. 21.
119 *Ma'ariv*, 14 June 1985.
120 *Ma'ariv*, 5 July 1985, p. 19.
121 *Nekudah*, no. 93, 22 November 1985, p. 26.
122 Harkabi, *Hakhra'ot Goraliyot*, p. 212.
123 Moshe Ben Maimon, *Misheh Torah, Hu Hayad Hahazakah, Sefer 'Avoda*, vol. 9 Jerusalem, Mosad Harav Kook, 1985, pp. 46-7.
124 Shalom Dov Wolpo (ed.), *Da'at Torah Be'inyanei Hamatzav Beertz Hakodesh* [The Opinion of the Torah Regarding the Situation in the Holy Land], 3rd edn., Kiryat Gat, Israel, 1983, p. 146, n. 4.
125 Rubinstein, *Mehertzel 'Ad Gush Emunim Uvehazarah*, p. 123. Rubinstein's reference is *Haaretz*, 9 May 1976.
126 Ibid. p. 145.
127 Harkabi, *Hakhra'ot Goraliyot*, p. 212.
128 *Yated Neeman*, 14 November 1993.
129 *Hamodia*, 8 November 1993.
130 For further discussion, see Nur Masalha, *A Land Without a People*, London, Faber and Faber, 1997, p. 81.
131 Robert I. Friedman, *Zealots for Zion: Inside Israel's Settlement Movement*, New York, Random House, 1992, p. 99.
132 See Eti Ronel, 'Inside Israel: The Battle over Temple Mount', *New Outlook*, February 1984, p. 12.
133 Ibid., p. 118
134 Ibid., p. 113.
135 Ibid., pp. 99-100.
136 Ibid., p. 100.
137 Cited in Jones, 'Ideo-Theology and the Jewish State', p. 19.
138 Ibid.
139 Avi Shlaim, *The Iron Wall: Israel and the Arab World*, London, The Penguin Press, 2000, p. 550.
140 Jones, 'Ideo-Theology and the Jewish State', p. 14.
141 Quoted in Shahak and Mezvinsky, *Jewish Fundamentalism in Israel*, p. 89.
142 Cited in H. J. Skutel, 'Purifying Zion', *Journal of Palestine Studies* 12, no. 2 (winter 1983), p. 83.
143 Dan Miron in *Yedi'ot Aharonot*, 3 February 1984, pp. 10 and 19.

Chapter 8

The Jewish-Muslim Encounter in the Holy Land: the Theological and Political Implications for Christianity

Robert M. Johnson

Since the mission of Muhammad and the founding of Islam, Jews and Muslims have had a sustained religious encounter, developing well-formed views of each other that, despite evolving over time, have remained relatively consistent through the centuries – until the founding of the State of Israel in the twentieth century. This event and subsequent episodes in the Holy Land have led to major paradigm shifts that have altered the nature of the Jewish-Muslim encounter. Though perhaps not readily obvious, the resulting impact on interreligious dialogue between these two faith traditions also poses serious challenges to Christianity in its encounter with other faiths.

To understand the nature and the impact of these paradigm shifts, it is important first to recognize both the common ground that the two traditions share as well as the traditional views each has had of the other.

Common ground?

Common heritage, practices and experiences

Islam and Judaism 'echo one another'.[1] Both faiths originated in the Middle East and share much geographically and culturally. Both faiths understand themselves as beginning with, and descending from, Abraham, each believing that it 'has preserved the paternal legacy especially well and in its purest form ... [and thus possesses] the rightful claim to lineage from Abraham.'[2] Both traditions place heavy emphasis on their respective books of revelation and the authority of past interpretations of those books. The narratives in their respective scriptures tell of many common 'ancestors', such as Abraham, Ishmael, and Moses. David Halperin writes, 'Few will deny that much of what the Qur'an and later Muslim sources have to say about the prophets before Muhammad has its roots in the Bible and the Jewish haggadah.'[3] For other scholars, Islam is indebted to Judaism because of the latter's contribution of monotheism to the world – 'they worked from the assumption that Islam rose in part upon Jewish foundations.'[4] Yet as Halperin emphasizes, the resulting Muslim texts are also 'profound and accurate interpretations of their sources' concealed meaning.'[5]

Both faiths proclaim that it is beyond human capabilities to state the name of God, to articulate who 'I am' is. 'The basis for assuming that [both] traditions are in a sense on common ground here is that for [both] God is an ultimately inscrutable mystery, and the self-revelation that is received is never exhaustive of the reality.'[6] Thus the name of God 'will either have to be revealed to us, or will be a form of the abstract noun "divinity", as in *elohim* or Allah.'[7]

Each community believes itself to have a vocation, and both want to see religious principles embodied in the political, legal, and economic systems of their lands. 'Judaism and Islam ... have no ... conceptual differentiation between the profane and the religious realms. Instead, these are cultures in which everything ideally participates in the holy.'[8] The two traditions also share common practices. Prayer, fasting, ablutions, alms-giving and gender rules are part of the legal tradition of both faiths.

Both religions share a common experience with regard to the West 'of being a minority, and at times a barely tolerated minority, in a nominally Christian society'.[9] In medieval times both Jews and Muslims produced anti-Christian polemics in defence of their respective faiths before Christianity. 'In the anti-Christian polemics of both Jews and Muslims, the main issue was the Unity of God',[10] which appeared to Jews and Muslims alike to be distinctly absent in Christianity, a perspective that remains today.

Both Judaism and Islam view defeat from a long-term view, based on their commitment to yielding to God's will. Judaism has always affirmed a view of eschatological vindication, so for Jews defeat is seen as a part of life and is not unexpected. Within the Shi'ite tradition of Islam the memory of Ali, Muhammad's successor, and his descendents impresses on the believer the reality of communal suffering and temporary defeat; and for both Shi'ite and Sunni Islamists the return to a pristine, 'original' Islam in response to the problems of modernism lead to a similar eschatological view. To them this 'return to Islam explains why the movement has lasted successfully for so long against a much better equipped enemy, *and ensures that it will continue until the final victory* [italics added]'.[11]

Descendents of Abraham

As mentioned above, both traditions trace their origins back to Abraham, though the Abrahamic narratives in their respective texts differ. For the Jews Isaac was Abraham's blessed son, while for Muslims Abraham's blessing was bestowed upon Ishmael. This distinction has serious implications for determining who might be included in 'the Abrahamic community'.

For Jews 'Abraham symbolizes God's indissoluble union with the people of Israel.'[12] Jewish religious self-understanding places great emphasis on covenant, land, people, and faith, and all of these are encompassed in Abraham. 'Without Abraham, there would be no land, no covenant, no people, no true faith.'[13]

For Muslims the Abrahamic connection is also foundational. Though the subject is still debated, Karl-Josef Kuschel argues that it was widely accepted, long before Muhammad, that Arabs were descended from Ishmael.[14] Indeed 'Jews have been willing to grant that Christians and Muslims claim ... a complementary participation in the Abrahamic covenant, [though] each claims in its own way to bring that covenant to its consummation.'[15] In this regard Muhammad did not ignore nor abandon the prior revelations because he 'did not intend to found a new religion; he rather wished to restore the old and true faith'.[16] Thus Islam emerged as a corrective witness to Judaism (and Christianity); hence, it was important for Muhammad to link his understanding of faith with the Jewish (as well as the Christian) tradition, making the figure of Abraham central for Islam.

History of peaceful co-existence

It is widely perceived that Jews and Muslims lived together harmoniously in Spain in an era of flowering culture. In more recent times, Jews and Muslims have lived together harmoniously in parts of the Middle East. The idea that Jews and Muslims can co-exist peacefully thus appears to have strong historical precedents.

'Jewish experience under Islam ... has been happier, by and

large, than under Christendom,'[17] as 'Muslim rulers have generally been tolerant toward the Jews and have seen their value.'[18] Indeed, Muslims often 'point out that Mohammed believed in a living relationship with all faiths',[19] as reflected in Sûra 2:256 in the Quran: 'There is no compulsion in religion.' Muhammad Haleem attributes this to Islam's 'inherent tolerance', which is 'born out of the very nature of Islam'; in this Islamic traditionalist view Islam 'did not tolerate non-Muslims grudgingly, but welcomed them to live freely in Muslim society'.[20] Michel Abitol offers a slightly different view: because 'Islam never considered Judaism as a religious threat or as a theological rival, theological disputes between Jews and Muslims were almost non-existent'.[21]

Nonetheless Judaism was a beneficiary of this attitude:

> From the mid-ninth to the mid-thirteenth centuries ... the creative centres of Jewish life were to be found in the domain of Islam rather than in Christendom. In fact, it was in the medieval Muslim world that post-biblical Judaism, which had developed in late Antiquity, evolved and crystallised in many respects into the religious civilisation that we know today.[22]

It was in these Muslim lands that both the revival of the Hebrew language and the study of the Talmud outside traditional Jewish academies flourished,[23] leading to the further development of Hebrew beyond devotional and theological use.[24] A synagogue in Toledo illustrates this unusual interchange – it contains inscriptions in both Hebrew and Arabic, with verses from the Quran among the Arabic writing. Haleem states that due to this experience in al-Andalus, when Jews fled the persecutions of the Spanish Inquisition, they 'came to the Muslims in North Africa and Turkey to continue enjoying the protection they had always received under Muslim rule in Spain'.[25]

Some scholars cite evidence that Jews and Muslims have lived together peacefully more recently, even in the Middle East. Kirsten Schultze states, 'Closer study ... contradicts the prevailing view that Jews everywhere in the Middle East were second-class citizens, and after the establishment of the state of Israel in 1948 were the target of 'anti-Semitism' and persecution.'[26] As an example, Schultze argues that Jews were widely considered simply another of the Lebanon's twenty-three minorities, with the same rights and privileges as any other minority, and 'were perceived as Lebanese by the other communities'.[27] Likewise, in Tunisia 'as far as is known in the collective memory of Tunisian Jews, Muslim-Jewish co-existence was convenient and tranquil' until the late twentieth century.[28] The perception extends to Israel, too. It is pointed out that Israel 'has adopted a personal code which honours religious law, regardless of religion, as long as the individual belongs to a recognised religious group'.[29]

The other side of the coin

Yet for all these perceived commonalities and experiences, there has also been another side to the Jewish-Muslim encounter, indeed a different perception of some of the examples described above. Commonalities have often ended up as points of dispute between the two traditions, as different thinkers on both sides apply other interpretations to them. For example, each tradition tells similar stories of vocation and election concerning Noah, Abraham, and Moses, but 'each tradition interprets history rather differently in the light of these stories, in applying the election of calling to itself'.[30] Yet 'while *revelation* is claimed to be the common supreme reference for Judaism, Christianity, and Islam, each community speaks for its own (and "true") conception of revelation.'[31]

Thinkers in each tradition have sometimes found ways to interpret the same story to support an entirely different or totally opposite cause. Many Jewish thinkers have focused on the notion of election to support the view that Judaism is somehow above other monotheistic religions, disregarding subsequent revelation altogether. Sayyid Qutb, the Islamist ideologue, used the Quranic story of Joseph, which differs only in minor ways from the biblical story, to illustrate the supremacy of Islam and the need for Muslims to restore the original, pure version of the faith Islam, without regard for any Jewish relation to the story.

With regard to living together, not everyone agrees that Jewish-Muslim co-existence has always been so cordial and peaceful nor that the tolerance attributed to Islam was totally benevolent. As Kenneth Cragg puts it, the tolerance afforded 'to certain minorities always assumed their political subordination as *dhimmis*'.[32] Several scholars point to both the Quran and to historical accounts, where it appears that acceptance of *dhimmi* status implies not only recognition of Muslim rule but also an act of 'humiliation connected with the payment of the *jizya* [tax] according to Qur'an 9.29'.[33] That Surâh states that the People of the Book should be fought 'until they pay the *jizya* out of hand, while being humiliated'. Thus it is argued that 'Islamic tolerance views this matter from a different perspective: "I tolerate you in spite of your being inferior, provided you submit to the rule of Islam".'[34] In the example of Spain that is so often cited, Rosa Menocal acknowledges that the tranquility there might have resulted simply from the fact that Islam there grew mainly via conversions so that the Muslims already had much in common with their long-standing Jewish and Christian neighbours.[35] The earlier example of Lebanon, too, may be more the result of the form of government, accepting of multiple cultures, imposed by Maronite Christians at the creation of the Lebanese state.

In Israel – the only place where Muslims (and Christians) are a minority and Jews the majority – there are also differing views about co-existence.

> Scripture's halakhah does not contemplate Israel's [the Jewish people's] co-existence, in the Land, with Gentiles and their idolatry. The halakhah of the Oral Torah commences its treatment of the same subject with the opposite premise: Gentiles live side by side (whether or not in the Land of Israel) with Israelites, and Israelites have to sort out the complex problems of co-existence with idolatry.

Even then, 'there are relationships with Gentiles that are absolutely prohibited', particularly in commercial life.[36]

Here Jewish efforts at better relationships have, in some instances, slipped. For example, while there are *Sharia* courts in Israel, the jurisdictions of those courts have always been limited, and Israel no longer allows a *Mufti*, the ultimate arbiter of religious law, to enter the country. Muslim religious schools have also disappeared there.[37] Thus, while there is an element of tolerance toward Muslims, it has been restricted over time.

More examples could be cited, but the point remains that co-existence has historically been marked by both positive and negative experiences, which has affected the way the traditions have dealt with each other.

Dealing with 'the Other'

How any religion deals with another inevitably has something to do with its own self-definition. 'Religious communities identify their members according to centuries-old criteria about who is to be included within the fold,'[38] yet there is considerable debate within each religion about what those criteria are and how they are to be applied.

Jewish self-definition

'Jews are obsessed with this notion of identity,'[39] and there is substantial debate among Jews, both secular and religious, about what constitutes being a Jew. Moses Maimonides, 'widely recognized as Judaism's greatest theologian',[40] 'defined 'who is a Jew' in terms, first and foremost, of faith commitment, as opposed to national, racial, or ethnic affiliation,'[41] a view subsequently upheld by many other Jewish thinkers. Neusner, for example, holds that 'Idolatry defines the boundary between Israel [the Jewish people] and everybody else.'[42] In this view self-identity for Jews is a theological matter, not a secular one. Dan Cohn-Sherbok, on the other hand, states that historically it was unequivocally clear that to be a Jew was 'a matter of physical descent [and] personal religious belief is irrelevant'.[43] The result is that 'One of the salient features of modern Jewry is the lack of consensus about what constitutes membership in the Jewish people.'[44]

The establishment of the State of Israel complicated the issue by creating two new segments of the Jewish population: (i) secular Jews whose identity is no longer based on ethnicity or religion and (ii) religious Jews whose identity is no longer bound up with the Diaspora. 'The state thus provides a frame of reference for Jewish membership and community consciousness independent of specific religious content,' resulting in 'a crisis in Jewish identity... in large part because the Bible has lost its power and relevance for the majority of Israelis.'[45] 'For the first time in 2000 years an entire Jewish society is developing in which the religious assumptions about the nature of Jews and Judaism appear to many to be utterly irrelevant.'[46]

While there are many issues confronting Jews about their self-identity, taking the other into account has not traditionally been seen as one of those issues. Being 'first' in the historical line of revelation and given their understanding of God's election of and covenant with them, many Jews have not seen any need to account for the other. For Jews the governing premise is that Israel (i.e., the Jewish people) 'cannot change the world but must negotiate with its repugnant reality', following the principles of the Torah; thus 'When it comes to dealing with the outsider, halakhah focuses not upon the Gentiles but upon Israel: what, given the world as it is, can Israel do in the dominion subject to Israel's own will and intention?'[47] As Asher Lopatin says, 'The Jewish conception, as in Jeremiah 31:3: "Eternal love I conceived for you then [in the time of Moses]; therefore I continue my grace to you", serves well the Jewish need for self-definition.'⁴⁸

Their experiences in the Diaspora repeatedly forced Jewish thinkers to respond to challenges from the other. Regarding Muslims, 'the challenges to Judaism presented by Islam ... evoked a necessary Jewish response and new synthesis,'⁴⁹ resulting, for example, in the first systematic work of Jewish religious and ethical values by Moses Maimonides; but such responses did not include defining Jewishness in terms of the other. The definition of who was Jewish was still seen as a matter internal to Judaism. Yet that view is showing signs of changing, as we shall see later.

Muslim self-definition

Islam, on the other hand, is intimately bound up with its understanding of the other. First, 'the Qur'an does not hesitate to acknowledge its continuity with the older Scripture religions,'⁵⁰ thus establishing a relationship with Judaism from the start. Second, Muhammad's encounters with the other, especially with Jews and Christians, led to laws and practices regarding Muslims in relation to the other. Thus integral to Islamic religious tradition is 'the drawing of boundaries between oneself and "the other"'.⁵¹

Muslims believe that the Quran is God's final, perfect, unmediated revelation, correcting and abrogating earlier revelations to Jews and Christians. Islam then is the religion to which all of mankind is called. Yet

> The identity of the community is not as clear-cut in Islam as it is in Judaism ... [Although] the principal points of differentiation remain focused upon matters of faith and practice ... the lines between identity of the community of Prophet Muhammad and those outside that community are not neatly drawn in scripture ... The Quran, in fact, uses a number of terms to designate the faithful.⁵²

Further, Neusner believes that the term '*Islam* does not have the kind of exclusivist connotation in the Qur'an that would develop later. It seems instead to indicate all those who believe in the one God ... those who submit (*muslimun*).'⁵³

Yohanan Friedmann, on the other hand, presents a forceful argument that early on Islam very clearly delineated the difference between being a Muslim and the opposite, or 'infidelity': those who deny the prophethood of Muhammad are non-believers, non-Muslims.⁵⁴ According to Friedmann, the more complex issues involved determining whether all infidels were one and the same, or whether some groups deserved a separate classification, especially as 'People of the Book', who were then given *dhimmi* status.

Either way, Neusner points out, after the subsequent development of *fiqh* (Islamic legislation), 'The Muslim community' became defined as those who accept not only the prophet but also Muslim legislation. Then 'The identity of the Muslim community came to rest on Islamic law, rather than on issues of behavior.'[55]

In summary, then, 'Islam (like Christianity) forms a theology of holy Israel that differentiates its predecessor from the rest of humanity, a theology of the genealogy of monotheism, while Judaism, with nothing to account for beyond itself, has no reason to do so.'[56]

Definition of 'the Other': the role of monotheism

Given these self-definitions, how do the two religions view 'the other'? 'Both Judaism and Islam ... concur that 'the other' is defined by unbelief ... The outsider is so indicated by a single mark: rejection of God in favor of idols.'[57] In defining idolatry both faiths place great emphasis on the unity of God. 'The unity of God ... the phrase itself – "God is one" – is but shorthand for specific confessions of faith,' yet monotheism itself 'is not a confession but an abstraction. However convenient it may appear, one is ill-advised to assume it describes a common faith.'[58] Though 'monotheism has been the central tenet of the various proclamations of Islam throughout the ages,'[59] as it has for Judaism, 'each of the three monotheistic religions postulates its own moral supremacy over the others.'[60]

Given this emphasis on idolatry, both traditions see Christianity as idolatrous; however, there is considerable disagreement about the issue between themselves. While 'it is a generally accepted notion that Islam considers Judaism and Christianity as monotheistic religions', most Muslim writers have considered the beliefs of those faiths as 'contaminated with polytheistic elements',[61] and in some Muslim writings all non-Muslims are classified as 'non-believers', even if they follow another monotheistic faith. Other Muslim thinkers have even gone so far as to categorize Jews and Christians as altogether polytheists because they have not accepted Muhammad and the Quran.[62]

These definitions have importance because they have affected the way in which Muslims and Jews have interacted. Since post-biblical Jews have, until 1948, always lived as a minority, notably in Muslim states, this interaction is seen most clearly in those Muslim lands.

Relations with the Other: the Islamic dhimmi

'The exclusive finality of Islamic truth [requires] its necessary disavowal ... of all alternative systems of faith and worship',[63] but such disavowal does note preclude co-existence nor tolerance. Indeed for Mohamed Talbi, a Tunisian Muslim reformer and advocate of dialogue, of the three Abrahamic religions 'Islam most naturally exemplifies the ethos of toleration and respect.'[64] The Quran refers to Jews (and Christians) as 'People of the Book', and People of the Book are considered 'protected people', or *dhimmi*, in a Muslim state as long as they pay a special tax (*jizya*) and live in accordance with Muslim laws concerning the community. Many of these laws deal with marriage, inheritance, and food restrictions; but they also restrict such things as proselytizing and building non-Muslim places of worship.

Thus how one was classified determined which laws were applied to a person. In early Islam there were disputes about who actually qualified for inclusion in the *dhimmi*, based on such factors as their ethnic group and whether they had accepted their Jewish faith before or after the time of Muhammad. Some Muslim jurists took the position that Jews (and Christians) who came to their religions during or after Muhammad's mission should be given the option of converting to Islam or expulsion from the Muslim lands. Interestingly, some jurists were much harsher in their judgements about Arabs who accepted Judaism after Muhammad than about non-Arabs.[65] Polytheists, on the other hand, had to convert to Islam or face death.[66]

Over time the category of the *ahl al-dhimmi* (the *dhimmi* community) was gradually expanded by different Muslim leaders to include other religions and even by some to include 'infidels' such as the Hindus. When Muslims conquered parts of India, there was no way for the new rulers to require of the much larger population what they had required of polytheists earlier – conversion or death. Thus Hindus were also protected as part of the *ahl al-dhimmi*. In this way Muslim practices as well as laws adapted to the changing needs of a growing empire with a diverse population.

> As long as the only idolaters encountered by the Muslims were inhabitants of the Arabian peninsula, the Muslims fought against them

without compromise ... Once Islam became the sole religion in most of the peninsula ... the religious considerations that demanded unflinching struggle against idolatry and other non-Muslim religions were replaced by the requirements of running a state and building an empire.[67]

The debate within Islam about non-believers continues today, especially in light of the Middle East conflict. For example, the radical Islamic Liberation Party refer to *hadith* to support a view that 'an unbeliever (*kâfir*) is anyone who follows a religion other than Islam. He is neither a believer nor a Muslim. Idolators, Jews, Buddhists, Christians and Communists are exactly the same in this respect – all will be consigned eternally to Hellfire on the Day of Judgement.'[68] This crucial issue will be examined further later. First, however, it is helpful to look at how the two traditions have viewed each other.

Judaism's 'traditional' view of the Muslim

What is clear from its literature is that Judaism has traditionally focused on Jewish matters so that any consideration of Islam has been addressed in terms of how Jewish issues are resolved rather than as a faith to be studied in its own right. As such, while it has been very important to the life of the Jews to understand where they stood with regard to Islam and to Muslims, there was no theological imperative to study and understand Islam the faith. During the Middle Ages, for example, when Jews emigrated to Western Islamic lands in North Africa and Spain, the immigrants adopted 'sophisticated communal structures, patterned in part' after those of the Muslim nation; but there was little call to learn about the faith of those being modelled.[69] The one outstanding exception was Moses Maimonides, the great medieval Jewish rabbi and scholar, whose theological work was constructed upon a platform that included substantial Islamic thought. Yet even that did not result in a great Jewish exploration of Islam.

Two things combined to change, and also complicate, that attitude. First, the historical experience living in exile had a cumulative effect on Jews, culminating in the Holocaust. These experiences 'burned out of the Jewish people any claim to sole ownership of the truth about the ways and expectations of the one God, while they remained convinced that their way was the right one for themselves'.[70] It also caused some Jewish thinkers to begin to study the religious positions of both Christianity and Islam.

Over time that effort has led to involvement in certain quarters in interreligious dialogue.

Second was the establishment and subsequent defence of the State of Israel. Nothing has so changed, or complicated, Jewish views of Muslims (as well as the reverse) more than these events. Since the founding of the state in 1948 and especially the experience of the Six Day War of 1967, Israeli literature has been obsessed with Israel's political reality and 'the changed identity of the Israeli Jew from pioneering idealist to conqueror'.[71] Now the Muslim is seen in light of the struggle for and the subsequent defence of the State of Israel, which 'put in question the spirit which had underpinned favorable European Jewish approaches to Islam'.[72] The effects of both of these factors will be discussed in more detail later.

Islam's 'traditional' view of the Jew

As described earlier, Islam defines itself in relation to both Judaism and Christianity, and traditionally there was a mixture of respect (as shown in the *dhimmi*) and suspicion. Yet early on there was a significant change in the way Islam viewed the Jews. Most historians agree that in the first part of his mission, in Medina, Muhammad fully expected the Jews to accept his message and become 'believers'. When it became clear that such general conversions were not going to happen, Muhammad's attitude toward the Jews changed, as reflected in the Quran.

This is seen in such acts as the change of the *qibla*, the direction in which Muslims pray, from Jerusalem to Mecca. It is also seen in the 'Islamization' of Abraham. Abraham, pre-Judaism, was seen as involved in establishing the Ka'bah shrine as well as the pilgrimage to Mecca. As such Abraham is identified as 'the first "true Muslim"'.[73] Great emphasis was then placed on Muhammad's direct descent from Abraham, thus justifying the claim that his was the 'true' faith of Abraham, in contrast to that of the Jews (and Christians).

The Quran reflects this change in presenting a constant theme about the Jews: God seeks to guide the Jews, but they persist in disobeying God. It is important in this context to note that the Quran also contains numerous positive comments about Jews – indeed such was the basis for including Jews among 'the People of the Book' in the first instance – but the overall image was mixed at best. With regard to the negative picture, there is a widespread Quranic view of Jews 'recognizing their own sorry condition, but then not being willing to do anything about it',[74] that is, not converting to Islam. The result is that the Jews have brought punishment on themselves, as seen throughout history.[75] Indeed the first Muslim state in Medina was built upon the defeat of the Jewish community there.

Medieval Muslim writers perpetuated this negative portrayal of the Jews; however, these claims were intended not so much to denigrate Jews as to clarify the mission of Muhammad and the message of the Quran. 'Islam has historically been more interested in using this Quranic perspective as a warning to Muslims against deviating from true religion as the Jews have done.'[76] Camilla Adang cites the work of several medieval Muslim writers to demonstrate that 'the issue that dominates in the works of the authors under review (as well as in the Quran) is that of the authenticity or spuriousness of the Torah,' not so much the nature of the Jew.[77]

On a similar note, 'Jewish scholars and writers were fully aware of the artistic and intellectual developments of the host community in which they lived ... [however] the converse by and large simply did not happen. Muslims showed virtually no interest in Jewish learning *per se*,' indeed even in the experience of co-existence in Spain, Muslim religious leaders rejected the notion that a Muslim might study non-Islamic religious material.[78] The Jew was essentially an anonymous person whose example was used to remind Muslims of their duty to their faith.

The founding of the State of Israel and subsequent events there changed everything.

> The Jews ... had been of minor practical interest for Islamic writers prior to the growth of Zionism. . . . Under the impact of the creation of the new state, [Muslim] teaching has been transformed into an 'apocalyptic myth' about the Jewish threat to Islam, and to humanity in general. The question of the Jews thus has become central to Islamic thought.[79]

All of this leads us to the single most important issue confronting both Islam and Judaism today: Israel and the Palestinians.

The issue of Israel-Palestine

Traditional Islamic thought portrayed the Jews in images of wretchedness and humiliation. That view changed after the founding of the State of Israel and the ensuing conflicts with Arab states. Now the image is one of the powerful Jew, with unduc influence in all corners of the world, seriously threatening the Muslim community, indeed the whole world.[80]

Following the establishment of the State of Israel in 1948, Muslim writings about the Jews began to include notions of pervasive Jewish political and economic influence in international affairs derived from European literature. These writings made a connection between the problem that Muslims had encountered with Jews in seventh-century Arabia and the modern Zionist Jews of the conflict in Palestine. Thus Jewish antipathies towards the prophet were now seen as 'exegetical archetypes, universal explanatory models to be applied to Islam's modern Jewish crisis in Palestine'.[81]

This literature also tends to focus on a pure 'original Islam', to which Muslims today need to return. Ron Nettler argues that these themes actually reflect internal Muslim concerns about their own faith – its corruption by the modern world and the need for Muslims to be more true to their faith. 'The Jewish other has been constructed here in a context of, and sometimes as a metaphor for, Islamic issues and interests, in response to Islam's modern situation, and utilizing traditional Islamic portrayals of the Jews in a very new way.'[82]

This new way is seen in the work of the prominent Egyptian jurist Mohammad Sa'îd al-Ashmâwî. Ashmâwî describes the existing corruption within Islam and ultimately lays the blame for such corruption at the feet of the Jews, whose mis-portrayal of 'the law' became the mistaken model for Muslims and eventually led them to their current state. In this way 'the misbehaviour of ancient Jews (particularly in Medina) and the modern misbehaviour of Zionist Jews in Palestine became an intellectual paradigm' for Ashmâwî and other Islamists.[83] For these Islamists 'Anti-Jewish stereotypes ... are all there in Islamic writings, notably the Qur'an and the hadith, and the *Isra'iliyyat* literature,'[84] but they have also been influenced by modern anti-Semitic literature.

Thus Jews 'are either seen as the first bearers of the prophetic tradition who are to be respected and protected as the "People of the Book" or ... as dangerous and treacherous enemies who are not to be trusted. When this latter view gets compounded with the issue of Israel and Palestine, it becomes an explosive mixture and an incitement to hatred.'[85]

Such changes of view are not limited to Muslims. The creation of the State of Israel has also had a comparable impact on Jewish views of the Muslim.

Paradigm shifts

The result of all these internal debates and interactions has been a number of paradigm shifts that have had profound effects on Jewish-Muslim relations. The early stage of Muhammad's mission illustrates how such paradigm shifts can occur. In a short period of time Jews went from being neighbours and potential converts to being tolerated members of the Muslim *dhimmi*. Of course, Muslims see the shift in a different way – a shift brought about by the unbelief of the Jews. Either way, this change set the stage for future paradigm shifts.

A second example, which evolved over time, involves the legacy of Abraham. Islam sees Abraham as the model Muslim, the model believer. Abraham is recognized by Jews as 'the first convert to Judaism'; indeed in the early disputes with emerging Christianity the upstart Christians were often challenged to justify their new faith by tracing it back to Abraham.[86]

Over time Judaism has further 'Judaized', and Islam has further 'Islamized', Abraham. For Jews Abraham has come to represent the faithful, Torah-abiding Jew (despite his pre-Torah origins). For Islam Abraham is included in the 'Islamicization' of all history prior to Muhammad, which 'allows the recognition and use of the achievements of the past and of other peoples without the need to pay tribute to those people'.[87] Abraham thus becomes the focal point for claims of exclusivity for both traditions, a shift that was gradual but that is now a central part of the self-identity of each religion.

Zionism

More recently the Israel-Palestine conflict has produced major paradigm shifts. As noted earlier, relations between Muslims and Jews have historically ranged from genuine communal harmony to legal tolerance. Jews, of course, have never accepted the religious claims of Islam; and Muslims have viewed Jews as monotheists whose beliefs had been corrupted, leading to misbehaviour most exemplified by their rejection of Islam. Zionism, the movement to reclaim the biblical land for the Jews, changed all this.

For the religious Zionists 'Many of the events of recent Jewish history are evidence of the imminence of redemption … Contemporary Israel is the answer to their religious hopes and waiting. Political Zionism is a tool toward this end, but religion is its motive force.'[88] Following the establishment of the State of Israel:

[Jews] were completely caught up in an extraordinary re-interpretation of [their] Jewish history. The equation was shockingly simple, and all the more potent for that. God had taken six million Jews in the Shoah, and given [them] back Jerusalem! It was, and remains, a potent myth ... [and] is part of the irrational power behind the settler movement and any number of fundamentalist, messianic tendencies till today.[89]

This renewal led to an exclusivist claim to the land of Israel-Palestine on the part of many Jews, a subject that will be addressed later.

On the Muslim side, 'Jews *qua* Jews are neither intrinsically evil nor historically hostile to Islam';[90] it was only when Zionism entered the picture that problems arose. Since the nineteenth century the position of Arabs in Palestine had been that 'The Jews should be opposed because they are foreign invaders, not because of any religious precept.'[91] During the middle of the twentieth century militant Islamic nationalists focused their ideological arguments on opposition to the colonialist powers, and within Islam the ideology of conflict and struggle was stressed. Thus 'Arab writers on the Palestine problem were inclined to use "Zionist" and "Jew" as synonyms ... [in order] to serve political goals.'[92] They did not distinguish between Zionists and non-Zionists, whether religious or secular. 'Jews as Jews only became evil in the discourse of modern Muslims after the Zionist movement demonstrated that the role of Jews as *ahl adh-dhimma* was at an end.'[93]

Before 1948 numerous groups, including later the PLO, attributed the push for a Jewish homeland to a Christian-inspired world imperialist movement,[94] a kind of crusader continuum. In so doing, they failed to recognize (a) the genuine desire of Jews to 'return from exile' and restore their nation and (b) the religious motives on the part of Jews seeking to return to 'their' land. Only after the 1967 Six Day War did Muslims begin to turn to both motives, resulting in numerous projections of Muslim political and religious views onto the Jews. It was then that Muslim writings began in earnest to portray the Jew so wholly negatively, both religiously and politically.

The ideology of today's Sunni Islamists is a good example. Hamâs, the Islamic Resistance Movement in the Israeli Occupied Territories, base their position on the work of Hasan al Bannâ of the early Muslim Brotherhood, the Egyptian Sayyid Qutb also of the Muslim Brotherhood, and the South Asian Sayyid al-Mawdûdî. The result is a theology that underscores the religious character of the Palestinian struggle with the State of Israel. Using historical events as though they represent reality today, 'Allegations [against the Jews] are presented in the framework of the struggle of Jewish tribes against the Muslim community in Medina and the misbehaviour of the Banû Isrâ'îl,' the Jewish tribes.[95]

Other non-Islamic and non-Arab sources, including European anti-Semitic sources, are also cited as further 'proof' in support of specific negative portrayals of Jews, whether in the Quran or in other Muslim writings. Probably the most egregious example is the *Protocols of the Elders of Zion*, a vehemently anti-Jewish document widely acknowledged as a medieval forgery, which still receives wide exposure in the Muslim world[96] and was recently made into a film for Egyptian television.

In Islam the 'attempt to place the issue within an Islamic framework, recruiting the Islamic tradition to define the nature of the conflict and to vilify the enemy'[97] shows another paradigm shift. No longer is the conflict a dispute between two local peoples over the land, but one with overtones of and implications for the fulfilment of God's plan for mankind. Thus it is not a local conflict between Israeli Jews and Palestinians, but a profoundly theological one involving the whole Muslim world.

On the Jewish side the paradigm shift has resulted in a change in the way Jewish scholars view the Muslim. 'Bernard Lewis ... came to personify the post-war shift from a sympathetic to a critical posture' regarding Islam.[98] For the West Lewis is a significant example, as he is considered by some 'the most influential post-war historian of Islam and the Middle East,'[99] and his recent books have received substantial press coverage.

The importance of the land

Another significant paradigm shift involves the land of Israel-Palestine. The attachment of Jews to the land is understandable, given the biblical story of God's covenant with the Jews regarding 'their' land and their rituals throughout history commemorating that covenant and yearning for a return from exile to that land. As Kuschel states, 'The people of Israel [the Jewish people] and a certain land are inseparable.'[100] 'The significance of the land in Judaism [is] not simply as a holy place ... but rather ... [involves] an inevitable restoration to the Land of Israel, in order to re-create there a new (ultimately universal) Eden, the locale where the dead, after the final judgment and repentance, will be raised for eternal life.'[101]

Yet even with Jews, following the establishment of the State of Israel there have been shifts. One example of this is the approach of *Gush Emunim*. A spiritual movement which traditionally disdained any political role, *Gush* nonetheless has substantial political influence in Israeli affairs. *Gush* has taken the initiative in settling on West Bank biblical sites; and Menachem Begin's government even made it lawful for *Gush* to be involved in 'legal violence', a right usually accorded only to police and the military.[102] To protect settlers, *Gush* maintains its own private army with small arms, some of which come from the Israeli military, though 'one of the movement's most abiding principles ... is its avoidance of violence.'[103]

For them 'the covenantal relationship between God and the Jews constitutes the *Gush's* most essential text ... [and] central to this covenant is the land.'[104] The Six Day War of 1967 reinforced the messianic expectations of *Gush* and encouraged them to focus on the religious requirements for divine intervention and redemption. Such an act also required redemption of *all* of the land, since a number of religious and ritual laws could not be observed completely until all the land was under Jewish religious rule.[105] Numbers 33:53 – 'And you shall take possession of the land and settle it, for I have given the land to you to possess it' – was read only one way: the State of Israel must possess all of the land, full stop.

The corollary to this is that anyone who attempts to give land to the Palestinians is the enemy. Later writings from *Gush* even show complete disregard for the legitimacy of government authority, stressing that no government has the authority to transfer any of the Holy Land to others and that such actions must be resisted. It was the further development of this line of thought that eventually led to the assassination of Yitzak Rabin.

'Arabs and Palestinians are not seen by *Gush Emunim* as inimical *per se*, but only in relation to their real or ideologised occupation of the land.'[106] *Gush's* writings show that they do not see problems with the Palestinians as some kind of political threat, and they even understand the Palestinians' yearning for their own land; rather, *Gush* are adamant that they simply should not occupy *Jewish* land. '[*Gush*] writers ... have indicated their understanding of the Palestinians' territorial aspirations, yet members of the *Gush* have no theological doubt that it is the Jewish right and superiority that prevails.'[107] As moves continue to secure peace in the region, *Gush* increasingly see themselves as the only hope to fulfill God's will by securing the land which God has given the Jews, leading *Gush* into 'ever more extreme positions',[108]

With regard to Islam there is some debate about the sanctity of the land. One camp argues that 'Jerusalem's sanctity, and by extension the sanctity of Palestine, gradually developed into an uncontested principle in medieval Islam.'[109] The other position is that 'The notion of the sanctity of Palestinian territory seems to have been taken over from Judaism.'[110] Following this argument, Jerusalem was once honoured as the direction for prayer and is the location of the third holiest shrine in Islam, and Muslims have long attempted to control and rule the land there; however, it is only recently that this goal has been enshrined in theological interpretation. 'The idea that the specific territory of Palestine is holy only appeared more recently. It certainly has no place in the fundamentalist ideology as developed by Qutb and Mawdûdî, who reject any attachment to a specific territory ... [and there is] difficulty of finding any Qur'anic evidence for these positions;' here 'the Palestinian fundamentalists have clearly been influenced by Judaism, in which notions of sacred territory and promised land are more prominent.'[111] Thus the issues surrounding the State of Israel forced a change in Muslim identity from one based on ideology to one based on territory.

Whichever claim is more accurate, there is no question that 'the land' has moved to the forefront of Muslim consciousness as well as theology. 'The struggle against the Jewish state in Muslim Palestine became central to Islamic thought and a measure by which to judge the successful return to original Islam.'[112] This theme is now at the centre of Islamist thinking, as seen in the reaction to the war in Bosnia and its impact on Muslims, which Islamists saw as a repeat of what happened to Muslims in Spain.

The theological argument put forward by the Islamists is that the liberation of any territory and the return to Islamic rule there is a step in the restoration of the Islamic *Ummah*, or community, which under this new interpretation can be considered the 'Islamic nation'. Following their failure to prevent the establishment of the State of Israel and multiple Arab defeats at the hands of the Israelis, 'the outcome of the struggle over Palestine is seen as decisive for the whole *Ummah*. A victory in this struggle would prove that Muslims are again on the right path and will continue to succeed in the world.'[113]

The Islamic Liberation Party, a radical group that is a near-exact counterpart to *Gush Emunim*, rely on their theological interpretation of the sacredness of the land to underpin their political position – no peace with Israel, rather the complete expulsion of all Jews from Palestine. The theology on which this is based is the belief that this land once belonged to Islam and that Muslims are required to rule all Muslim lands under strict *Sharia* law. They view Jews as unlawful occupiers of this land and emphasize that God commands Muslims to resist any such occupier and to return such lands to Islam. 'The corollary of this is that it is prohibited to conclude an open-ended or permanent peace with the occupier. Consequently, they are obliged to fight until the expulsion of the last man.'[114]

Thus two paradigm shifts have occurred. Islamists have developed a theological basis for (i) their focus on the land and (ii) the expulsion, rather than the conversion, of the Jews.

At the same time Israeli extremists increasingly refine their theological interpretations ever so narrowly so that only one thing is ultimately achievable: Israeli rule of all of Israel-Palestine and, for extremists, the expulsion of the Muslims.

Altered power structures

These paradigm shifts prompted by the Israel-Palestine issue have evolved against the background of another paradigm shift, one involving power. Historically Jews and Muslims have traditionally found themselves mainly in one situation *vis-a-vis* political power. Since biblical times Jews have lived within communities dominated by other religions, particularly by Christians and Muslims. With certain exceptions, until the last two centuries much of the Muslim community existed in countries dominated by Islam, where other religions, including Judaism, were in a (often small) minority.

These respective positions have had profound effects on both the self-image and the image of the other that developed within each tradition. Jews had to figure out ways to survive as a minority, often adjusting even their religious practices in order to do so. Despite such adaptations, Jews still found themselves at the receiving end of repeated persecutions. Naturally, such factors coloured the way in which Jews defined themselves as well as how they viewed the other; and as mentioned earlier, historically Jews often found cause to look more favourably on Muslim rulers than on Christian ones. In predominantly Islamic nations, where minority religions either abided by laws regulating non-Muslims or were expelled from those lands, 'Muslims faced the other religions from the position of power, and enjoyed in relation to them a position of unmistakable superiority. They were therefore able to determine the nature of their relationship with the others in conformity with their world-view and in accordance with their beliefs.'[115]

Today these situations of relative power have changed. Now there are Jews living in a land where they are the dominant political power, while growing Muslim communities live in more secular lands where they are either in a minority in terms of religion or are compelled to co-exist as 'equal' citizens with those of other religions. The impact of this shift has been enormous for both religions, and the effects are still being worked out within each tradition. It has challenged their traditional world-views, sometimes undermining the foundations of their own self-image as well as forcing them to re-think their views of the other.

The traditional Muslim self-image had always relied on a central notion of Muslim superiority,[116] a view that is being constantly challenged, and in many ways, in today's modern, pluralistic world. Ironically, the change in power structures has led to a Muslim image that sees the Jew as 'the powerful Jew, seriously threatening both the Muslim community and the rest of the world.'[117] As mentioned earlier this situation has forced Jews to wrestle with the very definition of being a Jew, while 'the experience, particularly of anti-Semitism culminating in the Holocaust and of Israel's constant struggles for existence in a hostile Arab world, has not generally encouraged interest in the development of positive theologies of the religious other,'[118] notably, including the Muslim.

Appropriating Maimonides

Another example of a paradigm shift involving the Israel-Palestine issue is the way the medieval work of Moses Maimonides, widely recognized among Jews as the master of rabbinic tradition,[119] has been re-interpreted in modern times. At the hands of Jewish religious radicals Maimonides has been 'reinvented' – transformed 'from being a rationalist and universalist philosopher ... into an anti-Arab religious zealot'.[120] Indeed he is claimed by two very different groups of Jews in Israel: militant religious Zionists and orthodox religious non-Zionists.

An orthodox rabbi, Maimonides has traditionally been recognized as the prime example of Arab-Islamic/Jewish symbiosis of that era, and many scholars today admire him for his understanding of and sympathy with Muslim thought. Maimonides is generally recognized as 'one of the most radical philosophers of the Islamic world ... for the outstanding part he played in the development of medieval Arabic thought and culture and Islamic civilization.'[121]

He was immersed in both the religion and culture of Islam, and his 'philosophy and theology, in particular, drew freely and copiously from Muslim patterns', and nearly all of his major work was written in Arabic.[122] Maimonides came to this position because he was trying to reconcile the Jewish faith with rational Greek-Arabic-philosophy, which was largely based on Aristotle.[123] Yet Jewish religious extremists have found a totally different way to use Maimonides in the service of their Zionist quest for the land of Israel.

Religious Zionists point to Maimonides' emphasis on *halacha*, or law, and insist that the binding nature of *halacha* as elucidated by Maimonides, in effect, elevates the Jew above non-Jews in terms of status and rights. They then use this position to argue theologically for a theocratic regime in Israel. The result is seen in the 'supremacist and essentialist notions of Jews as divinely "chosen people" ... and as the rightful owners of the "promised land"' that is the hallmark of *Gush Emunim* and other religious Zionists.[124] Indeed it is on this basis that *Gush* have been in the forefront of the settler movement in Israel and have called for the expulsion of all Palestinians (Christians as well as Jews) from the land.

Conversely the ultra-orthodox Haredi Jews in Israel, who are not Zionists, have a different interpretation vis-a-vis Maimonides. They believe that the messianic era cannot begin until the appearance of the messiah, in other words until there is divine intervention, and thus the actions of religious groups such as *Gush* are premature and wrong. Nonetheless, they do subscribe to the interpretation of Maimonides that when such divine intervention does occur, *then* Jews would be more powerful 'and would then be obliged by the *halacha* to conquer the "land of Israel", and expel all non-Jews'.[125]

Both David Hartman and Nur Masalha emphasize that this messianic notion of returning to the land was never central to Maimonides' thinking.[126] Religious Zionists, however, have used a different aspect of his theology – the importance of *halacha* – and tied that to their nationalist aspirations. The result is an entire generation of certain religious Jews who mistakenly believe that their messianic hopes and actions are underpinned by the greatest Jewish theologian in history. In another paradigm shift 'One of the greatest symbols of Arabo-Muslim-Jewish understanding ... has become, in a peculiar way, the hero of "messianic" Zionism and anti-Arab fundamentalism.'[127]

The eternal / implacable enemy

These paradigm shifts have inevitably ingrained another altered view in the minds of many Jews and Muslims: the 'unchanging nature' theory. Islamists claim that 'Throughout the entire period when Jews lived amongst the Muslims they fought Islam just as the Zionists do today.'[128] Their 'views concerning the Palestine question epitomize a trend within contemporary political Islam characterized by an absolutism founded on a belief in the unchanging validity of concepts that are fixed in the sacred text and the collective experience of the community'.[129] An example of this is seen in recent writings on the Jews in the Quran, which 'attribute to them an unchanging nature, which persists across the centuries ... a generally negative construction of Jewish nature [which] provides a convincing explanation for current Zionist successes and abuses in Palestine, and for perceived Jewish political and economic entrenchment and domination in other parts of the world'.[130]

Such writers do not debate the sometimes unclear language of biblical texts, 'but will 'fit' Scripture into [their] philosophical system. [They] see Scripture as a series of illustrations for [their] independently formulated ideas rather than as a set of propositions on which to base a rational argument.'[131] Thus interpretation of scripture, as well as an understanding of the Jews, is no longer an ongoing task – the picture of the Jew is established once and for all time.

The Jewish religious extremist position takes a different tack, but with a similar end point. *Gush Emunim* writings show that *all* non-Jews are the eternal opponents when it comes to the land of Israel and must be driven out at all cost.

Implications for dialogue

With so much in common from their religious histories, as well as their mutual antipathy toward the other major monotheistic tradition – Christianity – one might expect greater sympathy between Jews and Muslims for each other's faith. The paradigm shifts described above, however, do not appear to bode well for dialogue. Jonathan Magonet believes that religions today are being pushed by extremists 'towards a ghettoisation of their particular faith community, often accompanied by expressions of hostility towards others'.[132] Samuel Heilman attributes the reluctance among Jews and Muslims to engage with each other to a fear of possible contamination from the ways of the adversary.[133]

So there is, among extremists at least, a fear of being overwhelmed by modern, especially Western, culture, as well as a fear of becoming too close to the other. These fears combine to erect huge hurdles to understanding between many members of the two faiths. Yet, as Zalman Schacter argues, 'These anxieties cannot be averted by reverting to a strict fundamentalist position. Whenever tradition is challenged to renew itself, it must meet these crises.'[134] Indeed, there have been notable examples of this.

Perhaps because of their long experience living in exile as an oft-persecuted minority and having to find new ways to live with the other, Judaism has produced several leading exponents of dialogue, all the way from Maimonides to Martin Buber. While it may be harder to find many well-known examples among Muslims, one excellent example is the Tunisian Mohamed Talbi. Educated in both North Africa and the West, Talbi sees religious dialogue, both within Islam and with other faith traditions, as one of the most important issues confronting Islam today. It is significant that Talbi relies on traditional Islamic sources for support of his pluralist views.[135] For example, Talbi extends the Muslim acceptance and toleration of difference related to the four schools of Islamic law to an acceptance of difference in the realm of religious diversity.[136] He stands out among contemporary Muslim thinkers in his genuine desire for mutual understanding and dialogue, while not compromising his firm Muslim beliefs, an approach that sets Talbi and his few modernist colleagues apart from much of mainstream traditional Islam.[137]

Unfortunately, when one turns to the Middle East, the conflict there distorts the picture. 'Any inter-Jewish/Muslim theology in current terms is, of course, grievously deterred by political factors deriving from the establishment and defense of the State of Israel.'[138] In the Middle East 'The contribution made by religion in the region has been more to exacerbate things, to make absolute demands and claims, to raise emotions and heighten tensions, rather than to move anyone in the direction of peace – with the possible unique exception of that fateful encounter between Anwar Sadat, Menachem Begin and Jimmy Carter, all of whom seem to have had some level of religious motivation.'[139] As a result, genuine dialogue and trust-building among the three great monotheistic religions 'must begin away from the Middle East, because the political struggles too readily confuse the religious issues'.[140]

In some ways the challenge is made more difficult because of a lack of central authoritarian structures in the two religions. As Ruth Langer points out, 'Judaism lacks structures of authority that can demand broad deference and impose theological change;'[141] and the same may be said about Islam. Nonetheless, there are numerous initiatives at the ground level in both religions to encourage and facilitate dialogue between members of the two faiths; and the challenges of modernity, as well as the tragic realities of the Israel-Palestine conflict itself, are forcing some scholars in both traditions to re-examine their views of the other.

Implications for Christianity

For Christianity the implications of these changes in the Jewish-Muslim encounter may be encapsulated in an observation made by Jonathan Magonet at the 2003 JCM (Jewish-Christian-Muslim) Conference in Bendorf, Germany: 'We have spent centuries defining ourselves over and against the other religions; now we have to define ourselves in relationship with the other religions.'

Judaism and Islam are already engaging on a number of issues that have implications for Christianity, including the nature of God and His revelation and the place of the other in God's plan. Christianity has to take seriously how these other faiths view Christianity and what they have to say about it. Both Judaism and Islam, for example, see Christianity as some form of deviation from true belief in the one God, positioning the Christian revelation as incompatible with genuine monotheism. It is neither acceptable nor theologically defensible simply to ignore such views or reject them out-of-hand; rather, they have to be addressed in dialogue with the other. Indeed, the pluralistic reality of contemporary life demands it.

Monika Hellwig posits an important question in this regard: 'Christians ... must ask themselves, and therefore they must ask the Muslims, why the message of salvation in Jesus the Christ with its universal claim has in the course of history been complemented by a vast people, gathered from many nations, coming likewise to worship the God of Israel, but in a distinctively different tradition that denies the universality of the Christian claim.'[142] Inside her question is a second, very important, point – 'and therefore they must ask the Muslims' – here we see a call, indeed an imperative, for Christians to engage in dialogue with Muslims. Similarly from the Muslim side, 'Since Islam's self-understanding essentially refers to how it abrogates or supersedes Christianity [as well as Judaism], ... it must face questions about its own identity that it cannot settle without involving authoritative representatives of Christianity.'[143] Yet this will happen only when the Muslim encounters the Christian intent on dialogue.

Likewise with Jews. 'A community which claims to have been chosen in some special way as God's instrument of redemption of the world is compelled to ask itself how it stands in relation to other communities that claim a similar election from the same God, if only because of the need to define its own claim for its own members.'[144] Again, the answer to this question will come only from genuine dialogue, a process to which the Christian needs to contribute.

In this regard it is important for Christians to recognize that it is the person in dialogue, not the proselytizer, who can have a positive impact on the thinking of the other. Mohamed Talbi, mentioned earlier for his positive views about dialogue, acknowledges that Louis Massignon, a devout Christian 'mystical visionary' as well as Islamicist teacher, had a major impact on him when he was studying in Paris. Massignon introduced Talbi to 'varieties of Islam which he had not previously been aware of and [to] new approaches to tradition ... [thus] revealing to him a universal mystical religiosity in which all religious views come together, in spite of their exoteric doctrinal differences'.[145] This recognition of a universal spiritual truth became central to Talbi's understandging of religious pluralism.[146]

This example of engagement with the other raises the sensitive question about the role of missionary efforts in Christianity. Among Muslims there is little doubt that 'Christian missionary activity, especially in such places as Indonesia, Pakistan, and sub-Saharan Africa, plays a very important role in creating tension between Islam and Christianity.'[147] With regard to Jews, the aftermath of the Holocaust has led some Christian thinkers to conclude that proselytizing Jews is no longer acceptable, though this is certainly not a widely-accepted view throughout Christianity. Yet there are many differing positions on this subject, and the complexities surrounding the question of mission (in Islam as well as in Christianity) are beyond the scope of this work. Suffice it to say that emerging Jewish-Muslim dialogue places the question of mission in the spotlight for those who believe that Christianity has a role to play in this dialogue.

Another factor is the long-standing challenge of the enlightened layman. Just as ground-level initiatives may in the end bring about positive changes in the Jewish-Muslim encounter, so may similar initiatives force church authorities to confront issues of interreligious dialogue and to develop a theology of engagement with the other. Even in the cauldron of the Middle East such encounters are already raising questions for Christians about their support for either the State of Israel or the Palestinians. Both positions have implications for the way Christians understand the Bible, as articulated in a prophetic Christian document over thirty years ago: 'Christians of the West are finding that much of their traditional sympathy with Zionist aspirations was based on an interpretation of the Old and New Testaments which is now outdated, and are being shocked by the implications of this naive approach into serious reconsideration of their beliefs about the nature of the biblical message.'[148] 'Conversely, many Christians who are committed to the Arab side of the argument find that they can no longer acknowledge the debt of Christianity to the religion and civilization of the Jews without appearing to endorse modern Israeli aspirations.'[149] These challenges to Christianity are still valid today, and finding acceptable answers to them necessarily involves understanding the other through dialogue.

In this regard both Judaism and Islam have developed theologies regarding their presence in the land of Israel, with little response from Christians on their part. Yet 'Even though the Holy Places represent nothing vital for the practice of the Christian faith ... nevertheless the history of the Christian custody of, and devotion in, places associated with the life of Christ has made the possession of these places a matter of very great concern to certain Christian communities.'[150] Thus Christians have a responsibility both to take seriously these emerging theologies of the land and to formulate a Christian theology of the land in dialogue with Jews and Muslims. In so doing they may even play the role of 'mediator between the two antagonists' that Louis Massignon envisioned for Christians in the Holy Land.[151]

In a similar vein, Christians need to be sensitive to some more modernized Muslims who are beginning to explore further the evolution of Muslim dogma, a process that could eventually entail a kind of Muslim 'reformation'. Even if it occurs only in selected quarters, such re-thinking will necessarily include a further assessment of the nature of revelation and the resulting interpretation of each tradition's holy scriptures. Again, any conclusions about the relationship between the Hebrew Bible and the Quran will certainly impinge on those faiths' views of the New Testament. Christianity cannot simply stand by idly during such processes, as though immune from the ultimate results. Genuine engagement and dialogue are mandatory.

David Burrell writes, 'It is Jews, Christians, and Muslims who share the burden, if you will, of the one God.'[152] With this burden comes a responsibility – a responsibility, in accordance with each faith tradition, to respect and live together with our fellow man. If Christians are to live up to the commands of their faith, then they will have to find a way to define Christianity in relationship with, rather than against, other faiths in a way that enables Christians themselves to maintain the traditions of their faith. This also requires a theology that can be understood and respected by the other, so that divisive issues, such as questions surrounding the unity of God and the contradiction perceived by Jews and Muslims regarding the Trinity, can be clarified for all three faiths. In this regard 'the starting point of future Christology must be an acceptance of God's universal activity in and through other religious peoples and communities,'[153] and indeed this subject is now being addressed in earnest by Christian theologians.

Yet this is only a beginning, and failure – or worse, no action – on such issues will ultimately impoverish the Christian tradition. If, on the other hand, Christianity is able to address such issues and make its message and mission known to Jews and Muslims in a way that engenders respect and understanding, then there is hope that the three faiths will be able to find ways to live in peace with one another, proclaiming together the glory of the one God.

Notes

1. S. C. Heilman, 'The Vision from the Madrasa and Bes Medrash: Some Parallels between Islam and Judaism', M. E. Marty and R. S. Appleby, (eds) *Fundamentalisms Comprehended*, London, The University of Chicago Press, 1995, p. 72.
2. K. J. Kuschel, 'One in Abraham? The Significance of Abraham for Jews, Christians, and Muslims Today', M. A. Signer, (ed.), *Memory and History in Christianity and Judaism*, Notre Dame, Indiana, University of Notre Dame Press, 2001, p. 185.
3. D. J. Halperin, 'Can Muslim Narrative be Used as Commentary on Jewish Tradition?' R. Nettler, (ed.), *Medieval and Modern Perspectives on Muslim-Jewish Relations*, Luxembourg, Harwood Academic Publishers, 1995, p. 74.
4. M. Kramer, (ed.), *The Jewish Discovery of Islam: Studies in Honor of Bernard Lewis*, Tel Aviv, Tel Aviv University, 1999, p. 20.
5. Halperin, op. cit., p. 73.
6. M. K. Hellwig, 'Bases and Boundaries for Interfaith Dialogue: A Christian Viewpoint,' L. Swidler, (ed.), *Muslims in Dialogue: The Evolution of A Dialogue*, Dyfed, Wales, The Edwin Mellen Press, 1992, p. 332.
7. D. Burrell, 'Naming the Names of God: Muslims, Jews, Christians', *Theology*

Today, vol. 47, no. 1 (April 1990), p. 24.
8 R. Langer, 'Jewish Understanding of the Religious Other', *Theological Studies*, 64, 2003, p. 257.
9 J. Magonet, *Talking to the Other: Jewish Interfaith Dialogue with Christians and Muslims*, London, I. B. Tauris, 2003, p. 163.
10 S. Strousma, 'Jewish Polemics Against Islam and Christianity in the Light of Judaeo-Arabic Texts', N. Golb, (ed.), *Judaeo-Arabic Studies: Proceedings of the Founding conference of the Society for Judaeo-Arabic Studies*, Amsterdam, Harwood Academic Publishers, 1997, p. 248.
11 A. Nüsse, 'The Ideology of Hamâs: Palestinian Islamic Fundamentalist Thought of the Jews, Israel and Islam', Nettler, R., (ed.), *Studies in Muslim-Jewish Relations*, vol. 1, Chur, Switzerland, Harwood Academic Publishers, 1993, p. 111.
12 Kuschel, op. cit., p. 186.
13 Ibid.
14 Kuschel, op. cit., p. 195.
15 Hellwig, op. cit., p. 343.
16 Kuschel, op. cit., p. 195.
17 K. Cragg, 'Islam and Other Faiths', *Studia Missionalia*, vol. 42, 1993, p. 267.
18 Cohn-Sherbok, *Judaism*, London, Rutledge, 1999, p. 53.
19 H. Gordon, 'The Lack of Jewish-Arab Dialogue in Israel and the Spirit of Judaism: A Testimony', L. Swidler, (ed.), 1992, *Muslims in Dialogue: The Evolution of A Dialogue*, Dyfed, Wales, The Edwin Mellen Press, 1986, p. 400.
20 M. A. Haleem, *Understanding the Qur'an*, London, I. B. Tauris, 2001, pp. 72, 75.
21 M. Abitol, 'Jews and Arabs in Colonial North Africa', T. Parfitt, (ed.), *Israel and Ishmael: Studies in Muslim-Jewish Relations*, Richmond, Surrey, Curzon Press, 2000, p. 127.
22 N. Stillman, 'The Judeo-Islamic Historical Encounter: Visions and Revisions', T. Parfitt, (ed.), *Israel and Ishmael: Studies in Muslim-Jewish Relations*, Richmond, Surrey, Curzon Press, 2000, p. 2.
23 N. Stillman, 'The Jews of the Islamic West in the Perspective of 'La Longue Durée'', N. Golb, (ed.), *Judaeo-Arabic Studies: Proceedings of the Founding conference of the Society for Judaeo-Arabic Studies*, Amsterdam, Harwood Academic Publishers, 1997, pp. 237–8.
24 M. R. Menocal, 'Culture in the Time of Tolerance: *Al-Andalus* as a Model for Our Own Time', *Yale Law School Occasional Papers*, Second series, no. 6, 2000, p. 13.
25 Haleem, op. cit., p. 76.
26 K. E. Schultze, 'The Jews of Lebanon: A Minority among Many or the Enemy within?' T. Parfitt, (ed.), *Israel and Ishmael: Studies in Muslim-Jewish Relations*, Richmond, Surrey, Curzon Press, 2000, p. 87.
27 Schultze, op. cit., p. 92.
28 H. Saadoun, 'The Effect of the Palestinian Issue on Muslim-Jewish Relations in the Arab World: the Case of Tunisia (1920–1939)', T. Parfitt, (ed.), *Israel and Ishmael: Studies in Muslim-Jewish Relations*, Richmond, Surrey, Curzon Press, 2000, p. 108.
29 M. Natour, 'Muslims in Israel', T. Parfitt, (ed.), *Israel and Ishmael: Studies in Muslim-Jewish Relations*, Richmond, Surrey, Curzon Press, 2000, p. 239.
30 Hellwig, op. cit., p. 334.
31 M. Arkoun, 'New Perspectives for a Jewish-Christian-Muslim Dialogue', L. Swidler, (ed.), 1992, *Muslims in Dialogue: The Evolution of A Dialogue*, Dyfed,

Wales, The Edwin Mellen Press, 1989, p. 349.
32 Cragg, op. cit., p. 258.
33 Y. Friedmann, *Tolerance and Coercion in Islam: Interfaith Relations in the Muslim Tradition*, Cambridge, Cambridge University Press, 2003, p. 64.
34 I. Israeli, 'Radical Islam and Israel', T. Parfitt, (ed.), *Israel and Ishmael: Studies in Muslim-Jewish Relations*, Richmond, Surrey, Curzon Press, 2000, p. 227.
35 Menocal, op. cit., p. 9.
36 J. Neusner, T. Sonn, and J. E. Brockopp, *Judaism and Islam in Practice*, London, Routledge, 2000, p. 191.
37 Natour, op. cit., p. 247.
38 I. Bloom, 'Religious Diversity and Human rights: An Introduction', I. Bloom, J. P. Mattin, and W. L. Proudfoot, (ed), *Religious Diversity and Human Rights*, New York, Columbia University Press, 1996, p. 2.
39 D. Myers-Weinstein, 'Tradition and Change: Living the Questions: Jewish Identity and a Vision of the Future', from The Bendorf Conferences, Leo Baeck College, *European Judaism*, vol. 31, no. 1, London, Berghahn Books, 1998, p. 54.
40 N. Masalha, 'Reinventing Maimonides: From Universalist Philosopher to Religious Fundamentalist (1967–2002)', *Holy Land Studies: A Multidisciplinary Journal*, vol. 1, no. 1, 2002, p. 86.
41 Masalha, op. cit., p. 94.
42 Neusner, op. cit., p. 201.
43 Cohn-Sherbok, op. cit., p. 27.
44 D. Hartman, *Israelis and the Jewish Tradition: An Ancient People Debating Its Future*, London, Yale University Press, 2000, p. 12.
45 Hartman, op. cit., pp. 15, 9.
46 Magonet, op. cit., p. 132.
47 Neusner, op. cit., p. 199.
48 A. Lopatin, 'The Uncircumcised Jewish Heart in Sayyid Qutb's *Tafsîr*: Qur'anic Parallels to Jewish Conceptions', R. Nettler, (ed.), *Studies in Muslim-Jewish Relations*, vol. 1, Chur, Switzerland, Harwood Academic Publishers, 1993, p. 83.
49 Magonet, op. cit., p. 157.
50 Halperin, op. cit., p. 75.
51 M. Klein, 'Religious Pragmatism and Political Violence in Jewish and Islamic Fundamentalism', R. Nettler, (ed.), *Studies in Muslim-Jewish Relations*, vol. 1, Chur, Switzerland, Harwood Academic Publishers, 1993, p. 51.
52 Neusner, op. cit., p. 210.
53 Neusner, op. cit., p. 215.
54 Friedmann, op. cit., p. 56.
55 Neusner, op. cit., p. 225.
56 Neusner, op. cit., p. 181.
57 Neusner, op. cit., pp. 180, 181.
58 D. B. Burrell, *Knowing the Unknowable God: Ibn-Sina, Maimonides, Aquinas*, Notre Dame, Indiana, University of Notre Dame Press, 1986, p. 111.
59 H. Galford, 'Sayyid Qutb and the Qur'anic Story of Joseph: A Commentary for Today', R. Nettler, and S. Taji-Farouki, (eds), *Muslim-Jewish Encounters: Intellectual Traditions and Modern Politics*, Studies in Muslim-Jewish Relations, vol. 4, Amsterdam, Harwood Academic Publishers, 1998, p. 57.
60 G. Abramson, 'Jewish Religious Nationalist Writings on the Palestinian Question: The Case of *Gush Emunim*', R. Nettler, and S. Taji-Farouki, (eds),

Muslim-Jewish Encounters: Intellectual Traditions and Modern Politics, Studies in Muslim-Jewish Relations, vol. 4, Amsterdam, Harwood Academic Publishers, 1998, p. 121.
61 Friedmann, op. cit., p. 70
62 Friedmann, op. cit., p. 71
63 Cragg, op. cit., p. 257.
64 R. Nettler, 'Mohamed Talbi's Ideas on Islam and Politics: A Conception of Islam for the Modern World', J. Cooper, R. Nettler, and M. Mahmoud, (eds), *Islam and Modernity: Muslim Intellectuals Respond*, London, I. B. Tauris, 2000, p. 136.
65 Friedmann, op. cit., p. 66.
66 Friedmann, op. cit., p. 77.
67 Friedmann, op. cit., p. 86.
68 S. Taji-Farouki, 'A Case-Study in contemporary Political Islam and the Palestinian Question: The Perspective of Hizb Al-Tahrîr Al-Islâmî', R. Nettler, (ed.), *Medieval and Modern Perspectives on Muslim-Jewish Relations*, Luxembourg, Harwood Academic Publishers, 1995, p. 40.
69 Stillman, 1997, p. 235.
70 Magonet, op. cit., p. 14.
71 G. Abramson, 'The Absence of Reality: Islam and the Arabs in Contemporary Hebrew Literature', R. Nettler, (ed.), *Studies in Muslim-Jewish Relations*, vol. 1, Chur, Switzerland, Harwood Academic Publishers, 1993, pp. 1–2.
72 Kramer, op. cit., p. 38.
73 Nüsse, op. cit., p. 106.
74 Lopatin, op. cit., p. 75.
75 S. Taji-Farouki, 'A Contemporary Construction of the Jews in the Qur'an: A Review of Muhammad Sayyid Tantawi's *Banu Isra'il Fi Al-Qur'an Wa Al-Sunna* and 'Afif 'Abd Al-Fattah Tabbara's *Al-Yahud Fi Al-Qur'an*', R. Nettler, and S. Taji-Farouki, (eds), *Muslim-Jewish Encounters: Intellectual Traditions and Modern Politics*, Studies in Muslim-Jewish Relations, vol. 4, Amsterdam, Harwood Academic Publishers, 1998, p. 22.
76 Lopatin, op. cit., p. 82.
77 C. Adang, 'Medieval Muslim Polemics against the Jewish Scriptures', J. Waardenburg, (ed.), *Muslim Perceptions of Other Religions: A Historical Survey*, Oxford, Oxford University Press, 1999, p. 153.
78 A. Jones, 'A Bridge Between Two Communities', R. Nettler, (ed.), *Studies in Muslim-Jewish Relations*, vol. 1, Chur, Switzerland, Harwood Academic Publishers, 1993, pp. 31–2.
79 Nüsse, op. cit., p. 114.
80 Nüsse, op. cit., p. 104.
81 R. Nettler, 'A Post-Colonial Encounter of Traditions: Muhammad Sa'îd Al-'Ashmâwî on Islam and Judaism', R. Nettler, (ed.), *Medieval and Modern Perspectives on Muslim-Jewish Relations*, Luxembourg, Harwood Academic Publishers, 1995, p.176.
82 Ibid.
83 R. Nettler, 'Early Islam, Modern Islam and Judaism: The *Isra'iliyyat* in Modern Islamic Thought', R. Nettler, and S. Taji-Farouki, (eds), *Muslim-Jewish Encounters: Intellectual Traditions and Modern Politics*, Studies in Muslim-Jewish Relations, vol. 4, Amsterdam, Harwood Academic Publishers, 1998 (a), p. 11.
84 Israeli, op. cit., p. 233.

85 Magonet, op. cit., p. 165.
86 Kuschel, op. cit., pp. 187–8.
87 Nüsse, op. cit., p. 106.
88 Heilman, op. cit., p. 87.
89 Magonet, op. cit., p. 201.
90 J. T. Kenney,'Jews, Kharijites and the Debate over Religious Extremism in Egypt', R. Nettler, and S. Taji-Farouki, (eds), *Muslim-Jewish Encounters: Intellectual Traditions and Modern Politics*, Studies in Muslim-Jewish Relations, vol. 4, Amsterdam, Harwood Academic Publishers, 1998, p. 82.
91 I. Pappe, 'Understanding the Enemy: A Comparative Analysis of Palestinian Islamist and Nationalist Leaflets, 1920s-1980s', R. Nettler, and S. Taji-Farouki, (eds), *Muslim-Jewish Encounters: Intellectual Traditions and Modern Politics*, Studies in Muslim-Jewish Relations, vol. 4, Amsterdam, Harwood Academic Publishers, 1998, p. 90.
92 J. Nevo, '"Zionism" Versus "Judaism" in Palestinian Historiography', R. Nettler, (ed.), *Medieval and Modern Perspectives on Muslim-Jewish Relations*, Luxembourg, Harwood Academic Publishers, 1995, p. 159.
93 Kenney, op. cit., p. 73.
94 Pappe, op. cit., pp. 96, 102.
95 Nüsse, op. cit., p. 104.
96 Ibid.
97 Taji-Farouki, 1998, p. 27..
98 Kramer, op. cit., p. 38.
99 Kramer, op. cit., p. 39.
100 Kuschel, op. cit., p. 185.
101 B. S. Jackson, 'Comparing Jewish and Islamic Law', *Journal of Semitic Studies*, spring 2003, , 2003, p. 111.
102 Abramson, 1998, p. 114.
103 Abramson, 1998, p. 116.
104 Abramson, 1998, p. 109.
105 Abramson, 1998, p. 111.
106 Abramson, 1998, p. 110.
107 Abramson, 1998, p. 126.
108 Ibid.
109 Taji-Farouki, 1995, p. 48.
110 Nüsse, op. cit., p. 115.
111 Nüsse, op. cit., pp. 108–9.
112 Nüsse, op. cit., p. 100.
113 Ibid.
114 Taji-Farouki, 1995, p. 47.
115 Friedmann, op. cit., p. 1.
116 Friedmann, op. cit., p. 14.
117 Nüsse, op. cit., p. 104.
118 Langer, op. cit., p. 273.
119 Hartman, op. cit., p. 27.
120 Masalha, op. cit., p. 85.
121 Masalha, op. cit., pp. 88–9.
122 Masalha, op. cit., pp. 90–1.
123 O. Leaman, *Moses Maimonides*, Richmond, Curzon Press, 1997, pp. 16–17.
124 Masalha, op. cit., p. 94.
125 Masalha, op. cit., p. 110.

126 Hartman, op. cit., p. 118; Masalha, op. cit., p. 87.
127 Masalha, op. cit., p. 113.
128 Lopatin, op. cit., p. 83.
129 Taji-Farouki, 1995, p. 53.
130 Taji-Farouki, 1998, p. 15.
131 N. Solomon, 'Stereotyping Other Theologies', D. Cohn-Sherbok, (ed.), *Islam in a World of Diverse Faiths*, Basingstoke, Macmillan Press, 1997, p. 77.
132 Magonet, op. cit., p. 79.
133 Heilman, op. cit., p. 77.
134 Z. Schacter, 'Bases and Boundaries of Jewish, Christian, and Moslem Dialogue', L. Swidler, (ed.), *Muslims in Dialogue: The Evolution of A Dialogue*, Dyfed, Wales, The Edwin Mellen Press, 1992, p. 320.
135 R. Nettler, 'Mohamed Talbi: "For Dialogue Between All Religions"', R. Nettler, and S. Taji-Farouki, (eds), *Muslim-Jewish Encounters: Intellectual Traditions and Modern Politics*, Studies in Muslim-Jewish Relations, vol. 4, Amsterdam, Harwood Academic Publishers, 1998 (b), p. 172.
136 H. Goddard, *A History of Christian-Muslim Relations*, Chicago, New Amsterdam Books, 2000, p. 165.
137 R. Nettler, 'Islam, Politics and Democracy: Mohamed Talbi and Islamic Modernism', D. Marquand, and R. Nettler, (eds), *Religion and Democracy*, Aberystwyth, Blackwell Publishers, 2000, p. 58.
138 Cragg, op. cit., p. 268.
139 Magonet, op. cit., p. 68.
140 Magonet, op. cit., p. 71.
141 Langer, op. cit., p. 275.
142 Hellwig, op. cit., p. 331.
143 A. O'Mahony, 'Islam Face to face with Christianity', in, *'Spirituality Across Borders'*, *The Way Supplement 104*, 2002, p. 85.
144 Hellwig, op. cit., p. 334.
145 Nettler, 1998 (b), op. cit., pp. 174–5.
146 Nettler, 1998 (b), op. cit., p. 176.
147 S. H. Nasr, *The Heart of Islam: Enduring Values for Humanity*, San Francisco, Harper, 2002, p. 48.
148 A. E. Harvey, et al., *The Conflict in the Middle East and Religious Faith*, London, British Council of Churches, 1970, p. 30.
149 Harvey, op. cit., p. 2.
150 Harvey, op. cit., p. 29.
151 A. O'Mahony, *'Le Pélerin de Jérusalem:* Louis Massignon, Palestinian Christians, Islam and the State of Israel', A. O'Mahony, (ed.), *Palestinian Christians: Religion, Politics and Society in the Holy Land*, London, Melisende, 1999, p. 178.
152 Burrell, 1986, p. 1.
153 D. A. Lane, 'Jesus in Jewish-Christian-Muslim Dialogue', L. Swidler, (ed.), 1992, *Muslims in Dialogue: The Evolution of A Dialogue*, Dyfed, Wales, The Edwin Mellen Press, 1977, p. 374.

Chapter 9

Jerusalem, the Holy City in selected documents of the Holy See and in writings of Michel Sabbah, Latin Patriarch of Jerusalem

Charles H. Miller, SM

Michel Sabbah, Latin Patriarch of Jerusalem

Born in Nazareth in March 1933, Michel Sabbah found himself a seminarian in Jordanian-held territory at the time of the Israeli-Arab ceasefire in 1948, and was therefore excluded from residence or citizenship in his hometown. He was ordained priest in June 1955, served in various pastoral positions in Jordan and the West Bank, earned his doctorate in Arabic philology from the Sorbonne in 1973, was named president of Bethlehem University in 1980, and in 1987 became the first Palestinian to hold the position of Latin Patriarch of Jerusalem, being consecrated and installed on 6 January 1988. From that time on, he has spoken out unceasingly for justice, for peace, for forgiveness, for reconciliation of the warring parties.

Since 1988, Sabbah's life, as well as his writings and addresses, has been defined by the ongoing, indeed deteriorating situation of the Palestinian people, both Christian and Muslim, under the Israeli occupation. Although his archdiocese includes Israel, Jordan, Cyprus, Jerusalem, the West Bank and Gaza, it is primarily the Occupied Territories, including Arab Jerusalem, that have drawn most of his outspokenness. (The Synod of the Catholic Churches in the Holy Land, completed in the Jubilee Year 2000 under his leadership, however, was concerned with a much broader and more positive range of internal church issues and planning for the future.)

In this chapter I propose first to situate in an historical context the present-day attitude of the Holy See towards the Holy Land, the city of Jerusalem, and the Catholic faithful in that region, and secondly to examine some of the major documents of Patriarch Sabbah in an attempt to discern the outlines of his theological thinking, particularly about Jerusalem. Some of these documents are of his composition; some are committee productions to which he has substantially contributed. While his thoughts on social justice issues are relatively straightforward, some of the biblical presuppositions of his statements on Jerusalem call for some comment.

The context

Since the American/British invasion of Iraq in spring 2003, one has heard and read frequently in news reports about fighting and/or efforts to avoid fighting in 'holy cities' such as Karbala or Najaf. A major Islamic shrine associated with the story and tomb of the early Imam Ali has drawn millions of pilgrims through the centuries, and its immense associated cemetery is seen as a most desirable place to be buried, apparently for its proximity to the holiness of the shrine. Other 'holy cities' for Islam include Mecca and Medina, both associated with the very origins of Islam in the life of the Prophet Muhammad; Jerusalem in Islamic circles is known by its Arabic name, *al-Quds* 'the Holy'. Mecca, of course, has a status all its own, due to the Ka'aba as the centre of Islamic worship and goal of the Hajj; Medina has the Tomb of the Prophet; and Jerusalem with its al-Aqsa mosque and Dome of the Rock figures in the story of the Prophet's *miraj*, but never acquired the status of a mandatory pilgrimage goal like the other two.

But the idea of a 'holy city' hardly originated with Islam. In ancient Mesopotamia the foundations of cities were sometimes attributed to the gods, as Babylon to Marduk in the *Enuma Elish*, so that appropriate worship might be offered daily in the god's temple. The Greeks were at least sometimes a bit more down to earth in their foundation stories, remembering heroes (such as Cadmus at Thebes) or simple colonization expeditions from older cities. On the other hand, the Romans deified 'Roma' with a cult associated with that of the Emperor as divine from Caesar Augustus onwards.

One might, for clarity's sake, distinguish here between 'moral holiness', a quality of integrity of individual persons in their interior relationship with God and other human persons, and 'holiness' as a synonym for 'the sacred', an external status of things/times/places/human beings designated in a given society as specially set aside for divine service or presence. It is the latter sense of 'holiness' as applied to the city of Jerusalem that is in question here. Only God can judge the holiness (or lack thereof) of Jerusalem in the former sense.[1]

Jerusalem, a secular city?

The oldest documentation extant that seems to mention Jerusalem, the Egyptian execration tablets, attributes no particular divine quality to the city,[2] nor do the Amarna Letters;[3] nor does the Bible itself, in what it presents as the earliest reminiscences about it. Genesis 14 speaks of Melchizedek as 'king of Salem' and 'priest of El Elyon', but it is not at all clear that this 'Salem' should be identified with Jerusalem, while 'El' and 'Elyon' are Canaanite god-names. On the other hand, one interpretation of the old Canaanite name is 'City of [the god] Shalem'.[4]

In the Deuteronomistic history, the conquest and distribution narratives in Joshua (10; 12:10; 15:6) and Judges (1:21), whatever their respective antiquity, attribute no special quality to Jerusalem, the city of the Jebusites.

Even the story of David's conquest of Jerusalem, set as it is in the narrative just after his anointing by 'all the tribes of Israel' (2 Sm. 5:1–9), appears to describe a savvy political choice of a 'neutral' location hitherto not identified with either Judah or a northern tribe. The translation of the Ark of the Covenant from Baalah of Judah (via the home of Obed-Edom) in 2 Sm. 6 is, in the narrative as presented to us in the Bible, the first association of the city with something 'holy'. The Ark is said to have brought blessings to its hosts, so David wants it for his capital city, but the move also contributes substantially to his efforts to build up the idea of a centralized locus of power and authority, both political and religious.[5] A further development of a relationship with the divine is told in the census narrative of 2 Sm. 24, where the angel of Yahweh is restrained from striking Jerusalem, and David builds an altar for sacrifices on the threshing floor purchased from Araunah.

Jerusalem becomes the holy city par excellence

But the Deuteronomistic tradition, drawing upon prophetic precedent, seems to assign holiness to the city with the building of the Temple, i.e., Yahweh's explicit choice of a 'place', a *maqôm*, as his earthly dwelling. Solomon is reported to have built the first temple in Jerusalem, according to a divine promise to his father David, bringing the Ark of the Covenant up from the City of David to rest in it. Even so, there seems to be something of a distinction between city and Temple in Solomon's address to the people, recounting Yahweh's promise:

> From the day I brought my people Israel out of Egypt I chose no city, in any of the tribes of Israel, to have a temple built where my name should be; ... I have built the temple for the name of Yahweh, God of Israel. (1 Kgs 8:16–20)

Even granting the historicity of the 'First Temple' (for which there is extant no undisputed archaeological evidence), however, the location of Jerusalem for such a temple appears to be still simply the consequence of David's conquest and choice of it for his capital. Indeed, in 1 Kings the Temple is built as an integral part of Solomon's overall construction project, the major element of which is his own palace as symbol of his power and authority, enhanced by the proximity of the Temple. The placing of the Ark in the Temple consolidates for him, just as it had for his father in the City of David, the sense of continuity between the older tribal league and the new monarchy. In his dedicatory prayer Solomon is said to speak of the '*place* of which you have said "My name will be there,"...' 1 Kgs 8:29f, referring back to Dt 12:5ff. The 'city you have chosen' (1 Kgs 8:44) now seems to have taken on a sacred character in the biblical tradition, serving not merely as the geographical location of the *place*, the *maqôm* chosen by Yahweh, i.e., the Temple, but having a quality of chosenness in its own right, albeit derived from that of the *maqôm*/Temple.

There were, of course, other traditions that came to look upon 'Zion' as the chosen of Yahweh, in and from which he bestows his blessings (e.g., Ps 132:13 and the Songs of Ascents, *passim*; Is 2:1–5, etc.). The prophetic tradition played upon the idea of Yahweh's presence in the Temple both to extol the sacredness of Jerusalem and to excoriate the sins of her people.

An historical-critical view

Jewish and Christian readers through the centuries have tended to read the 'historical' books of the Old Testament as simply recounting events as they happened.

> Writing about Catholic readers before 1943, Robinson remarks: The biblical text [was] construed quite literally – a realistic narrative reading was the common mode of reading among the clergy ... That the literal sense referred to actual historical events was an assumption implied by the meaningfulness of the text, not a hypothesis to be demonstrated.[6]

Scholars today, however, try to read ancient documents, including the Bible, within the historical context of their composition, including social and political concerns of the times. Many, if not most of the biblical texts as we have them today, now appear to have been written, or at least redacted, and assembled into their present 'books' in the period that marked the return of certain groups of Jews from Babylon to Yehud in the late sixth and fifth centuries BC. As Michael Prior put it,

> In particular, the Israelite traditions which accord eminence to *Eretz Yisrael* (and concomitantly to Jerusalem and its Temple worship) reflect theological perspectives which resonate with quite specific social and political times and conditions. Literary considerations and historical-critical study alone are sufficient to show that these traditions are not atemporal, time-free directives of the Holy One ... And what applies to the land in general applies *mutatis mutandis* to the city of Jerusalem as the location of God's presence.[7]

Prior's evaluation is in harmony with the principles of Catholic exegesis, as set forth in three major documents of the twentieth century: the encyclical letter *Divino afflante Spiritu* of Pius XII (1943); the Dogmatic Constitution on Divine Revelation *Dei Verbum* of Vatican Council II (1965); and *The Interpretation of the Bible in the Church* of the Pontifical Biblical Commission (1993). In an address on the occasion of the completion of the last document, Pope John Paul II cites the earlier documents to draw on 'The Harmony between Catholic Exegesis and the Mystery of the Incarnation':

> Just as the substantial Word of God became like men in every respect except sin, so too the words of God, expressed in human languages,

became like human language in every respect except error (*EB*, n. 559).

Repeated almost literally by the conciliar Constitution *Dei Verbum* (n. 13), this statement sheds light on a parallelism rich in meaning.[8]

The Pope, and the Pontifical Biblical Commission itself, go on to give a positive, but critical, appreciation of the various methods and approaches developed by contemporary scholars for the study of the biblical texts, distinguishing among the more diachronic historical-critical method and more synchronic literary methods, tradition-based approaches, social-scientific approaches, and contextual (i.e., liberationist/feminist) approaches. The only schema of interpretation that is outrightly rejected is the Fundamentalist, 'a naively literalist interpretation ... refusing to take into account the historical character of biblical revelation ... incapable of accepting the full truth of the Incarnation itself.'[9]

In short, the 'holy' quality of Jerusalem, since it derives from the biblical tradition, should be seen in the light of modern scholarship as a designation assigned to the city within a certain socio-political context of the ancient world. Just how that 'holiness' is to be viewed by Catholics today is another question altogether.

The Holy City in the New Testament

Luke's Gospel has both explicit and implicit literary and redactional emphases on Jerusalem. Implicitly, Luke's Gospel begins in the Temple with the appearance of an angel to Zechariah, then takes Jesus explicitly to Jerusalem just after birth for the Presentation in the Temple where his parents are met by Simeon of Jerusalem; at age twelve there is the pilgrimage to Jerusalem; it is to Jerusalem that Satan takes Jesus in the third temptation (order changed from Matthew/Q, which say 'the holy city'), and finally Jesus sets his face towards Jerusalem (9:51) for the Passion and Resurrection. But the directives of the Risen Jesus make it clear that the mission of the disciples is a universal one, only 'beginning from Jerusalem ...' (Lk 24:47), and 'not only in Jerusalem but throughout Judaea and Samaria, and indeed to earth's remotest end' (Acts 1:8). And so the movement of Acts is away from Jerusalem ... 'to earth's remotest end', i.e., to Rome, capital of the Empire.

Paul's letters show a particular respect for harmonizing his teachings with that of the leaders of the church in Jerusalem (Gal 1–2) and a more material concern to help the poor there through collections abroad (Gal 2: 10; 2 Cor 8–9), but there is no mystical valuing of the physical city. On the contrary, 'Jerusalem in its present state ... is in slavery together with her children. But the Jerusalem above is free, and that is the one that is our mother ...' (Gal 4:25f).

The Letter to the Hebrews denies the significance and utility of the Temple and its worship ('Bulls' blood and goats' blood are incapable of taking away sin' Heb 10:4) in comparison to the efficacy of Christ's sacrifice (10:14). In Rev 11 'The city which kills the κύριος and the μάρτυρες has become the seat of ungodliness, blasphemy and obduracy.'[10] The heavenly sanctuary has replaced the earthly, and Christians have entry to the heavenly Jerusalem (12:22). Revelation 21–22 picks up the image of the heavenly Jerusalem as the symbol of fulfilment of Christian eschatological yearning. 'The allegorical interpretation already given to the name of Jerusalem Synagogue was adapted by the Christian theologians and transferred to the Church or believers.'[11]

In short, the 'holy city' symbolism of the Old Testament/Jewish tradition has been transmuted into an eschatological symbol, with apparently nothing more to do with the earthly than the borrowed name.

Jerusalem in Christian tradition

In the patristic era, particularly after Constantine and Helena's development of the city's Holy Places and embellishment of what had been for two and a half centuries the minor pagan backwater town of Aelia Capitolina, pilgrims flowed into Jerusalem and hermits and monks populated the nearby Desert of Judah.[12] Although Christianity never mandated pilgrimages as Judaism had already done for centuries and as Islam would later do, the idea of pilgrimage to the holy places associated with the life and death of Jesus, as well as to sites throughout the ancient world associated with the stories of the Old Testament and the work of the Apostles in the New, became a permanent fixture in Christian spirituality. Cyril of Jerusalem was able to convince the bishops that the see of Jerusalem, as the Mother Church of Christianity, deserved the designation of Patriarchate to put it on a par with Alexandria, Antioch and Rome. The Crusades derived their principal attraction, indeed their power, from the popes' call to deliver the Holy Places from Muslim subjection and to make the Holy Land safe for Christian pilgrims. In modern times, especially with the development of steamships and then airplanes, pilgrimage became mass movements of travellers, first from the West and Russia, but now increasingly from Africa, Asia, and Latin America to the Holy Land, with the concomitant development of support structures of the tourist trade. The idea of the 'Holy Land', the 'Holy City', the 'Holy Places', continues to draw Catholics, Orthodox, Protestants, Jews and Muslims to Jerusalem. The celebration of the Jubilee Year 2000 was essentially that of pilgrimages to Rome and the Holy Land, although those to the latter were cut short by the eruption of the second *intifada* on 29 September 2000, and numbers have remained drastically low ever since.

Jerusalem in Catholic thought today

There is not a unanimity of thought among Catholic theologians about the Holy Land and the Holy City today. Ideas range from a quasi-mystical, often literalist, pro-Zionism to an almost agnostic rejection on historical-critical grounds of attributing any 'sacred' quality to the earthly city.

The Pontifical Biblical Commission's 2001 publication, *Le peuple juif et ses Saintes Écritures dans la Bible Chrétienne*,[13] treats Jerusalem within the context of ancient Israelite cult, separately from 'the promise of the land' as such. The earlier members responsible for publication in 1993 of *The Interpretation of the Bible in the Church* having rotated off the Commission, the reader is hard pressed at times to find a clear continuity between its positive appreciation of the methods of contemporary biblical scholarship and some of the positions taken by newer Commission members eight years later. For example, in considering the 'Conquest' in the theme of *La Terre promise*, after critically admitting that 'The order of the anathema was therefore able to bring about a projection of later concerns into the past' (n. 56). 'The authors of the New Testament simply moved forward a process of symbolic deepening which was already inherent in the Old Testament and Judaism in the intertestament period' the Commission suddenly reverts to a pre-critical literalist position about the gift of the Land:

> This should never let us forget that a real Land was promised by God to Israel and received as an inheritance; this gift of the Land was conditional on faithfulness and convenant. (Lv 26; Dt 28). (n. 57)[14]

But to return to the treatment of Jerusalem itself: the PBC traces in the Old Testament the themes of election of the city by Yahweh, its designation as 'city of God', 'holy city', etc. 'Some texts even idealize the city of cities. Beyond the geographical reality it becomes a pole of attraction and the axis of the world' (n. 48). Later, the restored Jerusalem becomes a major symbol of eschatological salvation and source of divine teaching that will end all wars. In tracing the New Testament's views on Jerusalem, the Commission sees the city having a role in the plan of God, yet its blindness foreseen and its anticipated destruction wept over by Jesus. It is at the heart of Luke's theology (but only as a point of transiency, as noted above), but becomes a symbol of eschatological fulfillment through Paul, Hebrews and Revelation.

> 'Thus therefore, thanks to a symbolic deepening which was already well primed in the Old Testament, the Church always recognizes the links which intimately unite it to the history of Jerusalem and its Temples as well as to the prayer and worship of the Jewish people' (n. 51).

Jerusalem, then, is seen by the Commission as more spiritual, symbolic, historical in its significance for Christians, in contrast to the Commission's literalist interpretation of the promise of the land.

Catholic political thought on Jerusalem

The diplomatic position of the Holy See on Jerusalem has been closely aligned with the United Nations resolutions on the topic since 1947. From an initial opposition to Theodor Herzl's Zionist aims for the Holy Land in the time of Pius X until 1948, the Holy See moved to an acceptance and support of the United Nations Charter and the Security Council as legitimate sources of international law in our time. It accepted, therefore, the UN's recognition of the independence of Israel in 1948, but turned its attention much more to the plight of the Palestinian refugees than to the new Jewish state. After Vatican II's *Nostra Aetate*, the 1964 visit of Pope Paul VI to the Holy Land, and the accession of John Paul II to the papacy in 1978, a more positive approach to the State of Israel gradually developed among a generation of elder churchmen profoundly marked by the Second World War and the realization of the depth of the evil of Nazism.

While the UN in 1947 had called for Jerusalem to be a *corpus separatum*, a status strongly desired by the Holy See to protect access to the Holy Places for Christians, Jews and Muslims alike, the evolving political situation from 1948 through 1967 made such an outcome highly unlikely. The Holy See's position changed, then, to advocacy of a special status for Jerusalem, with access to the Holy Places guaranteed by international statute for persons of all religions. This was articulated in 1998 by then Archbishop (now Cardinal) Jean-Louis Tauran, Secretary for Relations with States (i.e., the Holy See's 'foreign minister'), in his address to the 1998 Symposium of Presidents and Delegates of Catholic Bishops' Conferences on Jerusalem. The *Final Communiqué* of the Symposium was abridged by the Vatican Information Service as follows:

> Jerusalem, the Holy City for the three monotheistic religions, is of unique value for the region and for the whole world. Thus, Jerusalem is and ought to be a universal symbol of fraternity and peace.
>
> Today Jerusalem is at a crucial time in her modern history ... Jerusalem, the city of three religions, is also home to two peoples, Israelis and Palestinians, and is the heartland of their respective national aspirations. Negotiations between the State of Israel and the Palestinian National Authority, with the support of the international community, will shape 'a final status' for Jerusalem ... Decisions will be made by political leaders but the concerns and hopes of believers must also be included in the pertinent negotiations.
>
> We have also reaffirmed that the uniqueness and holiness of the most sacred parts of Jerusalem require a special statute for her most sacred parts ... Such a statute should also guarantee the sacred character and the universal cultural heritage of the city. Free access to Jerusalem should be guaranteed to all, local people and pilgrims, friends and opponents. Finally, this special statute should be supported by international guarantees.' (VIS 1998)

The complete document is key to understanding the Catholic position on Jerusalem.

What is germane to our discussion here is the understanding of the 'holiness' of Jerusalem as articulated by the Symposium:

> 4. For Christians, as for Jews and Muslims, Jerusalem is a city of special religious reference. For Christians, in particular, Jerusalem is sacred as the place where Jesus, the Word and Son of God, lived, suffered, died on a cross, and rose from the dead, bringing to completion the work of our redemption. The descent of the Holy Spirit on Pentecost Day marked the birth of the Church which spread from Jerusalem to the

ends of the earth, so that down the centuries Jerusalem has been cherished throughout the world as 'the Mother Church'. Thus, the Holy City is always in our prayers as we await the final fulfillment of all the promises of God for a new Jerusalem, coming down from heaven where God will dwell with humanity.

5. For two thousand years, a living Christian community has been the bearer of the memory and the promise of the Holy City. Today, through all the changes and vicissitudes of history, this Christian community continues to dwell and worship in Jerusalem, and is deeply committed to continue to bear witness to the life, death and resurrection of Christ around the Holy Places where these mysteries were enacted. As they live in fidelity to this commitment, members of that community can rely on the solidarity of the universal Church.[15]

There are fundamentally two considerations here, one historical, one contemporary. The 'holiness' of Jerusalem for Christians is its historical character as the site of the life, death and resurrection of Jesus, the descent of the Holy Spirit, and the springboard for the spread of the Church. The universal Church today, moreover, has not only an historical interest in what happened long ago, but also a sense of solidarity with 'the Mother Church' of all Christendom, the living community descended from that first group of disciples of 2000 years ago.

The first consideration, as found in the Holy See's documents over the past two centuries, focuses primarily on preservation of the Holy Places, on their maintenance as places of genuine prayer, on the architectural and social integrity of the city that surrounds them, on free access for all believers, including both pilgrims from abroad and local Christians. The second consideration is concerned more with the human welfare of the local community of living Christians, with questions of social justice, of care for refugees, for victims of state-sponsored oppression and harassment, with the economic, social and political pressures that drive so many to emigrate from the land of their fathers.

While the definition of 'holiness' of places for Jews and Muslims is beyond the scope of this chapter, it might be useful to put the Catholic idea into a broader theological perspective. What is evident both from the PBC document *Le peuple juif...* and from the *Final Communiqué*, is that the Catholic Church considers Jerusalem and its Holy Places to be 'holy', 'sacred', primarily in an historical sense, not because of some magical quality possessed by them today. But as historical witnesses to the founding events of the Christian religion, they carry a psychological power for pilgrims that can be characterized as occasions of divine grace. Thus the *Catechism of the Catholic Church* recognizes the value of what it calls 'Popular piety':

> 1674 Besides sacramental liturgy and sacramentals, catechesis must take into account the forms of piety and popular devotions among the faithful. The religious sense of the Christian people has always found expression in various forms of piety surrounding the Church's sacramental life, such as the veneration of relics, **visits to sanctuaries, pilgrimages, processions, the stations of the cross**, religious dances, the rosary, medals, etc. [my emphasis – CHM]
>
> 1676 At its core the piety of the people is a storehouse of values that offers answers of Christian wisdom to the great questions of life ...[16]

The political interests of the Holy See in Jerusalem are, then 1) maintenance of free access for all to 'Holy Places' for the sake of the piety of pilgrims; and, integrally linked to that free access 2) maintenance of vital local Christian/Catholic communities living in a situation of justice and peace in the neighborhood of the Holy Places.

The theological thought of Patriarch Sabbah

One can identify five principal strands of thought on the matter of Jerusalem among the numerous homilies, statements, addresses, pastoral letters, and other publications of Michel Sabbah. Most of what he has to say about the Holy Land applies *a fortiori* to Jerusalem. Some of his principal documents are:

1. *Pastoral Letter 1 of H.B. Msgr. Michel Sabbah, Latin Patriarch of Jerusalem,* Jerusalem: Latin Patriarchate Printing Press, 15 August 1998.
2. *Pastoral Letter 2 of H.B. Msgr. Michel Sabbah, Latin Patriarch of Jerusalem, 'Pray for peace in Jerusalem (Ps. 122,6)'* on the Feast of Pentecost 1990, Jerusalem, Latin Patriarchate Printing Press, 1990.
3. *Pastoral Letter 4 of H.B. Michel Sabbah, Latin Patriarch of Jerusalem: Reading the Bible Today in the Land of the Bible,* Jerusalem, Latin Patriarchate, November 1993.
4. *Memorandum of Their Beatitudes the Patriarchs and of the Heads of the Christian Communities in Jerusalem on the Significance of Jerusalem for Christians,* Jerusalem, 14 November 1994.
5. *The Christian Significance of Jerusalem: Comments by Patriarch Michel Sabbah on the Memorandum of the Patriarchs: Christian Presence for 2000 Years,* 26 October1 996.

6. *Jerusalem: What is the Truth?: Jerusalem: A Holy City and a Place for Living.* Address at the ADC 14th Convention, 14 June 1997.
7. *Pastoral Letter 5 of H.B. Patriarch Michel Sabbah, Latin Patriarch of Jerusalem: Preparations for the Jubilee Year 2000,* Jerusalem, Latin Patriarchate, Feast of the Assumption, 1997.
8. 'Ouverture de l'an 2000 par les Églises de Jérusalem', Bethlehem, 4 December 1999.
9. *Religious Fundamentalism and Peace,* Jerusalem, 1 October 2003.
10. *Peace in the Holy Land,* Address on the occasion of receiving a Ph.D., *honoris causa,* at St. Mary's University, San Antonio, Texas, USA, 20 September 2004.

Some identifiable major strands of Sabbah's thought are:

1. Political – Sabbah's thought is closely attuned to that of the Holy See on the need for an international statute and guarantees for freedom of access to Jerusalem and its Holy Places for all nations and all religions.
2. Ecclesial/pastoral – Jerusalem is the Mother Church of the world, but also a living community of Catholics (and other Christians) with their own lives and destiny, which includes the service of hospitality to the Church on pilgrimage to the Holy Places.
3. Ecumenical – Sabbah sees the pragmatic and the theological need for Christian solidarity in Jerusalem and its growth under the pressure of the Occupation.
4. Interfaith – Ideally, Jerusalem should provide an example to the world of a city in which Jews, Muslims and Christians live in dialogue and brotherhood and peace.

1. The political strand

From his third pastoral letter (1993), *Reading the Bible* ..., Patriarch Sabbah has appealed to international law for the rights of his people. 'But the political rights of one or another of the three religions, or of any of the faithful, depend on the political action taken by the political authorities. And this is governed by international law' (n. 54). This same passage is recalled and cited in 1997, *Jerusalem: What is the Truth?* Part One: Jerusalem: A Holy City and a Place for Living (Address at ADC 14th Convention, 14 June 1997).

Sabbah explicitly endorses other political positions elaborated by the Holy See. His 26 October 1996 *Comments* ... *on the Memorandum* (of 14 November 1994) recalls in note 6 the position of the Holy See as articulated for a Muslim-Christian conference organized by the Middle East Council of Churches in Beirut in June 1996. Citing the

Fundamental Agreement between the State of Israel and the Holy See (par. 2 art. 11), Sabbah claims for the Church the right to express a moral judgement on the situation. In this matter, he acts very much in harmony with the Post-Synodal Apostolic Exhortation *Pastores Gregis* of His Holiness Pope John Paul II, 'On The Bishop, Servant of the Gospel of Jesus Christ for the Hope of the World', n. 67, 'The Bishop, Promoter of Justice and Peace':

> In the midst of tragically frequent situations of armed conflict, the Bishop, even as he exhorts people to assert their rights, must always remind them that Christians are obliged in all cases to reject vengeance and to be prepared to forgive and to love their enemies. There can be no justice without forgiveness. Hard as it may be to accept, for any sensible person the matter seems obvious: true peace is possible only through forgiveness.[17]

From his earliest years in office, Sabbah had already made his own the call of John Paul II for a 'special statute internationally guaranteed so that no party could jeopardize it' (Apostolic Letter *Redemptionis Anno* – cited in *Pray for the Peace* ... n. 49. This demand is reiterated in the *Memorandum* of 1994, in his *Comments* of 1996 (n. 5.3), and in *What is Truth* ... Part II (1997).

Under any circumstances, however, the local Christians of Jerusalem should enjoy certain rights, as the 1994 *Memorandum* calls for:

> a the human right of freedom of worship and of conscience, both as individuals and as religious communities,
> b civil and historical rights which allow them to carry out their religious, educational, medical and other duties of charity,
> c the right to have their own institutions ... and the right to have their own personnel man and run these institutions. (n. 12)

Sabbah's *Comments* pushes this call for an equality of rights for all citizens of Jerusalem 'without any distinction or discrimination' (4.1), with freedom of access for all Christians, both local and worldwide.

Drawing upon the sacramental character of Jerusalem in *Preparations* ..., he writes: 'We remind the great powers of this world and the leaders who are nowadays ruling this land that its holy character is very demanding; it is different from all other lands.' And he follows up by calling for removal of 'military barriers which have become a permanent obstacle to their [the sons and daughters of this land] faith and prayer' (n. 13).

In his 2004 address at St Mary's University Sabbah bases his position on the God-given dignity of every human person, rejects war, and calls to love and forgiveness. He realistically warns that

> Anything less than the [full Palestinian] state, and less than the land occupied in 1967, will keep the fire of hatred and war alive. (n. 5)

> Recognizing 'the God-given dignity of our enemies does not mean giving up all resistance to evil (n. 6) ... To claim our rights is to defend our dignity, but it is also to defend the dignity of the adversary and to help him enter into the way of reconciliation and salvation.' (n. 7)

2. The ecclesial/pastoral strand

This element of Sabbah's thought goes beyond civil life and politics and concerns the age-old vocation of the local Christians of Jerusalem vis-à-vis the worldwide Church. His *Pastoral Letter 1* at the beginning of his episcopate in 1988 proclaimed him to be 'At the Service of the Believer', i.e., of the people of the Church of Jerusalem, reversing the two priorities of the Holy See as indicated above:

> 51. The believer of the Holy Land has remained a faithful witness to his faith throughout the centuries in spite of all struggles and difficulties, during the darkest days, faced with all kinds of calamities. Therefore this faithful witness to the faith and the Holy Places draws from this very faithfulness, dignity and greatness. And he is the first object of our service.

> 52. Looking on the Holy Land as the place where our faith originated, we might forget or put on the second place this man with his own personality. He really risks to be submerged or even deformed under the pressure of the world looking at the Holy Places.

> 53. The Holy Land and the Church of Jerusalem have a universal nature, since the proclamation of the faith started from here throughout the whole world. But this note of universality has not to suffocate the person who remains faithful to his faith and to the land in spite of suffering and sacrifice.
>
> The Church universal owes to this man as to his land a particular service, on a spiritual and human level, so that he may realize his dignity and as a believer, may continue to bring the faith to his land, to all its guests, residents or pilgrims passing through it, who have come to study and to pray.

The 1994 *Memorandum* recalls 'The Continuing Presence of a Christian Community' from its very beginning:

> Across the centuries, the local Church has been witnessing to the life and preaching, the death and resurrection of Jesus Christ upon the same Holy Places, and its faithful have been receiving other brothers and sisters in the faith, as pilgrims, resident or in transit, inviting them to be reimmersed into the refreshing, ever living ecclesiastical sources. That continuing presence of a living Christian community is inseparable from the historical sites. Through the 'living stones' the holy archaeological sites take on 'life'. (n. 9)

Sabbah develops this idea in his 1996 *Comments*:

> We are aware ... that we have the duty and the right to welcome in Jerusalem all Christians of the world and to serve them in their pilgrimage and in their faith relation to the same Mother city.
> This relation between local Churches and the Universal Church is a normal and vital one, and it is conform [*sic*] to the nature of the Church ...
>
> Therefore Christianity in Jerusalem has two dimensions: local and universal. Each one of these two components completes and supports the other. Through the local Church the presence of the universal Church is guaranteed. On the other side, the small local Church becomes big and efficient, not only through the incessant coming of pilgrims, but also through the regular and continuous support of the universal Church. (n. 3.3)

In *Preparations*, as one might expect, the Patriarch again develops the idea of the vocation of the local Church towards the world:

> Our Holy Places, as well as our parishes, are holy for us and for the rest of the world. We are here for ourselves, for our Church of Jerusalem and for the Churches throughout the world. (n. 4)
>
> On this occasion, the entire Church sets out on pilgrimage, on a journey where she seeks God, in our various shrines, in order to meditate there the mystery of the plan of salvation, and to discover the true meaning of the Jubilee ... (n. 7)
>
> The parishes have to prepare for the welcoming [of] the various pilgrim Churches, as a sign of ecclesial communion open to the world. The parish communities are the living stones with which pilgrims wish to get in touch: through this communion their spiritual journey in the Holy Land will reach its fullness. (n. 9)

The last idea is worth considering further. How many pilgrims, particularly in our age of mass transit and large groups, have come to the Holy Land without ever gaining an awareness of the spirituality of the local Christians? How many have stayed only at Jewish-operated hotels, have had Jewish guides and/or Muslim bus drivers, have visited Holy Places, even for religious ceremonies and been cared for by foreign clergy, and have never spoken to local Christians about their lives, their spirituality, their identification with the Land of the Bible? Bowman's description of Latin Catholic 'Contemporary Christian pilgrimage in the Holy Land',[18] however, omits any consideration of such contact in actual practice. And yet Sabbah identifies this personal contact experience as the 'fullness', the culmination of a spiritual pilgrimage. While a few Christian travel agents had implemented some kind of programmed contact with the 'Living Stones' before the second *intifada*, it would seem that a much more concentrated effort in this regard would help to alert the worldwide Church to the severe political, social, economic, and personal difficulties faced by Palestinian Christians even in the best of times under the rule of the Israeli Occupation Forces, and give to the visitors a perspective perhaps not always seen in their national news media, a perspective of patience and struggle under what is clearly discrimination and persecution in Jerusalem, outright oppression in the Occupied Territories.

3. The ecumenical strand

One of the strongest indicators of Sabbah's commitment to mutual understanding among the Christian churches of Jerusalem is in the 1994 *Memorandum*, signed as it is by (as well as Sabbah) the Greek Orthodox Patriarch, the Armenian [Apostolic] Patriarch, the [Franciscan] Custos of the Holy Land, the Coptic [Orthodox] Archbishop, the Syrian [Orthodox] Archbishop, the Ethiopian [Orthodox] Archbishop, the Anglican Bishop, the Greek-Catholic Patriarchal Vicar, the Lutheran Bishop, the Maronite Patriarchal Vicar, the Syrian Catholic Patriarchal Vicar. In this document the bulk of the native Christian community of Jerusalem speaks out with one voice 'on the significance of Jerusalem for Christians'. The document gives a unified statement about the Christian vision of Jerusalem (sacramental, historical, ecclesiastical, political), calling for a special juridical and political stature for the city.

Given the nature of the Jubilee Year 2000, it was natural to find in *Preparations* a strong sense of ecumenical responsibility:

> The Church of Jerusalem, the Mother Church, has a special duty, on the occasion of this great Jubilee, to work for the communion of all the Churches. To pray for the communion among the various Churches here in Jerusalem is a way of preparing for the Jubilee ... Jerusalem, Mother of all Churches, must be in communion with all the Churches of the world. (n. 11)

Under the pressure of the Israeli Occupation upon all the Christian churches, a closer relationship has developed among the leaders of the latter than had ever existed previously, thanks in large part to Sabbah's leadership. Given the prolonged illness, eventual death and the subsequent long delays in replacement of the ranking Greek Orthodox Patriarch Diodoros I, the traditionally low profile of the Armenian Apostolic Patriarch, and the small numbers of the Anglican and Lutheran communities, Patriarch Sabbah has emerged as the principal spokesman for the combined efforts of the Christian communities of Jerusalem and the Holy Land. No other major clergyman's writings and speeches have had such worldwide distribution or such worldwide interest. At no point in his writings available to me is there to be found any criticism of another church in Jerusalem.

4. The interfaith strand

From the very beginning of his term as Patriarch, Michel Sabbah has sought to reach out both to Muslims and Jews, well aware of the difficulties and complexities of doing so in the Middle Eastern context. Nevertheless, from his *Pastoral Letter 1* onwards, he has sought to maintain open lines of communication with both Jewish and Muslim leaders. A significant part of that letter is devoted to a consideration of the nature of dialogue (nn. 32–38), which he sees as 'A Necessity in our Country':

> A country like ours, which has been known throughout the centuries for its pluralism, has to respect this characteristic if it wishes to remain true to itself. Fidelity to pluralism is expressed in dialogue. (n. 38)

Putting this respect into practice, Sabbah's *'Pray for Peace in Jerusalem'* has a section calling Christians to see Muslim neighbours in a positive, albeit realistic, light.

The Muslim faithful are your fellow compatriots. You share the same future, the same country, the same patrimony. The friction that arises in the course of ordinary everyday life cannot be allowed to destroy your sense of fraternity, or make you forget that you share the same homeland, the same patrimony and culture ... it is important to persevere in the long journey along the along the road towards a true understanding of our Muslim brothers and sisters. (n. 58)

Perhaps the most explicit, certainly the broadest, collaboration with Muslim religious leaders is *The Jerusalem Appeal* of 14–16 June 1996, a document signed by a large group of Christian and Muslim religious leaders from throughout the Middle East. Some principles enunciated in this appeal were:

- The cause of Jerusalem is pivotal to us ... None of us claims it exclusively for his faith.
- Jerusalem is its people. Its people are Palestinians.
- No power in the world has the right to Judaize Jerusalem, internationalize it, or deprive it of its Arab and Christian-Muslim character.
- Peace is the fruit of justice. Peace can not rest, nor will it endure, upon injustice and oppression.
- We call upon all Christians and Muslims of the world to support the legitimate Palestinian rights.
- As Christians and Muslims, we shall join efforts so that Jerusalem may become a city of reconciliation, justice and peace for all.

The most interesting item in the list is the third, stating that 'No power in the world has the right to ... internationalize it ...' At least superficially, while overtly directed against Israel's explicit policy of 'Judaizing' Jerusalem, this would appear to be a challenge to the UN resolution of 1947 declaring Jerusalem a *corpus separatum*, although the phrasing does not appear to oppose the Holy See's later position concerning a special international statute guaranteeing freedom of access to the Holy Places for members of all religions, as expressed in the *Final Communiqué* (Appendix I) of 1998.

Sabbah's statement for the Opening of the New Millennium (Bethlehem 4 December 1999) included an outreach to both Muslims and Jews, noting Jerusalem particularly in addressing the latter:

To the Jewish people, in its quest for security and peace we ask for them peace and security. But they know also that our security is their security and our peace is their peace; and our peace demands justice: the refugees await a return to a dignified, peaceful and stable life and cannot remain on the margin of [other] societies; the Holy City awaits a new order and a definitive stability; and other obstacles on the way to peace must disappear also. May the new millennium bring us the grace to enjoy together in this Holy Land a new order based upon justice and peace.[19]

At an interfaith meeting in Alexandria in January 2002, co-hosted by the Archbishop of Canterbury George Carey and the Grand Imam of al-Azhar al Sharif, Dr Mohamed Sayed Tantawy of Cairo, Sabbah was one of seventeen co-signers of 'The First Declaration of Alexandria'.[20] The opening sentence of the document distinguishes between Jerusalem and the Holy Land, as does item n. 6, reading as follows:

> In the name of God who is Almighty, Merciful and Compassionate, we, who have gathered as religious leaders from the Muslim, Christian, and Jewish communities, pray for true peace in Jerusalem and the Holy Land, and declare our commitment to ending the violence and bloodshed that denies the right of life and dignity.
>
> 6. As religious leaders, we pledge ourselves to continue a joint quest for a just peace that leads to reconciliation in Jerusalem and the Holy Land, for the common good of all our peoples.

But while n. 1 says that 'The Holy Land is holy to all three of our faiths', and calls for preservation of 'the sanctity and integrity of the holy places', as well as 'freedom of religious worship ... [to be] ensured for all', there is no other specific treatment of Jerusalem as such. Although one of two Catholics and of six Christians in the group, Sabbah's contributions were so significant that later that year he shared the Coventry Prize for Peace with two other co-signers of the Declaration, Rabbi Michael Melchior, Deputy Foreign Minister of Israel, and Sheikh Tal El Sider, Minister of State for the Palestinian Authority.

In short, Sabbah's commitment to interfaith dialogue has been an essential element of his pastoral ministry from its very beginning, but it is integrally tied to the call for justice and peace.

Conclusion

Michel Sabbah concludes his *Pastoral Letter 2:* 'Pray for Peace in Jerusalem' (Ps 122:6) by reflection upon Jerusalem as a sign of hope, and we could do no better than to end with that hope:

66. Jerusalem is at present a sign of contradiction and conflict. Nonetheless, she continue[s] to be a sign of hope, since she is the means by which the divine message ha[s] been transmitted to a believing mankind, believers of all peoples must meet together to hear the voice of God here. If they listen to his voice they will be able to restore to Jerusalem her sacred character and her power to bring peace, to humanize ... Every believer has the right to make Jerusalem his spiritual homeland; the place where peace and love can be found, from where one can call all men and women to peace with God.[21]

Notes:

Most, but not all patriarchal/ecumenical/interfaith documents referred to may be found via www.al-bushra.org

1 See M. Douglas, 'Justice as the Cornerstone: An Interpretation of Leviticus 18–20', *Interpretation* 53 (1999), pp. 341–50.
2 J. Pritchard, ANET, Princeton, Princeton University Press, 1955, p. 329.
3 Ibid., pp. 487–9.
4 C. Miller, 'Jerusalem' in Achtemeier, P., *The HarperCollins Bible Dictionary*, San Francisco, HarperSanFrancisco, 1996 p. 498.
5 A. G. Wright, 'A History of Israel', *NJBC* 75:83: 'The transfer of the Ark of the Covenant gave the city a religious importance that it was never to lose.'
6 R. B. Robinson, *Roman Catholic Exegesis Since Divino Afflante Spiritu: Hermeneutical Implications.* SBL Dissertation Series 111, Atlanta, Scholars Press, 1988, pp. 7–8.
7 M. Prior, '"You Will Be My Witnesses in Jerusalem, in all Judaea and Samaria, and to the Ends of the Earth": A Christian Perspective on Jerusalem.' In A. O'Mahony (ed.), *Palestinian Christians: Religion, Politics and Society in the Holy Land*, London: Melisende, 1999, pp. 100–101.
8 John Paul II, 'Address on the Interpretation of the Bible in the Church', in Pontifical Biblical Commission, *The Interpretation of the Bible in the Church*, Boston, Pauline Books & Media, 1993, p. 16. n. 6,
9 Ibid., p. 73.
10 Lohse, W. 'Σιών ...' in G. Bromley, TDNT VII, Grand Rapids, Eerdmans, 1971 p. 336.
11 Ibid. pp. 336–8.
12 See, for example, C. P. Thiede, and M. d'Ancona, *The Quest for the True Cross*, New York, Palgrave Macmillan, 2002.
13 Pontificia Commissio Biblica, *Le peuple juif et ses Saintes Écritures dans la Bible Chrétienne.* Documents du Vatican, Città del Vaticano, Libreria Editrice Vaticana, 2001.
14 Ibid. Ceci, toutefois, ne doit pas nous faire oublier qu'une terre concrète a été promise par Dieu á Israël et reçue effectivement en héritage; ce don de la terre était conditionnée [*sic*] par fidélité à l'alliance (Lv 26; Dt 28). (n. 57). A reader gains the impression of a committee document into which was inserted at the last moment a sentence to appease a concern of one or more members of a minority element, without its having been subjected to a hard scrutiny for consistency with the rest of the document or with the earlier PBC publication.

15 *Final Communiqué* of Symposium of Presidents and Delegates of Catholic Bishops' Conferences, 27–28 October 1998.
16 *The Catechism of the Catholic Church*, USCCB, 1994.
17 http://www.vatican.va/holy_father/john_paul_ii/apost_exhortations/documents/hf_jp-ii_exh_20031016_pastores-gregis_en.html
18 G. Bowman, 'Contemporary Christian Pilgrimage to the Holy Land', in O'Mahony, op. cit., pp. 141–65.
19 M. Sabbah, 'Ouverture de l'an 2000 par les Églises de Jérusalem', Bethlehem, 4 December 1999:

> 4. A nos frères musulmans dans tous nos pays arabes, notre message dans le 3ème millénaire est un message pour plus de connaissance mutuelle, de confiance, de respect et de construction en commun: Dieu nous a voulu dans cette Terre Sainte et dans toutes les patries arabes, des arabes chrétiens dans des sociétés arabes musulmanes et chrétiennes: nous acceptons la volonté de Dieu sur nous. Tous, musulmans et chrétiens, nous avons besoin de nouvelles visions, comme le dit. l'Ecriture Sainte: 'Il se fera dans les derniers jours, dit le Seigneur, que je répandrai de mon Esprit sur toute chair. Alors vos fils et vos filles prophétiseront, vos jeunes auront des visions et vos vieillards des songes' (Actes 2,17; cf Joel 3,1–5).
>
> Au peuple juif, dans sa quête de la sécurité et de la paix: nous demandons pour lui la paix et la sécurité. Mais il sait aussi que notre sécurité est sa sécurité et notre paix est sa paix; et notre paix demande justice: les réfugiés attendent le retour à une vie digne pacifique et stable et ne peuvent pas rester en marge des sociétés; la Ville Sainte attend un nouvel ordre et une stabilité définitive; et d'autres obstacles sur la voie de la paix devraient disparaître aussi. Puisse le nouveau millénaire nous porter la grâce de jouir tous ensemble d'un nouvel ordre en cette Terre Sainte, basée sur la justice et la paix.

20 http://www.bc.edu/research/cjl/meta-elements/texts/documents/interreligious/alexandria2002.htm
21 One could also identify Sabbah's spirituality of Jerusalem, but that will have to wait for a future article.

Appendix

Memorandum of their Beatitudes the Patriarchs and the Heads of the Christian communities in Jerusalem on the significance of Jerusalem for Christians

14 November 1994

Preamble

1. On Monday, 14 November 1994, the heads of the Christian communities in Jerusalem met in solemn conclave to discuss the status of the holy city and the situation of Christians there, at the conclusion of which, they issued the following declaration:

Jerusalem, Holy City

2. Jerusalem is a holy city for the people of the three monotheistic religions: Judaism, Christianity and Islam. Its unique nature of sanctity endows it with a special vocation: calling for reconciliation and harmony among people, whether citizens, pilgrims or visitors. And because of its symbolic and emotive value, Jerusalem has been a rallying cry for different revived nationalistic and fundamentalist stirrings in the region and elsewhere. And, unfortunately, the city has become a source of conflict and disharmony. It is at the heart of the Israeli-Palestinian and Israeli-Arab disputes. While the mystical call of the city attracts believers, its present unenviable situation scandalizes many.

The Peace Process

3. The current Arab-Israeli peace process is on its way toward resolution of the Middle East conflict. Some new facts have already been established, some concrete signs posted. But in the process Jerusalem has again been side-stepped, because of its status, and especially sovereignty over the city, are the most difficult questions to resolve in future negotiations. Nevertheless, one must already begin to reflect on the questions and do whatever is necessary to be able to approach them in the most favorable conditions when the moment arrives.

Present Positions

4. When the different sides involved now speak of Jerusalem, they often assume exclusivist positions. Their claims are very divergent, indeed conflicting. The Israeli position is that Jerusalem should remain the unified and eternal capital of the State of Israel, under the absolute sovereignty of Israel alone. The Palestinians, on the other hand, insist that Jerusalem should become the capital of a future State of Palestine, although they do not lay claim to the entire modern city but envisage only the eastern, Arab part.

Lesson of History

5. Jerusalem has had a long, eventful history. It has known numerous wars and conquests, has been destroyed time and again, only to be reborn anew and rise from its ashes, like the mythical Phoenix. Religious motivation has always gone hand in hand with political and cultural aspirations, and has often played a preponderant role. This motivation has often led to exclusivism or at least to the supremacy of one people over the others. But every exclusivity or every human supremacy is against the prophetic character of Jerusalem. Its universal vocation and appeal is to be a city of peace and harmony among all who dwell therein. Jerusalem, like the entire Holy land, has witnessed throughout its history the successive advent of numerous peoples: they came from the desert, from the sea, from the north, from the east. Most often the newcomers were gradually integrated into the local population. This was a rather constant characteristic. But when the newcomers tried to claim exclusive possession of the city and the land, or refused to integrate themselves, then the others rejected them. Indeed, the experience of history teaches us that in order for Jerusalem to be a city of peace, no longer lusted after from the outside and thus a bone of contention between warring sides, it cannot belong exclusively to one people or to only one religion. Jerusalem should be open to all, shared by all. Those who govern the city should make it 'the capital of humankind'. This universal vision of Jerusalem would help those who exercise power there to open it to others who also are fondly attached to it and to accept sharing it with them.

The Christian Vision of Jerusalem

6. Through a prayerful reading of the Bible, Christians recognize in faith that the long history of the people of God, with Jerusalem at its centre; is the history of salvation which fulfils God's design in and through Jesus of Nazareth, the Christ. The one God has chosen Jerusalem to be the place where His name alone will dwell in the midst of His people so that they may offer to Him acceptable worship. The prophets look up to Jerusalem, especially after the purification of the exile: Jerusalem will be called 'the city of justice, faithful city (Is 1:26,27) where the Lord dwells in holiness as in Sinai (cf Ps 68:18). The Lord will place the city in the middle of the nations (Ez 5:5), where the Second Temple will become a house of prayer for all peoples (Is 2:2; 56:6–7). Jerusalem, aglow with the presence of God (Is 60:1), ought to be a city whose gates are always open (Is 60:11), with Peace as magistrate and Justice as government (Is 60:17).

In the vision of their faith, Christians believe the Jerusalem of the Prophets to be the foreseen place of the salvation in and through Jesus Christ. In the Gospels, Jerusalem rejects the Sent-One, the Saviour; and He weeps over it because this city of the prophets that is also the city of the essential salvific events – the death and resurrection of Jesus – has completely lost sight of the path to peace (cf Lk 19:42).

In the Acts of the Apostles, Jerusalem is the place of the gift of the Spirit, of the birth of the Church (2), the community of the disciples of Jesus who are to be His witnesses not only in Jerusalem but even the ends of the earth (Acts 1:8). In Jerusalem, the first Christian community incarnated the ecclesiastical ideal, and thus it remains a continuing reference point. The Book of Revelations proclaims the anticipation of the new heavenly Jerusalem (Rev 3:12; 21:2 cf. Gal 4:26; Heb 12:22). This holy city is the image of the new creation and the aspirations of all peoples, where God will wipe away all tears, and 'there shall be no more death or mourning, crying out or pain, for the former world has passed away' (Rev 21:4).

7. The earthly Jerusalem, in the Christian tradition, prefigures the heavenly Jerusalem as 'the vision of peace'. In the Liturgy, the Church itself receives the name of Jerusalem and relives all of that city's anguish, joys and hopes. Furthermore, during the first centuries the liturgy of Jerusalem became the foundation of all liturgies everywhere, and later deeply influenced the development of diverse liturgical traditions, because of the many pilgrimages to

Jerusalem and of the symbolic meaning of the Holy City.

8. The pilgrimages slowly developed an understanding of the need to unify the sanctification of space through celebrations at the Holy Place with the sanctification in time through the calendared celebrations of the holy events of salvation (Egeria, Cyril of Jerusalem). Jerusalem soon occupied a unique place in the heart of Christianity everywhere. A theology and spirituality of pilgrimage developed. It was an ascetic time of biblical refreshment at the sources, a time of testing during which Christians recalled that they were strangers and pilgrims on earth (cf. Heb. 11:13), and that their personal and community vocation always and everywhere, is to take up the cross and follow Jesus.

The continuing presence of a Christian community

9. For Christianity, Jerusalem is the place of roots, ever living and nourishing. In Jerusalem is born every Christian. To be in Jerusalem is for every Christian to be at home. For almost two thousand years, through so many hardships and the succession of so many powers, the local Church with its faithful has always been actively present in Jerusalem. Across the centuries, the local Church has been witnessing to the life and preaching, the death and resurrection of Jesus Christ upon the same Holy places, and its faithful have been receiving other brothers and sisters in the faith, as pilgrims, resident or in transit, inviting them to be reimmersed into the refreshing, ever living ecclesiastical sources. That continuing presence of a living Christian community is inseparable from the historical sites. Through the 'living stones' the holy archaeological sites take on 'life'.

The significance of Jerusalem for Christians

10. This has two inseparable fundamental dimensions:
(1) a Holy City with holy places most precious to Christians because of their link with the history of salvation fulfilled in and through Jesus Christ;

(2) a city with a community of Christians which has been living continually there since its origins. Thus for the local Christians, as well as for local Jews and Moslems, Jerusalem is not only a Holy City, but also their native city where they live, whence their right to

continue to live there freely, with all the rights which obtain from that.

Legitimate demands of Christians for Jerusalem

11. In so far as Jerusalem is the quintessential Holy City it above all ought to enjoy full freedom of access to its Holy Places, and freedom of worship. Those rights of property ownership, custody and worship which the different Churches have acquired throughout history should continue to be retained by the same communities. These rights which are already protected in the Status Quo of the Holy Places according to historical 'firmans' and other documents, should continue to be recognized and respected. The Christians of the entire world, Western or Eastern, should have the right to come in pilgrimage to Jerusalem. They ought to be able to find there all that is necessary to carry out their pilgrimage in the spirit of their authentic tradition: freedom to visit and to move around, to pray at holy sites, to embark into spiritual attendance and respectful practice of their faith, to enjoy the possibility of a prolonged stay and the benefits of hospitality and dignified lodgings.

The local Christian communities

12. They should enjoy all those rights to enable them to continue their active presence in freedom and to fulfill their responsibilities towards both their own local members and towards the Christian pilgrims throughout the world. Local Christians, not only in their capacity as Christians per se, but like all other citizens, religious or not, should enjoy the same fundamental rights for all: social, cultural, political and national. Among these rights are:

   a- the human right of freedom of worship and of conscience, both as individuals and as religious communities,

   b- civil and historical rights which allow them to carry out their religious, educational, medical and other duties of charity

   c- the right to have their own institutions, such as hospices for pilgrims, institutes for the study of the Bible and the Traditions, centres for encounters with believers of other religions, monasteries, churches, cemeteries, and so forth, and the right to have their own personnel man and run these institutions.

13. In claiming these rights for themselves, Christians recognize and respect similar and parallel rights of Jewish and Muslim believers and their communities. Christians declare themselves disposed to search with Jews and Muslims for a mutually respectful application of these rights and for a harmonious coexistence, in the perspective of the universal spiritual vocation of Jerusalem.

Special stature for Jerusalem

14. All this presupposes a special judicial and political stature for Jerusalem which reflects the universal importance and significance of the city.

(1) In order to satisfy the national aspirations of all its inhabitants, and in order that Jews, Christians and Muslims can be 'at home' in Jerusalem and at peace with one another; representatives from the three monotheistic religions, in addition to local political powers, ought to be associated in the elaboration and application of such a special statute.

(2) Because of the universal significance of Jerusalem, the international community ought to be engaged in the stability and permanence of this statute. Jerusalem is too precious to be dependent solely on municipal or national political authorities, whoever they may be. Experience shows that an international guarantee is necessary.

Experience shows that such local authorities, for political reasons or the claims of security, are sometimes required to violate the rights of free access to the Holy Places. Therefore it is necessary to accord Jerusalem a special status which will allow Jerusalem not to be victimized by laws imposed as a result of hostilities or wars but to be an open city which transcends local, regional or world political troubles. This statute, established in common by local political and religious authorities, should also be guaranteed by the international community.

Conclusion

Jerusalem is a symbol and a promise of the presence of God, of fraternity and peace for humankind, in particular for the children of Abraham: Jews, Christians and Muslims. We call upon all parties concerned to comprehend and accept the nature and deep significance of Jerusalem, the City of God. None can appropriate it in exclusivist ways. We invite each party to go beyond all exclusivist visions or actions, and without discrimination, to consider the religious and national aspirations of others, in order to give back to Jerusalem its true universal character and to make of the city a holy place of reconciliation for humankind.

Signed by Greek Orthodox Patriarch, Latin Patriarch, Armenian Patriarch, Custos of the Holy Land, Coptic Archbishop, Syriac Archbishop, Ethiopian Archbishop, Anglican Bishop, Greek-Catholic Patriarch Vicar, Lutheran Bishop, Maronite Patriarchal Vicar, Catholic Syriac Patriarh Vicar,

Jerusalem, 14 November 1994

Chapter 10

The Plural Significance of Jerusalem as Seen *Ex Infra*: Kenneth Cragg on the Interrelated Jerusalem

Bård Maeland

Introduction

Should any solution to the Jerusalem issue be religiously determined? And, what is actually the most important with regards to Jerusalem: to do the right things, or to think the right thoughts? In this chapter I will explore and discuss how 'Jerusalem' is conceived by a prominent Christian theologian who has spent large parts of his career in the Middle East, and who has dealt extensively with issues related to religious traditions other than Christian situated in this region: Bishop Kenneth Cragg.

It should be noted that Kenneth Cragg's encounter with Jerusalem is very much determined by his approximation of it from various points of departure, and on diverse levels. These are mainly theological and biographical in nature, including political concerns. Together, all these, I will suggest, contribute to his own understanding of Jerusalem, which I will describe as an approach from below – *ex infra*. This approach 'from below' can be particularly seen from his criticism of what he regards as 'high', 'privileged', 'dominating', 'power-ensuring', 'exclusifying', etc. Such criticism, I will contend, is developed and raised from his normative point of departure which takes place, in some sense, 'below' that which he criticizes. Needless to say, in this Cragg is certainly not 'approximating' Jerusalem *per se* but its *meaning*. It is this meaning I will research based on its entailed wider religious context. This includes primarily his relation to the Islamic and Jewish traditions. It is my objective to show how the *interrelation*

From Beirut to Jerusalem – via Gaza

I have already mentioned already Cragg's biographical approximation to Jerusalem. In his case, it is not a minor issue how he eventually ended up, professionally, in Jerusalem. In short, between his childhood in Blackpool in England and his consecration as bishop in Jerusalem in 1970, comes his time as missionary in Lebanon for the British Syria Mission.[1] This time (1939–1947) included service at Lebanon Bible Institute as well as being chaplain to All Saints' Church, Beirut, for the Bishop of Jerusalem.

Cragg's very first visit to Jerusalem took place in this period, in July 1939. This was the time and place for visiting a summer school in Arabic. In retrospect he describes this coming to Jerusalem by taxi from Haifa, after passage of the Ras al-Naqurah (Hebrew: Rosh Haniqra) border out of Lebanon, as one of two traditional ways of approaching Jerusalem.[2] The other was from the Jordan valley, via Bethany, 'cresting the eastward slopes of the Mount of Olives'. At the very start of his stay in the Middle East, one year before the outbreak of the Second World War (his fiancée, Melita, just reached the last ship to cross the Mediterranean before the outbreak of the war[3]), these two ways to Jerusalem came to symbolize major parts of his further career. The one coming from the Palestinian landscape, the other from the threshold of the Arabian peninsula.

Let me just mention some events that illustrate this point. During his period in Lebanon, where he was stationed from 1939–47, he also shared the fate of Palestinian people while he stayed in Gaza in 1941 because of an evacuation of civilians from Lebanon. The period in Beirut also included being warden for Palestinian students at St Justin's House (1942–47), which had to close in 1948 because of the Arab-Israeli war.[4] This experience indeed informed the way in which he thought of Jerusalem.

This became very urgent in what he calls the 'Anglican unease in Zion'.[5] Cragg describes the sociology of the Anglican community in Jerusalem in 1939 as consisting of 'three centres':

> The original Christ Church [in the Old City], with its Hebrew adorned sanctuary and its implicit Zionist sympathies, St George's Cathedral

where mandatory power was at home and Liturgies were always held in English, and St Paul's where the Palestinians gathered.[6]

How should he cope with these competing loyalties and diverse cultural and political affiliations? It seems that Cragg's way to Jerusalem, and to Judaism, is markedly informed by his way to it through the fate of the Lebanese and Palestinian peoples. This may explain some of his sympathetic preferences for Palestinians and Arabs, whether Christian or Muslim, not only over people representing Judaic 'exclusiveness' and Israeli power dominance, which can be discerned across his writings, but also over the ambiguous story of the British Mandate.[7] This joint geographical and biographical way to Jerusalem certainly also shaped his political view of the Jerusalem issue. One should however note that the political issue is subordinated by what he sees as the meaning and idea of Jerusalem.[8] One consequence of this in Cragg's writings is that the question 'What is to be thought of Jerusalem?' is always made prior to the question about 'What is to be done?'[9]

It is my aim to show how the former question has been directly and indirectly answered by Cragg in relation to the two other competing religious traditions situated in this area: Islam and Judaism. I will start with the 'nephew' (Islam) of Christianity, which constitutes the overwhelming majority of Cragg's writings, before I consider Cragg's relation to the 'progenitor' (Judaism). In this, we will see that the relation between father and son is somewhat more complicated than between the cousins. Since the former relation has been less thematized in studies on Cragg, I have also chosen to spend some more time on this.

From Mecca and Medina to Gethsemane and al-Aqsa

From the beginning of his writings, Cragg's theological encounter with Islam circles the issue of how Muhammad and Christ relate to what he calls the theme of 'Antagonism and Suffering in the Economy of Truth and Righteousness'.[10] This theme serves the role of a *tertium comparationis* between Islam and Christianity, which, Cragg contends, makes 'a particular and illuminating form of comparison'. Certainly, compared with this yardstick, the results must turn out as very different. Yet, on the other hand, Cragg asserts that 'in the most insistent of antagonisms there is what binds the parties'.[11] Already here, one may discern a strong impetus towards developing relations to other religions.

Hermeneutically speaking, this approach which accentuates differences as important for 'binding the parties', may have a parallel in Schleiermacher's hermeneutics of 'mis-understanding' (German: *Mißverständnis*). It is Schleiermacher's contention that attempting to know the Other, we should always reckon with non-understanding as more basic than understanding, which again enables one to reorient oneself in a new direction towards the unknown, or 'misknown' Other.[12]

This realism about antagonism does not however stop Cragg searching for common areas between Christians and Muslims, also where these attempts by further scrutiny end up as 'contrasted idioms'. In what follows I will aim to figure out Cragg's search for these common areas which are, mainly: the creation of God as 'sacramental', the nature of human wronging and forgiveness, the understanding of God's relationality and revelation, and, lastly, prophethood as an activity on behalf of God. In his elaboration of these areas, central Islamic and Christian matters are simultaneously addressed. Another way of putting this, is to say that his theological energy revolves round an intention to reformulate the Islamic and Quranic notion of God's sovereignty (*takbir*). On the way towards this, he aims to base his attempts on 'Qur'anic reasons', yet always pursued in direction of a Christian understanding of the incarnation, suffering, death and resurrection of Jesus Christ. Let us have a closer look into these areas.

Cragg uses creation as a common area of Muslim-Christian relation, both the way God expresses Himself to humans and how He is experienced.[13] Creation, which includes everything from human beings and activity to prophethood, represents, according to Cragg, a 'capacity for revelation'. The meaning of this concept is that God is, on the one hand, able to express Himself and His intention for the world by using mundane vehicles within a broad range, and, on the other: humans may experience God in nature as well as in the life of other persons. Hence creation is regarded as 'sacramental'. However, this 'capacity' is fundamentally distorted by human wrongdoing, not least if religiously motivated. By addressing how this involves God, Cragg reveals a contrasted understanding of forgiveness in Islam and Christianity. Whereas forgiveness is conceived as effortless in Islam, Christianity requires that evil is borne personally in order to bear it away. Relation and revelation thus have to be related to redemption. Thus, these contrasted approaches to a common theme (creation) uncover different interpretations of God's 'expressionality' (forgiveness and redemption).

The understanding of God's relationality is particularly

addressed by the notions of 'association' and 'dissociation', in particular related to the Quranic and Islamic concepts of *shirk* and *tanzil*.[14] Cragg maintains firstly that the Quranic doctrine of the dissociation of God from the human realm (anti-*shirk*), originally from pseudo-deities after the pagan fashion of the Qureish, is inconsistent with his relation (association, *shirk*) to humans as seen in creation, and as also witnessed by the Quran. If one opts for a God outside relations, one runs the danger of deism and even atheism, neither of which Cragg perceives Islam to adopt.

Secondly, this also has bearing for his reinterpretation of the sending of the Quran (*tanzil*) and revelation (*wahy*). Whereas the traditional Islamic view is that Muhammad functioned mechanically as a mouthpiece for the reception of the Quran, Cragg maintains that it is impossible to hold this together with the view of a relational God who is dependent upon and involves the personality of his messengers. Nevertheless, Cragg opts for a Christian acknowledgement of Muhammad as a prophet of God, bringing an important contribution to the doctrine of the unity of God.

The themes of evil, and its necessary consequence of suffering, however, become crucial when Cragg engages in the encounter of Islamic and Hebrew-Christian prophethood. How is God to be interpreted when His messengers experience rejection, ignorance and suffering? and what is the proper divine agency in such a situation? At this point Cragg establishes a preliminary common ground for seeing Muhammad in Mecca and Jesus in Gethsemane as experiencing personal, prophetic suffering caused by their messages. Cragg sees this as suffering on behalf of God. Yet, the continuation of their lives by either the way of *Hijra* (power ensuring, rescue) or Gethsemane (long-suffering as bearing away the evil by which the suffering was caused) reveals two different ways to understand the messengers, and consequently God.[15] Whereas Islamic prophethood is self-sufficient, Hebrew prophethood, especially as with Jeremiah who suffers 'biographically', requires something 'beyond' themselves. This 'beyond' Cragg sees in the filiality of God the Son who vicariously, on behalf of God and the people, bears away evil. Cragg sees the latter as exceeding the Islamic understanding of God as sovereign, because God's sovereignty appears as love and thus shows itself able to cope with evil in a more convincing way. These two differing patterns are however seen in a more complementary perspective in his last works.

Yet, how do these 'contrasted idioms' relate to the meaning of

Jerusalem? The answer most be compounded.

First, Cragg's interpretation of prophecy takes Islam to the threshold of Jerusalem, to Gethsemane. In short: Redemption happens neither in Mecca, Medina nor at the Temple, but in Gethsemane and on Golgotha. Hence there are religious reasons for coming to (East-!)Jerusalem. Cragg calls the Christ-way of suffering: 'the pattern of the Cross', yet starting with the suffering on behalf of humankind and God of the prophets, also tasted by Muhammad in Mecca in his experience of agony and adversity there.

Second, his Christian-Muslim view of Jerusalem is also determined by his inter-theological discussion of 'association' vs. 'dissociation' in Islam and Christianity. In his Christian language this discussion relates intimately to a view of God who comes down to humankind in the incarnation of his Son, and gets even lower on Jesus' way from Galilee to Gethsemane and the Cross. Let me include one verse from his collection of Christmas poetry which shows how God is to be sought as 'profundus' and not as 'excelsus':

> Lower still the road leads down
> From the inn that had no room
> To a cross and thorn-wreathed crown
> And the cold and awful tomb.
> Gloria in profundis Deo.[16]

From this perspective – from below – it is also possible to ask about the meaning the Mosques at the Temple Mount convey. Is it just arbitrarily chosen to erect the edifices at the vicinity of the Holy of Holies? Or does it reveal a meaning which is common to Christians and Muslims?

In an article on, mainly, the Islamic concept of Jerusalem, the 'incarnational' theme of 'divine associationism' is employed in order to discuss the meaning of the Old City Mosques.[17] Against the traditional meaning of *shirk* Cragg asks whether Muslims can affirm a notion of 'necessary 'messengers'". This issue, which I have presented above in relation to the different views of prophecy in Islam and Christianity (and Judaism), leads Cragg to connect the role of the necessary 'messengers' of, and behalf of God, to 'hallowed' places:

> It is only through Allah's 'near ones', *awliya,* that locales invite reverence and are magnets to faith'. Whether Abraham, Jesus or Muhammad, cities – Makkah, Madina, Jerusalem – have their mysterious aura only because they have their 'messengers', and these in turn

have their standing only as having been 'sent' by and from God.

Hence, there is a justified 'association', which, in fact, facilitates any knowledge of the guilt of *shirk*, that is: without 'earth-seeking', 'human-meant', 'truth-sending', the will of God to only worship Him would have been unknown to us.[18] Thus, the 'sacralising' of al-Aqsa is connected to the association of God with Muhammad, and, most significantly: Muhammad's belief that preceding prophethoods had been associated with Jerusalem.[19]

What are the consequences to be drawn from this? Firstly, that 'how we take things will hinge on how we hold faiths'. Related to the Jerusalem issue, this means that any solution to the Jerusalem issue will be religiously determined since it is not some acre of land we are talking about, but the meaning of these acres. And given the Islamic position, where Muhammad's belief includes other prophethoods, the Islamic faith would imply that Jerusalem should be a place, not only for exclusive unilateral ambitions, but for plural meanings of it.[20] Yet, this plural perspective is indirectly taken from the 'below' perspective of a legitimate 'divine associationism'. More on this belongs to a later subchapter on Palestinian Christians. Now: What about the 'progenitor'?

From exclusified holiness to a shared conviction of divine earnestness

Cragg's 'negotiation' with Judaism and Jewry, which he entitles a 'search for a Christian Judaica', came to be important already from his very first encounter with Jerusalem in 1939.[21] Parallel to one of the core issues he concentrated on in the Christian-Muslim relation: how God relates to humans (cf. the aforementioned problem of 'association'; *shirk*), the core issue in the Christian-Jewish relation came to be the meaning of at the same time 'believing in God' and 'believing in ourselves'.[22] This issue implies therefore concepts such as 'people', 'chosen', but also 'the divine nature'.

It is clear from his use of 'Christian Judaica' that Cragg neither wants to opt out of the very conflict between Christianity and Judaism, nor any possible relations whatsoever. In his characteristic aesthetic language he therefore says that:

> We end discord if we unstring the instrument but we also forfeit all that music, and musing, should explore.[23]

Two immediate consequences of this approach are that he avoids two-covenant theories from the Christian side (Christianity as only meant for 'Gentiles') and a non-Semitic explanation of Christianity from the Jewish side, seeing Christianity as entirely a Graeco-Roman, Hellenistic product.[24] On the contrary, Cragg sees the conflict between these two religious traditions as essential, which for the Jewish side has implied the following:

> [Judaism] called into question the whole *raison d'être* of the Church compelled, as it saw it, by the *raison d'être* it has always cherished and could not betray, namely its abiding privacy with God in unchanging covenant.[25]

On the other hand, he affirms the following statement of Ignatius of Antioch in order 'to let the issue stand, with no evasion and without palliative':

> To profess Jesus Christ while continuing to follow Jewish customs is an absurdity. The Christian faith does not look to Judaism, but Judaism looks to Christianity, in which every other race and tongue that confess a belief in God has now been comprehended'.[26]

This does certainly not imply that the Christian 'vision' is disconnected from its Jewish origin:

> We need to realize how it was Jewish vision and venture which conceived the open Church. ... The Gospel could never have been the thing it was without Jewish minds, Jewish labours and Jewish love to God and men. Paul may have had the idiosyncrasies of genius but he was a 'Hebrew of the Hebrews' in his inclusion of the 'Gentiles' in Christ.[27]

Closely related to these quotations is also his view of the anti-Semitism issue. From the Christian perspective, Cragg sees the birth of Christianity, as a proposal

> [An] opening out of a covenanted people-hood to all and sundry, on the sole condition of penitence and faith, without prior distinction of birth, or place, or culture ... Jewish made and 'Gentile'.

thus giving promise of an end to the trauma of 'essential differentia before God'.[28] However, that which might have brought an ultimate end to anti-Semitism came simultaneously to be seen as a source of it. Cragg mentions here the Christian notions of 'fulfilment', 'preparation', 'completion' and 'supersession', as clues to the way in which Christianity 'took over' Judaism and Judaic. It does not seem that Cragg estimates these concepts as contrary to Christianity's 'own birthright', seeing them as describing a story with a proper, universal climax. In this respect, Cragg resonates with the statement of Ignatius.

Seen together with his entire interreligious approach, this does not surprise since Jesus Christ is conceived as the ultimate answer to questions raised, and impasses perceived, in all religious traditions. Hence, he does not affirm the kind of radical pluralist[29] solution to the Christian-Jewish controversy which for example Jacob Neusner has phrased about the controversy of the first century, as 'different people talking about different things to different people'.[30]

With regards to 'anti-Semitism', there is no doubt that Cragg sees the dark role Christians have played in the anguish of the Jews. The guilt should be confessed, he says, and the confession should be deep and unequivocal.[31] However, Cragg also sees another kind of anti-Semitism, namely that of excluding Jews from the reach of the Gospel.[32] As Cragg sees it, the Gospel cannot be gospel if someone was to be excluded from the beginning. On the contrary, it presents an 'opening out to all and sundry', aiming at relations and meeting of minds.[33]

It is exactly here that the conflict between Christianity and Judaism is perceived as essential. Whereas the Church is described as 'the open Church', and Christianity as an 'ever-open-ness', Judaism is characterized by 'exceptionality', 'chosen-ness' and 'closed-ness'.[34] If these are the alternatives, no wonder that the latter one may plead to be left in peace, seeing itself as not convertible and receiving the Christian invitation to the 'open Church' as an embarrassing hospitality.[35] To develop relations, however, Cragg suggests that past disagreements and hostilities should be left, and the energies should be dedicated to what he sees as the current challenge, namely

> A positive Christian relation to the covenant which was 'already there', before 'God was in Christ,' and abides beyond and despite that disclosure which is, for Christians, the covenanting fullness of altogether open grace.[36]

This does not imply to forgetting past events like Holocaust, but to present attempts at a 'better reconciliation' based on a 'perceptive Christianity'.[37] One of the issues he ponders in this respect is the 'mystery of election'. Cragg asserts that

> What the Christian sees as the validity of the Jewish past, as historical preparation for Christ, need not be thought to be forfeited because Jewry withheld recognition of such fulfilment ... On the contrary, the sense of Christian roots in Hebraica ought to relate Christians expectantly to fruits of those same roots in the ongoing spirituality they have sustained since the Christian vintage was drawn off.[38]

Whence he proceeds by asking rhetorically: 'Does not the mystery of election stand – like all religious meaning – in the conviction that it is so?' This is not to be reckoned as a purely relativist offer. On the contrary, it is to be interpreted as an attempt to acknowledge what has been 'inwardly possessed' while still searching 'for the outward relationships of truths inwardly possessed'.

It seems that Cragg aims to ride on two horses: There is 'something there' in Judaism, as it was before the time of Christ. But, on the other hand, there is 'something more' after God's intervention in history through the Christ-event. At a first glance one might think of this double understanding as causing the two to become either isolated form each other, or that the former becomes entirely subordinated a Christian perspective. An answer to this must engage with Cragg's wider framework for understanding 'covenant', 'election' and 'convergence'.

A clue to an answer can be found in the following conclusion of the present task of the developing relationship between Christians and Jews, which he sees as epitomized in the relation between the Torah and Christ:

> That the two [i.e. Christ and Torah] differ sharply need be no impediment to their continuing mutuality so long as the Christ-bearers do not exclude Jews from His reach or the Torah-bearers Christians from their forgiveness or from the mind of their Judaism now. In that way each may be worthy of a convergence of their worlds.[39]

This rather irenic 'worthy of convergence' at the end of Cragg's 'Christian Judaica' in his theological autobiography, *Faith and Life Negotiate*, does not mean that the subjects of controversy between Christian and Judaic faith have been resolved, but that tensions are coped with, 'where we most differ we have still to belong', which indeed comes close to his 'contrasted idioms'-approach in his search for relations to Islam and Muslims.[40]

This fact becomes obvious in Cragg's considerations about the meaning of 'covenant', which he links to the meaning of 'redemption'. Redemption, again, he sees as an answer to what he sees as 'a single quest of a common human meaning that covenants shall not exclusify nor plot deface'.[41] In this he wishes to level Christianity and Judaism in order to view their 'answers' as contributions to a shared human quest.

This theme, which is a basic element in all of Cragg's writings,[42] searches out human commonalities in Judaism, Islam and Christianity. These are in particular to be found in relation to his view of humankind under God as entrusted with a stewardship (*Khalifah*) over nature:

> Since this is a common human privilege, there are no privacies and no monopolies, no exclusive holiness, no 'peculiar peoples', only distinctive races, climates, living spaces and environments and a rich diversity of cultures – all under God in an equal benediction and at a comparable risk to their 'ever generous Lord'.

Cragg sees this theme of creation as a common Jewish-Islamic-Christian heritage from the *Noahid* bond of Genesis.[43] His language is strong, indeed, albeit somewhat indirect with respect to delicate political counterparts. Yet, the practical consequences to be drawn from this statement are quite obvious, which I will return to at the end of this chapter.

His anthropology does not, however, end by this positive statement about humans as God's trustees, which would certainly not be in need of any redemption. Cragg's concept of redemption is closely related to his view of evil. More precisely, Cragg's notion of redemption relates intimately to his understanding of the reach of evil. As we noted in the section on Christian-Islamic relations, redemptive love is seen as the 'more than' what can be done through just(ified) use of law and power. This view depends on a perception:

> The real vulnerability inseparable from human society, the inhumanity of these to those, and the vocation through suffering to reconcile, to reinstate relationship on the other side of wrong and, so doing, to let 'grace more abound'.[44]

Yet, how does this view relate to the inescapable, in this context, ultimate reach of evil: Holocaust? To speak about 'evil that is borne away by bearing it biographically', which is one of Cragg's formulas for the redemptive love of Christ, should be tested against the background of *Shoah*. How does Cragg meet this challenge?

Cragg calls Holocaust 'a concentration of evil'.[45] The question, however, is whether this Hell on earth should be read as reaching 'back and down into the inclusive tragedy of mankind',[46] or be seen as 'the unspeakable proof of exceptionality' which for ever ends all theodicy of the God who chose the Jews as His people? Although Cragg is careful while writing about these things, he sees a possibility of healing, through 'human solidarity and the freeing of the shut-in spirit [of the Jews, by Holocaust, cf. Elie Wiesel]'.[47]

With Elie Wiesel, he contends that we must belong humanly with others, a human whole, if we are to accuse 'inhumanity'. Thus to accuse is to confirm a belief in man as responsible: There is an 'ought' in being human, which, firstly, warrants the 'problem' of evil, and which, secondly, in evil and in good, does not exonerate guilt. If perceived thus, Cragg maintains that 'unless we are to fall back upon a despairing atheism which will also silence our indictment of the cosmos', there has to be a will to redemption.[48] In this, Cragg sees the Hebrew prophet of affliction (Isa 63:9) as representing a truth which Christianity ripens in the suffering of Christ, reconciling the entire world and maintaining both moral criteria as paramount and the equal accessability to grace and hope. On exactly this background, the nature and range of evil and redemption, other alternative Messiahships have to be excluded.[49]

The 'ever generous God' was mentioned in one of the Cragg-citations above. Holding this view together with the ultimate reach of evil and redemption, Cragg has found a mate in the late Rabbi Abraham Heschel, New York. Heschel was saved from Warsaw after the Germans arrived there, but lost his whole family. Yet, 'Holocaust' is scarcely used in his writings. Instead, he talked about 'retaining our share in God',[50] which implied a travail of hope, knowing that ourselves as creatures was 'God's stake in history' and that God's task was to vindicate him. Via the prophets, Heschel found this to be the central clue of divine pathos, that is: God conceived as 'the most moved mover'. In this Jewish view, albeit not approved by many Jewish scholars, Cragg sees 'the same soul as the theology which fashioned the New Testament Church'.[51] And this soul, Cragg maintains, which is a possible outcome of the project of a 'Christian Judaica', may represent a single conviction among the competing religious traditions of the Middle East, albeit the same 'sense of God' does not share the 'eventuation'.[52]

Yet, to conceive the differences between the traditions as held together in the thought of 'the God of patience' may enable Christians to see election as a continued 'divine travail' with His people, while at the same time seeing the cross as the realization of this divine patience. Not in the meaning of a revised two-covenant theory, but as 'an approximation of what Christians believe and what Jews in that context wish to hold in reservation'.[53] This is precisely the opposite of what the two-covenant theory aims at,[54] and he sees in this a 'better reconciliation' between Christians and Jews.

One may conclude this extensive section by the claim that if it is thus possible to reach a religious reconciliation between Jews and Christians, a political solution must also be drawing nearer than if controversy is perpetuated.

One might moreover ask what this elaboration of Cragg's Christian-Judaic relation has to do with Jerusalem. In short, the somewhat extensive elaboration has been done in order to reconstruct a framework for his particular expressions about Jerusalem. This is the more required since, when it comes to Jerusalem proper, Cragg moves onto another level of language which implies a whole lot of theology. The following citation may illustrate this:

> The Temple Mount becomes the ultimate irony. [Cragg mentions the Muslim and Jewish significance of the site]. Legitimacies quarrel here, deplore their forfeiture and supersession, or celebrate their warrant and their prestige. The surcharged holiness, electrified by passion and history, examines and explores the sanity of religions and constitutes surely the most telling plea for a mutuality riding out the passions of envious diversity. Where Zionism is most adamant its own quest is most at risk.[55]

In short this conclusion takes the difference between Zion (exclusiveness) and Gethsemane (suffering) as its presupposed theological point of departure. Whereas Judaism is conceived in its 'inflexible pride of a Jewish otherness', reassuring a political exclusivism, Cragg sees in the whole mission of Jesus a will for relation through redemption. The current challenge that leads from this authentic event is 'compatibility' and 'compassion', deriving from the same Latin root, in particular if it is 'willed'.[56] Between these two, there seems to be a certain dependency, namely that compatibility, or living together despite past conflict, needs compassion. If phrased thus, the source of origin for this demand is certainly situated in Gethsemane, yet not exclusively so. There is also a 'divine association' to be conceived through Judaism in this respect, as also through Islam, as I have already shown.

As seen in the case of Rabbi Heschel, Cragg's criticism of Judaism, or better: Zionism, is not unequivocal. Like in Islam, he discovers clues to a Christian interpretation of the common human quests and situation. A telling example of this is his 'meditation' on the way Marc Chagall combines the theme of crucifixion with Jewish terror and tragedy in history, and with Jesus wearing a prayer shawl (i.e. *The White Crucifixion,* 1938):

> Is the painter suggesting that the sorrows of Israel somehow meet in the travail of Jesus?[57]

This kind of relation is what Cragg hopes for in his cross-reference studies[58] where the 'tent of meeting outside the camp' (Exodus 33:7–11) may substitute 'fixity', 'prejudice' and 'entrenchments', all of these phenomenologically illustrated with the Tabernacle as a thing 'merely communal and partisan'.[59] And in this, the perspective is decisively taken from 'below', from Gethsemane and the locale of divine association at risk itself.

Inferiority and kenosis

As I have shown, the crux in Cragg's interreligious approaches to Islam and Judaism is located in 'love who suffers', which is risked in all its divine vulnerability as caused by 'real evil'. This 'vulnerable position' is what I have denoted 'low', because it is seen as an argument 'from below' (*ex infra*). In what follows I want to determine more precisely what kind of approach this really is.

In a theoretical study, Andreas Grünschloß has tried to enlarge and revise the traditional tripartite way of thinking of interreligious relations: exclusivism, inclusivism and pluralism, in order to place 'inferiority' (cf. *infra*) somewhere along the previous available options.[60] Yet, in Grünschloß' revision of this scheme these options are renamed as: 'distance', 'hierarchy', and 'parity', with further qualifications and sub-forms of each. One of the sub-forms he develops within 'hierarchy' is that, logically speaking, one might discern between those who see themselves as superior (superiority) to others and those who see others as superior to themselves (inferiority).

I will now develop this framework by making more precise how 'below' or 'low' is used in Cragg. In order to simplify I will maintain that the concept of inferiority may imply two different things: 1) That the ones 'higher' than you are 'better' or more valuable in some sense, or 2) that to act adequately in a specific experience or situation must imply to place oneself 'below' or 'low' in some way. Since the first option is excluded by Cragg's criticism of Islam and Judaism, my suggestion will be that it is this latter sense that forms Cragg's writings along his 'kenotic' Christology. Only by 'love who suffers' is love able to overcome human wrongdoing and waywardness, and thus change humans from within.

This relates also to the meaning of 'kenotic' as employed by Cragg. In a telling passage which he makes in a retrospect manner, he defines how he has been using *kenosis* in his writings. His notion of *kenosis* is not that of

> 'emptying' (e.g.) a vessel of its contents, so that nothing remains. It is a divesting of what might normally be assumed to belong to a status so that standing, or dignity, or privilege, might seem to be no longer possessed but are *in fact more superbly fulfilled.* [61]

Cragg, most interestingly, refers to the King in Shakespeare's *Henry V*, where the King leaves aside his crown and take on a borrowed robe and goes among his soldiers. On the rhetoric question whether the King is still 'royal' and 'kingly' or less so, Cragg answers: 'more so!' Further, and connected to a story in Isaac Walton's *Life of George Herbert* (1827), where a usually well-groomed poet arrives to a music session all muddied and bedraggled, having helped the peasant whose animal had fallen down in the road, Cragg states generally that:

> There are some dignities that exist only to be laid aside e.g. that of shepherd or friend. They cannot be what they are and be self-preserving, self-immunizing. The Christian faith is that it is this way with God, with 'God-in-Christ' – and Jesus is the proof. The divine is not self-economizing, but self-expending. This is kenosis.[62]

Hence, *ex infra*, 'from below', does not mean that God's mission in Jesus failed (inferior), but that it was executed differently, and in fact in the best way (superior). This is certainly an important lesson to be learned by all parties tied to the Middle East conflict: Power is limited in range, and vulnerability is the only way of overcoming real evil. If not realized in security politics, it does however unfold a critical perspective on all use of power for dominion.

The kenotic community of reconciliation and forgiveness

It is of no surprise that the embodiment of Cragg's Christian interreligious hermeneutics is located to the Palestinian Christians. This means, that as far as his interreligious hermeneutics is regarded as a hermeneutic of conflict-resolution, the Palestinian Christian community should also be regarded as a mediator of peace and reconciliation. If so, this would eventually require that the history and experience of this community both reveals a history of suffering as well as another way of reacting to it than the ones Cragg has described by the Islamic *Hijra* and the Zionist case.

The first requirement has certainly been true since the British Mandate, which is also the way Cragg himself experienced it in 1941 when forced to share the fate of the Palestinians at the Gaza strip. He may therefore say, that

> Palestinian Christianity is uniquely experienced to meet the demands of its present vocation. For it belongs with the whole *mise-en-scène* of Christian faith as its native possession.[63]

This 'native possession' does however not merely say that Palestinian Christians are familiar with all kinds of biblical sites, but that they are also familiar with the conditions in which the suffering and humiliation of Jesus took place. In this meaning, Palestinian Christianity has 'the capacity to read tragedy',[64] as well as merging its own history with the decisive history to which it is built upon, thereby fulfilling the duty of humankind:

> It is thus that, for Christians, the bringing of forgivingness and forgiveness to all human situations is, by the seal of divine mandate and example, the whole duty of man.[65]

One might lastly ask whether this duty as exemplified by Christians does have any need for the physical Jerusalem. Does 'bringing of forgiveness to all situations' require access to its birthplace? In this respect Cragg seems on the one hand to maintain that 'the only Christian 'birthright' anywhere is that of faith'.[66] On the other hand he seems, presumably driven by his incarnational and aesthetic theological mind, to require access to the land of Palestine caused by the need for proximity of the Christian mind to its generative events, parallel to what I described as to his view of Muslim perception of 'hallowed' places:

> The Christian distinctiveness of Palestine can best be described as sacramental ... Event as history is crucial to Christian faith. It follows that the locale of the event-history has a sacramental quality, enabling musing of the mind on that piece of earth, or pilgrim feet traversing it, to possess thereby the meanings it once enshrined. Imagination is thus quickened to participate. Meanings 'come home' where their home was. Such is the way of sacraments, and sacred geography can be one of them, the physical bespeaking the spiritual at the rendezvous with history.[67]

Hence, Cragg does not provide us with an entirely spiritualist, 'eternalizing', or 'de-politicized' solution, but a rather realist claim, what he calls: 'the way of sacraments' or 'the sacrament of geography'.[68] This means that a Christian reconciliatory witness also needs a home for its agency and identity, a 'means of grace'. In short: 'While the heart seeks them out where sight can know them, it knows them well within already'.[69]

The Jerusalem issue – religiously concluded

We started by mentioning how Cragg prioritized 'What can be thought about Jerusalem?' over 'What is to be done?' The article in which this pair of questions is presented does however not avoid concluding as to the future of the Holy City. Cragg's conclusion, which is stressed to be a religiously based claim, is that

> Jerusalem – by irreducible historical factors – has to have a plural, that is a triple, 'ownership' of love and may not properly be unilaterally annexed ... How this cardinal principle of its being is to be registered politically is the still open question, but it is incontestable religiously.[70]

I hope to have shown how these various 'significances' of Jerusalem are bound to religious traditions, and by pondering the traditions and their interrelatedness, I hope to have shown how it *is* possible to develop fruitful relations between the three 'owners', albeit through contrasts and antagonisms. If such relations are achieved, other issues of conflict may draw closer to resolutions than if religious controversies are perpetuated.

Notes

1 For further (auto-)biographical information, see his *Faith and Life Negotiate: A Christian Story-Study*, Norwich, The Canterbury Press, 1994. This 'Christian story-study' does not only present the life of Cragg but merges 'faith' and 'life' from the perspective of 'negotiation'. From this perspective, the book is an intriguing example of how a Western educated Christian faith is 'sifted' in the Middle Eastern 'soil'. This impact comprises, in particular, influences from all kind of religious parties. An important expression of this impact took place during his D.Phil-studies in Oxford 1947–50 (diss.: *Islam in the Twentieth Century: The Relevance of Christian Theology and the Relation of the Christian Mission to its Problems*, Oxford University, 1950) when he stayed at the Longworth Rectory, Berkshire, where the influential *Lux Mundi* movement had flourished six decades earlier.
2 *Faith and Life Negotiate*, p. 155.
3 Ibid., p. 79.

4 After this Cragg returned to Oxford, as Rector at Longworth, the previous site of the *Lux Mundi* movement of the latter third of the nineteenth century, so important for the development of the Church of England. Here, Cragg carried on with a D.Phil. thesis on the relevance of Christian mission to the problems Islam experienced in the first part of the twentieth century. The topic of the thesis was certainly not arbitrarily chosen. Through this study he achieved to ponder his experiences of 'The Sifting East' (ch. 4, *Faith and Life Negotiate*), where his life and faith were 'negotiated', especially related to Christian-Muslim issues.

5 *Faith and Life Negotiate*, ch. 6, pp. 154ff.

6 Ibid., p. 157f.

7 Ibid., pp. 154 and 162.

8 Issues concerning Jerusalem have been primarily addressed in *This Year in Jerusalem: Israel in Experience*, London, Darton, Longman & Todd, 1982; *The Arab Christian: A History in the Middle East*, Westminster and Louisville, KY, John Knox Press, 1991; *Faith and Life Negotiate*, 1994, and *Palestine: The Prize and Price of Zion*, London and Herndon, VA, Cassell, 1997. See also *Troubled by Truth: Life-Studies in Inter-Faith Concern*, Edinburgh/Cambridge/Durham, 1992, where chapters are devoted to Rabbi Abraham Heschel (ch. 6) and Elie Wiesel (ch. 4), which reveal his encounter with several Jewish-Christian issues.

9 Cf. Cragg, 'The Excellences of Jerusalem,' (delivered as a keynote speech 22 August 1998 at the International Academic Conference on Islamic Jerusalem, Islamic Research Academy of the School of Oriental and African Studies), *Journal of Islamic Jerusalem Studies*, 2 (1998), no.1 (winter), 1.

10 See his D.Phil. diss., *Islam in the Twentieth Century: The Relevance of Christian Theology and the Relation of the Christian Mission to Its Problems*, Oxford University 1950, Part II, p. 270. How this theme is resonated, and in practice reiterated across his studies, can be seen from his late *Palestine: The Prize and Price of Zion* (1997), where the testing of the Christian and Islamic faith relates to the issues of 'justice', 'tragedy', 'vicarious experience' and 'the way through suffering to reconciliation', pp. 206, 219.

11 *Palestine: The Prize and Price of Zion*, p. 204.

12 Andreas Grünschloß, *Der eigene und der fremde Glaube. Studien zum interreligiösen Fremd-wahrnehmung in Islam, Hinduismus, Buddhismus und Christentum*, HUTh 37, (eds) H.D. Betz et al. (eds), Tübingen: Mohr Siebeck, 1999, pp. 295–99: 'Der 'Mißverständnis' als hermeneutische Grundsituation'. Grünschloß refers to Schleiermacher's Hermeneutik in two different works: *Hermeneutik und Kritik. Mit einem Anhang sprachphilosophischer Texte Schleiermachers*, introduced by V. M. Frank (ed.), Frankfurt, 1977, and *Hermeneutik*, V. H. Kimmerle (ed.), Heidelberg, ^{2}1974.

13 See for example *Christ and the Faiths*, ch. 3 ('Capacities of Revelation').

14 See for example 'The Qur'an and the Christian Reader.I', *Muslim World* 46 (1956), pp. 61–8, *passim*.

15 This strong contrast has however been somewhat moderated in his later studies. There is a change with regards to the issue of use of force within the writing of Cragg. Whereas he in the majority of his studies comes very close to pacifism, seeing use of force as almost identical with the perversion of it, in a later study he sees powerlessness and use of power, including *Hijra*, as complementary to the powerlessness and suffering of Jesus. For this later development, see '"My tears into thy bottle": Prophethood and God', *The*

Muslim World 88 (1998), no. 3–4, pp. 238–55. See also the contemporary *The Weight in the Word. Prophethood: Biblical and Quranic*, Brighton, Portland, OR, Sussex Academic Press, 1999, 133, for a similar argument.

16 'Gloria in Profundis Deo', v. 6, *Poetry of the Word at Christmas*, 2nd rev. and expanded edn. (¹1987), London, New Millennium, 1996, p. 21.
17 'The Excellences of Jerusalem', p. 11.
18 Ibid., p. 12.
19 Ibid., p. 13.
20 This is a paraphrase of how Cragg interprets the *Fada'il* ('praises' or lit. 'Excellences') where Muslim poets of the 'middle centuries' (2nd Islamic century onwards) celebrated the Holy City to which they went as pilgrims, ibid., pp. 2, 13–15.
21 *Faith and Life Negotiate*, p. 181: 'The search for a "Christian Judaica" became central to my groping mind as early as my first sight of Jerusalem.'
22 *Faith and Life Negotiate*, p. 179.
23 Ibid., p. 182.
24 Ibid., p. 182–6.
25 Ibid., p. 181.
26 Ibid. The citation is taken from Ignatius to the Magnesians, in J. B. Lightfoot (ed.), *The Apostolic Fathers, Ignatius and Polycarp*, 2nd book, vol. 2, London, 1889, ch. x, p. 133.
27 *Faith and Life Negotiate*, p. 184.
28 Ibid. p. 179f.
29 I use 'radical pluralist' in a similar way as S. Mark Heim does in his *Salvations: Truth and difference in religion*, New York, Maryknoll, Orbis, 1995. In that study the religious traditions are seen as aiming at diverging points, fulfilments etc, hence: 'salvations' in plural. This view is explicitly proposed as an alternative to pluralist approach like the ones of Paul F. Knitter, J. Hick and Wilfred Cantwell Smith, which Heim sees as an expression of modernity's exclusivist (totalitarian?) ambitions under the guise of 'a comfortable and unitary reference point' which makes them 'not religiously pluralistic at all', ibid., pp. 129f and 139f.
30 Quoted in *Faith and Life Negotiate*, p. 185. The quotation is taken from Neusner's *The Religious Study of Judaism, Description, Analysis and Interpretation*, vol. 1, New York, 1986, somewhere (I did not have access to the original whilst writing this chapter) on pp. 141–2 or 152.
31 *Faith and Life Negotiate*, p. 200f.
32 Ibid., p. 183, and *Christ and the Faiths*, 163.
33 Ibid., p. 191f, and *Christ and the Faiths*, 164.
34 Ibid., pp. 183 and 193.
35 Ibid., p. 193.
36 Ibid., p. 192.
37 Ibid., p. 165.
38 Ibid., p. 166.
39 Ibid., p. 202.
40 Ibid., p. 186.
41 Ibid., p. 203.
42 Particularly elaborated in *The Privilege of Man: A Theme in Judaism, Islam and Christianity*, Jordan Lectures in Comparative Religion, no. 8 [School of Oriental and African Studies (SOAS), London], London, Athlone Press, 1968.

43 *The Excellences of Jerusalem*, 16. It is noteworthy that he does not use the common Abrahamic heritage, which he does not expect any decisive help from, ibid.
44 *Palestine: The Prize and Price of Zion*, p. 219.
45 *Christ and the Faiths*, p. 153.
46 Which is one of Cragg's own interpretations of E. Wiesel's statement: 'Were hatred a solution, the survivors, when they came out of the camps, would have to burn down the whole earth', taken from *Legends of our Time*, New York, 1972, p. 233. See also Cragg in *Palestine: The Prize and Price of Zion*, p. 208: 'Victimization is not reversed in the making of victims'.
47 *Christ and the Faiths*, p. 155.
48 Ibid., p. 157.
49 *Faith and Life Negotiate*, p. 187f.
50 *Christ and the Faiths*, p. 167.
51 Ibid.
52 Ibid., p. 168.
53 Ibid., p. 167.
54 Cf. *Faith and Life Negotiate*, p. 186: 'To be left face to face with how we relate without treason, in our joined and separate identities, is precisely the reason for rejecting the alternatives [i.e. the two-covenant theory and the (Jewish) view of Christianity as entirely Graeco-Roman, non-Semitic creation] ... Tension and loyalty come together – as it must seem to me.'
55 *Palestine: The Prize and Price of Zion*, 193f.
56 Ibid., p. xiv.
57 *Christ and the Faiths*, p. 148.
58 *Christ and the Faiths* explicitly employs 'cross-reference' as its method. The notion of 'cross-reference' is used already in 1985 in *Jesus and the Muslim: An Exploration*, London. In *Christ and the Faiths*, p. 4, the concept and method of 'cross-reference' is introduced thus: 1. Christ is *not* primarily anonymously present in the religions (as with Rahner), but is as *prepossession* known already by their own meanings. 2. These meanings and imagery are *distinct from* the New Testament understanding of his 'Christhood', of which Christianity exists. 3. The task for a cross-reference theology is, therefore, to bring Christ as understood by Christianity to the religions as they have understood him. Cragg compared this with the activity of *translation*.
59 Ibid. p. 147.
60 *Der eigene und der fremde Glaube. Studien zum interreligiösen Fremd-wahrnehmung in Islam, Hinduismus, Buddhismus und Christentum* (Hermeneutische Untersuchungen zur Theologie, 37), Tübingen, Mohr/Siebeck 1999.
61 See *Faith and Life Negotiate*, p. 302, n. 8, my emphasis.
62 Ibid.
63 *Palestine: The Prize and Price of Zion*, p. 218.
64 Ibid., p. 207.
65 Ibid., p. 222.
66 Ibid., p. 219.
67 Ibid., p. 218f.
68 Ibid., p. 219, and 'The Excellences of Jerusalem', p. 10.
69 'The Excellences of Jerusalem', p. 10.
70 'The Excellences of Jerusalem', p. 11.

Chapter 11

A Possible way to Share Jerusalem in Peace

David Kitching

Introduction and summary

The huge significance of Jerusalem for the three great faiths of Judaism, Christianity and Islam, listed in their historical sequence, cannot be overstated. The feelings of many millions of people, over many centuries, for the sanctity of the great city have enriched the world in many ways; not only in the city itself, from the pathos of the Wailing or Western Wall through the sereneness of *Haram-al-Sharif*, the Noble Sanctuary, to the poignancy of Gethsemane, but also in the ideas and poetry inspired by Jerusalem from the Psalms through the Book of Revelation to the tradition of the Prophet's ascension of and for English speakers to the aspiration of William Blake's hymn, 'Jerusalem'.

But all our joy and praise is touched with pain. The strife and warfare over Jerusalem has been tragic and deeply alarming, from the destruction by the Roman Emperor Titus through the Persian sack of the early seventh century, the wars and massacres of the Crusades, and much more, to the battles of 1948 and 1967 and the present severe tensions, terrorism and repression. Much in all this has given great occasion to the enemies of the Lord to blaspheme; both honest atheists and those who wish to attack and hurt the faiths are given so much material to claim that we, the believers, do terrible harm to humanity.

Wise believers in all the faiths now see that God is not confined to any particular place or time: so that too much emphasis on particular sanctities can lead to mistakes. This philosophical truth, however, does not really help the feelings of millions, or the situation on the ground. But something else might do so.

The idea of the Sovereignty of God, *Siyadat Allah*, whether we call Him the Lord, God or *Allah*, has been raised in various quarters and by distinguished individuals, such as the late King Hussein. Believers of course hold that He is sovereign over all the Earth but a particular application of the principle of his sovereignty over so unique a place as old Jerusalem, cannot be inappropriate.

This sovereignty, over the Old City and the adjacent shrines hallowed by each or all of the three faiths, needs so to speak to be earthed, or made concrete. What follows is an attempt to do this.

Sovereignty over the small and tightly defined area in question might be vested in three representatives, one from each faith. They might be entitled Consul, in the ancient sense of supreme magistrate; or Guardian; or any other term that might prove the least controversial. The key is that they should hold the legal authority. Each faith should work out a candidate, who would then have to be accepted by the others. This would of course be difficult, but given good faith and goodwill should not prove impossible. For the Christians, since we have lost Mother Teresa who would have been a prime possibility, a representative of the Orthodox communion might present the least difficulty for the first item of office. For the Muslims, perhaps a well respected Sharif or Imam not connected with a particular Government or political movement, or a highly respected individual such as the Rector of al-Azhar University in Cairo; and for the Jews a respected rabbi probably not connected with the religious political parties in Israel (although there are enlightened possible candidates among them).

If the term of office of the 'Consuls' were to be between two and four years, that would enable different churches and persuasions to take part in turn. This applies not only to the Christians, where the Roman Catholic Church would almost certainly take on the second term, but to Sunni and Shi'a in Islam, and to orthodox and reformed synagogues, and probably also Ashkenazi and Sepphardi, among the Jews.

There may perhaps be a case for the Christian Consul to have slightly less authority than the others, for example no veto if the other two were in agreement; so as to remove any fear of some echo of the Mandate or even the Crusades, and to reflect the political situation in the region at present. On the other hand, the Christian interest in Jerusalem is very great indeed, and it would be a tragedy if this were to decline. The appointment of a Christian

Consul, even if with powers slightly less than the others, would be an enormous fillip to the morale of Jerusalem Christians of every denomination. This is a point that can hopefully be resolved at the negotiating stage. In any case, it is to be hoped that the Consuls should normally achieve unanimity.

A Council representing both faiths and the resident population should support the Consuls. This double requirement will mean the need for great care, and respect for complexity, in determining its composition. Election of some, even most, of the members by the residents of the Sovereign Area would be desirable, but with a balancing factor to ensure an equal number of Muslims and Jews; and also Jews and Arabs, since Christian Arabs have to be taken into account. There should certainly be a good representation of Christians, probably anyway nearly as large as the other faiths.

Within each faith, there would have to be representation of different churches and persuasions; and also some place for the faiths worldwide as well as the local adherents. This applies to Islam nearly as much as to the Christians, and to the Jews perhaps to a lesser, but significant, extent. Possibly these wider faith representatives would have to be appointed rather than elected, which would make the democratic element of election of a good proportion of members by the residents the more important.

The powers and procedures of the Council, for example whether it should be legislative and/or executive or only advisory and deliberate, would clearly need careful thought and negotiation. The Sovereign Area, like the Vatican, could hardly be a full democracy; the Consuls are likely to need to have ultimate authority.

There would need to be a small civil service, as far as possible indigenous.

The role of the United Nations should include an enabling resolution, from the Security Council and probably the General Assembly as well, to set up the Sovereign Area, and a key part in the negotiation of its relationship to Israel and Arab Palestine. This would almost certainly need to be set out in a treaty or treaties, registered at the UN. That body may also need to provide the top echelon of a small peacekeeping force, though hopefully this may prove to be short-lived. It will perhaps need to provide one or two posts, or advisory assistants, in the small civil service. The Sovereign Area should however be wholly self-governing, and not a Trust Territory.

This whole proposal is fully compatible with the larger part of Jerusalem functioning, with total international acceptance, as the capital of Israel, and with the Arab parts of East Jerusalem functioning similarly as the capital of Arab Palestine. The extent of the Sovereign Area should be modest; the walled Old City and a few closely adjacent shrines, with possibly a small enclave outside (The Augusta Victoria Hospital?) to provide a breathing space and room for an administrative headquarters (this has been suggested to the present writer by a distinguished Palestinian citizen of Jerusalem). No Jewish neighbourhood or Arab village should be included. The Consuls themselves would presumably want to live in the Old City.

Another aspect that needs to be covered is that there are subjects on which greater Jerusalem, as a whole, needs to work as a unit; water supply, other public utilities, transport (though this would affect the Sovereign Area only rather minimally), probably a few others. Given good will, this should be far from impossible. An administrative mayor, without political functions, could head the necessary departments: perhaps appointed most of the time by the Israelis, given their majority in the greater city, with the consent of Arab Palestine and the Sovereign Area.

This whole proposal is dependent on a very large assumption: that a majority of influential people in all three faiths can come to see that there are more and deeper things that they share than that divide them. At a time when attitudes and lifestyles are, for very many people certainly in the Western world and widely elsewhere, so different from the beliefs and values of all three, I hope and trust that this assumption is valid. A wide ignoring, if not outright repudiation of Christian, Judaist and Islamic values, crass materialism and selfish hedonism run riot, with all their results in corruption, greed, the breakdown of family and other relationships, and much else, are surely doing so much damage to human happiness and the human race that all believers need to work together as far as ever they can. This, indeed, applies to believers in the world's other great religions, and to thoughtful humanists, as well as to the three faiths involved in Jerusalem. But it is these three who must work together, and at least contain their differences, for peace to break out in places holy to them all. These proposals depend on our realizing that we are members one of another.

The other premise, not an assumption but a condition precedent, is that restrained and moderate people in Israel and in Arab Palestine will, at some time before irreparable damage is done, recover control of their societies. This will be difficult in Israel, but not, I believe, impossible for that great country. The concept of 'land for peace' could not be applied to Old Jerusalem if it were a matter of ceding it to the Arabs; but a shared sovereignty between the Faiths could be quite different. For the Arabs, it is difficult to abandon aspirations; but to modify them to accepting a Sovereign Area shared by the faiths is not at all the same thing as surrendering to Israeli Sovereignty.

Relevant history

'Jerusalem', sang the great Psalmist, 'is built as a city which is compact together', or 'is a unity in itself'. This in fact has seldom proved true for long. Anyone who is seeking a means to bring peace to the city by sharing her needs should look back to see whether this has been tried before; with what success, and what went wrong. It is also necessary to look at efforts to give the city a special status, alongside the neighbouring power or powers, but enjoying a degree of autonomy from them.

The latter has been suggested and considered a number of times over the long march of history, and has once, even if long ago, been realized and stable for a long period. When that remarkably enlightened ancient king, Cyrus of Persia, applied to the exiled Jews his policy of allowing communities to return home, with religious toleration and some home rule, those who returned to Jerusalem from exile and around Babylon were encouraged, even subsidized, to rebuild their Temple and, some time later, the walls of their city. The accounts of this in the Old Testament books of Ezra and, particularly, Nehemiah – one of the most straightforward and vivid personal narratives in history – are confirmed by other sources. What was set up was a 'Temple City', with its surrounding countryside, of which there were a number of other examples in the Persian Empire. There was internal self-government, with a governor appointed by the Persian imperial government but acceptable to the people. This was more often than not a Jew: Nehemiah himself was an early example, and probably the most effective. Later the High Priest was often allowed to assume this role. There were certain privileges, including tax exemptions. But there was no real political, and of course no military, independence; the Persian kings, Cyrus, Darius and their successors, were firmly in control, and could have abrogated the autonomy of the Temple city-state at any time if they had wanted to. But wisely, they did not. This continued to be the position of Jerusalem under Alexander the Great and then Egypt of the Ptolomies, for a total of about 350 years.

This is strongly relevant in any nominally Sovereign Area in

Jerusalem, shared by the faiths, because even if under United Nations protection it would in practice depend on the restraint and goodwill of Israel and the Arab Palestinian state. Hopefully both would come to see, or to be persuaded, that such restraint and goodwill was in their best interests.

Jerusalem's role as the central shrine of Judaism and the idealized eternal capital of Israel was greatly strengthened during the long Temple city-state period. The Old Testament Book of Chronicles, written probably late in the Persian time, emphasizes this role, adding to the references in Deuteronomy and various Psalms. Jerusalem is where the Lord has chosen to place His name and make His dwelling forever. It is the only valid place for pilgrimage and making offerings. This reverence for the city has carried over from the Jews to many Christians, even apart from the connections of Jesus Christ himself with Jerusalem.

The huge importance of the city for the Jews has to be understood and deeply respected. Several ideas for the internationalization of the whole of Jerusalem have foundered on the failure to recognize it. It cannot be emphasized too strongly that the present proposal must be geographically modest, as well as being based on the sensitive sharing between the faiths.

The aggressive interference by the Seleucid king of Syria, Antiochus IV, with the Temple city-state led to the revolt of the Maccabees, which resulted in an independent, and quite extensive, Jewish state for a century. Then, after the half-independent rule of Herod, the Romans took over. They did not restore the Temple-state, but made Judea a province under their direct rule. The presence of their governors, Prefects or Procurators, was obtrusive and alien. Even so, there was a measure of autonomy in the city itself. Day to day control was largely devolved to the High Priest's Council, the 'Sanhedrin', and the High Priest himself had more or less unhindered control of the Temple itself (not always of its Treasury; but even here the fourth governor, Pontius Pilate, was slapped down by the Imperial Government for appropriating Temple funds to build an aqueduct for the city).

It was of course at this time that Jesus taught and died in Jerusalem, resulting in the city becoming precious and holy for a second world religion.

All autonomy was withdrawn after the Jewish revolt, and Titus' storming of Jerusalem. Under Hadrian in the early second century, it became a Roman colonial city, at first pagan, and with all Jews excluded, and the temple destroyed. Then in the fourth century it became a Christian city, under Roman and then Byzantine rule.

First the Church of the Holy Sepulchre and then many other Christian shrines were built. At one time there were more of these than have survived; for example the Byzantine emperor Justinian erected a huge church in conscious rivalry of Solomon, but this was destroyed, not by the Muslims but by an earthquake. In the seventh century first the Persians and then the Muslim Arabs captured the city. The first were destructive this time, with massacres of Christians, and many shrines desecrated. The brief Christian recovery of the city under the emperor Heraclius had insufficient time to repair these. The Arabs, under the caliph Umar, were more positive; he received the keys of the city from the Christian Orthodox Patriarch, and respected the Holy Sepulchre and the other remaining Christian shrines. The Muslims then built their own great and revered shrine, the *Haram-al-Sharif* (Noble Sanctuary), on the Temple Mount. This and especially the supremely beautiful Dome of the Rock, is one of the three most revered shrines of the House of Islam, and a hugely important place for pilgrimage.

The first period of Muslim rule lasted for four and a half centuries. There was no self-government for the Christians, or for the Jews, who had gradually returned to the city in considerable numbers. But the Christian shrines were respected, and pilgrimages normally allowed. There were however a few less tolerant caliphs, and one of these in the late eleventh century, helped to cause the Crusades.

After their ferocious capture of the city, the Crusaders set up their Kingdom of Jerusalem, which held the city for eighty-eight years, and took over, but preserved, the Noble Sanctuary including the al-Aqsa mosque. When Saladin retook Jerusalem for the Muslims, he fully respected the Christian shrines, and welcomed Christian pilgrims.

The Crusaders never recovered Jerusalem by force. But owing mainly to the internal war of the Muslims, an unusual Crusader, the emperor Frederick II, temporarily regained most of it (Bethlehem and Nazareth also) by diplomacy. His treaty with Saladin's grandson, al-Kamal, is the only historical precedent for the city to be shared between two faiths (the Jews were not included). Three quarters of the city returned to the Christians, but Muslim sovereignty was kept over Haram-al-Sharif. This arrangement lasted for fifteen years (1229–44).

The arrangement was precarious. Neither Frederick nor al-Kamal represented their faiths effectively. Frederick indeed, an outspoken agnostic, did not pretend to do so; he explained to al-Kamal that it was only for political and diplomatic reasons that he had to press so hard for the return of places that meant nothing to him! The most powerful forces in both faiths rejected the Treaty. The Pope, who in his capacity as a temporal ruler in Italy was at war with Frederick, excommunicated the liberator of Christian Jerusalem. The Knights Templar, who had possessed *Haram-al-Sharif* during the main period of Crusader rule, were furious at Frederick's leaving it in Muslim hands. Nearly all the latter were equally contemptuous of the Treaty denouncing al-Kamal as a traitor to Islam. His plea that he had preserved the *Haram-al-Sharif* for Islam was treated with disdain. Even the Christian barons and soldiers who were in charge of the coastal part of Palestine, now of course in Israel, which then still formed a small Crusader kingdom made no effort to help Frederick to reorganize the city; and before long he went home to Sicily in disgust, leaving the walls unrepaired. After fifteen years more fanatical Muslims from further east decisively defeated both the Crusaders and Saladin's family and the city remained in Muslim hands from 1244 until the First World War.

Whether, without this military event, the only arrangement for sharing the city between faiths (though only two) might have lasted longer, and even taken root, can never be known. Given the hostile attitude of the majority of influential people in both faiths, probably not. But the fact that this one precedent for sharing Jerusalem between faiths by friendly agreement had only a short and precarious life need and should not discourage a more positive effort to share sovereignty now between all three faiths. The hostile division of the city as a whole by a truce between Israel and Jordan after the 1948 war is even less relevant in the medieval precedent; the personal unpopularity of both Frederick and al-Kamal with their own sides got their Treaty off to a bad start. Frederick, an agnostic with arrogant manners in an age of faith, and for good measure a short and bald man at a time when physical beauty was as highly prized as today, was despised by both sides in spite of his intellectual brilliance. Their treaty of sharing had no popular motivation at all. Moreover, this was not an arrangement for shared sovereignty, but only for agreed partition. An agreement for all three faiths to operate together as sovereigns over the Old City and adjacent shrines would be a horse of quite a different colour. If achieved with wide support and wider acceptance, it should also contribute to peace between its secular neighbours rather than Jerusalem exacerbating the difficulties in their relations, as it does today.

The long period of Muslim rule over Jerusalem, from the mid

thirteenth century to the British General Allenby's entry in December 1917, the Ottoman Turkish empire being in charge for the second half of this long time, had features similar to the earlier Muslim regimes: no self-government or sharing of power, but most of the time a reasonable tolerance of Christian and Jewish residents and pilgrims, and respect for their shrines, under the control of their own religious authorities.

Christian Europe and the other countries of the West accepted this situation more or less cheerfully. Jerusalem became, to a large extent, an idealized concept expressed for example, in English, by Blake's famous hymn, 'Jerusalem', and by others such as 'City of God, how broad and far outstretch thy walls sublime'; there are somewhat similar hymns in French and German. This tendency existed in both Catholic and Protestant circles. Eastern Christians were also in the main reconciled to the situation, although there were some troubles for those of them within the Ottoman Empire, such as discrimination in taxation. But in its heyday Ottoman Turkey employed many eastern Christians in senior positions, and received good service from them. As the Ottoman Empire declined, some European powers became more assertive as Christian champions. Tsarist Russia, from the late eighteenth century, claimed to protect Orthodox Christians; and a little later France, under governments wishing to court Catholic support, Catholics and Maronites. This, under Napoleon III, was a secondary cause of the Crimean War. Indeed by the mid-nineteenth century internal disputes between Catholic, Orthodox, and other guardians of Christian shrines, especially the Church of the Holy Sepulchre, were both severe in themselves and a source of international tension. At the same time, several Western powers, led by Britain and Germany, were setting up consulates in Jerusalem which acquired something approaching extra-territorial status.

The Jews were in less of a position to react, but in the nineteenth century, with the start of the Zionist movement, they started to return to the city in large numbers. Indeed they were already the largest community in greater Jerusalem by 1914, though not, of course, in Palestine as a whole.

The British Mandate, between the two World Wars, had a number of ideas for Jerusalem, especially as it became obvious that the two promises on which it had been founded – a 'national home' for the Jews and self-government for the Arabs – were hopelessly contradictory for the country as a whole. By the late 1930s there were blueprint plans for both an Arab and a Jewish state, with

Jerusalem, meaning the whole city and the immediately surrounding area, under separate and neutral (meaning British) control. None of this got beyond the blueprint stage. However, the shrines of all three faiths were safeguarded and respected, and controlled by their own authorities; and were kept in notably good repair. There was also an impressive degree of cooperation between Jews, Arabs and British in historical and archaeological work (and some academic work; for example the first director of the British Middle East Centre of Arab Studies was a Jew highly proficient in Arabic, Abba Eban, subsequently Foreign Minister of Israel!). There was also a sincere attempt to set up an elected city council, for the whole city, with the three faiths all represented, in the proportion three Jews, three Muslims, one Christian. This however foundered on the increasing Jewish majority in the city as a whole, and the Arab insistence on parity. No one at this stage suggested singling out the Old City and the shrines.

During the chaotic last months of the Mandate, and the 1948 war that followed, various plans for making Jerusalem some sort of international zone, outside both the Jewish and Arab states, were mooted. All of these except one aimed to include the whole of the increasingly large, and by now two-thirds Jewish, city. One put forward by the Conciliation Commission of the UN itself suggested a rather nominal Trusteeship Zone with two separate municipalities, Jewish and Arab. The one, which suggested a smaller enclave based on the Old City came from the Archbishop of Canterbury, Geoffrey Fisher, who had been following events in the Holy Land and especially Jerusalem for several years, and receiving a mass of contradictory pressure from all sides. He thought the Commission plan unsound, and proposed instead a limited international zone rather similar in area to that proposed in the present paper: the Old City plus adjacent areas of significance to the three faiths. He however added a great deal of land east of the walled city, including the whole of the Mount of Olives and other Arab areas (as well as Mount Scopus; but not the small area just south-west of the Wall, which the present proposal does include). Archbishop Fisher did not propose a self-governing area, but a trust territory.

His plan was endorsed by the World Council of Churches, and submitted to the UN. Here, however, it was wholly rejected by the Arabs, who complained that it left Jewish Jerusalem intact, but sought to internationalize Arab Jerusalem (which had just been occupied by Jordan). It was also rejected by Israel, who doubtless looked forward to gaining the whole city in due course. Lord Fisher did not have the support of any major country, not even his own; he had omitted to consult the Foreign Office, which opposed his plan. It sank without trace (except perhaps, in another form, now). Meanwhile the UN's ideas did not get off the ground either, partly because there was at that time no UN peacekeeping force available, also because Israel and Jordan produced a tactical alliance against any internationalization of Jerusalem. Both preferred partition and had quietly agreed a division line by late 1949.

The division of greater Jerusalem from 1948 led to renewed Muslim control of the Old Walled City and most of the shrines adjacent to it. They respected the Christian shrines – King Hussein welcoming the Pope to them in a small red helicopter! – but the Jews were expelled from the Western Wall, even though the terms of the truce between Israel and Jordan had stipulated that they should have access there. After the Israeli victory of 1967, the Wall was of course restored to the Jews, who also took over a significant area just west of it, which had been a Maghrabi or Moorish section of the Muslim Quarter. This was bulldozed for a platform for the Jews to pray, involving the destruction of several mosques. But the *Haram-al-Sharif* and the Christian shrines were protected; and efforts by extreme Zionists to invade the *Haram* and proclaim the refounding of the Temple were given short shrift by the Israeli Government (and, for doctrinal reasons, discouraged by mainstream Judaism). After thirty-six years, Israeli police still control the entrances to the *Haram*, with tact to the Muslim worshippers and, as I can testify, their guests; and in tacit partnership with the Warden of the Shrines of al-Quds.

The enlightened Jewish Mayor of Jerusalem, Teddy Kollek, made several attempts to allow limited self-government to Arab Muslims and Christians in the section of the greater city where the constituted a majority. He also made various sensible concessions, such as the use by Arabs of Jordanian currency and commercial law. But his liberal ideas were blocked by hardline influences in the Knesset, both religious and secular nationalist. The hopes of the more open-minded elements in Israel that in return for religious respect, economic prosperity, full participation by Jerusalem Arabs (in contrast to the West Bank people) in Israeli social security, some devolution of authority to the minorities, and Israeli rule over a unified greater Jerusalem would receive general acceptance, have not been achieved.

This has been at least partly because the Israeli government and law courts have tended to support the claims of Israeli settlers, even when extreme. The Jews naturally reoccupied the Jewish quarter of the Old City, but they also extended it considerably at the expense of the other quarters. Moreover, when the Israeli authorities refused permission to any non-Jews to reside in the enlarged Jewish quarter, or to buy or even retain property there the courts upheld this. But at the same time Jews were free, indeed encouraged, to buy property and settle in the other quarters. Encroachments by Jewish settlers in the other quarters have been considerable, and sometimes carried out in an offensive manner. These grievances in the Old City have certainly resonated outside it. Mayor Kollek has recently been quoted, since retirement from his long and strenuous innings, that it will take six or more generations for a united greater Jerusalem to settle down as a cohesive society.

Since Ariel Sharon's at best tactless demonstration at the Temple Mount/*Haram-al-Sharif*, in the autumn of 2000, which seemed to contradict the generally careful and respectful attitude to the *Haram* noted above, was furiously resented by all Muslims, and the increasingly bitter *intifada* that followed and still continues, attempts at accommodation have been few and halting. All this has to strengthen the case for a more even-handed solution, such as sharing the Old City and a small extension outside it between the faiths, with Jewish and Arab Jerusalem the capitals of Israel and Arab Palestine.

To sum up: Jerusalem's long history contains only one attempt to share the city on friendly and equal terms, and this was partial – it did not include the Jews – and short-lived. Only once in the distant past, has there been a precedent for independence or at least autonomy, respected by powerful neighbours: the Temple city-state from Cyrus to the Ptolemies. Tolerance by the ruling power of other faiths and communities has a better record, but at present is failing or at best clearly inadequate. To explore a three-way division by agreement, Israeli Jerusalem, Arab al-Quds, and a small Sovereign Area run jointly by the three faiths, but also maintaining unity for necessary practical purposes, would seem very well worthwhile.

The importance of shrines

It is worthwhile here to emphasize the huge importance of shrines.

Human awareness of God has many aspects. Two of the main ones are that nearly all of us, except determined atheists, realize that 'It is He (or perhaps for polytheists, They) that has made us, and not we ourselves'; and that He exists before and over all

Creation, in nature, renewals, and prompts us towards good. But there are also for most believers special places, where His presence is felt with great power; Mecca for Muslims, Lourdes for Roman Catholic Christians, to take just two examples. Standing on the Argyll hills between Loch Long and Loch Goil, I myself have echoed Jacob's cry at Bethel: 'This is the gate of heaven!'

Jerusalem is special even beyond these. The huge significance of the Old City, and especially the Western Wall, to the Jews needs no further emphasis, except perhaps to remark that although originally the city, and especially the site of the Temple, were deeply more important to Eastern than to Western Jews, this is no longer so. All venerate them, most especially the Western Wall. For the Muslims, *Haram-al-Sharif*, and particularly the Dome of the Rock and the Rock itself, are of supreme importance: second only to Mecca as a place of pilgrimage. This is probably strengthened by the great emphasis in Islam on the transcendence of God, and the prohibition of pictures or other icons; also there is no equivalent for Muslims of Christmas, with its vision of the human side of Godhead, even a reverent cosiness. The beauty of the Dome, raised by the skill of believers to the glory of God, supplies something deeply needed.

It is possible that for the whole company of Christian believers, shrines are not quite so central as for the other two faiths: because of belief in the resurrection of Jesus Christ, and His living presence for us. Even so, the Holy Land where He was born, lived and worked, and Jerusalem where He taught, suffered and died, and then was raised, are of very great importance for millions of Christians: many pilgrims from all over the world have come to Jerusalem in every generation, to visit the Holy Sepulchre, the site of the Last Supper, perhaps the Garden Tomb, other places, and especially Gethsemane (and of course Bethlehem). For Christians of every persuasion who live in Jerusalem the sacred role of the city is infinitely clear.

Extent of the Sovereign Area

A Sovereign Area can be set up on two scales. The principle is the same: that the shrines dear to all three faiths should be in an area deemed to be under the special sovereignty of God, dedicated to peace and freedom of access, and to His worship each in their own way. It should be outside the power of any one state, but guaranteed by its neighbours. The two scales are however important, and each has its plusses and minuses. The minimum scale would confine the sovereignty strictly to the shrines themselves, with no hinterland, or even any ground between them. This would mean a series of small and mostly very small enclaves, with no additional buildings, even for a headquarters. The sovereignty would be notional and theoretical, and would need virtually no administration or civil servants; unlike the obvious near-parallel for the whole idea, the Vatican City-state, it would have none of the trappings of a state; and hardly any resident population, since most of the people working in the shrines would have to come from outside. It would be totally dependent in every respect on Israel and Arab Palestine.

The maximum scale would be much more like the Vatican, and with an area probably very similar to the latter's 108 acres. It would include the land immediately around and between most of the shrines. This would almost certainly mean the whole of the old walled city, with a very limited adjacent area to the east and perhaps very small one to the south (not west, or significantly north). There would need to be an administration, needing a headquarters; an enclave outside the Old City (the Augusta Victoria hospital site has been suggested for this). It would have a significant resident population. There would need to be arrangements for security as well as for most functions of government. Like the Vatican, it would have effective sovereign status; even though of course no military viability, and still closely dependent in practice on the goodwill of its neighbours. It would have much more reality, but many more practical problems. The whole area, however, would be small, almost certainly well under 10% of greater Jerusalem.

The remainder of this chapter is concerned mainly with the second alternative. This does not mean that the first should be dismissed. It could have a few advantages, in that it might be seen by the governments of Israel and Arab Palestine as less of a threat, or anyway less of an infringement of their aspiration. But it would also have less reality in itself, leave unresolved such hard problems as how the Old City, apart from the shrines themselves, should be shared between Israel and Arab Palestine. Both would certainly claim the whole, and therefore a large part of the problem remains unsolved. The smaller scale has some resemblance to the discarded UN Conciliation Commission plan referred to above. The larger scale should be the preferred option.

Even so, the minimum scale could be applied valuably for the suggested smaller enclaves, such as the Rockefeller Museum, and the buildings in Bethlehem and Bethany.

Even the larger scale would not, of course, be economically viable, at first anyway (just possibly it could become so, through a wealth of pilgrims and visitors). Still less could it ever be militarily defensible. It would therefore, as noted, be dependent on the restraint and goodwill of Israel and Arab Palestine. That is by no means necessarily a bad thing. It could achieve, before very long, enough moral and spiritual strength, and hopefully sufficient width and depth of international support, to earn respect and acceptance from its neighbours; always provided that the authorities in the Sovereign Area showed enough sensitiveness and wisdom. Indeed given that, it could in the longer run become a positive factor in the relationship between its neighbours. It could eventually contribute to the security of Israel as a universally nation and state.

It is again worth remarking that the present plan, while resembling Archbishop Fisher's idea of 1949 to some extent as regards its area, has vital difference. It depends on self-government by representatives of the faiths, with a mostly elected Council, and with the UN as servant, adviser, and guarantor, not master. While perhaps a little open to the Arab objection of 1949 it is much less so, since its land claims east of the Old City are a great deal less, and it is wholly compatible with Arab Jerusalem being the recognized capital of Palestine, just as Jewish Jerusalem of Israel. Moreover it makes a claim, just south west of the present Wall, to a small piece of land, which was in Israel before 1967; which tends to balance its format (for this please see the Annexe on 'Extent of the Sovereign Area').

The UN is also far better equipped now than it was in 1948–9 to provide a very small protective and peacekeeping force. And the very worsening of the situation now means that there is little or no prospect of the tacit alliance of Israel and the Arabs against a separate regime with international guarantee that arose against a UN trusteeship of all Jerusalem in 1949. A possible boundary of the Sovereign Area on the 'maximum' or substantial scale is annexed to this chapter. This of course is tentative, and will doubtless be subject to a great deal of negotiation. But hopefully the principle is clear. It cannot be repeated too strongly that the Sovereign Area must be modest enough not to encroach on the integrity of Israeli and Arab Jerusalem as the capitals of the two neighbour states.

A modest alternative would be to limit the area to the walled city only. This would have the merit of simplicity, and would provide a very clear boundary, which would be easier to negotiate. But it would have strong disadvantages. It would mean leaving many of the most important shrines, the majority but not all Christian, outside. It would also leave no room for an administrative headquarters, or for UN advisers.

The Vatican State as a precedent?

The differences between that tiny Sovereign State and the proposed Sovereign Area in Jerusalem are large and obvious, but there are some basic similarities. The Vatican is also part of a much larger city, which is the capital of a great neighbour country (though of course only one). It is a religious foundation; and it is protected by an international treaty.

The sovereign state of the Vatican was set up by the Lateran Treaties of 1929 between the papacy and the Italian Government. That the latter government was at the time Fascist is curiously enough, irrelevant. Many of the worst aspects of Mussolini's regime had not become apparent, and it was accepted internationally as the legal government of Italy, and was at the time a member of the League of Nations. More importantly, the Treaties have continued secure and flourishing with democratic Italian Governments for well over fifty years.

'Treaties' is plural because the main one setting up the City-State was accompanied by another which awarded some compensation to the papacy for Italy's annexation of the much larger Papal States, in the middle of peninsular Italy, in 1859 and 1870. There need of course be no equivalent for a Jerusalem Sovereign Area. On the other hand, there may need to be two treaties, with Israel and with Arab Palestine. Registration at the United Nations should give the Jerusalem Treaty or Treaties a buttress which the Lateran one has not proved to need.

That treaty declared the Vatican to be a Sovereign State, with the Pope as its Head: with all the attributes of sovereignty, including sending and receiving ambassadors, issuing its own currency, and the right to raise its own revenue. It could also transfer funds as well as other communications with full diplomatic privilege (this was important to the papacy, which had lacked such rights since 1870; and they were respected by both sides during the Second World War, even when Nazi Germany controlled Rome in late 1943 and early 1944). The Vatican could also raise its own army, even if this has been essentially for decorative purposes. Civil and commercial law have been aligned to those of Italy. Citizenship has been extended sparingly: few of those who work in the Vatican but reside elsewhere acquire it, and by no means all the residents. On the other hand, many senior Roman Catholic churchmen hold it, wherever in the world they live.

The Jerusalem Sovereign Area would probably have a rather larger resident population than the Vatican, and a much more varied one in race and belief. This may make arrangements more complex, and harder to set up in the first instance. On the other hand, the Jerusalem state will have no need of the Vatican's elaborate foreign policy, and diplomatic representation. The questions of currency, citizenship, and commercial and civil law are discussed later in this chapter.

There is some, but not very much, similarity between the political background of the Lateran Treaties and the situation in and around Jerusalem today. There was at the outset considerable mistrust of the Vatican State from extreme Italian nationalists, as well as dislike from the anti-clerical Italian Left. Both these factors have largely disappeared. In Jerusalem, nationalist objections can be expected from both sides; in Israel mainly from the right-wing parties, secular and religious. Hopefully these, and similar Arab objections, would gradually recede, provided that the Consuls and the Council behave with wisdom and tact, and that great care is taken to prevent any activities subversive to either neighbour from taking place in the Sovereign Area.

The negotiations leading to the Lateran Treaty were long and arduous, even though Pope Pius XI and Mussolini were both, for their own reasons, anxious to agree. After eighteen months of discussion, these were resolved by narrowing down participation to the Pope and Mussolini personally, with two carefully chosen go-betweens who commanded the respect of both sides. The last difficulties to be overcome were territorial (the Vatican's wish to add a corridor to the sea to their sovereign territory) and diplomatic (Mussolini's effort to claim support from the Vatican in his quarrels with France, Britain and Yugoslavia). The Vatican finally dropped the first demand, and the Italian Government the second.

In Jerusalem the plan breaks new ground. There has never been a sovereign or autonomous area covering only a rather small part of the city – although the Vatican precedent could here be genuinely helpful. The Temple State of long ago was much larger: the whole city with its surrounding countryside; the abortive ideas of the last Mandate and 1948–9 were mainly similar. The right-wing nationalist and religious parties in Israel, and the stronger nationalist groups in Palestine, are both bound to make the negotiations hard and fiercely contested, and there being three sides will add a new range of difficulties, even though some aspects of this could prove helpful. Particularly if the negotiations should become a debate narrowed down to a very few responsible leaders, someone of great calibre will need to be chosen to represent the embryonic Sovereign Area.

This is a role involving, though not confined to the UN. It is hard to see that representatives of the faiths, central though their interest and position is, could manage this by themselves, without strong leadership of their delegation from outside which would concentrate their minds in a centripetal way. Of course the faiths representatives must be there, with force and conviction. No one country would be likely to take the leadership of this delegation with much prospect of success, although several countries would certainly have a valuable role in the wings. One way forward might be for the UN, probably the Security Council and the Secretary-General acting together, to persuade a rare and brave individual of the very highest calibre and reputation to take the job on: giving him or her a comprehensive but flexible brief, and huge moral support (Nelson Mandela or F. W. de Klerk? Mikhail Gorbachev? Aung San Yi?). It would certainly be a role extremely vulnerable to wreckers, including terrorists; so that one trusts that the Lord will guide him or her waking, and guard them sleeping.

The Vatican is not quite the only historical arrangement worthy of study. In its time, The League of Nations tried to set up at least two 'free cities' Danzig, now Gdansk, and more briefly Fiume, now Rijeka in Croatia. These aimed at a sharing or compromise solution for a town in dispute between two competing nations. There was no religious aspect, but strong political nationalist ones. Fiume lasted for very few years; Danzig limped on for twenty with the aid of a first-aid (Swiss) League administrator. The League of Nations had far less political clout than the UN, with all its faults, has achieved.

Treaties of guarantee to respect the independence and neutrality of small states have appeared on the international scene from time to time. The best known are those which purported to protect Belgium and Luxembourg. They did help to keep the two countries out of trouble through one major war, in 1870, but failed at the second hurdle, in 1914; being famously described as 'a piece of paper'. This was of course before the League and the UN.

How the Sovereign Area might operate

The key is a collegiate presidency composed of representatives of each of the three faiths, entitled Consul, Warden, Guardian or whatever else might be decided. The authority of the Sovereign Area would rest with them, as with the Pope in the Vatican or the President of the USA. The Crown in Parliament in the United Kingdom is a less exact analogy, because the proposed Council, whatever its powers, would not share sovereignty. The hope would be that, after however strong a discussion, decisions of the three would normally be unanimous. If however this should fail, the Christian Consul should probably not have a veto, if both the others were in agreement. He or she would be to that extent a junior partner; the main reason being the situation on the ground, and the need to avoid any echo of the Mandate, let alone of the Crusades. The Jewish and Muslim Consuls would have a veto. But it is to be hoped that disagreements would very seldom, if they were ever pressed to the point of a vote among the Consuls; and the Christian Consul if of the right calibre, should be able to help with this. Balancing the arguments above, it is extremely important that the Christian share in the Sovereign Area should be influential and respected.

It is of course realized that the election of the three Consuls/Wardens will pose formidable difficulties; not least because all three faiths have widely different churches and persuasions. Perhaps the constitution of the Lebanon could be of help here, with its complicated but fairly intended division of posts and power between Maronite and Orthodox Christians, Sunni and Shi'a Muslims, Druze etc. There could be an agreed order, as already indicated, within Christianity between Orthodox, who would perhaps have the best claim for the first innings; Roman Catholic, various Protestants, and other confessions. Similarly in Islam between Sunni and Shi'a, and in Judaism between Orthodox, reformed, and other groups. A fairly short term of office, say two to four years, with no immediate re-election, would help here; although on the other hand it would be a pity to make this entirely rigid, if anyone were to show himself or herself especially effective and respected in the office.

Putting forward an agreed candidate within each faith would be a strong challenge to their spirit of mutual love and readiness to co-operate: which hopefully, with considerable difficulty, they could all surmount. But then it would certainly be crucial that the two other faiths should agree each appointment. A mechanism for these two processes will not be easy but ought to prove attainable. Useful conferences between two and sometimes all three faiths have been held in recent years, both under the auspices of faith leaders such as the meeting in Alexandria in the autumn of 2001, sponsored by Archbishop George Carey with the consent and encouragement of the Egyptian Government; and arranged by secular leaders in various countries, such as one initiated by Don Juan Carlos for representatives of all three faiths in Spain, and one arranged by the Wilton Park organization in Britain on Western-Islamic relations. These and similar resources can be used.

Among the Christians, an important and often neglected constituency is what might be termed the 'buried' Christian churches: Armenian, Syriac, Coptic, Assyrian and others. They are numerous in Jerusalem, and should certainly have specific representation on the Council; and probably an agreed 'turn' for the post of Christian Consul. There would be two ways of covering this: to give this 'buried' constituency two or three seats on the Council; and/or have a very small 'upper Chamber', in which the three patriarchs in Jerusalem would sit ex-officio, alongside eminent clerics or other representatives of the other faiths, and possibly a representative of the Protestant churches. The Armenian Patriarch could represent the other Eastern churches, and the Orthodox Patriarch the Russian church as well as the Greek. As regards the Christian consul, one might envisage a rota of four, Orthodox, Catholic, Armenians and others, and Protestant (Lutheran, Anglican, Church of Scotland ...). This is admittedly complex, but should be achievable with goodwill.

On the substance, each faith would clearly have to show great wisdom in selecting an acceptable candidate. The late Mother Teresa would have been a marvellously appropriate candidate for the Christians. With this not possible, the Orthodox confession should, as already indicated, have the diplomatic skill to suggest a good candidate for the first term, and the Roman Catholics for the second. Jews would probably need to avoid anyone connected with the most extreme religious parties in Israel, but there are wise and peaceable members of that fraternity; there are also a number of highly respected rabbis in various parts of the world (and indeed Jewish lay persons; the Consuls need not be clerics). The Muslims would clearly have to avoid anyone with a connection with any organization tainted by terrorism (this of course applies equally to the other two faiths). The Muslims might also be wise to avoid anyone at all closely connected with a particular Arab, or indeed other, government. But here again, there are many peace-loving and respected Muslim leaders, whether Imams or Ayatollahs or not, in many parts of the world. The Rector of al-Azhar University of Cairo is an example.

One has to recognize that this process of choice and acceptance could well, in the first instance anyway, take some considerable time. It is possible that, if it should become clearly wise to get the Sovereign Area going, for example if a combination of political circumstances were favourable but precarious (as they seemed to be for a short time in the middle of 2000). It might be expedient for the international community, after as much consultation as possible, to make interim appointments. These would of course be provisional.

Like the Vatican, the Sovereign Area could hardly operate as a full democracy. Almost certainly, both legal sovereignty and decisive power must reside with the Consuls. But a Council, as far as practicable elected, should certainly be set up to support them. The resident population would probably have a considerable Arab majority, possibly an Arab Muslim majority. This means that a number of Jews will need to be elected or nominated, in order to make Arab and Jewish membership equal; and also, not of course the same thing, Jewish and Muslim representation equal, i.e. Jews equal Arab Muslims and Christians together, and Jews equal Arab and other Muslims together. This need not be as difficult as it may sound: it could be achieved by appointing a small numbers of non-Arab Muslims from outside, equal to the Christian Arabs. The 'extra' Jewish members would preferably be elected, though exactly by whom would need to be worked out.

Christian representation should probably be rather smaller, but significant; for reasons given above. The presence and rights of the resident Christian population, and the importance of their shrines, call for something not too far short of equality. The shadow of the Mandate need not be very strong; as it happens, very few of the Christian population of a Sovereign Area within her likely borders have any significant connection with the former mandatory power, Britain, and only one shrine (the Garden Tomb). The proportions proposed in the 1930s, of three Jews, three Muslims and only one Christian, referred to an elected council for greater Jerusalem as a whole, where the Christian proportion was and is much smaller than in the likely Sovereign Area. How the Christian element in the Council can best be elected or selected will hopefully emerge. It is very important that the resident Christian population, very much including the 'buried Churches', should be well represented, but also that they be balanced by some representatives of the worldwide Christian churches.

The power of the Council will probably need to be defined, for the first few years at least, by the proposed UN conference to establish the Sovereign Area, and provide it with a Treaty of Guarantee.

The Council should certainly have no power to elect or dismiss the Consuls, but it should be able to debate, and approve or criticise, their decisions. It might take on increasingly the role of a municipal council responsible for the secular administration of the Area; or at least act as closely advisory to the consuls in that role. The arrangements for the shrines, under the authority of the Consuls, should certainly be in the hands of the appropriate guardians of each faith; with special arrangements for such delicate matters as the boundary between *Haram-al-Sharif* and the Western Wall. The Council would here have at most a deliberative function.

Most aspects of day-to-day life in the sovereign Area will be referred to, even if briefly, under the heading 'Practical Problems' below. Some points, appear to be vital:

1. Citizenship of the Sovereign Area will need careful definition from the start. This will have to include what may be a contentious point; whether there can be dual citizenship of Jews with Israel, Arabs (whether Muslim or Christian) with Palestine or another Arab state, and non-Arab Christians with wherever. This will probably be unavoidable.

2. The right for non-citizens to reside in the Area will need careful attention and definition. It should almost certainly lean to a liberal interpretation: it would be a great pity if the movement of people were to become more restricted. But some control will be unavoidable, particularly to prevent any subversion of neighbour states from within the Sovereign Area, as noted immediately below.

3. Security will pretty certainly need UN support (see later section), but should not, hopefully, be a major problem after the initial period. Perhaps more difficult will be to ensure that neither Israel nor Arab Palestine should feel threatened by any activities in the Sovereign Area.

4. A perhaps less immediate point: it will be essential that the Consuls take a modest view of any functions that they may have outside the Sovereign Area: here quite unlike the Vatican. It seems unlikely that the Sovereign Area will need any diplomatic representation, except in Israel and Palestine, possibly Jordan, and at the UN.

5. The Sovereign Area will need a court to decide questions of land and house ownership, and the right to settle in the various quarters of the Old City. While it will almost certainly be impracticable to reverse the enlargement of the Jewish Quarter, which indeed was rather small originally, further encroachments by Jewish settlers

outside their quarter may need to be contained; and the imbalance between the total exclusiveness of the Jewish Quarter and the openness of the others be removed. This aspect will probably be hard for some powerful forces in Israel to accept.

It is important, even vital, to recognize that this whole enterprise calls for more disbursement of power, even sacrifice, from Israel than from anyone else. This is unavoidable, since Israel controls all of greater Jerusalem at this time. In the long run, the gain for Israeli security may hopefully make this sacrifice worthwhile and acceptable. Meanwhile it means that Israel must be expected to press certain conditions to be in place before the enterprise is established. This will almost certainly include a significant period of calm, and absence of attacks on any part of Israel; and also probably the firm acknowledgement, in a treaty subscribed to by all her Arab neighbours, that Jewish Jerusalem up to at least the 1967 frontier (with the possible exception of the tiny area referred to above), that is to say two-thirds to three-quarters of the whole greater city, is inalienably part of Israel, and her capital. Such conditions would be reasonable, and probably necessary. Moreover, Israel's position within the Sovereign Area would naturally be nearest to the position of Italy in the Vatican; meaning that the civil and economic arrangements would be attuned in the first instance to Israel, although with Arabs, Muslim and Christian, having their honoured and secure share in sovereignty and influence, and a significant input into the civil arrangement. Hopefully the establishment of an Arab Palestinian capital in north-east Jerusalem, should accompany, or even better precede, the coming into being of the Sovereign Area. This brings us naturally to the next point.

The Role of the United Nations

This will have to be large and many-sided.

It will be crucial at the outset. The Sovereign Area should not, given its unusual religious character, be a Trust Territory of the UN, as was the thrust of the ideas current in 1948–9. Self-government is better. But the world organization will have to play a decisive and formal part in establishing it.

As noted more briefly below, there are likely to be four stages in the creation of the Sovereign Area, in all of which the UN will have a key share. First, keeping pace with discussions within and between the faiths, there will need to be informal discussions between, first and crucially, Israel and the Palestine Arabs: perhaps with Jordan and/or Egypt in attendance. Although an 'honest broker' role could possibly be assumed by the European Union – the USA would be perceived as too pro-Israel, and individual countries (including Russia) would have too much historical baggage or not enough clout – the UN would be the best placed to act as host and intermediary. It could with great advantage provide facilities, a Secretariat, and availability of advice, probably including from the Secretary-General himself.

At the second stage, when hopefully the parallel inter-faith discussions were making real progress, a more formal conference of all the closely interested parties would need to take place. This should without doubt be under UN auspices, although a committee something like the 'Mitchell' committee of 2000–01 might be set up to provide collegiate chairmanship. Besides the obvious participants, Israel and Palestine and the representatives of the faiths, this conference should include probably all the permanent members of the Security Council; Israel's Arab neighbours; perhaps another major Islamic country, non-Arab, and one or two mainly Christian ones; plus one or two suggested by Israel to provide a better balance, although her most powerful friend, the USA, would be there as a permanent Security Council member.

The third stage would be the decisive Conference to establish the Sovereign Area. This should be open to all UN members, and be as formal and high profile as, for example, the first UN Environment Conference at Stockholm in 1972. A major international statesman, perhaps from a country well outside the region and not identified with any of the three faiths – India? Japan? – could valuably be brought in as Chairman (another possibility would be Nelson Mandela, if as a devout Christian he was acceptable to the other faiths. And just possibly, with the same proviso, ex-President Bill Clinton might be a starter). Another respected figure of the first calibre would be needed as the Conference's Secretary-General; Mr Kofi Annan would hardly be able to do this unless the rest of the world was unusually quiet.

The fourth and last stage would be the Treaty of Treaties of Guarantee. This would hopefully have been drafted and agreed at least in outline at the third stage. The importance of a formal treaty cannot be overstated. It or they should be endorsed by Resolution of both the Security Council and the General Assembly; and then registered at the UN with reference to these resolutions and clearly carrying their authority.

The role of the UN in the Sovereign Area once it has been set up will equally crucial. The following are the main functions that come to mind:

1. While the personnel of the peacekeeping military or police force in the Sovereign Area (perhaps initially military, later only police) should as far as possible and as soon as possible be mainly indigenous, probably with quotas for members of each faith, and should be under the command of the Consuls, the UN will almost certainly have to provide its top echelon, and its effective operational commander, for the first few years at least. This should come from countries with experience of peacekeeping and a lack of close recent connection with Israel or the Arabs. A Scandinavian commander might be suitable.

2. The 'civil service' of the Sovereign Area will have many sensitive tasks and will initially anyway need an experienced and impartial administrator of top calibre to head it. This would most naturally be a UN appointment. A small number of advisory appointments in the civil service might also be very useful. One such could well be to help set up and operate the law court, suggested above, for settling questions land and home ownership in the Old City.

3. The Financing of the Sovereign Area is discussed below, under 'Practical problems'. There will almost certainly need to be some funding through the UN, at least to start with. This might best be raised by means of a 'Pledging Conference', similar to those for UNRWA [United Nations Relief and Working Agency for Palestine Refugees in the Near East], rather than being a claim on the central UN budget. Specialised technical assistance as necessary, probably in the form of short-term attachments, could be a role for the UNDO [United Nations Development Organization].

It seems worthwhile to comment briefly on the role of the United States, which has not so far been discussed positively. It is crucial, but will need to be performed with great skill and restraint. At government level it will probably be an enabling rather than a prominently active role. Sensitive encouragement to Israel to adopt a positive attitude could very well prove to be decisive for the whole enterprise. There is certainly also a very much wider role for the American churches, and for the hugely important and influential Jewish community. There are also more Muslim organizations and individuals of influence than is often realized.

All this applies on a smaller scale to Britain. Co-operations between the faiths, such as the Three Faiths Forum, exist in this country and could be very valuable. British Jewry, though less powerful than American, includes groups and individuals of renown and influence. The worldwide Anglican Communion, of which the Church of England, even if often quietly, remains the core member, covers a great deal of ground, and perhaps because of its unusually rather humble stance (in the present generation) is widely respected. Its representatives have been notably active in efforts to promote peace in the Middle East. Several other Protestant churches, notably the Church of Scotland, carry weight; as also certainly do British Roman Catholics. Co-operation between the Christian churches in Britain (and Ireland) is often happy and effective. British Muslims are vibrant, increasing, and in the majority more peaceful and positive than the media tend to portray them. British government postures, like American, probably need to be modest; but a small British input into the peacekeeping force (not the command) need not be ruled out (General Allenby's entry into the Old City on foot as a pilgrim is still in the folk memory of Jerusalem). Britain may well be in a position to influence events quietly more than her detractors assume.

Many other countries, such as France, Spain and the Netherlands, Canada and Australia, South Africa and Brazil, Russia, Egypt, Pakistan and India, and perhaps more quietly Germany, may well have various insights and resources to contribute. This chapter must take note of Voltaire's wise warning that to say everything is to bore.

Returning to the United Nations, it will certainly be for a member country or team of countries that does not have too much historical or present political involvement to live down to take the initiative in proposing the necessary Resolutions in the General Assembly and the Security Council. This rules out the USA, the UK, France and probably Russia, and of course Israel and the Arab states. That leaves plenty of talent available.

Lastly, as already noted, the Sovereign Area would almost certainly need diplomatic representation only in Israel, Arab Palestine, just possibly Jordan and the USA, and the UN itself. Perhaps one or two semi-official missions whose real purpose would be to attract aid and tourism might be added. The Sovereign Area should probably be admitted as a nominal member of the UN perhaps without voting rights or by convention not using them.

Practical problems

While these will abound for the larger Sovereign Area, the minimum one would have some too. A technical area, consisting only of the agreed shrines, would not have room even for a small headquarters; and even if this were to be provided in another tiny enclave, the arrangement would be very precarious. The authority of the Consuls could not help being less convincing. We shall therefore concentrate again on the slightly-larger-than-Vatican alternative. That is not to say that 'the minimum Sovereign Area' might not be a fallback position of significant value, as compared with no effort at sharing at all.

The practical problems can be classified as legal; economic; financial; many social, such as cultural, and educational, for adults and children residents, and tolerance between different communities and customs; and, certainly not least, citizenship, and competing loyalties, for the resident population.

Let us take the last first. Unlike the Vatican, there could be both justice and advantage in conferring citizenship on all permanent and long-term residents in the Sovereign Area. There would however have to be the option of dual citizenship, as noted above. One can hope that a considerable loyalty to the Sovereign Area might develop before too long. It should become a unique policy, with not even the Vatican closely comparable. Obviously the Sovereign Area could never dream of going to war with anybody, so that the military aspects of patriotism might come, helpfully, to apply. This would be helped if, even from the start, a large proportion of recruits to the peacekeeping police force were residents.

Whether the Sovereign Area could usefully emulate the Vatican in granting citizenship to certain people outside, eg. distinguished leaders of all three faiths, is a secondary question which the Consuls could consider in due course. As regards voting for the Council, the right to do so should naturally apply to all adult residents with the proviso already mentioned of equalizing Jewish and Muslim members, and fixing a Christian share at perhaps a slightly lower level. This, again as already noted, will involve some election or selection from outside the Area.

Not all the economic problems can be foreseen, but a good start could be made by stipulating free trade with both Israel and Palestine; perhaps also Jordan. An alternative might be customs union with Israel and a carefully regulated free trade arrangement with Palestine; but this would be a second best, since it could appear discriminatory.

There are a number of problems that would be thrown up by the threefold division of greater Jerusalem. These should be overcome, if as soon as ever possible, a co-operative authority, as already suggested, could be set up comprising all three and taking responsibility for example for water and electricity supplies for the whole of the greater city. This could even be part of the treaty or treaties setting up the Area. The first organizations of the young European Community, and the Nile Waters Agreement between the Sudan and Egypt, might repay study.

Social and economic arrangements converge in such matters as currency and commercial law. On the first, we cannot at present know whether an independent Arab Palestine would agree to use Israeli currency or insist on its own (or use Jordanian). If the first, there will be no problem. If the second, the untidy but probably necessary answer might be to have both (Israeli-Palestinian/Jordanian) currencies legal in the Sovereign Area. The same solution as regards commercial law to be used by Jerusalem Arabs may prove to be a helpful precedent.

For both education and civil law, a dual Jewish and Arab system may be necessary at the start, with provision, mostly perhaps private, for non-Arab Christian children (no hindrance should be placed to their going to school outside the Area, for example to Notre Dame or St George's Cathedral College). Hopefully in due course, even if rather a long course, the resident population will grow together sufficiently for a unified system to become practicable. It would be highly desirable that the system of criminal justice should be united, at any rate after a short initial period. This is an area where expert legal advice under UN auspices could turn the trick.

Finance: possibly as in the Vatican, there will be no income tax at the start. But here again, the Sovereign Area should hopefully, before long, develop enough of a community spirit for a unified system of personal taxation to be acceptable. There could well be some initial funding from and through the faiths, with generous contributions from outside, hopefully by all three. This would be something like the Vatican's 'Peter's Pence'. There should probably be an initial Grant from the UN, since some members have few citizens from any of the three faiths, on a voluntary basis, through a Pledging Conference similar to the arrangements for UNRWA. This might have to be repeated from time to time for a while, but with any fortune not so frequently as for UNRWA, and not permanently.

The process of negotiation will certainly be complicated, and various delays are likely to take place. Since this is so, it would be wise to have a mechanism for interim arrangements: for example, as already noted, for the interim appointment of Consuls. One can envisage a situation where most arrangements were in place, and the key players precariously willing to co-operate, but delay could sabotage the whole enterprise. How this could best be done would be a task for the third stage, the Preparatory Conference. Both the UN and the European Community/Union have plenty of experience of negotiation against a deadline; the key is a will to agree.

The same Preparatory Conference will have to discuss, and find the basis for provisional agreement on, most of the subjects set out above. Perhaps all or at least many decisions should be open to review within a fairly short term of years. There should certainly be room for the elected Council, with the assent of the Consuls, to amend many of the detailed arrangements, and suggest new ones. There may also be a case for a renewed Treaty of Guarantee after ten or fifteen years.

How to get started

The official international phases for this are set out above in the section on the role of the 'United Nations'. But alongside the first phase of this, and even ahead of it, there will need to be convergent discussions within, and hopefully before long between, the faiths. Forums exist in several countries for co-operation between the three faiths. Within the Christian world, such organizations as the World Council of Churches should have a very useful role, even though it does not include some of the most important churches. There are other potentially helpful points of meeting, such as ARCIC (between the Roman Catholic and the Anglican Communions). In Jerusalem itself the three patriarchs have a convention of co-operation, and a wider body for consulting together also exists. It will be extremely important that the very senior dignitaries of all three faiths, from the Pope and the Orthodox Ecumenical Patriarch through the Chief Rabbis to the most respected Sunni leaders (since the suspension of the Caliphate there has not, of course, been an undisputed leader of Sunni Islam; but persons of the calibre of the Rector of al-Azhar and the Warden of the Shrines of al-Quds would be important) and the senior Ayatollahs of Shi'a Islam, are at least benevolently inclined to the convergent discussions, and hopefully ready to take part in them. The first two stages of the international secular negotiations should probably run nearly parallel with the faith ones. It is only when both these have made meaningful headway that the Preparatory Conference can be convened with any real hope of success.

The very first step, before the above, has to be the adoption of this whole enterprise, at the very least as something to be explored, by significant elements – at least a number of groups and individuals of influence – in all three faiths. Neither secular Governments nor the UN are at all likely to spark without this. The central purpose of this present paper is to appeal to the faiths as well as the secular world to look hard, and positively, at an enterprise of this sort.

This whole enterprise would of course be helped enormously by a withdrawal by both Israel and the Palestinians from their most extreme positions, notably withdrawal from the most provocative of the 'settlements' and a complete assurance that the defensive wall under construction will be dismantled when terrorist attacks cease, and on the Arab side the end to such attacks and the withdrawal of the full demand for a 'right to return' to former homes in Israel before 1948–9. But the faiths will probably need to get this process started even before the secular authorities on both sides manage these relaxations.

Summing up and conclusions

That the so dearly loved city of Jerusalem should be the source of such deep strife is a human and religious tragedy. Efforts have been made, over the long history of the city, to overcome the strife, by the ruling power extending genuine tolerance to other; by setting up a more or less independent city-state; and once by sharing the Old City by treaty. The present proposal tries to combine the second and third of these, for a limited area forming only a small part of greater Jerusalem, the Old City and the adjacent shrines.

At the least, a Sovereign Area shared by the three great monotheist faiths would have the benefit that no one is completely victorious and no one completely defeated. More positively, a successful Sovereign Area should give peace and security to all three faiths within Jerusalem, and should at least gradually reduce bitterness elsewhere, and make for wider peace. It could make the other causes of conflict between Israel and Arabs less hard to resolve. On a wider canvas, associating the faiths in a project of friendship in a place so dear and sensitive to them all, could bring them together in mutual respect and so reduce one of the deep tensions in the world.

Our present time has several advantages for attempting this. We have in the United Nations a mechanism, which should be able to help and buttress an enterprise of this sort more effectively than the League of Nations could do so in, say, Danzig. Some of the ways this could be done are suggested above. All that is said above about how a Sovereign Area might be run, and the extent of its territory, is of course no more than a blueprint, a basis for discussion; in rugby football terms, the scrum half putting the ball into the scrum. But the enterprise needs a start, and the present alarming situation calls for urgency.

The present Government of Israel and the leaders of Arab Palestine may well find it hard to countenance this proposal. But this cannot mean that suggestions like this, which go beyond tourniquets and try to solve key parts of the massive problem, should not be put forward. This surely cannot wait for ameliorations in the present Israeli-Arab conflict; hopefully, indeed, if and as it makes progress, it will contribute to amelioration. Some people may dismiss this project as hopelessly idealistic. So it is, unless a significant number of leaders and persons of influence in all three faiths are prepared to grasp it and run with it. They will meet opposition and perhaps anger from some of their own people, and some scepticism from the outside world. But there are enlightened circles in that world, both believers, members of other faiths, and freethinkers, who welcome and support an enterprise like this as a contribution to peace.

If enough of the leaders and influential people of the three faiths try to explore this proposal with determination and skill, it will I believe be found that it is not impossible at all. If we believers in Judaism, Christianity and Islam and can love the Lord our God with all our hearts and minds, we can initiate a move for human peace and goodwill that only these faiths together can make. The benefit to the international community and the wider world could be great indeed.

Annexe 1: On the extent of the Sovereign Area

The case for including the whole of the walled Old City is compelling. This is the place that holds many of the most beloved shrines of all three faiths. The only doubt that might arise is the Western or Wailing Wall, whose sanctity to the Jews is tremendous. It would be physically possible to link this with contiguous Israeli land just south of the Wall. But an exception is to be made. The Muslim case for excepting also the whole of the *Haram-al-Sharif* apart from the Wailing Wall would be very strong, given the enormous importance of especially the Dome of the Rock and the al-Aqsa mosque to Islam (they are second only to Mecca as objectives for pilgrimages). This of course would take the heart out of the whole enterprise. There has been an idea that there could be a vertical division of sovereignty. With the 'Wilson's Arch' area connected underground with the Western Wall, in Israel and the part of the courtyard of the *Haram* above it in Arab Palestine. This is ingenious, but would need such intricate border policing in a small sanctified area as to be brittle and difficult in practice. Including the whole *Haram-al-Sharif* and including the Western Wall in the Sovereign Area would be far more promising; to share physical control of the shrines carefully, and to police it sensitively should be exactly what the Consuls can best manage.

However, given that the Western Wall, Ha-Kotei Ha-Ma' aravt has since 1967 acquired great secular importance to the State of Israel as well as the Faith of Judaism – it has become the site of patriotic ceremonies and such as, in particular, the oath of allegiance by officers in the Israel Defence Force – there may be a case for especially imaginative treatment. One answer could be that the Treaty setting up the Sovereign Area might provide for a formal temporary resumption of Israeli sovereignty over this site on a prescribed and limited number of days each year.

The most extensive area of shrines outside the Old City – mainly but not entirely Christian – is just East of the Wall, on or near the Mount of Olives. The case for including these in the Sovereign Area is very strong indeed, and it could be fairly straightforward geographically. The boundary might start just north of St Stephen's Gate, taking in certainly Gethsemane and the Church of All Nations, and probably the Tomb of the Virgin and the Greek and Russian churches nearby: and further up the Mount Dominus Flevit, the Church of Paternoster and Chapel of the Ascension, and the tombs of some of the Jewish prophets. This could leave probably the summit of the Mount and certainly the Arab village of ai-Tur outside the Sovereign Area.

Annexe 2

There are several shrines in Bethany, now the Arab village of al-Azharriya, about a mile east of the Mount of Olives. If any of these were to be included in the Sovereign Area, that should be on the 'minimum scale', i.e. the shrines only, with no land around them (though of course with guaranteed access). This should also apply to the only point north of the Wall which has a strong claim to be included in the Sovereign Area; the Garden Tomb, just north of the Damascus Gate, St George's Cathedral and College, and also Notre Dame de France, both north of the Old City, should probably stay outside the Area, since they operate well and relate to the local communities, and have no long historical claim to be 'shrines'. The same applies to St Andrew's Church of Scotland, south west of the Old City.

There could be some case for suggesting that the Rockefeller Museum, just north of the Wall, which contains material important to all three faiths, might appropriately be included, even if still run by the Israel Department of Antiquities. Since the land outside the Wall immediately around the Museum is essentially Arab, this could be convenient. But it should not be pressed.

There should certainly be no extension of the Sovereign Area west of the Old City. This is the heart of Jewish Jerusalem, with many of the Israeli Government buildings, and there are few if any non-Jewish shrines (and some important, including modern, Jewish ones).

On the south side there is one small area which has strong claim to inclusion: the high ground just outside the south west angle of the Wall, which runs geographically with the Armenian Quarter of the Old City, and is separated from the land to the south and east, as well as west by quite deep valleys. It was within the Byzantine walls, and probably those of Saladin. It contains very important Christian shrines, such as the site of Jesus' last supper, and the Church of the Dormition; and one important Jewish one, the Tomb of David. It very probably acquired the name 'Mount Zion' by historical error, as the ancient city, which David gained from the Jebusites, where he brought the Ark, and made his capital, was certainly farther east. That whole area outside the Wall to the south and south east should obviously remain in Israel, outside the Sovereign Area, even if it includes some places associated with Jesus Christ, such as the Pool of Siloam.

One addition, suggested to the writer by a distinguished citizen of Jerusalem, is that in order to give some breathing space and to provide room for the necessary administrative staff (apart from the Consuls themselves, who would doubtless want to live in the Old City), the Augusta Victoria Hospital complex should be an enclave part of the Sovereign Area. This, given the lack of room in the crowded Old City, would certainly be a great advantage. There would probably be room for the UN agencies at present there as well; and indeed the UN, with its necessary involvement in the Sovereign Area, would probably welcome this. Augusta Victoria, as the first headquarters of the British Mandate, and located just south of the Mount Scopus area which will presumably be an Israeli enclave as in 1948–9, seems extremely well placed for this proposed role.

Annexe 3

What is proposed, therefore, apart from the enclave just mentioned, is that the Sovereign Area should be confined to the Old City with two very limited extensions to the east and south west; a compact, well-defined and contiguous area, with possibly one or two buildings, but without any land around them, outside. There could be a case for adding to these the Church of the Nativity in Bethlehem (but no part of the town outside it). The Christian shrines and churches in Nazareth and elsewhere in Galilee are too far away for inclusion, even as buildings, to be appropriate. The central principle must be that the Sovereign Area, while certainly having its own integrity, should obtrude on Israel and Arab Palestine to the least troublesome extent possible. Naturally this Annexe is a blueprint and subject to detailed negotiation.

Annexe 4

My recent stay in Jerusalem did not lead me to want to make any significant changes to the body of my text at this time. The central idea, of a Sovereign Area governed by three representatives, one from each faith, is, I remain certain, is the right one. To some extent, the Sovereign Area will be notional, in that its existence depends on the restraint of its neighbours. But this need not diminish its reality. Everyone loves, or at least has a high regard for, Jerusalem. A Sovereign Area, with the same existence and dignity as the Vatican, could be a hugely valuable construction. As stated before, it also carries the virtue that no one entirely wins the present confrontation, and no one is completely defeated. It therefore runs well with, and could be a natural part of, the negotiated peace between Israel and Arab Palestine which could be appearing on the horizon.

Furthermore, all three faiths are struggling in the world at large. A successful co-operation on Jerusalem would have to be of untold value.

The 'frontiers' between the Sovereign Area and both Israel and a Palestine state need to be kept as open as are those between England and Scotland, Canada and the USA, or the Vatican and Italy. The Jaffa and Damascus Gates of the Old City come immediately to mind. The openness of the borders of the Sovereign Area is vital, with people wandering in and out of these and other Gates, and up and down the Mount of Olives, at least as freely as now; and with permits to transit as liberal as ever possible. This should be compatible with a firm control by the police of the Sovereign Area of subversive persons, let alone terrorists. One would expect that, once a Palestine state is in being, co-operation between Israel and the state would be close and reliable: that being so manifestly in the interests of both. The authorities, including the police, of the Sovereign Area should fit into this without much difficulty. There will obviously be no possibility of an airport in the Sovereign Area, so that source of entry, with its problems, does not arise.

Admittedly the advance of the frontier of the Palestinian entity from beyond the Green Line, or with the new Wall even further into the West Bank, to points which run with the East and perhaps part of the North Wall of the Old City, would be seen by many in Israel as a diminution of security. But it need not be so. I am increasingly persuaded that the establishment of a Sovereign Area, and managing a provisionally and finally a firm peace between Israel and Arab Palestine, run together, and buttress each other.

The Extent of the Sovereign Area

My stay in Jerusalem leads me to feel that this should probably be somewhat more modest than is proposed in the Annexes above; but not much more. What has just been said, about the Sovereign Area and a firm peace running together, tends to reinforce the case for the Sovereign Area's boundaries to be slightly wider than the walls of the Old City. If, on the East side, a triangle of territory including Gethsemane and the Church of All Nations, and two-thirds of the way up the Mount of Olives to take in Dominus Flevit, but not any ground at the top of the mount (except possibly the Benedictine convent on a 'minimum' basis) were included, it would be obvious that the Sovereign Area was not making excessive claims; and the very awkwardness of the boundary, and its indefensibility, would mean that it had to be open. The Arab village of Al Tur will surely finish in the Palestinian state.

The main principle stands, that the Sovereign Area is essentially concerned with the walled Old City of Jerusalem; but does include the whole of that.

There are a few particular points:

West Wall
There could be a case for leaving the Citadel, with its splendid history museum, in Israel. But on balance, the Jaffa Gate is so thoroughly well defined a 'border' that it has to be right. Otherwise the Wall entirely.

Inside the Old City, the Western Wall of the Temple Mount/Haram–al–Sharif should, as suggested, revert to Israeli sovereignty on a limited number of days each year, such as the commissioning of Israeli Defence Force officers.

North Wall
Mainly the Wall itself, including the new gate and the Damascus Gate. The Garden Tomb, however, might form part of the Sovereign Area on the minimum basis, i.e. the site itself, no land around it. Whether the Rockefeller Museum might be included in the Sovereign Area probably depends on where the boundary of Israel and the Palestine state hits the North Wall. If that should be well west of the Museum, there is a case for the Museum to form part of the Sovereign Area.

East Wall
This is referred to above.

South Wall
This is the difficult one. The area now known as Mount Zion, although it surely has no connection with the original Mount Zion of David's time, contains a number of important shrines, both Christian and Jewish. It was certainly within Justinian's walls, and probably Saladin's. Geographically, it runs with the Armenian Quarter, and is separated by deep valleys to the west, south and east from the rest of Israeli south Jerusalem. The case for its inclusion in the Sovereign Area is strong. But it has been Israeli territory since 1948, not 1967, and this fact, plus its name, would clearly make it hard for Israel to accept its inclusion.

This should perhaps be left for negotiation after the Sovereign Area has been set up. The rest of the South Wall is a clear border.

Christian shrines
Away from the Old City, these shrines at Bethlehem and Bethany/ al Azariya should form part of the Sovereign Area on the minimum basis only. But the setting up of the Sovereign Area should certainly prove helpful to Bethlehem Christians.

The August Victoria Hospital
There remains the suggestion that this might very usefully be included in the Sovereign Area, to give some space for an administration, given the crowded nature of the Old City. The curious history of the Hospital compound, I am told by German Lutheran friends, could lead to legal problems, in that if a change of ownership were to take place, the Government of Israel could claim reversion to them. However the Lutherans personally support my proposal, and there is a distinction between sovereignty, ownership (which should remain with the international Luthrisch-Evangelische Kirchen) and use.

All this detail about boundaries is of course a tentative blueprint; it will depend on negotiation between the parties concerned. The key point is that the creation of a Sovereign Area could be a real factor in the pursuit of peace, and seems well worth putting forward at this time. It is offered as a building block. It is for governments, and even more for the people and the faith representatives of Jerusalem, to achieve the building; as Nehemiah did, in olden time.

Chapter 12

Christianity and Jerusalem: Present and Future Perspectives

+ *Michel Sabbah*
The Latin Patriarch of Jerusalem

1. On 14 November 1994, the heads of the Christian Communities in Jerusalem met to discuss the status of the Holy City and the situation of Christians there, at the conclusion of which, they issued a declaration, which until today expresses their common vision and stance. I quote the second paragraph, which introduces the whole declaration:

> Jerusalem is a holy city for the people of the three monotheistic religions: Judaism, Christianity and Islam. Its unique nature of sanctity endows it with a special vocation: calling for reconciliation and harmony among people, whether citizens, pilgrims or visitors. And because of its symbolic and emotive value, Jerusalem has been a rallying cry for different revived nationalistic and fundamentalist stirrings in the region and elsewhere. And, unfortunately, the city has become a source of conflict and disharmony. It is at the heart of the Israeli-Palestinian and Israeli-Arab disputes. While the mystical call of the city attracts believers, its present unenviable situation scandalizes many.
> (*Memorandum*, par 2)

The second important common stand of the Patriarchs of Jerusalem was their letter dated 17 July 2000, addressed to the three leaders gathered in Camp David: Clinton, Arafat and Barak.

2. To speak about Christianity and Jerusalem, we have always to bear in mind two forms of Christian presence and concern in Jerusalem, distinct but strongly united: the local and the universal, local Palestinian Christians and Christians from all over the world. Both are present in Jerusalem, and both are intimately linked

among themselves and with the Holy City.

This is to say that Jerusalem is the Holy City for all Christians in the world; locally or abroad. It is the city of their roots, it is historically the Mother Church. It was always the place of worship and daily living for local Christians. It was always a place of pilgrimage, worship and studies for Christians coming from all the Churches.

3. The universal presence in Jerusalem is manifest by the presence of religious communities from all over the world and from the several Churches; Catholic, Orthodox or Protestant. Many members of these communities spend their lives for the sake of Jerusalem and the mystery of Redemption which took place in it. They are not born there: but by their prayer, studies, charity, by their life and death in it, they become a part of Jerusalem.

Pilgrims to the Holy Places are another sign of this universality: we indeed consider them as an important part of world Christianity, and at the same time a part of our own dioceses in the Holy Land. Their presence is a support to our faith, and witnesses to the same Saviour, Jesus Christ, which is the main objective of all Christian presence, local or universal.

Lastly this universal presence is manifest in the growing attention of the world Churches to what is going on in the Holy Land today: to the local Christian presence and to the political conflict in the region. This situation requires the involvement of all Churches, because of their allegiance to Jerusalem, in the difficult quest for justice and peace.

Here I have to express special thanks for the large and generous solidarity shown to the Churches of Jerusalem, during these last months of suffering, by so many Churches, Catholic, Orthodox and Protestant, among which this Bishops' Conference of England and Wales was very significant.

4. The local Christian presence is small: it amounts to 2% of the total population of Jerusalem and the Holy Land. It was more substantial in some times past: in 1922, according to some sources, it was 51% in Jerusalem, and in 1947, it was still one third of the population of the Holy City. The proportion lessened in the following years, due to social, economic and especially political factors, i.e. the conflict between Palestinians and Israelis. Up until today, emigration, for this same political reason, is a phenomenon which is reducing more and more the proportion of Christians in Jerusalem and the Holy Land.

On this issue of emigration, our position as Churches is the following: Christians in the Holy Land are called by God to be **Christians in the Holy Land,** and not elsewhere in the world. Even when political instability makes daily life more difficult, Christians should be aware of their identity and mission, and remain where they are – where God wants them to be – and thus make their own contribution to the building of the future, together with and within their own Palestinian society. Christian emigration cannot be considered only from a 'human' point of view, or according to merely political perspectives. Christian presence, especially in Jerusalem and all the Holy Land, is part of the mystery of God in this land, who allowed, in His divine wisdom, Jews, Christians and Moslems to gather and to survive here over centuries. Therefore, any measure to achieve reconciliation in Jerusalem, to determine its present and future, must not ignore the dimension of the presence of God in this city, or the Christian Palestinians who are a part of that presence.

5. We local Christians are few in number. At the same time, we belong to many Churches, each of us bearing our own memories and wounds. Memories and wounds: we put them all together before the same Jesus Christ who has gathered us in the past, and gathers us today, around the places where he has redeemed and sanctified the world. Today, each one of these Churches, Catholic, Orthodox and Protestant, remain faithful to its faith, to its liturgy, and to its ecclesial traditions as received down the centuries. Each Church also shares in the same effort towards Christian unity in the city where all Christians were born. Indeed, we meet each other on many occasions. Fraternal spirit reigns among us, and common messages are addressed from time to time to our faithful.

The present and the future of Christians depends upon this fraternal spirit, and upon this common walk towards unity.

6. The Holy Places are a main component of the Christian presence in Jerusalem. From 1856, in the Congress of Paris after the Crimean War, then in 1878 in Berlin following another war between Russia and Turkey, the Status Quo was established to regulate relations between Christian communities in the Holy Places, mainly in the Holy Sepulchre and the Basilica of Bethlehem. This same Status Quo later passed to the League of Nations, then to the UN.

The expression 'status quo' means literally, 'Things are to remain as they are', without prejudice to the rights claimed by any party. This situation helped organize inter-Christian relations, as well as the duties of political leaders towards the Christian presence. Sometimes misunderstandings occur: but any such instance today is no longer powerful enough to separate any community from the general fraternal spirit prevailing among us all.

The status quo is already a kind of 'international law' which permeated Jerusalem, and which regulates the relations between Christians themselves with respect to the main Holy Places of Christianity. Successive governments, Ottoman, British Mandate, Jordanian, Israeli, have all so far respected these regulations as expressed by the Status Quo.

One day, once Jerusalem enjoys more quiet and peaceful times, this Status Quo needs to be revised, in order to create new mechanisms – once again, without any prejudice to any party. Only in this way can the present difficulties be overcome over the practical steps necessary to make improvements, to rebuild and repair, or to safeguard the honour and the reverence due to such places, and to prevent abuses by irresponsible or ignorant visitors.

7. The Christian presence is also a presence with Islam and with Judaism. Dialogue with Moslems is conducted on the basis that both Christians and Moslems are Palestinians, form one people with the same history and destiny, and hence share the same sufferings and aspirations. The day-to-day applications of such dialogue are continuously worked out as they affect action in the individual or public realm, and for all new legislation in every domain. Relations between Palestinians, Moslems and Christians constitute a permanent collaboration tending to build the best way of living together, despite those differences in belief that are manifested in many aspects of social life.

Many wish have imagined and wished for the creation of some formal Christian-Moslem institution, some body for reflection and creativity, in order to exchange views, to reconcile them, and to proceed together through the complications of daily life. It may sometimes happen, consciously or unconsciously, that religion becomes sometimes reduced to irrational feelings and reactions, on both sides, whether Christian or Moslem. In order to preserve the rationality and authenticity of our religious lives and relations, such a stable body will be very useful.

In this matter of Christian-Moslem relations, some would express their fear of religious extremism. When speaking about all kinds of extremism, one should see the whole reality: extremism and violence are born of situations of injustice, oppression, humiliation and poverty. Those who maintain such situations of injustice, humiliation and poverty a for violence. Another factor which invites the growth of religious fundamentalism or extremism is the religious vacuum that is expanding in the modern Western world. Therefore, in order to avoid dangers stemming form such 'extremism', leaders should work for more justice and equality among the peoples of the earth in general, and should work for a fuller appreciation of the presence of God in society. Specifically, in what concerns Palestine and Israel, leaders should work for the justice required by the Palestinians. Because justice for the Palestinians is the only way to assure security to all the region.

8. Interfaith dialogue with Jews. Many interfaith Christian-Jewish associations exist in Israel. Their dialogue continues the Christian-Jewish dialogue that started in the West after the Second Vatican Council. However this dialogue remains international, with a distinctively Western historical background. It does not engage with the daily lived realities of the region and it often ignores issues of peace and justice. A Jewish-Christian dialogue in Palestine and Israel should deal with the daily relations between Christian Palestinians and the Jews of Israel – and that means that it should deal with the issue of justice, peace and equality among all, based on religious values as well as on positive legislation.

9. Finally, local Christians are of course a part of the ongoing political conflict between Palestinians and Israelis. The role of this Christian presence is important, because it is echoed in the universal Church, in all the Churches of the world, and it is supported by a large chain of church solidarity and concern for Christians and for the Holy Places, these being the places of the Church's roots. Locally, Christian Palestinians are precisely **Palestinians**, hence their direct involvement in the conflict. Being Palestinians and Christians they call for justice and peace. This claim for justice means a claim for freedom, human dignity, and the right to an independent state. It means the end of the Israeli military occupation in Jerusalem and in all those Palestinian Territories occupied in 1967.

I have said that this claim is Palestinian. Nevertheless it is simply a claim for normal human rights, not special and not essentially different from the rights of any person or people in the earth, including the Jewish people. What the Jewish people achieved for themselves (freedom, an independent state), the Palestinian people should be also able to achieve (freedom, and an independent state). With this aim, the UN passed a number of resolutions, and with this aim peace talks started in 1993, following the Oslo agreement.

With regards to these relations between Palestinians and Israelis, and the necessity to put an end to the conflict, I would like to quote the words of H. H. Pope John Paul II, in his address to the diplomatic corps, on the occasion of the New Year. I quote:

> This light (of Christmas) signals the path of all who in our times in <u>Bethlehem</u> and <u>Jerusalem</u> are struggling on the road to peace. In this part of the world which received God's revelation to man there should be no resignation before the fact that a kind of guerrilla warfare has become an everyday event, or in the face of the persistence of injustice, the contempt for international law or the marginalisation of the Holy Places and the requirements of the Christian communities. Israelis and Palestinians can only think of their future together, and each party must respect the rights and traditions of the other. It is time to return to the principles of international legality: the banning of the acquisition of territory by force, the right of peoples to self-determination, respect for the resolutions of the United Nations Organization and the Geneva Conventions, to quote only the most important. Otherwise, anything can happen: from unilateral rash initiatives to an extension of violence which will be difficult to control.

9.1 Christianity and violence in Jerusalem. The Church, of course, does not support violence. Peace, and peaceful ways, can give birth to more peace. Unfortunately, all the nations of the world were born in wars and bloodshed. It seems that the Palestinian state is not different from all nations of the world. The Jewish state had its period of resistance and violence during the British mandate before 1948, after which the State of Israel was born. History makes all peoples equal in their refusal and condemnation of violence, and at the same time in their forced recourse to violence. Violence is to be condemned. But any form of oppression, of illegitimate military occupation is a form of violence and a direct invitation to violence. Will humankind be able one day to live without weapons and violence? Those days will be the days of the Second Coming of Christ, and the dawn of the Kingdom of God, when all earthly kingdoms will have their end.

Violence in Jerusalem is in direct contradiction to the nature and the call of the holy city. However, Jerusalem during its long history, though permeated by the mystery of God, has known many forms of violence. Although God wished it to be the city of reconciliation between human beings and God, and between human beings themselves, today it seems to be the **city of non-reconciliation**, or, to put it in a positive way, a city in which believers in the same God, – yes, He is the same God, Creator of all, Jews, Christians and Moslems – are desperately striving for a difficult reconciliation.

9.2. Concretely, the question of Jerusalem has a double aspect, political and religious. The political question is to be settled by both political parties involved, Palestinians and Israelis, on the basis of the above-mentioned principle, the removing of all forms of oppression and occupation begun in 1967, and on the basis of the international resolutions.

Once the political aspect of the conflict is settled, the second aspect, the religious aspect, can and must be approached. The holiness of the city, the patrimony of humankind, the Holy Places with all their historical requisites, are to be taken into consideration by political and religious leaders alike. As to the Christian Holy Places, Christian leaders of Jerusalem, representing all Christians, will speak with the political authorities. The political authorities will have to find the special means to ensure all that is needed to preserve the holiness of the city, to respect and safeguard historical and contemporary religious and civil rights, and to ensure freedom of worship and freedom of access at all times, whether of peace or war. The authorities will need to present this special regime for recognition by the international community, in order to guarantee its stability. This procedure is by no means the kind of internationalization that takes the property of the city or that property's control from the hands of its legitimate local governors; rather it permits the normal recognition by the international community required today for any lasting agreement.

9.3 'Christianity in Jerusalem' today means also the daily life of the local Christians of Jerusalem, with all the exigencies of life: not only freedom of worship, but dignity of life, and equal opportunities for all, to be ruled not according to the mere weight of the number of citizens but according to the equal right of every religion and every person to enjoy full freedom in the Holy City. Christians do not ask for privileges, or for a special protection. They are citizens and believers just like all other citizens. The only proper protection for all, Jews, Moslems and Christians, will be a set of non-discriminatory and just laws, because the nature of Jerusalem and its divine call cannot admit discrimination or exclusivism.

The Patriarchs and Heads of Christian communities concluded their 1994 document with these words:

> Jerusalem is a symbol and a promise of the presence of God, of fraternity and peace for humankind, in particular for the children of Abraham: Jews, Christians and Muslims. We call upon all parties concerned to comprehend and accept the nature and deep significance of Jerusalem, the City of God. None can appropriate it in exclusivist ways. We invite each party to go beyond all exclusivist visions or actions, and without discrimination, to consider the religious and national aspirations of others, in order to give back to Jerusalem its true universal character and to make of the city a holy place of reconciliation for humankind.

10. Conclusion Our future as Christians in Jerusalem will depend upon our present: on how we deal with Jerusalem, how much we accept it, and contribute to its building. It depends upon the awareness of local Christians themselves of their call: to be **the witnesses of Jesus Christ in His land**, to be Christians there, and as such to be an integral part of their society, Palestinian, Arab and Moslem; moreover to have a constructive and objective dialogue with Judaism and with Israeli society as a whole. Our future depends on our readiness to respond to this call and identity.

The conflict will come to an end one day. But authentic Christian life will always remain a struggle, in order to love and to build; a struggle for a constant ecumenical spirit, for a constant constructive inter-faith dialogue, for a constant action for justice and peace. Moreover Christians will remain a small number, but the small number will be also true believers, for whom religion consists of love, dialogue, sharing, building, and overcoming all kinds of difficulties.

We do not promise a quiet future to our faithful, but a difficult one, which needs a clear vision of our Christian identity and a strong will, in order to remain the living stones; to guard, with our prayers and our service to society, the Holy Places of our blessed land, and to welcome the whole Christian world.

+Michel Sabbah, Patriarch
London, 23. 01. 2001

(Some minor amendments in respect of English usage made by Frank Turner, SJ and approved by Patriarch Sabbah.)

Notes on Contributors

Michel Sabbah, The Latin Patriarch of Jerusalem 1987–2008. Elected in 1987, the first Palestinian Christian to be appointed since the revival of the Latin Patriarchate in 1847. An outstanding leader of the Christian community in the Holy Land who has written some of the most important contributions for Christian theological reflection on the present conflict in the Holy Land through his Pastoral Letters: *An Appeal for Peace for Jerusalem* (1990); *Reading the Bible Today In the Land of the Bible* (1993); *The Christians of the Holy Land Today and the Dialogue of the Religions* (1996); '*Seek Peace and Pursue it*' (Ps. 34 [33]; 15); *Questions and Answers on Justice and Peace in Holy Land* (1998).

David Neuhaus SJ, The Pontifical Biblical Institute, Jerusalem. He is an Israeli Jesuit who teaches in the Seminary of the Latin Patriarchate of Jerusalem and at Bethlehem University. He is also a research fellow at the Shalom Hartman Institute, Jerusalem. He completed a Ph.D. at the Hebrew University of Jerusalem in political science and degrees in theology and scripture in Paris and Rome. His publications include *Justice and the Intifada: Palestinians and Israelis Speak Out*, edited with Kathy Bergen and Ghassan Rubeiz, New York, Friendship House, 1991; *Kritische Solidarität: Einge Überlegungen zur Rolle privilgetierter Christinnen und Christen im Kampf der Enteigneten*, Aphorisma Kulturverein, Trier, 1995; and `L'Idéologie judéo-chrétienne et le dialogue juifs-chrétiens', *Recherches de Science Religieuse* (1997); 'A la rencontre de Paul: Connaître Paul aujourd'hui – changement de paradigme', *Recherches de Science Religieuse* (2002), as well as articles in reviews such as *Al-Liqa* (Encounter), *Pastoral Psychology* and *Mishkan*. He has recently completed work with Alain Marchadour, on the question of the Land from a biblical, traditional and contemporary Catholic perspective published as *The Land, the Bible and History: Toward the Land That I Will Show You*, Fordham University Press, 2008.

Charles H. Miller, SM, Professor of Theology at St Mary's University in San Antonio, Texas, USA, is a Marianist priest. He holds the S.Th.L. from the University of Fribourg, Switzerland; the S.S.L. from the Pontifical Biblical Institute of Rome, and the S.Th.D. from the Pontificio Ateneo di Sant'Anselmo, Rome. His teaching career included 1970–78 at Saint Louis University and 1979–present at St Mary's University. He served as Dean of Humanities and Social Sciences at St Mary's University 1987–99, and as Rector of the Ratisbonne Pontifical Institute – Centre Chrétien des Études Juives in Jerusalem 2001–3. He is the author of *'As It Is Written': The Use of Old Testament References in Vatican Council II* (1973). He has published in *ZAW, CBQ, The Bible Today*, is an abstractor for *OTA,* contributed forty-five entries to the *HarperCollins Bible Dictionary* and a paper on 'Hermeneutical Problems of Palestinian Christians Reading the Old Testament' in *ARAM,* Vol. 18–19, 2006–07.

Leon Menzies Racionzer, after a long career in business, completed postgraduate study and research into contemporary Christian-Jewish relations in the modern State of Israel at the Centre for Christianity and Interreligious Dialogue at Heythrop College, University of London. His publications include 'Christian communities in Contemporary Israel: A Study in Religion, Politics and Church-State Relations', in *One in Christ: a catholic ecumenical review* (2004); 'Hebrew Catholic Thought and Theology in Israel' *The Heythrop Journal* (2004); 'Christianity in Modern Israel', in *International Journal for the Study of the Christian Church* (2005). He is writing a monograph on Christian theological reflection in the modern state of Israel based upon the life and work of the Dominican scholar Marcel Dubois, OP.

Leonard Marsh is an Anglican priest to a London Parish. He has a specialist interest in the contemporary theological, especially Liberation Theology, and political movements within the Palestinian Christian community in Jerusalem and the Holy Land. He undertook postgraduate research and study at the School of Oriental and African Studies, University of London. He has published many articles on contemporary Palestinian Christianity and theology including 'Palestinian Christianity: A study in Religion and Politics' in *International Journal for the Study of the Christian Church* (2005); 'Palestinian Christians: Theology and Politics in the Holy Land' in *One in Christ: a catholic ecumenical review* (2004).

Michael Marten (University of Stirling) read Divinity at the Universities of Aberdeen and Erlangen, and wrote his Ph.D. on Scottish Presbyterian missions to Palestine at the University of Edinburgh. I. B. Tauris (London) is publishing a revised and expanded version of his thesis later this year under the title *Attempting to Bring the Gospel Home. Scottish Missions to Palestine, 1839 – 1917*. He has also published on Scottish missions in Lebanon, and is the editor of *Christian witness between continuity and new beginnings: modern historical missions in the Middle East*, a collection of essays published in 2007 in the series *Studien zur Orientalischen Kirchengeschichte* (LIT, Germany). He has recently been teaching Middle East politics at the University of London's School of Oriental and African Studies.

Sotiris Roussos is an Associate Professor at the University of the Peloponesse. He completed postgraduate research and study at the School of Oriental and African Studies, University of London entitled *Greece and the Arab Middle East: The Greek Orthodox Communities in Egypt, Palestine and Syria, 1919–1940*. His publications include, 'The Greek Orthodox Patriarchate and Community in Jerusalem: Church, State and Identity' in *The Christians communities in Jerusalem and the Holy Land: Studies in History, Religion and Politics* (2003); 'Patriarchs, Notables and Diplomats: The Greek Orthodox Patriarchate of Jerusalem in the modern period' in *Eastern Christianity: Studies in Modern History, Religion and Politics* (2003); 'The Greek Orthodox community in Jerusalem in international politics: international solutions for Jerusalem and the Greek Orthodox community in the 19th and 20th centuries' in *Jerusalem: Its Sanctity and Centrality to Judaism, Christianity and Islam* (1997).

Drew Christiansen, SJ Editor of the Jesuit weekly *America* and counsellor for international affairs to the United States Conference of Catholic Bishops. From 1991 to 98, he was director of the Office of International Justice and Peace of the USCC. With a doctorate in religious social ethics from Yale University, he has taught on the faculties of the Jesuit School of Theology at Berkeley, the Graduate Theological Union (Berkeley), and the University of Notre Dame. For his work on behalf of Palestinian Christians, he was invested in 1998 as an honorary canon of the Holy Sepulchre. His publications include 'Palestinian Christians: Recent Developments' in *The Vatican-Israel Accords: Political, Legal and Theological Contexts*, edited by Marshall J. Breger, Notre Dame, Indiana, University of Notre Dame Press, 2004; and the collection of papers which focus on 'forgiveness in conflict resolution', see William Bole, Drew Christensen and Robert T. Hennenmeyer (eds), *Forgiveness in International Politics: Alternative Road to Peace*, Washington DC., United States Conference of Catholic Bishops, 2004.

Nur Masalha Director, The Centre for Holy Land Studies, St Mary's College, University of Surrey. He has authored *Expulsion of the Palestinians. The Concept of Transfer in Zionist Political Thought, 1882–1948* (Washington, DC, The Institute for Palestine Studies, 1992); *The Palestinians in Israel* (ed.) (1993); *A Land Without a People: Israel, Transfer and the Palestinians, 1949–1996* (1997); *Imperial Israel and the Palestinians: The Politics of Expansion, 1967–2000* (2000); edited, *Catastrophe Remembered: Palestine, Israel, and Internal Refugees. Essays in memory of Edward W. Said* (2005). He is editor of *Holy Land Studies: a multidisciplinary journal*, Edinburgh University Press.

Robert Johnson has recently completed postgraduate study and research at the Centre for Christianity and Interreligious Dialogue, Heythrop College, University of London. He has a special interest in the theology and politics of the Jewish-Muslim-Christian Encounter. He has been lecturer in business studies at the University of London, University of Navarra and other international schools.

David Kitching is an Anglican priest and a vicar of six villages in Cambridgeshire. He formerly had a career for twenty-seven years as a British diplomat, during which time he served in numerous posts in the Middle East and Whitehall. For many years he has assiduously promoted an international regime for the Holy City, representing the 'Sovereignty of God'. He recently set out his proposals in the influential Israeli journal *Haaretz*.

Bård Mæland Senior Researcher and Staff Chaplain to the Chaplain in Chief, Norwegian Defence. Dr Mæland is the author of *Rewarding Encounters: Islam and the Comparative Theologies of Wilfred Cantwell Smith and Kenneth Cragg*, London, Melisende, 2003, and has published a book (in Norwegian) about the morality of Norwegian officers serving in KFOR, Kosovo 2000–2002 (*Wounded Idealism: The Morality of Norwegian Officers in Kosovo*, Bergen, Eide, 2004). He is also the founder and chief editor of *Journal of Military Ethics*.

Anthony O'Mahony Heythrop College, University of London. His specialist research interests are Christianity in the Middle East, Christian-Muslim Relations and the contemporary Christian theological and political thought. His publications include *Palestinian Christians: Religion, Politics and Society in the Holy Land* (1999); *The Christian communities in Jerusalem and the Holy Land: Studies in History, Religion and Politics* (2003); *Eastern Christianity: Studies in Modern History, Religion and Politics* (2003); with Michael Kirwan SJ, *World Christianity: Politics, Theology, Dialogues* (2004); *Christianity in the Middle East: Studies in Modern History, Theology and Politics* (2008); with Peter Bowe, OSB, *Catholics and Interreligious Dialogue: Studies in monasticism, theology and spirituality* (2006).

Index

Abitol, Michael 186
Abramson, G. 191, 194, 200, 212 n. 60, 213 n. 71
Abu Ghneim/Har Homa, Israeli settlement 105, 108
Aburih, Said K. 74
Abusahleih, Fr Raed 29 n. 51
Adang, Camilla 195
Alexander, Michael Solomon, Anglican Bishop of Jerusalem 43 n. 47
Alexandria, interfaith summit 235, 283–4
Algazy, Joseph 56
alien, resident *see ger toshav*
Amalekites, Palestinians seen as 160–3
Amir, Yigal 176
Anglican Church:
   and conversion of Jews 116, 117, 118
   and conversion of Muslims 117, 118–19
   and Greek Orthodox Church 99, 101
   indigenization 18, 115, 121–2, 125–6, 131–2
   and Jerusalem Sovereign Area 290
   presence in Holy Land 115, 116, 118–19, 120–2, 128–31, 246
   and Six Day War 125
   see also Sabeel
Anti-Defamation League 26 n. 5
anti-Semitism:
   and Cragg 252–3
   criticism of Israel seen as 38
   European 1–2, 4–5, 18, 77, 88, 163, 168, 199
   and Islam 196, 199
Appleton, George, Bishop of Jerusalem 125
al-Aqsa Mosque 9, 174, 217, 251, 271, 296
   access to 9, 275–6
   see also intifada, second
Arab nationalism 61–2, 70–3, 97–8, 106, 155, 198
   secular 97, 103–4

Arab–Israeli War (1967) *see* Six Day War
Arabic language 146–8, 186, 204
Arabs:
   Christian 2, 4, 8–10, 16–17, 20, 35, 49, 73–4, 82, 88
   and Greek Orthodox Patriarchate 92, 94, 96–109
   Israeli 2, 4, 8–10, 20, 56, 58, 73–4, 82
   and Israeli–Palestinian conflict *see intifada*
   Syrian 97
   see also Christians, Arab; Palestinians
Arafat, Yasser 52–3, 54, 64, 105, 107, 302
Ariel, R. Yisrael 156–7, 162
Ashkenazi Jews, and Gush Emunim 141
al-Ashmâwî, Mohammd Sa'îd 196
Ashwari, Hanan 72
al-Assal, Riah Abu, Anglican Bishop of Jerusalem 18, 29 n. 57, 49, 126
Ateek, Naim 70, 72, 75–83, 84–5, 88–9, 126–7
Ateret Cohanim 113 n. 47, 155, 157, 174
Attrash, Maher 57
Auschwitz, Jewish and Arab visit to 21
Aviner, R. Shlomo 155
'*avoda zara* (idolatrous worship) 164–8, 177
Awd, Mubarak 72
'Azran, Yosef 172

Balasuriya, Tissa 70
Balfour Declaration (1917) 70–1
al-Banna, Hasan 198
Bar Yosef, Hamutal 24
Barak, Ehud 52–4, 62, 302
Barth, Karl 75–6
Basic Agreement, Holy See and PLO 60, 64
Bebbington, David 116, 132 n. 1
Begin, Menahem 142, 200, 206
Beilin, Yossi 52, 53
Ben Gurion, David 14

Ben Nahum, Yonatan 30 n. 69
Ben Zvi, Yitzhaq 14
Benedictos, Greek Orthodox Patriarch of
  Jerusalem 103
Benveniste, Meron 104
Bertram, A. 102
Beth HaTefutsot (Diaspora Museum) 4
Bethlehem:
  Church of the Nativity 55, 63–4, 298
  and second *intifada* 56–7, 104
Bible:
  allegorization 80, 82
  and contextualization 80–2
  and critical methodology 81, 83, 88–9,
    220–1, 223
  and promised land 78–81
  and settler colonialism 159–63
  and typology 80–1, 82
Binfield, Clyde 117, 133 n. 11
Bishara, Azmi 26 n.14
Blake, William 265, 273
Blyth, G. F. Popham, Bishop in Jerusalem
  119, 121, 129
Bonar, Andrew A. and McCheyne,
  Robert Murray 133 n. 8
Bowman, G. 232
Bradley, Ian 116, 132 n. 2
Britain, and Sovereign Area of Jerusalem
  289–90
British Mandate in Palestine 71, 101–3,
  110, 120, 247, 260, 266, 273–4, 281,
  283, 285
Burleigh, J. H. S. 134 n. 23
Burrell, D. B. 191, 210, 212 n. 58

Camp David negotiations 26–7 n. 18,
  52–3, 302
Cappucci, Hilarion 29 n. 57
Carey, George, Archbishop of
  Canterbury 235, 284
Carter, Jimmy 206
Catechism of the Catholic Church 58, 227
Chacour, Elias 29 n. 63, 71–2
Chagall, Marc 257–8
Cheyette, Bryan 133 n. 7
Christ Church, Jerusalem 119, 125,
  129–30, 246
Christian Allies Caucus 10, 11
Christianity:
  as Abrahamic faith 185, 192, 244, 309
  common heritage with Islam 248
  dialogue with Islam 46, 63, 207–10,
    233–4, 305–6
  dialogue with Judaism 19–22, 24–5, 38,
    46, 63, 194, 209, 233–5, 306
  Hebrew-speaking 23
  as idolatrous 77, 144, 164, 171, 172, 191
  and Jerusalem Sovereign Area 266–7,
    282–4
  and Jewish–Muslim encounter 207–10
  and Judaism 207–10, 251–8
  and Maimonides 144, 147, 149–50,
    164–8
  as missionary faith 5, 8–9, 17, 31, 34,
    117, 122–3, 208
  and 'the Other' 247–8
Christianity, Jewish Israeli views 1–25
  and freedom of religion 7–12, 123, 229
  and *haredim* 171
  ignorance of 4, 5, 22, 34
  and Israeli–Palestinian conflict 16–19
  and Jewish–Christian dialogue 19–22,
    24–5, 38, 46, 63
  monochromatic view of history 4–5, 6
  negative attitudes 3–4, 5
  and new Christian Israelis 12–16
  rabbinical attitudes 163–4
  and Zionist fundamentalists 149–50,
    164–8, 171, 172
Christians:
  Arab 2, 4, 8–10, 16–17, 20, 35, 49,
    73–4, 82, 88
  emigration from Israel 36, 47, 49, 57,
    62, 73–5, 104, 131, 142, 303–4
  expatriate 2, 10, 11, 17–18, 19, 26 n. 14
  foreign workers 2, 16
  immigrant 2, 12–16, 32, 37
  indigenization of leadership 17–18, 48
  Israeli 4
  as minority in Israel 1–2, 4, 46, 82, 87
  Palestinian 9, 44–5, 56–9, 62–5, 93,
    96–103, 142, 157, 259–61, 303–6
Christodoulos, Archbishop of Church of
  Greece 107, 109–10, 114 n. 70
Chrysanthos, Metropolitan of Trebizond
  99–100
Chrysostomos Papadopoulos (later
  Archbishop of Athens) 98–9
Church of Greece *see* Greek Orthodox
  Church
Church Missionary Society (CMS) 117,
  118–19
Church of Scotland, presence in Holy
  Land 120–1, 122–3, 127–8, 131–2
Church's Ministry among Jewish People
  (CMJ) 119, 125, 130
citizenship:
  and Jerusalem Sovereign Area 281,
    286, 291
  Jewish Catholics 35
  and new Christian immigrants 12–13,
    16

and Zionist fundamentalism 157–8
Cleopas, Metropolitan of Nazareth 101–2
Clinton, Bill 53, 288, 302
CMJ *see* Church's Ministry among Jewish People
CMS *see* Church Missionary Society
Cohn-Sherbok, D. 189
Colley, Linda 133 n. 9
colonialism, settler 159–63, 276
Cone, James 69
Confraternity of the Holy Sepulchre 92–4, 96, 98–100, 102–3, 110
Congress of Patriarchs and Bishops of the Middle East, First (1999) 47, 65 n.9
Constantinople, Ecumenical Patriarchate 93, 95–6, 98–9, 110
contextualization:
  and biblical exegesis 80–2
  in Presbyterian theology 115, 120–1, 128, 131–2
conversion to Christianity 16, 31, 116–17
  of Eastern Christians 118, 120, 121, 129
  of Jews 116–17, 118, 119, 123
  of Muslims 117, 118–19
conversion to Islam 188, 192
conversion to Judaism 13, 14–15, 161
covenant, in Cragg 254–7
Cragg, Kenneth 207, 215 n. 138
  and creation 248–9, 255
  and forgiveness 82, 248, 259–61
  and inferiority and kenosis 258–9
  and Islam 187, 192, 213 n. 63, 247–51
  and Judaism 247, 251–8
  and Palestinian Liberation Theology 79, 82, 88
  and Palestinians 246–7, 259061
  and plural significance of Jerusalem 245–61
  and prophethood 248, 249–51
  and relationality and revelation 248–9, 251
  and Zionism 126
creation, in Islam and Christianity 248–9, 255
Crombie, Kelvin 134 n. 21
Crusades 46, 82, 149, 222, 265, 266, 271, 283
Cubain, Majib, Bishop of Jordan, Lebanon and Syria 134 n. 20
culture, Islamic Arab 23
Cyril of Jerusalem 222, 241
Cyrillos, Greek Orthodox Patriarch 94, 95–7, 110

Damianos, Greek Orthodox Patriarch 94, 97–103, 110
Daoud, Ignace 36–7
Darby, John Nelson 78
Davidson, Andrew Bruce 116, 132 n. 3
Dei Verbum 220–1
democracy, and Israeli state 7–8, 23, 177
dhimmi status 65 n. 3, 133 n. 15, 146, 154, 187, 191–2, 194, 197–8
dialogue:
  Christian–Muslim 46, 63, 207–10, 233–4, 305–6
  Jewish–Christian 19–22, 24–5, 38, 46, 63, 194, 209, 233–5, 306
  Jewish–Muslim 21, 183, 194, 205–7, 208
Diodoros I, Greek Orthodox Patriarch 55, 105, 113 n. 47, 233
discrimination:
  against non-Jews 6, 8–9, 23, 35–6
  against Palestinians 51–2, 308
dispensationalism, and Christian Zionism 77–8
Divino afflante Spiritu (Pius XII) 220
Dome of the Rock 174, 217, 271, 277, 296
Dreyfus, R. Yair 176
Druckman, R. Haim 162, 172
Druze:
  as Lost Tribe 14
  and military service 10
Dubois, Marcel, OP 26 n. 14, 39 n. 5, 40 n. 15
Durst, Stefan 129

East Jerusalem:
  as capital of Arab Palestine 268, 279, 287
  Christian Arabs in 2, 173–4
  Israeli occupation 103, 105, 108, 119, 125, 173–5
  and St George's Cathedral 121–2
Eban, Abba 274
ecumenism:
  and Anglican presence in Jerusalem 122, 126–7, 128–9
  and final status talks 52–3, 63
  and Great Jubilee 53–5, 233
  and Hasmonean Tunnel 50–1
  and Holy Sepulchre 54–5
  and human rights and justice 44–5, 47, 48, 50–3, 57–8, 59–62, 127, 303–4
  and *Memorandum on Jerusalem* 50, 232–3, 238–44, 302, 309
  and Palestinian residence in Jerusalem 51–2
  see also Sabeel

Edelstein, Yuri 12
election:
　in Islam 187
　in Judaism 21, 76, 81, 187, 189, 208, 224, 253–4, 256
Elichai, Jochanan 34, 40 nn. 16, 19
Eliyahu, R. Mordechai 174, 176
Ellis, Marc 84, 85–6
Ethiopia, Christian immigrants from 2, 12, 14
evil, in Cragg 255–6, 258–9

Falasha Mura 28 n. 40
Falashas, Ethiopian 14
Falwell, Jerry 77, 78
Filastin (newspaper) 97, 102–3
Fiorenza, Joseph 52
Fisher, Geoffrey, Archbishop of Canterbury 274–5, 279
Flannery, Edward 41 n. 29
forgiveness:
　in Cragg 82, 248, 259–61
　and Palestinian theology 45, 82, 89
Franciscan Custody 18
Frederick II, Emperor 271–2
Free Church of Scotland, presence in Holy Land 119
freedom, religious 7–12, 16, 19, 60, 64, 123, 229, 242
Freij, Elias 72
Freire, Paulo 89
Friedmann, Yohanan 190–1, 192–3, 202–3, 214 n. 115
Fundamental Agreement, Israel–Vatican 60, 62, 228–9
fundamentalism, Christian, and Zionism 77–8, 162
fundamentalism, Jewish 138–77
　and Christianity 171, 172
　divisions between 168–71
　and *halacha* 138–9, 140–1, 151–3, 161–2, 177, 204
　and Palestinian Christians 142–3, 150

Gafni, Shraga 160
Galford, H. 191, 212 n. 59
Gaudium et Spes 60
Gaza:
　Israeli occupation 72, 73, 103
　as Palestinian state 87, 176
genocide, against Palestinians 161, 162–3
ger toshav 25 n. 2, 151, 153–9, 163, 172, 177
Germanos, Greek Orthodox Patriarch 94
Germanos, Metropolitan of Thyateira 99–100

Gobat, Samuel, Anglican Bishop in Jerusalem 134 n. 18
Golan, Gadi 42 n. 37
Goldstein, Baruch 86
Gori, Albert, Latin Patriarch of Jerusalem 32
Gourion, Dom Jean-Baptiste 15, 33, 38, 42 n. 32
Gräbe, Uwe 136 n. 52
Graham, Keith 94
Great Jubilee 53–5, 223, 233
Greece, and support for Patriarchate in Jerusalem 100–2, 105, 107, 109
Greek Orthodox Church:
　and Anglican Church 99, 101
　and Greek government 107
　scandals in 108
Greek Orthodox Patriarchate of Jerusalem viii, 71
　and Arab Orthodox 92, 94, 96–109
　and Church–state politics 27 n. 23, 92–110
　and dialogue with Jews 65 n. 8
　expatriate leadership 18, 49, 63, 92, 103–5
　finances 100–3
　and guardianship of Holy Places 55–6, 92–4, 96, 100–2, 107, 109–10
　Israeli influence in patriarchal election 106–7
　in Istanbul 95, 9203
　land holdings in Israel 11, 49, 96, 101–2, 104–5, 107–10, 129, 175
　monastic nature 49, 92, 98
　and Ottoman Empire 92–9
　and Palestinian Authority 105–6
　and Roman Catholic Church 54–5
　and Russian influence 95–7, 98–9, 106, 110, 273
　see also Cyrillos; Damianos; Germanos; Ireneios
Grossman, David 30 n. 69
Grünschloss, Andreas 258
Gush Emunim (Bloc of the Faithful) 125, 139
　and *halacha* 142, 151–2
　and *haredim* 169–70
　and importance of land 168, 170, 176, 200–2, 204–5
　and Maimonides 144
　and Palestinians 153–9, 168, 175–6
　political influence 142
　and West Bank settlements 139, 141–2, 151, 200

Habash, George 103

Haddad, Faik Ibrahim, Bishop in
  Jerusalem 119, 125
Hagar, Moshe Ben-Yosef 172
halacha:
  and '*avoda zara* 164–8
  and Christians in Israel 171
  and ger toshav 153–9, 177
  and Gush Emunim 142, 151–2
  and haredim 170–1, 172, 204
  and Jewish fundamentalism 138–9,
    140–1, 151–3, 161–2, 177
  and Maimonides 139, 144, 145, 150,
    162, 167, 172–3, 204
  and Muslims 188
Halamish, Aharon 161
Haleem, Muhammad A. 186
HaLevy, R. Hayyim David 3–4, 6
Halperin, David J. 184, 190, 212 n. 50
Halsell, Grace 78
Hamas 74, 87, 198–9
Hammer, Joshua 64
Hanna, Atallah 29 n. 57, 109
haredim:
  and Christianity 171
  and Jewish fundamentalism 138–9,
    168–71, 172–3
  and Maimonides 169, 204
  and Palestinians 170–1, 173, 204
Harkabi, Yehoshafat 140
Hartman, David 30 n. 66, 189, 204, 212
  n. 44
Harvey, A. E. et al. 209, 215 n. 148
Hasmonean Tunnel 50–1
Hastings, Adrian 94
Hebrew:
  as liturgical language 23, 33, 35
  in medieval world 147–8, 186
Hebrew Catholicism:
  cultural issues 33–6
  ecclesiological issues 36–8
  and inculturation 23, 37–8
  number of adherents 31
  origins 32–3
  statutes 34
Hebrew University of Jerusalem, Centre
  for the Study of Christianity 22
Hebron Massacre (1994) 86–7
Heilman, Samuel 205–6
Heim, S. Mark 263 n. 29
Hellwig, Monica 207–8
Henné, Jean-Roger 39 n. 6
Herzl, Theodor 224
Heschel, R. Abraham 256, 257, 262 n. 8
Hess, R. Yisrael 160–1, 162–3
Hick, J. 263 n. 29
Higton, Tony 130

Hillel, Shlomo 158–9
Hitti, Philip K. 143
Holocaust 2, 4–5, 21, 34, 46, 53, 77, 88,
  123, 193
  in Cragg 255–6
Holy Land:
  Christian presence in 51, 57, 62–5,
    226–7, 241–3, 302–4, 306–9
  and Jewish–Muslim encounter
    183–210
Holy Places:
  access to 9, 19, 225–7, 228, 234, 242,
    304–5, 308
  and Greek Orthodox Patriarchate
    55–6, 92–4, 96, 100–2, 107, 109, 110
  Muslim 9, 107, 217
  pilgrimage to 11, 94, 96–7, 104, 122,
    209, 222–3, 241–2, 303
  and Sovereign Area of Jerusalem
    277–80, 285, 295–6, 297
Holy See:
  Basic Agreement with PLO 60, 64
  and control of Christian Holy Places
    107
  Fundamental Agreement with Israel
    60, 62, 229
  and Jerusalem 224–7, 228–30
Holy Sepulchre 271, 273, 277
  Christian access to 9, 175
  and Greek Orthodox Church 94–5
  restoration of dome 54–5
housing, Palestinian 51–2
human rights, Christian commitment to
  44–5, 47, 48, 50–3, 59–62
Hummel, Thomas 122, 135 n. 28
Hussar, Bruno, OP 26 n. 14

Ibn Tibbon, Yehuda 149
identity:
  Arab 97
  Jewish 5–6, 10, 16, 23, 140, 151, 155,
    177, 189–90, 203
  Muslim 190–1, 201, 203, 208
  Palestinian Christian 34, 44–65, 74–5,
    84, 87–8, 102, 106
IDF *see* Israeli Defence Force
idolatry, and Christianity 144, 164–8,
  171, 172, 177, 191
Ignatius of Antioch 252–3
Imperial Orthodox Palestine Society 95
inculturation 62
  and Hebrew Catholics 23, 37–8
indigenization, and Anglican Church 18,
  115, 121–2, 125–6, 131–2
International Christian Embassy,
  Jerusalem 77

The Interpretation of the Bible in the Church 220
intifada:
  economic effects 104
  first (1987–93) 44, 46, 48, 72–4, 126
  and non-violence 58–9, 62, 72, 82
  and Palestinian Christian identity 34, 44–65, 74–5, 84
  and residency in Jerusalem 51–2
  and *Sabeel* 84–7
  second (2000–) 6, 16–19, 34, 46–7, 55–9, 62–3, 87, 104, 132, 223
Ireneios I, Greek Orthodox Patriarch 29 n. 55, 94
  deposition 109–10
  and Greek Orthodox land holdings 107–8
  and Palestinian Authority 49
  recognition by Israel 27 n. 33, 49–50, 59, 106–7
Islam:
  as Abrahamic faith 183, 185, 192, 194, 197, 244, 309
  and Christianity 207–10
  common heritage with Christianity 248
  common heritage with Judaism 183–5
  conversion to 188
  and Cragg 187, 192, 213 n. 63, 247–51
  dialogue with Christianity 46, 63, 207–10, 233–4, 305–6
  dialogue with Judaism 21, 183, 205, 209, 233
  and Jerusalem Sovereign Area 266–7, 282–4
  and Judaism 5, 143–4, 145–8, 164, 168, 193–9, 205
  and land of Israel–Palestine 199–202, 209
  and Maimonides 143–4, 145–8, 164, 167–8, 193, 203–4
  and monotheism 5, 164, 167–8, 184, 191
  Muslim Holy Places 9, 107
  points of dispute with Judaism 187–8
  self-definition 190–1, 207–8
  and State of Israel 195–6, 197–8
  and 'the Other' 188–95, 247–8
Islamic Liberation Party 201–2
Islamism, and importance of land 201
Israel:
  and Christian Zionism 77–8
  Christians as minority 1–2, 4, 46, 82, 87
  as democratic state 7–8, 23, 177
  Fundamental Agreement with Holy See 60, 62, 229
  and Islam 195–6, 197–8
  and Israeli identity 5–6, 7, 140, 151, 155, 177
  Jewish views on Christianity 1–25
  as Jewish state 7–8, 11–12, 15, 22–3, 33, 199
  Office of Christian Communities' Affairs 51, 55, 68 n. 50
  Religious Affairs Ministry 26 n. 18, 53, 62
  religious and cultural diversity 1, 35
  see also land of Israel–Palestine
Israel Trust 119
Israeli Defence Force (IDF) 55, 161, 296, 300
Israeli–Palestinian conflict 16–19, 33, *see also intifada*
ITAC Response to the Anglican Peace & Justice Statement 130

Jackson, B. S. 199, 214 n. 101
Jerusalem:
  Anglo-Prussian bishopric 118–19
  as capital of Israel 239, 267, 279, 287
  in Catholic political thought 224–7
  and Christianity 240–3
  in contemporary Catholic thought 223–4
  in Cragg 250–1, 257, 260–1
  history 269–76
  as holy city 217–18, 219, 221–6, 229, 241–2, 265, 302, 308
  and Islam 201, 250–1
  Israeli dominance in 104, 108
  in New Testament 221–2, 224, 240–1
  in Old Testament 219, 222, 224
  Palestinian residency 51–2, 172–3, 174, 276
  partition 275
  in patristic thought 222–3
  as secular city 218
  as sign of hope 235–6, 244, 309
  significance for three faiths 50, 225, 228–30, 234, 238, 243, 245–61, 302
  Sovereign Area 266–70, 276, 277–85
    and citizenship 281, 286, 291
    and Consuls 266–8, 281, 282–6, 289, 291, 293, 296
    Council 267, 279, 281–2, 283–6
    extent 277–80, 291, 295–8, 299–301
    financing 289, 292
    practical problems 291–3
    security 286
    and United Nations 267, 270, 274–5, 278–80, 282, 285–6, 287–90, 292–3

Vatican State precedent 280–2, 286, 287, 291
Western Wall 3, 54, 265, 275, 277, 286, 296
see also al-Aqsa Mosque; Dome of the Rock; East Jerusalem; Holy Places; Holy Sepulchre; Temple
Jerusalem Reclamation project 174
Jesus, Jewish attitudes to 5
Jewish Defense League (US) 156
Jewish National Fund (JNF) 175
Jews, peaceful co-existence with Muslims 185–8
John Paul II, Pope:
  and biblical exegesis 220–1
  and Christians in Holy Land 47
  and conflict resolution 62
  Holy Land pilgrimage (2000) 3–4, 22, 25, 40 n. 13, 53–4, 55, 307
  Pastores Gregis 229
  and State of Israel 224
  Tertio Millennio Adveniente 53
John XXIII, Pope, *Pacem in terris* 60
Johnson, Howard A. 75
Joint Institute for Jewish Studies (Israel) 14
Jordan, and Palestine 103, 106–7, 216, 274
Jowett, William 117
Judaism:
  as Abrahamic faith 183, 185, 192, 197, 244, 309
  Arabic-speaking 23
  and Christianity 24, 207–10, 251–8
  common heritage with Islam 183–5
  conversion to 13, 14–15, 161
  and Cragg 247, 251–8
  dialogue with Christianity 19–22, 24–5, 38, 46, 63, 194, 209, 233–5, 306
  dialogue with Islam 21, 183, 194, 205–7, 208, 233
  and Islam 5, 143–4, 145–8, 164, 168, 193–9
  and Jerusalem Sovereign Area 266–7, 282–4
  Jewish Israeli views on Christianity 1–25, 163–4
  Liberal 21
  under Muslim rule 145–7
  Orthodox 7, 12, 14, 21, 123, 124, 145, 164–6, 169
  points of dispute with Islam 187–8
  Reform 82, 124, 145
  religious and cultural diversity 1, 35
  self-definition *see* identity
  settler 139, 159–63
and 'the Other' 188–95
see also land of Israel–Palestine
justice, Christian commitment to 44–5, 47, 48, 50–3, 59–62, 127, 306

Kabha, Mustapha 103
Kach ('Thus') movement 156, 157, 177
Kafity, Samir, Anglican Bishop of Jerusalem 72–3, 126–7, 129
Kahane, R. Meir 156–9, 173
Kakoyiannis, Arsenois, Archimandrite 99, 100
al-Kamal al-Din 271–2
Kee, Alistair 76
kehilla see Hebrew Catholicism
Kenney, T. J. 198, 214 n. 90
kenosis, in Cragg 258–9
Khalaf, Karim 162
Khalidi, Rashid 71, 97
Khoury, Elia 29 n. 57, 134 n. 21
Khoury, Fawzi 29 n. 57
Klein, M. 190, 212 n. 51
Knesset:
  building 107–8
  Christian Arab members 26 n.14, 176
  Zionist members 158–9, 162, 171, 172, 173, 275
Knitter, Paul F. 263 n. 29
Kollek, Teddy 173, 275–6
Kook, R. Abraham Yitzhak HaCohen 141, 169
Kook, R. Tzvi Yehuda 124, 141, 151–3, 155, 160, 169, 174
Kramer, M. 194, 199, 213 n. 72, 214 n. 98
Kraybill, Donald 85
Kronish, Ron 22
Kuschel, Karl-Josef 185, 199, 214 n. 100
Kuttab, Jonathan 72

Laham, Lufti, Greek Catholic Archbishop 72–3
land of Israel–Palestine:
  and Christianity 209
  and Islam 185, 197–8, 199–202, 209
  and Zionism 162, 165, 168, 170–2, 174, 176, 203–5
Landau, Y. 3, 26 n. 6
Langer, R. 203, 207, 214 n. 118
Latin Patriarch of Jerusalem *see* Sabbah, Michel
Law of Return 12–13, 35–6
Lebanon, and Cragg 246–7
Leibowitz, Yesha'ayahu 140, 152, 177
Leor, R. Dov 176
Levinger, R. Moshe 168
Levy, R. Yitzhak 176

Lewis, Bernard 199
liberation theology, Palestinian 69–89
  and biblical exegesis 78–83, 88–9
  and Christian Zionism 75–8
  and *Sabeel* 84–7
literalism, biblical 79–80, 116–17, 149–50, 220–1, 223–4
LJS *see* London Jews Society
Lohse, W. 222, 236 n. 10
London Jews Society (LJS) 118
Lopatin, Asher 189–90, 194–5, 213 n. 74
Lorberbaum, M. 25, 30 n. 74
Luther, Martin 82–3

Macanna, Clephane R. 123–4
Mackie, Robert 135 n. 30
Magonet, Jonathan 189, 193, 196, 198, 205–6, 207, 212 nn. 46,49, 213 n. 70, 214 n. 85
Mailula, Mike 86
Maimonides, Moses:
  and Christianity 144, 147, 149–50, 164–8
  and *ger toshav* 153–4, 172
  The Guide of the Perplexed 148–9, 169
  and *halacha* 139, 144, 145, 150, 162, 167, 172–3, 204
  and idolatry 166–7
  and Islam 143–4, 145–8, 164, 167–8, 193, 203–4
  and Jerusalem 174
  and Jewish fundamentalism 138–9, 150–1, 162, 176–7, 203–4
  and Jewish identity 189–90
  and Jewish nationalism 143–5, 169
  medieval context 144, 145–50, 167
  Mishneh Torah 145, 148–9, 172–3
  and Palestinians 160, 172–3, 174
  as philosopher 145–9, 152, 169, 204
  as theologian 149–50, 152, 169, 176–7
Mar Elias Monastery, land 108
Marcuzzo, Boulos-Giacinta 29–30 n. 63
Masalha, N. 203, 204, 212 n. 40,189, 214 n. 120
Massignon, Louis 208, 209
Matossian, Martyos 175
Mavrogordatos, George 100, 107
al-Mawdûdî, Sayyid 198, 201
Meged, Aharon 30 n. 69
Meged, Eyal 30 n. 69
Melchior, R. Michael 29 n. 58, 235
Meletios Metaxakis, Archbishop of Athens 98–100
Memorandum on Jerusalem (1994) 50 232–3, 238–44, 302, 309
Menocal, Rosa 188

Meron, Dan 177
Messianic Jews 13, 15, 31, 40 n. 20
messianism, Zionist 138, 139, 141, 150–2, 157, 162, 169–70, 174, 176, 204
Middle East Council of Churches (MECC) 129
millenarianism 77–8, 116
millet system 44, 92, 100, 118
Min-Harar, R. Shlomo 168
mission:
  anti-missionary law (1977) 8
  see also Christianity, as missionary faith
monotheism:
  of Christianity 191, 205, 207
  of Islam 5, 164, 167–8, 184, 191
  of Judaism 5, 146, 149, 164, 184, 191, 197
Mor, Uri 51, 55
Moral Majority, and Christian Zionism 77
Morton, Colin 127–8
Mouallem, Boutros, Melkite Archbishop for Galilee 67 n. 42
Musgrave, Clarence 136 n. 47
Muslims, peaceful co-existence with Jews 185–8
Mussolini, Benito 280–1
Myers-Weinstein, D. 189, 212 n. 39

Al-Nakba (the Catastrophe) 71, 121, 123
Nasr, S. H. 208, 215 n. 147
National Christian Coalition 109
National Religious Party (NRP; Mifdal) 139, 141, 153, 162, 169–70, 176
nationalism:
  Greek 100, 110
  Israeli 124–6, 139, 141, *see also* Zionism
  Palestinian Arab 61–2, 70–3, 97–8, 102–3, 106, 155, 198
  Syrian Arab 97
Natour, M. 187, 211 n. 29
Navon, Yitzhak 140
Netanyahu, Binyamin 50, 51, 67 n. 42, 142
Nettler, R. 196, 208, 215 n. 145
Neuhaus, David 34, 40 n. 17
Neusner, J. 189, 190–1, 253
Nevo, J. 198, 214 n. 92
New Testament:
  and Jerusalem 221–2, 224, 240–1
  and Jewish fundamentalism 172
Nielsen, Jørgen S. 133–4 n. 15
Nikolaos, Metropolitan of Axoum 99–100
Nisan, Mordechai 153–5
Nostra Aetate 46, 224
NRP *see* National Religious Party

Index

Nüsse, A. 195, 197, 199, 201, 213 n. 79, 214 nn. 87, 95, 110

Œuvre de Saint Jacques l'Apôtre 14–15, 31
  liturgical use of Hebrew 35
  as non-missionary 31, 33
  origins 32–3
Old Testament:
  allegorization 80, 82
  Christocentric approach to 81–3, 88, 163
  historical-critical view 220–1
  and history of Jerusalem 269–70
  and Jerusalem 219, 222, 224
  and Jewish fundamentalism 172
  and Palestinian liberation theology 80, 81–3, 88, 126
  prophetic tradition 82–3
  and settler colonialism 159–63
  and typology 80–1, 82
Olmert, Ehud 173
O'Mahony, A. 207–8, 215 n. 143
Oriental Catholic Churches 32, 37, 44, 66 n. 10
Oslo Accords 44, 50–1, 104–5, 175–6, 307
Ottoman Empire:
  and Greek Orthodox Patriarchate 92–9
  and Jerusalem 273
  millet system 44, 92, 100, 118

Pacem in terris (John XXIII) 60
Pacini, Andrea 73
Palestine:
  and Arab nationalism 97–8, 102–4, 106
  British Mandate 71, 101–3, 110, 120, 247, 260, 266, 273–4, 281, 283, 285
  and Jerusalem 239
  and Jordanian rule 103, 106, 216, 274
  seen as Jewish home 117
Palestine Liberation Organisation 107, 198
Palestinian Authority:
  criticisms of 61, 176
  and Palestinian Christians 142–3
  and Patriarchate of Jerusalem 49, 105–7, 109
  and rights of Christians 64
Palestinian Territories:
  Christians in 2, 16–17, 108, 306
  and *Gush Emunim* 155
  and *intifada* 34, 44–65
Palestinians:
  Anglican 125–6, 130, 247
  and biblical exegesis 78–83, 88–9
  in Christian Zionism 75–8, 88
  and Cragg 246–7, 259–61
  discrimination against 51–2
  and emigration 51–2, 57, 62, 73–5, 104, 131, 142, 161, 303–4
  as *ger toshav* 153–9, 163, 172, 177
  Greek Orthodox 93, 96–109
  and haredim 170–1, 173, 204
  identity 34, 44–65, 74–5, 84, 87–8, 102, 106, 142
  in Jewish Zionism 69, 71–2, 97, 138–9, 142–3, 150–9, 200
  and John Paul II 54
  and national homeland 54, 61, 87, 230, 306–7
  and nationalism 61–2, 70–3, 97–8, 102–4, 106
  residence in Jerusalem 51–2, 172–3, 174, 276
  seen as Amalekites 160–3
  see also liberation theology; Sabbah, Michel
Pastores Gregis (John Paul II) 229
Paterson, Alexander 119
Paul VI, Pope 224
People of the Book 146, 187, 191, 192, 194, 196
Peretz, Yair 27 n. 22
Phanariotes, and Greek Orthodox Patriarchate 93, 95–6
pilgrimage:
  to Holy Places 11, 94, 96–7, 104, 122, 222–3, 241–2, 303
  and local Christians 231–2
Pius XI, Pope 280–1
Pius XII, Pope, *Divino afflante Spiritu* 220
Pizzaballa, Rierbattista–OFM 29 n. 56
pluralism, universalistic 45, 253
politics:
  and Christian Palestinians 103–4
  and *haredim* 170
  and human rights 45–6, 48, 51, 59, 61–2
  and religious Zionism 140–2
Pontifical Biblical Commission 220–1, 223–4, 226
Popular Front for the Liberation of Palestine 103
Presbyterian Church:
  and conversion of Jews 116–17, 119, 123
  presence in Holy Land 115, 116, 119–20, 127–8, 131–2
Prior, Michael 69, 73, 78–9, 85, 124–6, 130, 220
Procopios, Greek Orthodox Patriarch 96

prophethood, in Islam and Christianity 248, 249–51
Protestantism:
  and Christian Zionism 17
  and conversion of Jews 116–17
  and Evangelicalism 17, 116–17
  and Messianic Jews 13, 15
  see also Anglican Church; Presbyterian Church
Protocols of the Elders of Zion 199

Qutb, Sayyid 187, 198, 201

Rabin, Yitzhak 176, 200
Rabinovich, Nahum 176
racism:
  European 119
  Israeli 157, 177
Radford Ruether, Rosemary 76–7, 84
Ram, Uri 135 n. 38
Rashi (R. Shlomo Itzhaki) 156–7
Ratzinger, Joseph (later Pope Benedict XVI) 36
Ravitsky, Avi'ezer 140
redemption, and covenant 254–7
relationality and revelation, in Islam and Christianity 248–9, 251
religion, freedom of 7–12, 16, 19, 60, 64, 123, 229, 242
religion and state 7–8, 35, 59
  and Anglican diocese of Jerusalem 126
  and Greek Orthodox patriarchate 27 n. 23, 92–110
  and Zionism 139–40
Riegner, Gerhard 53
Robinson, R. B. 220
Roman Catholic Church:
  and biblical exegesis 220–1
  and Christian Zionism 17
  and Christian–Jewish dialogue 20, 38, 46
  and conversion of Jews 31
  and Greek Orthodox Church 54–5
  and Hebrew Catholicism 31–8
  and Jerusalem 223–4
  in political thought 224–7
  Jewish Israeli perceptions 2–3, 4–5
  and justice and human rights 45–6, 59–62
Rosenthal, Franz 147
Ross, Robin 127
Rowland, Christopher 84
Rubinstein, Amnon 161, 162
Rubinstein, Danny 29 n. 51
Rufeisen, Oswald (Fr Daniel) 13, 40 nn. 19, 21

Russia:
  and immigration to Israel 2, 12, 15, 35–7, 108
  influence on Greek Orthodox Church 95–7, 98–9, 106, 110, 273
Russian Orthodox Church 15

Saadoun, A. 186–7, 211 n. 28
Sa'adia ben Yosef Gaon 146, 147–8
Sabbah, Michel, Latin Patriarch of Jerusalem 20, 24, 33, 37–8, 65 n. 8, 216–36
  accused of supporting terrorism 17
  and Christianity and politics 44–5, 48, 49, 51, 57, 61, 228–30
  ecclesial/pastoral thought 230–2
  and ecumenical thought 232–3
  and interfaith dialogue 233–5
  and intifada 44–5, 48, 49, 51, 57, 61, 72–3
  and Memorandum on Jerusalem 50, 232–3, 238–44, 302, 309
  and Palestinian Authority 61
  perspectives on Jerusalem 302–9
  theological thought on Jerusalem 227–35
Sabeel 84–7, 126–7
Sabella, Bernard 74
Sactouris, Antonios 100–1
Sadat, Anwar 206
Safie, Diana 44
Said, Edward 85
St George's Cathedral, Jerusalem 119, 121–2, 125–6, 128, 129, 246–7
St John's Hospice (Jerusalem) 175
Sakakini, Khalil 111 n. 22
Schacter, Zalman 206
Schleiermacher, F. D. E. 248
Schneerson, R. Menachem Mendel 170, 172
Schultze, Kirsten E. 186
Scofield, Cyrus I. 78
Scots Hotel, Tiberias 122, 131
Second Vatican Council:
  Dei Verbum 220–1
  and Judaism 46
  and justice and human fights 59–60
secularism, Jewish 7, 14, 22–3, 139–40, 141, 159, 168–9, 177, 189
Shach, R. Menahem Eli'ezer 170
Shaham, David 153
Shaka'a, Bassam 161–2
Shalom Hartman Institute 30 n. 66
Shamir, Yitzhak 142
Shammas, Anton 26 n. 14
Shapira, R. Avraham 140

Sharansky, Natan 52
Sharon, Ariel 68 n. 50, 87, 106, 142, 175, 276
Shas (*Shomrie Torah Sephardim*) party 170, 171, 172
Shavit, Ari 3, 26 n. 4
Shoah *see* Holocaust
Shoufani, Emile 21
shrines, importance 276–7; *see also* Holy Places
Shvili, Benjamin 30 n. 69
El Sider, Sheikh Tal 235
Simon, Uriel 162
Siniora, Hanna 72
Six Day War (1967) 69, 72, 103, 124, 139, 275
  and Jewish fundamentalism 150–3, 200
  and Jewish identity 194
  and Muslim views of Judaism 198–9
Smith, Wilfred Cantwell 262 n. 29
Sodano, Angelo 41 n. 23
Solomon, N. 205, 215 n. 134
sovereignty, divine 248–9, 266, 277
Soviet Union, Christian immigrants from 2, 12
Sprinzak, Ehud 139, 141
Statement on the Israeli/Palestinian Conflict 129–30
Status Quo agreement (1948) 7
Status Quo on Holy Places 93, 101, 242, 304–5
Stern, Yuri 27 n. 22
Stewart, Weston Henry, Bishop of Jerusalem 121–2
Suissa, Eli 52

Taji-Farouki, S. 201, 202, 205, 214 nn. 109, 114, 215 n. 129
Tal, Uriel 140, 163
Talbi, Mohamed 192, 206, 208
Talmon, Ya'akov 140
Tantawy, Mohamed Sayed 235
Tarazi, Khalid 72
Tauran, Card. Jean-Louis 225
Temple, Jerusalem:
  First 219
  Second 240, 269–70
  movement to rebuild 150, 152, 157, 174
terrorism:
  condemnation 17–18, 38, 58–9, 87
  Jewish 157, 162
Tertio Millennio Adveniente (John Paul II) 53
theocracy, Zionist 140, 150–1, 162, 174, 204

Theology of Land and Covenant (Church of Scotland) 128
Timotheos, Greek Orthodox Patriarch of Jerusalem 103
Tisserant, Card. Eugéne 32, 35
Toldot Yeshu 5
Torrance, David 119
Torrance, Herbert 122
Tsimhoni, Daphne 72, 74

United Nations:
  and Jerusalem 267, 270, 274–5, 278–80, 282, 285–6, 287–90, 292–3
  see also Oslo Accords
United States, and Sovereign Area of Jerusalem 289
universalism, and justice 45, 61

Valerga, Giuseppe, Latin Patriarch of Jerusalem 42 n. 36
Van Buren, Paul 75–7
Van der Leest, Charlotte 134 n. 18
Vanunu, Mordechai 18
Vatican *see* Holy See
Vatican City 278, 280–2, 286, 287, 291
Venizelos, Eleutherios 100
Vergani, Antonio, patriarchal vicar for Israel 32
violence:
  against Christians 9
  causes 305–6, 307
  and *Gush Emunim* 200
  and *intifada* 58, 63, 66 n. 14
  in Jerusalem 307–8
visas, refusal 11

Waldenberg, R. Eli'ezer 173
Walker-Arnott, Jane 119
Weinberg, Tzvi 162
West Bank:
  and *Gush Emunim* 139, 141–2, 151, 155, 176, 200
  Israeli occupation 74, 85, 103, 124, 141–2, 151–3, 155, 176, 200, 299
  Palestinian Christian exodus from 47, 51–2, 59
  as Palestinian state 87, 176
Wiesel, Elie 256, 262 n. 8, 264 n. 46
Wolpo, R. Shalom Dov 172–3
Wright, A. G. 236 n. 5

Yad Leakhim organization 172
Yad VaShem (Holocaust Museum) 3, 4, 54
Yehoshua, A. B. 28 n. 48, 30 n. 69
Yosef, R. 'Ovadia 170–1, 172

Younan, Munib, Lutheran Bishop of Jerusalem 49
Young, J. W. A. 102
Young, William 118

Zemel (Avidan), R. Avraham 161
Zionism 1–2, 5, 15, 23, 273
   Christian 17, 27 n. 22, 39 n. 5, 75–8, 88, 116–17, 119, 123–4, 128, 246
   and Greek state 100–1
   and Islam 197–8
   and messianic theology 138, 139, 141, 150–2, 157, 162, 169–70, 174, 176, 204
   and Palestinians 69, 71–2, 97, 138–9, 142–3, 150–9, 200
   phases 124, 126
   religious (neo-Zionism) 124–6, 139–40, 143–5, 151–63, 176–7, 197–8, 203–4
   right-wing revisionist 139
   secular political 139–40, 141, 159, 168–9, 197
   and ultra-orthodox Jews 169, 203

www.ingramcontent.com/pod-product-compliance
Lightning Source LLC
Chambersburg PA
CBHW050430240426
43661CB00055B/2332